HALLIWELL'S
HARVEST

LESLIE HALLIWELL

HALLIWELL'S HARVEST

A further choice of entertainment movies from the golden age

Charles Scribner's Sons
New York

United States Edition published
by Charles Scribner's Sons 1986

Copyright © Leslie Halliwell 1986

Library of Congress Catalog Card Number 85–061328

ISBN 0–684–18518–0

1 3 5 7 9 11 13 15 17 19   I/C   20 18 16 14 12 10 8 6 4 2

Printed in Great Britain

CONTENTS

INTRODUCTION

In presenting more recollections and revaluations of films which, with very few exceptions, were produced between forty and fifty years ago, I have to make it clear that the subjects are not necessarily personal favourites. Rather they are movies about which there is something of abiding interest to say; movies which seem to deserve honourable mention in their particular aspect of the cinematic art; movies which hold some historical value for students who were not born when they were first released. That they all, even those which many would consider unsuccessful, are still fun to watch is almost by the way; but most of them have indeed given pleasure, very recently, when Channel Four reintroduced them to millions of viewers who were delighted to discover or reconfirm that wit, style and pictorial panache were readily available so many years before the slick, brash heyday of Messrs Spielberg, Coppola and their millionaire ilk.

Though the cinema has sometimes been thought of by highbrows as a mere panacea for popular ills, something to keep off the streets people who might otherwise attend football matches, drink beer, or at best read comic strips, the fact is that during both silent and talkie periods it frequently achieved the level of art, and even more frequently provided acute enjoyment for those able to appreciate the sheer professional craft of writer or director, of photographer or actor or editor or production designer, sometimes of all at once. Many of the results have passed deservedly into the archives, but archives are dry places, seldom frequented, and the films of which I speak are still capable of entertaining a great public. In retrospect, their reshowing may seem to be one of the greatest blessings to society bestowed by television; more people will enjoy them on the box in the corner than ever paid to see them in cinemas on their first release.

Halliwell's Hundred and *Halliwell's Harvest* are dedicated to the proposition that art should not be despised because it is popular. Some people will also find these films pleasurably nostalgic, and that is an effect not to be derided, for no civilization can continue to grow without the constant opportunity to review its own past achievements. Alas, the picture palaces themselves cannot be revived; as I discovered while writing my memoir *Seats in All Parts*, almost all the temples of yore have been demolished. Of the twenty-seven cinemas which I used to frequent in my own home town, fewer than half remain as structures and only one is still a cinema, a sparsely filled triple with none of the atmosphere it breathed when crowds ringed the building for its 1937 opening.

In this book I have appended to my eighty-four revaluations three longer essays which I hope will amuse and even inform: one on film titles, one on film books, and one on films which can be recalled with the perverse enjoyment one so often finds in failure.

L.H.
Kew 1985

PS   It may be objected that in some cases I have more bad than good to say of my choices. This is because I am judging by the highest standards I can summon, paying these films the compliment of assuming that, even though they may have been intended only as entertainment for the moment, they still repay analysis half a century later. In other words I am following the precept of Polonius, being cruel only to be kind.

Battle of the Sexes
ADAM'S RIB

Husband and wife lawyers are on opposite sides of an attempted murder case.

The Art, which used to stand at a crossways called the Rock, must long ago have gone the way of most cinemas, for the grimy Lancashire town of Bury is an unsentimental place, famous for the invention of black puddings and for little else. There never was anything at all genteel about it; yet in 1949 it still boasted this little independently-owned relic of the age of potted aspidistras and dusty plush. The Art had a decorated proscenium; a claustrophobic, poorly ventilated atmosphere; and curtains which smelled as though they had not been cleaned for a decade but were frequently sprayed with cheap scent. Throughout the heyday of the double feature and continuous performances, the Art still clung to separate two-hour shows, at 6 p.m. and 8.15; and the aged commissionaire who took my ticket wore a uniform which seemed likely to have been handed down from the Crimean War.

It was a totally inappropriate venue at which to experience so strident and worldly an example of the post-war American comedy. *Adam's Rib* is stripped of all the old mindless romantic pretences. The couple in it are already man and wife: *Man and Wife*, indeed, was the first title thought of. They are both middle-aged lawyers, and the theme is the equality of the sexes. Although played for laughs, the plot is based on an attempted murder, which struck me that evening as somewhat unexpected: black humour was still fairly rare. The movie doesn't exactly grab you with action either: scenes are played out in long steady takes, placing total reliance on the skill of the actors, and the staginess of the whole thing is emphasized by continuity shots of a cartoon proscenium with announcement placards reading 'That Evening' or 'Next Day'. Brittle, sophisticated, urbane, intellectual were some of the descriptions applied to the entertainment by international critics, and it quickly acquired classic status. Its merits were firmly based on the work of two couples. Ruth Gordon and Garson Kanin wrote the script specifically to fit the talents of their friends Spencer Tracy and Katharine Hepburn, whose off-screen romance was for many years, during which they made nine films together, one of Hollywood's best-kept secrets. (The friendship was later shattered when Kanin wrote a bestselling tell-all biography of the other couple, and Hepburn never spoke to him again.)

As though the foregoing aspects were not enough to spark interest, *Adam's Rib* served also as an introduction to four young character stars whom MGM hoped would show to advantage on its contract roster. Judy Holliday made her first appearance as Mrs Doris Attinger, who in the first five minutes of the film is seen following her adulterous husband (Tom Ewell) through Manhattan streets to an assignation with his light-of-love (Jean Hagen). There are no laughs until she stops outside the love-nest to get out her gun; then, after a

1

bewildered pause, she reaches into her handbag for the book of instructions. With this assistance she does a pretty good job of shooting the place up, winging her husband and causing sensational headlines in the morning papers. These are read by, among others, our married lawyers Adam and Amanda Bonner. He naturally takes the man's side and she the woman's, and (surprise, surprise) they find themselves in court adopting these very positions. Amanda's visit to her client in jail is a model of screen economy. A six-minute scene is filmed in a single shot, with the star, in profile, giving the spotlight to the newcomer as the dizzy deceived wife with the Brooklyn accent:

AMANDA: Now start with the day of the accident.
DORIS: No accident. I wanted to shoot him . . . so I sent the kids to school and I went and bought a gun. So then I was very hungry . . . so I went in a hamburger place and ate two. Rare. And one lemon meringue pie.
AMANDA: And then what?
DORIS: I was still hungry . . . So then I bought two chocolate nut bars and I went outside of his office and I waited the whole afternoon and I kept waiting and eating the candy bars till he came out so then I followed him so then I shot him.
AMANDA: And after you shot him, how did you feel then?
DORIS: Hungry.

Each day the case proceeds a little further, and in the evening come the domestic discussions. During one of these the camera remains focused on a chair in the middle of the Bonner bedroom, the participants being seen only when they pop into the picture from their dressing rooms on either side. They are hosting a dinner party with distinguished guests, and life is complicated by the uninvited presence of a song-writing Romeo from down the hall, one Kip Lurie (David Wayne, the fourth newcomer). He makes unabashed eyes at Amanda and has a neat line in unsettling remarks, as to a gaggle of elderly guests when he enters: 'Are you the judges? They said there'd be judges here.' And to a girl who makes a sarcastic response to one of his wisecracks, he replies: 'I knew a girl collapsed a lung, laughing like that.' To Adam he is a positive pain in the posterior, but Amanda shows a little femininity by being mildly susceptible to his flattery and tolerant even of his mordant commentary on her home movies. ('Barn-kissing, an old Connecticut custom.')

As the case proceeds, Adam's own tolerance becomes a little strained by his wife's no-holds-barred courtroom tricks, and Amanda even suspects antagonism in the rear-end massage he gives her every evening during their toilet:

AMANDA: I know your touch, I know a slap from a slug.
ADAM: Okay, okay.
AMANDA: I'm not so sure it is. I'm not so sure I want to be subjected to typical, instinctive, masculine brutality. And it felt not only as though you meant to but as though you thought you had a right to. I can tell.
ADAM: What you got back there, radar equipment?

2

ADAM'S RIB. 'Vive la difference,' says Spencer Tracy to Katharine Hepburn, who does not seem to be dressed for the occasion.

The two sides are essentially summarized by Amanda's conversation with her assistant:

AMANDA: How do you feel about a man who is unfaithful to his wife?
GRACE: Not nice.
AMANDA: All right. Now, how about a woman who is unfaithful to her husband?
GRACE: Something terrible.

It is this attitude which Amanda seeks to correct, and she does so by bringing forth in court a parade of women who are more than the equal of their spouses. They include a circus strong woman who at a prearranged cue picks Adam up by one leg and raises him high above the judge's podium. That evening, acutely embarrassed, he explodes: 'Just what sort of a blow you've struck or think you've struck for women's rights I don't know, but you've certainly fouled *us* up beyond all recognition . . . I've done it all the way I said I would. Richer, poorer, sickness, health, better, worse. But this is too worse! This is basic. I'm old-fashioned. I like two sexes.'

But Amanda in court triumphantly sums up her case: 'An unwritten law stands back of a man who fights to defend his home. Apply the same to this maltreated wife and neglected mother. We ask you no more.'

She wins, of course, and it remains only for Adam to regain his self-respect. This he does by bursting in on a romantic but innocent tryst between Kip and Amanda, and threatening to shoot the interloper. All he wants is to hear her say: 'Stop, you've no right.' And she does. Whereupon he puts the muzzle of the gun in his mouth – and eats it. It is liquorice.

The discussion ends in bed. Where else?

AMANDA: What I say is true. No difference between the sexes. None. Man, woman, the same.
ADAM: They are, huh?
AMANDA: Well, maybe there is a difference. But it's a little difference.
ADAM: Yuh. Well, as the French say . . .
AMANDA: How do they say?
ADAM: *Vive la difference!*

I twice met George Cukor, who directed this elegant film. In 1967, as Tracy lay dying, I spent an afternoon in Cukor's mansion above Sunset Boulevard and he was expansive enough to show me the villa where Tracy and Hepburn used to meet. Then, in 1981, not too long before Cukor himself died, I met him again at a dinner party and found that age had made him crusty. Whatever great name from the past was mentioned, Cukor had but one response: 'Pain in the ass.' He even applied it to Tracy and to the making of *Adam's Rib*. But he smiled as he said it.

Adam's Rib. US 1949; black and white; 101 minutes. Produced by Lawrence Weingarten for MGM. Written by Ruth Gordon, Garson Kanin. Directed by George Cukor. Photographed by George J. Folsey. Music by Miklos Rozsa. With Spencer Tracy as Adam Bonner; Katharine Hepburn as Amanda Bonner; Judy Holliday as Doris Attinger; Tom Ewell as Warren Attinger; David Wayne as Kip Lurie; Jean Hagen as Beryl Caighn. The song, 'Farewell Amanda,' by Cole Porter.

The Devil and Mr Foster

ALIAS NICK BEAL

A politician is almost corrupted by a sinister stranger offering wealth and power.

This is the kind of film that was fated never to succeed, even in the days when Hollywood turned out ten films a week and the star was usually all that mattered. It came to be made because a writer and a director accumulated enough power, riding high on a previous success, to overestimate the capabilities of their audience; but it was probably the only chance they got to do so. The critics, alas, far from applauding the attempt to be different from the common run, disdained *Alias Nick Beal* for dressing up serious themes in the guise of a gangster-political melodrama. In Wardour Street, the Tin Pan Alley of the British film industry, American politics were in any case considered to be the kiss of death at the box office and, since the title character was not understood to be Old Nick in another guise, *Alias Nick Beal* was retitled *The Contact Man*, which was certainly no more attractive and anything but more clear. With this handicap it was sent out without benefit of press show to take its chances on independent local release, which meant that many towns never saw it at all. I caught up with it early in 1950 on a three-day run at the Cambridge Playhouse, which in winter fully earned its local nickname of the Icehouse. Sharing the bill was Betty Hutton in *Red Hot and Blue*, a more straightforward gangster show with music, and it seemed by far the more popular with the few stalwarts who came in. Ironically, it had the same director as *Alias Nick Beal*, John Farrow: no doubt it had been handed to him so that he could work off his penance.

When and if you look at the graph of Ray Milland's career, *Alias Nick Beal* is the point at which the line begins to fall. After the heights of *The Lost Weekend* and *The Uninvited* and *The Big Clock*, he had seemed to lose his box office lure, and *Alias Nick Beal*, an undoubted star role, was no doubt given to him in the expectation of his proving that a real star can triumph over the least promising material. In the eyes of the front office he flunked it, and was given no second opportunity, at least not by the studio which created him. Ahead, until he became a character support, lay no more than a few thin romantic comedies and stodgy westerns, routine vehicles in which he could wear wide-brimmed hats to conceal his receding hairline and the increasing lack of command in his eyes. It seems ironic now that as Beal he gives one of his most striking performances. Though used chiefly as an elegant prop, he never for a second fails to emanate hovering menace. With mouth slightly apart, jelly-like eyes, and immaculate double-breasted suit, he is as plump and sinister as a chip-shop cat.

Elegance is what this film has in spades. John Farrow (father of Mia) never hit the top rank as a director, but his work was always smooth and interesting, and such items as *The Hitler Gang* and *Night Has a Thousand Eyes* should help to earn him a National Film Theatre season one day. *Alias Nick Beal* may well be the work which came closest to satisfying his own ambitions: saltily scripted, immaculately photographed, in all departments a piece of superior craftsmanship. It is a showy film set in large spaces, all beautifully underlit in that needlepoint sharpness which was Paramount's unselfconscious trademark in the days before the experiment with VistaVision brought a less pleasing kind of deep focus. It is a film of characters symbolically grouped in a roomy frame, of sequences in which the director's eye flits maliciously from details of expression to composed images of the whole man.

5

ALIAS NICK BEAL. In any ordinary movie Audrey Totter would be playing the temptress, but here she is about to be seduced by a tall dark stranger (Ray Milland) who has just walked out of the fog.

The plot gathers momentum like a juggernaut, though to start with it is slow to take shape, which is perhaps the reason for a hasty flash-forward after the credits, presumably added after the film was complete and occupying just as much time as it takes a worried-looking Thomas Mitchell to hurry up a flight of steps in the rain. (Farrow had undoubtedly seen *Foreign Correspondent*, qv.) Over this vivid shot the voice of Milland intones: 'In every man lies the seed of destruction . . . a fatal weakness.' And so the scene is quickly set for a modern version of Faust: Mitchell's character name is even given as Foster, which is about as close as you can get.

One might almost think to begin with that one was watching a Frank Capra comedy-drama. We revert to Foster's happy times, and find him to be that rare species, an honest politician, concerned for 'the little people' and deep in the foundation of boys' clubs. With the moral support of an admiring priest, a role in which George Macready is successfully cast against type, he fights the scourge of a local racketeer called Hanson, who, alas, is said to have burned his incriminating books before the cops could get to them. Frustrated, Foster cries:

6

'I'd give my soul to nail him'; and right on cue, without so much as a split second's pause, in walks an urchin with a scribbled anonymous message: 'If you want to nail Hanson, meet me in the China Coast tonight around ten.'

The China Coast proves to be one of those insalubrious waterfront cafés once so beloved of Hollywood set designers because they involved minimum construction costs, being perpetually swathed in studio fog. Here Mr Beal, in his jaunty snap brim, makes his appearance, much to the proprietor's bewilderment, by walking in from the direction in which there's nothing but water. He seems to be something of a mind-reader too, for when Foster arrives, the drink he has just thought of is waiting for him. (For himself Mr Beal chooses a Barbados rum, which the proprietor did not even know was on his shelf.) The mysterious stranger's card reads simply: Nicholas Beal, Agent. 'Agent for what?' asks Foster. 'That depends. Possibly for you.'

Before you can say Jack Robinson – or Nick Beal – Mr Foster's new agent has arranged for the cops to be tipped off to raid a certain spot. Here they find the books which the bewildered racketeer Hanson thought he burned. Foster's triumph as racket-breaker is also the beginning of his moral downfall: he worries because as district attorney he pushed the search through without a warrant. Poor Mr Foster; and poor Mr Mitchell, who is doomed to give a performance which however well shaded must lack suspense. We know that from being totally honest he must become Mr Beal's puppet, and that finally, and even more boringly, he will turn honest again at the expense of his own soul. But that's what happens when you tell a well-known story. At least Mr Mitchell does all that is possible to preserve our interest, his every inflection being carefully judged. Come to think of it, this was probably his last star performance as well as Milland's; he too went down on a high note.

Every last one of Mr Foster's honest friends distrusts Mr Beal, which is not surprising when one considers the conjuring tricks he constantly plays: appearing and disappearing without opening doors, and writing dialogue for people before they utter it. If he really were the inscrutable Joe Boss of the city underworld, which is his cover, he should surely have drawn less attention to himself; but then the film would have been less enjoyable. Meanwhile, bartenders scratch their heads and tell him: 'You sure got a different line, mister.' And when asked where he just came from, he is likely to reply disarmingly: 'Down the chimney.' When the politician's wife looks him straight in the eye and asks what his real racket is, his reply is smooth and ambivalent: 'My racket concerns good government, Mrs Foster.' But then all his remarks are ambivalent. 'You a friend of Joe's?' he is asked. 'I met him once, October 13th, 1944.' 'That's the night he was killed.' 'That's right.'

On one occasion a Salvation Army rhetorician seems to be getting a little personal. 'I've wrestled the devil and thrown him. I've pinned his shoulders to the mat.' Mr Beal moves away and is stung to mutter: 'I wonder if he knows it's two throws out of three?' The priest overhears and looks thoughtful; later he persuades Foster that his new agent may be both dangerous and not quite natural. Mr Foster scoffs at the idea, as you and I might if we were on the brink of being elected governor, with the help of Mr Beal's clever tricks.

FOSTER: Where's the horns and the tail? Where's the smell of sulphur and brimstone?

PRIEST: Maybe the devil knows it's the twentieth century too, Joseph.

But by now Foster has signed a document which says that in return for being made governor he will accompany 'the aforesaid Mr Beal' to the island of Almas Perdidas, which he really should have looked up in the gazetteer: it translates as the island of Lost Souls. The rest of the film, once Foster has wrestled with his conscience and disowned his governorship after disclosing that the voting was rigged, is devoted to our hero's salvation. For time is pressing: by doing right he invoked the forfeit clause, and the now wolf-like Mr Beal makes one more magic appearance to insist: 'Tonight is collection night. The China Coast at eleven o'clock, and don't let the fog throw you. It won't bother us where we're going.'

Luckily the priest is also present on the waterfront to force a confrontation. Foster may have signed the contract, but the priest throws it to the ground with a Bible on top of it, and Mr Beal recoils from that as Dracula would from a garlic-covered crucifix. 'You seem to have jockeyed me into some kind of morality play,' he snarls. 'It's always been bell and candle and that worn out book of yours.' 'And it always will be,' says the priest rather smugly, conscious of an easy victory. With a half-uttered MacArthur-like promise to return, Mr Beal whirls away in a wisp of fog. 'He's gone,' breathes the happy Mrs Foster. 'But where?'

The priest, who has seen at least one Hollywood film too many, claims the last line. 'I wouldn't ask.'

I have not mentioned the sub-plot, in which Foster's moral downfall is principally accomplished by Beal's transformation of a waterfront floozie into a high-class tart for whom the governor-to-be falls hook, line and sinker. The familiar sexual badinage is worth enduring for the sake of the Daliesque murals which stretch from end to end of her 100-foot apartment, but Miss Audrey Totter is just a few steps below par as a *femme fatale*. This was her last big part too: *Alias Nick Beal* seems to have been unlucky for everybody.

Alias Nick Beal (GB title: *The Contact Man*). US 1949; black and white; 93 minutes. Produced by Endre Boehm for Paramount. Written by Jonathan Latimer from a story by Mindret Lord. Directed by John Farrow. Photographed by Lionel Lindon. Music by Franz Waxman. With Ray Milland as Nick Beal; Thomas Mitchell as Joseph Foster; Audrey Totter as Donna Allen; George Macready as Reverend Thomas Garfield; Fred Clark as Frankie Faulkner; Geraldine Wall as Martha Foster.

O Brave New World, That Hath Such People in It
THE BEST YEARS OF OUR LIVES
Three men come home from war to a changed mid-America.

The war was over. I was committed in eighteen months or so to spend two years in the army, but that would be a safe adventure with a happy ending. (Little did I know how dull.) Meanwhile, the school play, the film society and the small problem of getting a university scholarship occupied me fully; but I did have time to notice that some of the more earnest among my fellow sixth-formers had founded something called the Reconstruction Club, and I went along to several meetings. The aim was to set right in post-war Britain all the things which had not been right in the thirties. 'Homes for heroes', 'social security' and 'six feet of good English earth' were phrases much bandied about. We had heard about Samuel Goldwyn's new film, which was supposed to deal with all these matters from the American point of view, and we demanded of each other why there was no British equivalent. So we queued as a group to see *The Best Years of Our Lives*, in order to find inspiration from its account of how America was dealing with its post-war problems.

The movie proved to be a magnificent confidence trick. It does touch on serious matters, but in an airy kind of way, as one would expect from something based on a poem (the credits bashfully say a novel) and adapted by that pretentious old wordsmith Robert Sherwood. It won the approval of the critics because it was beautifully photographed and cinematically constructed, of the public because it involved several big stars in three absorbing romances. Boone City, the setting, is an anonymous place which could be any town, anywhere, and the three returning heroes also have a universal ring. The middle-aged sergeant, Al Stephenson (Fredric March), is revealed as a bank executive, well heeled and earnest. Oddly enough, he is the one who gets most drunk on the first night home, but he has no problems when he goes back to the bank next day: he is, in fact, offered promotion to vice-president in charge of small loans, and only slowly does he come to realize that selfishness has taken over his town during his five-year absence. 'Last year it was kill Japs, this year it's make money.' The air force captain, Fred Derry (Dana Andrews), turns out to have been a lowly soda-jerk before call-up, but he can't get even that job back without an argument, and his glamour-conscious wife leaves him because he seems dull out of uniform. The naval rating, Homer Parrish (Harold Russell) experienced only one piece of action in the Pacific, but it left him with articulated hooks instead of hands, and he gets edgy whether people admit to noticing his disability or pretend not to. These are the three with whom the audience faces the future, and none finds any virtue in looking back at the recent years of glory: Al's son is not even interested in his war souvenirs, and Fred wanders dazedly through a whole airfield of unused planes destined for the scrapheap, having found that his old drug store has become a supermarket where other assistants complain that nobody's job is safe with all these servicemen crowding in.

The approach worked superbly. Audiences would not have paid money to hear how difficult the future was going to be; without anybody telling them, they had already suspected it. It was the powerful emotionalism of the picture that sent them home feeling they had participated in something worthy: and the rather contrived happy endings can have done no harm either.

Despite its length there is nothing very expensive-looking about *The Best Years of Our Lives*. It is, however, an undoubted masterpiece of professionalism, its calm control of the audience almost entirely attributable to Gregg Toland's camerawork and William Wyler's subtle direction of actors and careful grouping of them within the frame. For a major movie it begins somewhat abruptly, with an interior shot of an airport ticket lounge where Fred is walking from one desk to another (across a map of America on the floor) trying to get a flight back home. (The service rehabilitation units don't seem to have been very helpful to any of these heroes.) He is told rather curtly, 'we can probably get you on flight 37 on the 19th'; just then a businessman bustles up to say that his secretary wired for a ticket, which is promptly supplied. The interloper has sixteen pounds excess baggage, but he waves a genial hand: 'Oh, that's all right, how much is it?' Thus swiftly the film sets one of its themes, that while at war the servicemen have allowed their world to slip through their fingers. Fred eventually finds that Air Transport Command is his best bet, and after a long wait he is put on a two-day stopping flight, along with Al and Homer. None of them knows the others, but the movie makes them friends and their different situations provide constant contrast. The scenes of the three of them huddled into the nose of the B17 as it wings its way at low level across America are unlikely to be forgotten by anyone who comes fresh to them even now, and in the days when flying was a rare experience they were even more meaningful, especially when the plane approaches Boone City and the veterans see people playing golf – 'just as though nothing ever happened'.

Following sharply are two scenes which never fail to bring a lump to the throat. Homer reluctantly gets out of the taxi and stands on his front lawn, while his family and the girl next door pour out of their houses and stand round him both excited and embarrassed, not wanting to draw attention to his hooks. His mother's involuntary gasp of anguish (an unexpectedly fine cameo from Minna Gombell) is cunningly judged. Then Al goes home to his superior upper-floor apartment, only to be sharply challenged by the desk clerk. He shushes his children, who open the door and stand in silent excitement, while from the distant kitchen the voice of Myrna Loy calls to know who is the visitor. There is a tense moment during which the penny drops, then a superb long-held shot as she appears, apron-clad, at the far end of the wide corridor, while Al stands with his back to the camera, his arms half outstretched but his legs apparently frozen to the ground. It is a grouping which would have delighted any of the old Dutch masters who might have captured it.

The joy of *The Best Years of Our Lives* is that it details at least one character

THE BEST YEARS OF OUR LIVES. The opening sequence in the observation cone of the bomber, now flying three heroes back to an uncertain civilian future. Harold Russell, Dana Andrews, Fredric March.

with whom anybody in the audience can identify, so that although the problems it posed were not universal, it was a world-wide box office smash. All its actors prospered because Wyler's skill had painstakingly caught every character nuance of which they were capable, and even handless Harold Russell might have developed a career had he so wished. (He turned up again on the screen just once, thirty-five years later, in *Inside Moves*.) Goldwyn's film won Academy Awards for best picture, for best direction, for Hugo Friedhofer's exciting score, for Fredric March as best actor, for Russell as best supporting actor and best newcomer, and for Daniel Mandell's editing. Goldwyn also received the prestigious Irving Thalberg award, given to those who bring honour to the industry.

There never was a serious British contender for honours in the field of post-war reconstruction, and my school's Reconstruction Club soon fell apart from sheer impotence, but *The Best Years of Our Lives* was fondly remembered for other reasons, and when it played its UK television premiere in 1964 it was eagerly watched by 72 per cent of the available population, a feat still not equalled even by 'Coronation Street'. Times change, though: a 1975 attempt to turn it into a television series called 'Returning Home' failed rather miserably, despite professional competence in every department.

The Best Years of Our Lives. US 1946; black and white; 182 minutes. Produced by Samuel Goldwyn. Written by Robert E. Sherwood from the poem 'Glory for Me' by Mackinlay Kantor. Directed by William Wyler. Photographed by Gregg Toland. Music by Hugo Friedhofer. With Fredric March as Al Stephenson; Myrna Loy as Milly Stephenson; Teresa Wright as Peggy Stephenson; Dana Andrews as Fred Derry; Virginia Mayo as Marie Derry; Harold Russell as Homer Parrish; Cathy O'Donnell as Wilma Cameron; Hoagy Carmichael as Butch Engle; Gladys George as Hortense Derry; Roman Bohnen as Pat Derry; Steve Cochran as Cliff Scully; Ray Collins as Mr Milton; Minna Gombell as Mrs Parrish; Walter Baldwin as Mr Parrish.

Right Between the Eyes
BOOMERANG

The district attorney of a small New England town tries to track down the murderer of a priest.

When the veterans got back from the war in 1945, it was to the image of a rosy-tinted America, with roses round the door, and Lionel Barrymore under the apple tree eating Ma's best pie. It took only a short time for this image to wear thin: *The Best Years of Our Lives* (qv) practically demolished it in one fell swoop, and by 1947 audiences had accepted a crasser, more sinister, urbanized version of the America of *The Grapes of Wrath* and *Mr Smith Goes to Washington*, a land full of racketeers who in the absence of the men at war had flourished like the green bay tree, filling the biggest cities and the smallest towns with knaves, fools, graft and corruption. They justified themselves in terms of keeping everybody happy. A banker gets a profitable contract, and the town gets a boys' home, right?

Boomerang is a product of these unhappy years. One of its central characters is a war veteran, 'five years behind the parade', who can't get a job and is too full of despair to defend himself properly when accused of the murder of a priest with whom he had a comparatively minor argument. The setting is a small town in Connecticut, but Darryl F. Zanuck in making the film had a wider message: a narrator tells us that the community is meant to stand for any town in the United States, 'for as some wag once said, after New York it's all Connecticut'. Apart from some subtle changes of accent and religion, that is. You see, the victim of circumstantial evidence is only one of the national ills which the crusading Zanuck intends to expose. Apart from the exemplary young district attorney and his gracious wife in their charming home, everybody we meet is corrupt to some degree: the cops, the banker, the newspaper magnate, the reporter, the defence counsel. We can exempt the judge, but even he is obtuse enough to suspect the DA of political chicanery, and that can't be right, not when the DA is played by Dana Andrews in a Twentieth Century-Fox film produced by the *March of Time* team with government approval.

The picture has in its cast a remarkable number of competent actors. Lee J. Cobb, Karl Malden, Ed Begley, Robert Keith, Taylor Holmes, Arthur Kennedy, Sam Levene. But none of them gets a big scene: each is observed fleetingly, on the run, as in life; they wander in and out of the action, slipping the odd remark to the camera as they turn to some other matter. This is fine for realism, but it adds up to a somewhat breathless eighty-eight minutes, and we wonder at the end if this kind of realism doesn't have just as unrealistic a cumulative effect as Jimmy Cagney kicking in a few doors. We wonder too about the loose ends: life always has them, but in this case there may have been rather fewer than the film suggests. We are told at the finale that the DA in question was Huntley Cummings, who rose to become attorney general of the United States. But was he really, as the film says, offered bribes to keep his mouth shut? And if so, wouldn't he have had to arrest a few people, and did he? Did he really risk his life in sanctioning the making of the movie? And wasn't it rather pointlessly melodramatic in view of the fact that in real life the crime was never solved, for the makers of the film to put the finger on a mousey little guy who *might* have done it? No motive is given, and the guy is named only as Jim, but we see him among the courtroom spectators looking guilty, and earlier on arguing with the priest. Then right at the end a reporter opens a newspaper with a picture of a man who has been killed in a car crash trying to evade the police, and it's our mysterious suspect, and the reporter looks thoughtful and for no reason I could see says: 'I wonder . . .' That's Hollywood, of course, but it isn't very satisfactory in a film with such a high ethical stance.

The chief remaining interest of *Boomerang* lies not so much in the social issues it picks up and then drops, and certainly not in its rather specious study of an honest prosecutor who sees his mission as not necessarily to convict but to discover the truth; it lies rather in its prominent place in a line of crime documentaries which was evolved in Hollywood in the late forties, primarily at Twentieth Century-Fox though with earlier encouragement from the *Crime Does Not Pay* series at MGM and from the likes of *Confessions of a Nazi Spy* at Warners. Some titles in this loose series, of all of which *Boomerang* will at some point remind the assiduous student, are *The House on 92nd Street* (qv), *Crossfire*, *Gentleman's Agreement*, *Call Northside 777*, *Pickup on South Street*, *Naked City* and *Pinky*. There are even echoes backwards to *Citizen Kane* and forwards to *Invasion of the Body Snatchers*. Taken together, these films give us a *Sunday Times* view of post-war middle America, only slightly processed for popular presentation. *Boomerang*, though a leader in terms of critical acclaim at the time, is not my favourite among them. It is slightly too cold, too cynical, too unresolved, certainly too lax in plot construction. By its own account it sets

BOOMERANG. Sensation in court: Lee J. Cobb harangues Dana Andrews, while Arthur Kennedy looks on in bewilderment.

out to make things clear, yet it doesn't even trouble to explain its own title except in the form of a speech from the troubled DA: 'I thought I had the case going perfectly straight and suddenly it comes back and hits me right between the eyes.' But you do feel when it's over that you know half the townspeople and could find your way around the streets. Kazan's camera picks out the memorable images: the open greengrocer's store, the echoing city hall, the faces you see for only five seconds each in a montage, scratching or sniffing or rubbing their noses. Were they all actors? Straight from the method school, if so. I would have liked a little more animation in the lead from Dana Andrews who, having only a year previously played the troubled war veteran in *The Best Years of Our Lives*, here takes on the role of the DA, the bastion of the establishment. He uses the more serious of his two expressions, the one which looks like a headache commercial, and for the part as written he is perfectly adequate, though one wonders whether the casting of James Stewart or Gary Cooper might have made *Boomerang* a softer, wiser, more meaningful movie.

As an entertainment, it's full of strong unstressed moments; you're always happy to see it again because you can never catch them all in one sitting. There are clichés too, of course; they always seem to creep in. Politician to reporter: 'I don't care if he's guilty or not, I've got to win an election.' Crooked banker

14

to D.A.: 'Is one man's life really worth the whole town?' (Predictable, soft-spoken answer: 'Yes, Paul, it is.') But there are plenty of freshly observed moments, such as the cop taking his suspect to jail and finding himself threatened by a lynch mob. Being Lee J. Cobb, he drops his cigarette to the ground and murmurs: 'Some people are going to get hurt. Want to be first?' And one weary cop to another after practically every man in town has been suspected: 'They even picked up my Uncle Jerry the other night, sixty-four years old.' Reply: 'Did he do it?' Finally back to Lee J. Cobb who has, in spite of himself, obtained a desperate confession by keeping a suspect sleepless and browbeaten for thirty-six hours. He carries the collapsed, inert figure back to its prison cot and mutters: 'What a way to make a living!'

Boomerang. US 1947; black and white; 88 minutes. Produced by Louis de Rochemont for Twentieth Century-Fox. Written by Richard Murphy from the magazine article 'The Perfect Case' by Anthony Abbott. Directed by Elia Kazan. Photographed by Norbert Brodine. Music by David Buttolph. With Dana Andrews as Henry Harvey; Jane Wyatt as Mrs Harvey; Lee J. Cobb as Robinson; Arthur Kennedy as John Waldron; Sam Levene as Woods; Taylor Holmes as Wade; Robert Keith as McGreery; Ed Begley as Harris.

Tenny and Nielsen and Algy and Him
BULLDOG DRUMMOND COMES BACK

Criminals intent on revenge kidnap Drummond's bride-to-be.

Hollywood studios of the thirties were filled with refugees. Should a far eastern setting be required, hundreds of Chinese or Japanese actors could be lined up at the drop of a hat. To suit any story set in Europe, a studio could pick from a scintillating selection of stage actors, recent emigrants who in support of their new allegiance would willingly abandon their true origins to turn Russian, German, Egyptian or oriental as the script demanded. Thus the likes of Albert Bassermann, Peter Lorre, Marcel Dalio, Sig Rumann and Eduardo Ciannelli acted their way into our hearts against backlot sets which had no more relevance to the real Europe than did a surrealist painting. A stiff-upper-lipped English colony had burgeoned too, with its own cricket team under the captaincy of Charles Aubrey Smith. It seldom seemed to worry these gentlemen when they were expected to frolic, Wodehouse or Wimsey style, against utilitarian settings through which the canvas often showed, and which had been hurriedly taken over from the previous production. At Universal, for instance, a Scottish castle, a Sussex country village and a

Viennese resort were all represented by a village street built to depict the German town in *All Quiet on the Western Front* and subsequently adapted for *Frankenstein*. In such circumstances it did not seem ludicrous that the entire cast of *The Bride of Frankenstein* was English, or that the burly American playing the Welsh heir in *The Wolf Man* had a dapper father a good foot shorter than himself. A puff or two of artificial fog was expected to cover all the joins. Few Hollywood designers in those days had even crossed the Atlantic, and mistakes were legion; but English audiences laughed indulgently when Big Ben turned up on the wrong side of the Thames, or when a country railway station had signs facing the wrong way. After all, English films themselves were seldom convincing. What mattered was that Hollywood's heart should be in the right place, and that the films it made were fun to watch.

It is in this spirit that the Bulldog Drummond series of the mid-thirties must be approached. Drummond had made sporadic appearances, in various incarnations, since 1925, and would go on doing so until 1948, with a brief and sudden comeback in the sixties. Only in the first talkie bearing his name was there any similarity to H. C. McNeile's original conception, which was somewhere between a restless post-war adventurer and a Jew-hating fascist thug. In this somewhat uneasy film of 1929, the hedonistic and even brutish qualities of the man were cunningly filtered through the charm of Ronald Colman, who remained debonair even when strangling the villain with his bare hands. By the time Paramount got hold of the property in 1937, Drummond had predictably become a characterless London playboy, a mere stick of a hero designed to show off various comic and villainous foils. The bad guys, naturally, had foreign names and spoke with guttural accents. The comics included Drummond's vacuous friend Algy, whose wife was always about to have a baby; his desiccated manservant Tenny, who despite his advanced years was astonishingly adept at climbing on to fast-moving vehicles; and Colonel Nielsen of Scotland Yard, whose fate was always to be wrong in his deductions but to turn up in the nick of time to save the foolhardy heroes from whatever devilish death the villains had contrived. In the first three episodes, audiences were amazed to find former matinée idol John Barrymore in the Nielsen role. Fading and befuddled by drink, he caused audience confusion by getting top billing but not playing the hero. Instead he was allowed to overbalance the story by turning up in several easily penetrable disguises and by hamming his few scenes to the top of his bent.

The item under review came second in this lightweight series, which sank rapidly from the status of nervous 'A' to that of cheap support. Paramount's first Drummond, Ray Milland, had departed from this duty in order to woo Dorothy Lamour in her backlot jungle. Replacement John Howard was not even English, but made a passable stab at the accent, and showed what might be called the lighter side of his *Lost Horizon* characterization as Ronald Colman's hysterical brother. It became a standard gag for the series that Drummond was forced by circumstances to put aside his thoughts of imminent marriage. The circumstances in this case were in fact the kidnapping of his bride-to-be by a sinister couple bent on revenge: Drummond had

BULLDOG DRUMMOND COMES BACK. Algy (Reginald Denny) is kidnapped by the dastardly
villain (J. Carrol Naish).

secured the arrest and conviction of a dear departed relative. Also as usual, the
backgrounds suggested the twenties rather than the thirties, providing a
fogbound clubland atmosphere reminiscent of Dornford Yates and Greyfriars
and Agatha Christie and Just William: in no sense was this a real Britain on the
brink of a real war. Drummond is discovered in his heavily oak-furnished
country seat, firing his revolver to summon his manservant. 'You rang, sir?'
asks the imperturbable Tenny. Yes, says Drummond, he requires comment on
a poem he is writing to his lady love. Tenny studies it with a frown: 'A bit on
the feathery side, don't you think, sir?' 'Nonsense,' says Drummond, 'what
rhymes with married?' 'Harried, sir.'

Just then Nielsen drives by and honks his horn, for no other reason than to
explain that he has to meet the seven o'clock express: 'some important papers
from the Yard.' By the time he returns for the promised drink, the would-be
Mrs Drummond has also come and gone; gone under protest, that is, having
been attacked and chloroformed by the villains. 'Confound it, Drummond,'
says Nielsen amiably, 'how is it that whenever I see you someone has just been
murdered or disappeared?' A clue is now discovered, for these villains are of

17

the literary type and love to draw attention to themselves. 'It's round and flat and not a hat, but it carries a message for all of that.' Taking no more than a couple of minutes to deduce a gramophone record, Drummond finds a specially labelled one which intones a second instruction: 'Eight paces ahead you'll find a clue; it's twisted and hanging plain in sight.' (No rhyme? Did the original script say 'in front of you'? And why was it changed?) The three investigators now find a drugged Algy and a third message: 'Exactly forty miles from here you'll find an inn where fishermen are lying.' (Don't they always?) By a small miracle of map analysis Drummond locates a waterfront pub called the Angler's Rest and, since an addendum insists that the police must not be involved, Nielsen dashes off to his make-up box and assumes the character of a hirsute fisherman. 'You know, my dear Sanger,' he coos to his assistant, 'I really feel I should have been an actor.' Perhaps he should: the smell of the greasepaint positively oozes from his next scene, when he has to order 'arf o' bitter' not once but three times.

At the Angler's Rest the clues fall thick and fast, which is just as well since nothing else is happening. 'What you've done once, do once again.' And, more ambitiously:

> In Limehouse below the setting sun
> You'll find what seems like number one.
> Go inside, and number three
> Will bring you straight to me.

Not even pausing to wince at the poet's inability to scan, the assembled company now transports itself en masse to a rather splendid studio Limehouse, and in particular to one of those low dockland dives so beloved of Hollywood at the time. (They reached their apogee in *Sherlock Holmes and the Voice of Terror*.) The sign outside the Setting Sun helpfully names the owner as Sanghil *Won*. Inside, ignoring a female chanteuse belting out 'What Shall We Do with the Drunken Sailor?', Drummond is led by a three-fingered man into a padded room with a collapsible floor. This promptly deposits him into the murky Thames, but it is all part of the villains' playfulness, for under the pier is yet another message: 'Now find the clue which is hidden beneath the line.' The trick this time is invisible ink, and heating reveals an instruction to 'go back to Rockingham', which is where they started. By the time they reach the house, the villains' invention is notably flagging. 'Go back to the Angler's Rest', says yet another note. But on the way Drummond is momentarily kidnapped, and allowed to glimpse his true love, gagged and bound in the back seat of a Daimler. Prodded and threatened, she mouths yet another piece of nonsense: 'Is Greyminster the fifth or sixth most beautiful village in England?' At the inn, a book of Wordsworth's poems has been left by 'a gentleman', and in it the words 'the mere' are ringed. The penny drops. Of course: the Mere at Greyminster, a stately pile well known to Drummond, and at present conveniently uninhabited. Deflected only momentarily from their purpose by a falling tree, our heroes soon find themselves locked up in a gas-filled room with a ticking bomb, the intent of the clues having been solely to lull them into an unwatchful state. Luckily Nielsen has stayed behind to don a second unspeakable disguise, and the yarn fizzles out with the physical vanquishing of the dastardly evildoers in an affray distinguished by such lines as 'Dot him one' and 'I shall bash him on the bazooka, sir'.

By no standard is this more than feeble stuff, and in performance it is even less lively than in recollection; but as something designed to fill an hour before the ice-cream break it does have a fascination mainly deriving from its air of innocence, a commodity regrettably absent from modern film-making. At least it transfixed with delight a couple of ten-year-olds to whom I showed it in 1983. Personally, although I dearly wished its cast had been better served by script and direction, I still found it vastly preferable to the sexed-up and mildly sadistic Drummond who turned up during the sixties in *Deadlier than the Male* and understandably returned to limbo after a horrendous sequel called *Some Girls Do*. Now, that was true decadence.

Bulldog Drummond Comes Back. US 1937; black and white; 60 minutes. Produced by Paramount. Written by Edward T. Lowe. Directed by Louis King. Photographed by Harry Mills. With John Howard as Bulldog Drummond; John Barrymore as Colonel Nielsen; Reginald Denny as Algy; E. E. Clive as Tenny; Louise Campbell as Phyllis Clavering; J. Carrol Naish as Valdin.

Green and Pleasant Land
DAD'S ARMY

When England is threatened with invasion, the elderly inhabitants of Warmington-on-Sea join the Home Guard.

It may seem eccentric that the second most recent film in my movie collection should be a spin-off from a television comedy series which ran on BBC for nine years. But although this film version is in some technical respects rather slacker than the highest professional standards I would demand, it is still the best television spin-off I have seen, and like the series it harks back in sympathy, in spirit and in historical detail to the golden age from which most of my other choices come. With a little more attention to plotting and editing it might well have been thought to emanate from Ealing in, say, 1952, the year of *The Titfield Thunderbolt*. On its release there were the usual sniffy criticisms which film people apply to anything which derives from television, and a few more reasonable thinkers queried the wisdom of bringing real Nazis into a gentle English jape about invasion being prevented by a group of aged buffoons during those wartime summers of the early forties. Personally, I

DAD'S ARMY. The men who kept Hitler at bay. Ian Lavender, James Beck, Arthur Lowe, Arnold Ridley, John Le Mesurier, Clive Dunn, John Laurie.

don't see why we shouldn't make fun of the Nazis just as we do of ourselves, and memory tells me that the comic spirit of muddling through which is depicted in this film is not unlike that which really beat Hitler. He could not make sense of the blithe self-confidence displayed by the poorly-equipped British, and so, thinking they must have a secret weapon waiting to trap him, he refused to invade, and eventually lost the war.

The pre-credits joke is among the best, with the Nazi general on the far side of the channel staring through his binoculars at the white cliffs of Dover, and seeing only the perpetually incontinent Private Godfrey emerging from a clifftop gents. We are then shown a real Sussex street in its summer dress. Deployed along it may be seen, on the day of the call to action, an imperishable gallery of sublime comic creations. Mr Mainwaring, the self-important bank manager, passes on his way to work several comrades-in-arms-to-be: the butcher, the undertaker, the greengrocer, the spiv, and above all his diffident assistant Wilson, caught on his way back to the grocer's to change his weekly egg, which has a doubtful ambience. Wilson thinks the war news sounds serious, but Mainwaring is full of bravado:

MAINWARING: Nothing to worry about. The whole German attack will just fizzle out. They'll never get through the Maginot Line.
WILSON: No, sir, they've just gone round it. It was on the news.

Mainwaring's banking day starts badly, too, when he refuses to change a cheque for a stranger who turns out to be a very peppery general; but he is given his chance for glory when Anthony Eden on the radio issues a call for the formation of Local Defence Volunteers, later to be familiarized as the Home Guard. Never a man to act as number two, Mainwaring hastens to the recruiting office, where he takes over the entire situation by dint of a simple announcement that he is doing so. A pleasant touch is that having been hoisted at his own request into a position of command on the counter, he has to issue orders with his head at an angle to avoid the ceiling, and looks like the Hunchback of Notre Dame. Taking over the church hall as his HQ, he is induced by the gift of a pound of sausages to appoint as his corporal the ancient butcher, whose experience of war goes back to the Sudan campaign against the fuzzy-wuzzies, with their fear of cold steel: 'They don't like it up 'em, sir, they don't like it up 'em.' The first parade is a predictable shambles, not assisted by the appearance of the accommodating Mrs Pike in search of her delicate son, Mainwaring's junior clerk, and her occasional lover, Mr Wilson, through whose unassuming exterior deep waters clearly run:

MRS PIKE: Will you be round later, Arthur, for your usual?
WILSON: Really, Mavis . . .

The training sequences are accomplished in basic Laurel and Hardy style, with a number of nicely-judged moments. When the greengrocer/ARP warden tries to evict the amateur soldiers so that he can start his own proceedings, Mainwaring's stiff answer is: 'I must ask you to keep your hands off my privates.' There is some pleasant cross-cutting, too, between Nazi preparations on the French coast and those at Warmington-on-Sea. 'A message from the Führer: he wants you to take the invasion plans to headquarters.' 'A message from your wife, sir: she wants you to take home a pound of Brussels sprouts.' (A running joke of the television series, for which the film hasn't time, is the visible quailing of the officious Mainwaring at the mere mention of his never-seen Elizabeth.) And the sequence ends with a genuine golden moment which might easily, it seems at first, have come from Sherlock Holmes's *His Last Bow*. The platoon is assembled atop the cliff, and the unflappable Wilson takes time to draw Mainwaring's attention to the scenery:

WILSON: Beautiful sunset, sir.
MAINWARING: Beautiful land, Wilson. And they're not going to get it, you know. We'll fight till we're down to the last round of ammunition. By the way, how much have we got?
WILSON: One round each, sir.

Until that moment one has been inclined to equate the comedy level with the best of Will Hay; but Hay for all his brilliance trailed behind him the absurdities of stage farce, and here in *Dad's Army* there are frequent touches of truth mixed with propaganda. Churchill would have been proud of them.

The peppery general from the bank queue proves (of course) to be Mainwaring's commander, and now mutters 'bloody clerk' at each encounter. All the encounters are disastrous. Having ingeniously converted his butcher-van transport to gas, Mainwaring accidentally punctures the balloon and has to borrow a steamroller, which fails to stop at its destination and mows down a neat row of army tents, while the whole parade stands stiffly at the salute. An almost surrealistic sequence follows, with the general on his white horse floating gently down river on the central section of a pontoon bridge which has been sabotaged. The Warmington platoon breathlessly tries to keep up with him along the bank: 'Couldn't you swim ashore, sir?' 'I'm a general, not an admiral.'

The finale brings a weary return to the church hall, which the audience has meanwhile seen to be occupied by three stray German parachutists who are holding practically the whole village as hostages. There is some good googly dialogue. The ARP warden has been trapped in the gents, and is climbing out of the window when he encounters the sexton and jerks his thumb behind him; 'It's full of Germans.' The sexton makes the wrong connection: 'Then why don't you use the one in the vicarage?' Then Mainwaring tries the front door, finds the whole village sitting to attention, and can't interpret the cryptic nods and messages from the limp-wristed vicar, who has a gun trained at his back. 'He kept winking at me,' Mainwaring tells Wilson when he rejoins his men, 'and telling me to come back later.' 'And are you going to?' asks Wilson innocently. The penny drops only when an emissary is sent out with instructions: 'If I'm not back in fifteen minutes the vicar is going to be very upset.' 'Why?' they ask. 'They're going to shoot him.'

Huddled conferences now take place in the shrubbery. The general finally strokes his chin and utters: 'We'll have to be very careful how we handle this. I've sent for the navy.' The naval gent who arrives has similar thoughts and sends for the police, who send for the marines, who send for the fire brigade. The way in which Mainwaring eventually brushes aside this shilly-shallying and relieves the church hall by personal action may be heroic or it may be foolhardy, but it is credible as part of the man, so he can't be entirely a caricature. It brings the film to a satisfactory end, though like the series episodes it stops on an off-beat rather than a laugh. Those with eyes to see and ears to hear will have gained during the preceding ninety minutes a very fair impression of life in Churchill's England, though it may be only reasonable to send them as a corrective to see a starker version of similar events, such as *Went the Day Well?* (qv), equally persuasive in its own way, with death at the post office and a quisling in the manor.

Dad's Army has decided historic interest as well as entertainment value, and the fact that its reputation is unestablished is due mainly to the contempt professed by adherents of one medium for the product of any other.

Dad's Army. GB 1971; Technicolor; 95 minutes. Produced by John R. Sloan for Norcon/Columbia. Written by Jimmy Perry and David Croft. Directed by Norman Cohen. Photographed by Terry Maher. Music by Wilfred Burns. With Arthur Lowe as Captain Mainwaring; John Le Mesurier as Sergeant Wilson; John Laurie as Private Fraser; James Beck as Private Walker; Clive Dunn as Corporal Jones; Arnold Ridley as Private Godfrey; Ian Lavender as Private Pike; Liz Fraser as Mrs Pike; Bill Pertwee as ARP warden; Frank Williams as the vicar; Edward Sinclair as the verger.

Hurrah for the Next Man Who Dies

THE DAWN PATROL

In France during World War I, flying officers wait their turn to embark on suicidal missions.

This is a film as notable for its connections as for its original substance. Its author, John Monk Saunders, once married to the actress Fay Wray who sat in King Kong's paw, is remembered for his stories of World War I flyers, of whose short unhappy lives he had a Hemingway-like vision (best expressed, perhaps, in that uniquely cynical 1931 movie *The Last Flight* [qv], in which a group of them, hanging on in Paris after the war, go to the bad in various ways). *The Dawn Patrol* first emerged as a film in 1930, and by then, it must be said, enough time had elapsed for it to be influenced by a British play called *Journey's End* which had set London and Broadway box offices afire and was itself being filmed by James Whale. To be sure, *Journey's End* is set in a dugout during the incredible trench fighting which slaughtered so many innocents, and *The Dawn Patrol*, apart from its interpolated airplane sequences, is set in the officers' living quarters of a makeshift airfield behind the lines. But not only is the mood identical – the mood of artificial gaiety and bouts of pessimism – so are the characters. In both the commander is at his wit's end because he must obey orders which send so many boys straight from school to their deaths. In both he has an older adjutant who acts as a calming force by talking about England's green and pleasant land to which they all hope to return. In both there is a young officer who starts by admiring the commander and then turns against him. And in both the players are killed off one by one until death is the only winner. Stiff but sharp, the 1930 *Journey's End* movie won its laurels, but the piece was not filmed again until in the seventies it turned up as *Aces High*, its background changed to the air war, so that it looked pretty much like *The Dawn Patrol*. (The title *Aces High* reminds one of *Twelve O'Clock High*, which had a very similar situation transposed to World War II, with Gregory Peck as the officer showing the strain of command.)

Meanwhile, the original *Dawn Patrol*, now known on American television as *Flight Commander*, had been upstaged as early as 1938 by a remake using all the original action footage but concentrating on tensely dialogue-ridden interiors, which instead of Richard Barthelmess, Neil Hamilton and Douglas Fairbanks Jnr now featured Errol Flynn, Basil Rathbone and David Niven.

It is the 1938 version which I have chosen to study, and a rich study it makes. For Hollywood at the time it was quite a remarkable enterprise, entirely eschewing feminine relief and casting only British actors in its British roles. The aerial dogfights are distanced by their slightly fuzzier 1930 photography, and this makes it more obvious that the acting bits are basically a play. All three leading roles are strong, though Rathbone starts off on so twitchy a note that his performance has nowhere to go but down: 'You know what this place is? It's a slaughterhouse, and I'm the butcher. Send 'A' Flight out on another rotten show? Protect our bombers in planes stuck together with spit and glue? And do our boys complain? Never. They just say right, and go and do it.' This is Stanhope of *Journey's End* to the life, except that Rathbone, admirable villain or Sherlock Holmes that he was, never seemed quite the stuff of which heroes are made. We are relieved when halfway through the film he marches stiffly off to promotion and leaves the tensions of command to Flynn, who though usually saying 'right' without a lot of fuss, has tended also to sneer at Rathbone's spinelessness in obeying impossible orders instead of arguing the toss with his superiors.

The first half of the film keeps the tensions in the background, preferring to concentrate on the superficially frivolous lives of these death-or-glory boys who drink themselves stupid every night in the knowledge that the dawn flight over enemy lines may be their last. And so after dinner they foregather at the bar, get through crates of whisky, play 'Poor Butterfly' on the gramophone, and sing a particularly melancholy quatrain:

> So stand by, your glasses ready.
> This world is a world of lies.
> Here's a toast to the dead already:
> Hurrah for the next man who dies!

'Listen to them,' says Rathbone. 'Bluffing themselves, pretending death doesn't mean anything to them, trying to live just for the minute, the hour, pretending they don't care if they get up tomorrow and never come back.' Most devil-may-care of all is Lt Scott, played by David Niven: perpetually drunk and wearing spotted pink pyjamas over his uniform, both to bed and on next day's mission. After one sortie he is thought to have been shot down, and his presumed passing casts a momentary shadow of gloom over the mess. 'He was wearing his piebald pyjamas: funny if he showed up before the devil in those.' But it turns out that Lt Scott managed a pancake landing, and he returns that evening with half a dozen bottles of champagne. Meanwhile the real truth is being underlined by Donald Crisp as the adjutant, who stays aloof from the revelry but fancies having a dog in the mess to cheer him up. It is his job to write letters of sympathy to bereaved parents and wives. 'Do you

THE DAWN PATROL. Basil Rathbone gives David Niven and Errol Flynn a talking-to. They probably had plenty of the same in real life.

think,' he asks Rathbone, 'they're becoming stereotyped?' 'No matter how you write it,' is the answer, 'it will break his mother's heart just the same.'

Just before dawn the necessary replacements arrive, young officers fresh from flying school, with only a few hours' experience in the air. 'That's all right, gentlemen,' says the sergeant respectfully, 'We'll deal with your baggage'; but he knows that within minutes they will be piloting planes on what may be their first and last mission. Above the engines' roar the sergeant can be heard repeating the officially required question: 'Has the officer any papers on him that might give information to the enemy?' Bitterness creeps into the mess when a German officer is captured; but Niven recognises the man who shot him down, and is delighted to meet him, so they all get drunk together. That night Flynn and Niven steal off by motor bike to paint the town red: 'Gentlemen, keep the war going please, we're off to roll in a few gutters.' But on their drunken return they find an impudent challenge from German air ace Von Richter, and they risk court martial by carrying out a two-man strafing of the German ground emplacements. Then comes Flynn's promotion and a change of mood, for, having found that argument with the top brass is impossible, he takes to drink in order to issue the orders he loathes. Niven rebels when his own younger brother comes in and is promptly sent on a mission by Flynn, only to die in action. The shape of the film then demands that Flynn himself be killed in a suicidal assignment which he steals from Niven, who is left to take over the thankless task of flight commander.

At the back of one's mind while watching this brooding film there lurks not so much a sense of the absurdity of war as a feeling that if Flynn and Niven had been in the Royal Flying Corps this might have been their own story. They take their acting as lightly as the characters take their lives, but it works because there is nothing simulated about it. At the time *The Dawn Patrol* was made they were sharing a house on Santa Monica Beach, a house they christened Cirrhosis by the Sea. From all accounts, life there can't have been so very different from life in Flight A mess of the 59th Squadron.

The Dawn Patrol. US 1938; black and white; 102 minutes. Produced by Hal B. Wallis for Warner. Written by Seton I. Miller and Dan Totheroh from the original by John Monk Saunders. Directed by Edmund Goulding. Photographed by Tony Gaudio. Music by Max Steiner. With Errol Flynn as Captain Courtney; Basil Rathone as Major Brand; David Niven as Lt Scott; Donald Crisp as Phipps; Melville Cooper as Sergeant Watkins; Barry Fitzgerald as Bott; Carl Esmond as Von Mueller; Peter Willes as Hollister; Morton Lowry as Ronnie.

Out for the Count
DRACULA

A Transylvanian vampire count moves to Yorkshire but is outwitted by Professor Van Helsing.

I first read Bram Stoker's novel as an undergraduate, one night after a West End play when I was on the milk train back to Cambridge. By the time we lurched to a prolonged halt at Saffron Walden, the book had scared the living daylights out of me, and I sorely wished there had been someone, anyone, to share my musty compartment, through whose door, open to the East Anglian blackness, a vampire might attack me at any moment. Next day I skipped a lecture in order to finish the book in bed, and although the epistolary form tends to bog it down later on, I still re-read the opening chapters with perverse pleasure while a few hackles rise on the back of my neck. These chapters comprise Stoker's account of a trip to Transylvania undertaken by a Victorian solicitor's clerk named Jonathan Harker, whose mission is to discuss with a strange nobleman his proposed purchase of an English manor. The stage versions, popular in the twenties and multifariously revived in the seventies, all restrict the action to an English country house whose inhabitants are variously affected by the fact that Count Dracula has recently become their neighbour. Dramatically the plays suffer from this compression, for the Count can make no more than occasional appearances, sometimes as the fluttering bat into whose form he is able to change at night. Only in those early Transylvanian scenes of the novel does he take centre stage, coming some way towards endearing himself to us as the last of a noble line afflicted by a strange malady.

The 1930 film version, though theoretically adapted from the play, kept these Transylvanian scenes as part of the opening-up process, and they are certainly the best thing in it. Clearly the producers were in two minds as to whether or not the whole subject was too nasty for filming in any form, and so they geared their publicity towards the Count's hypnotic power over the female sex, with the tag-line 'The strangest love a woman has ever known!' Even allowing for the fact that talkies were but three years old, the entire approach of this version, despite the handling by Lon Chaney's well respected director Tod Browning, was tentative rather than full-blooded. Its appeal today lies chiefly in its being the first of a long line, and on the whole the Christopher Lee version of 1958 is a better adaptation. Even the heavily-syllabled Bela Lugosi, who had played Dracula on the Broadway stage, seems more of a liability than an asset. Apart from a few bars of Tchaikovsky over the main title, the film is musically silent, and poor Mr Lugosi has to make his sinister effects with very little assistance save for two pinpoints of light which are supposed to be directed at the pupils of his eyes, but as often as not miss their target. Furthermore, when approaching his prey he sometimes seems unsteady on his feet; the positioning of his limbs is often more comic than sinister; and he is so tall as to blend poorly into whatever few visual compositions his director attempts. Of course he has a magnificently mittel-European voice, and his way with such lines as 'I never drink . . . wine' is inimitable. (Poor Frank Langella in the 1979 version found that the only way to be original was completely to throw away the famous utterances, a great disappointment to those of us who grew up on music-hall impressions of 'Children of the night: listen to them, what music they make'.)

In surprising but sober fact, the Transylvanian prologue in 1930 was crammed into a single reel. And surprise, surprise, in this Universal version it is not Harker who goes to Transylvania, but the gentleman named Renfield who later becomes a mad insect-eater. This leaves the heroic Harker quite sane but with little to do save stand on the drawing room carpet casting sheep's eyes at his lady love and listening politely to Professor Van Helsing's discourses on the nature of vampires. As the timid Renfield, Dwight Frye is actually quite good in what was to be his only sizeable part prior to a succession of crazed hunchbacks, and even his English accent is reasonably creditable. We meet him at the last rest stop on his interminable journey into the unknown, in a coach full of peasants crossing themselves and muttering about the approach of Walpurgisnacht. (Those who have visited Universal City will find the setting still recognizable as its backlot, though a glass shot of

DRACULA. Helen Chandler seems pretty convinced that Bela Lugosi is not taking her to her bedroom as promised.

spiky mountains goes some way towards disguising it.) The landlord, hastily casting glances towards heaven, tries to dissuade the wide-eyed traveller from visiting Count Dracula and his brides (brides! Renfield had never heard of *them*) by explaining in fractured English: 'Dey leave deir coffins at night and dey feed on de blood of de living!' To emphasize this danger we are now treated to a shot of the forbidding castle, which seems to have been hewn from the rock on which it stands; then we cut to the dungeons, where sure enough rats and giant insects and armadillos (armadillos in Transylvania?) dart and scatter as withered hands open coffin lids from within. In a trice, we see before us the immaculate, caped and steel-eyed count with his three pale ladies, who look like guests at a twenties society party except that they hiss when thwarted.

We return to Mr Renfield being dropped off, at his own insistence, at the Borgo Pass at midnight. This version makes no secret of the fact that the muffled coachman awaiting him in the side road is really Dracula himself, who for reasons we may guess at is forced to run his castle single-handed; but five minutes later when Renfield calls to the man to slow down, there is no man at all, just a bat appearing to guide the horses. When the coach stops at the castle even the bat has disappeared, but a heavy door opens fairly promptly to reveal a comparatively genial elderly gentleman, candelabra in hand. 'I am . . . Dracula,' he enunciates in polite if not cheerful greeting; but Renfield's relief is short-lived when his host, leading the way up a crumbled stairway, appears to walk through a wall of cobweb without disturbing it, whereas Renfield must use his stick to scatter the angry occupants. Dracula, raising an eyebrow, takes the opportunity for another memorable line: 'The spider spinning his web for the unwary fly. The blood is the life, Mr Renfield!'

Upstairs as the count watches his guest pick at a cold supper there is a splendid moment when Renfield pricks his finger on a paper clip and Dracula, seeing the spot of blood, advances on him as though hypnotized, until a crucifix round Renfield's neck makes him cower away. (I remember with affection the only good line in Polanski's crude spoof *The Fearless Vampire Killers*, when Alfie Bass as the Jewish bloodsucker, having a crucifix waved at him by his defiant victim, simply grins and says: 'Hoi! Hev you got the wrong vampire!') The Count also comes up with one of the conversation-stoppers of all time: 'To be dead! To be really dead! That must be glorious!' But the promising scene is allowed to taper out far too quickly and with next to no frissons of fear. Renfield, at the window, hears a wolf howl and mysteriously faints; the three ladies appear from stage left and look hungry; but the count stalks into the group and prepares to take precedence for the first nibble, though the image fades before he gets anywhere near Renfield's neck. Query, just thought of: has the effect of the crucifix worn off so soon?

The remaining hour of this version is scarcely of interest. Indeed it is muddled almost beyond belief, the Count being rumbled and staked almost before he has obtained a toehold on English high society. Dracula even gives himself away by hissing to his persecutor before witnesses: 'For one who has not lived even a single lifetime, you are a wise man, Van Helsing.' And those who looked forward to a visual recreation of Bram Stoker's graveyard thrills must have found them sadly missing. The 1979 remake certainly did not stint on such horrors, though Laurence Olivier as Van Helsing was scarcely on form, being content merely to give his routine Albert Bassermann impersonation. What this version did, curiously, was transplant the entire Transylvanian prologue to Whitby, which both versions seem to agree is 'near London'. Dracula's guest this time is the unwisely unchaperoned heroine Lucy, for whom he gives a private dinner party in his recently purchased Carfax Abbey, which he has 'restored' for the occasion by dint of a thousand candles. Now there's a trick missed, for the art direction which in Yorkshire seems merely absurd could in Transylvania have been magnificent.

Perhaps, on reflection, the best *Dracula* was Murnau's illicit one of 1922, retitled *Nosferatu* to escape copyright problems. The 1930 version has wistful charm, the 1958 one majors in shock, 1979 was determined to be different; but *Nosferatu*, remade rather too slavishly in recent years by Werner Herzog, was the only one to engender genuine revulsion, which I take it would be quite an appropriate reaction to any long-dead vampire one might meet socially.

Dracula. US 1930; black and white; 75 minutes. Produced by Carl Laemmle Jnr for Universal. Written by Garrett Fort from the play by Hamilton Deane and John L. Balderston, based on the novel by Bram Stoker. Directed by Tod Browning. Photographed by Karl Freund. Music by Tchaikovsky. With Bela Lugosi as Count Dracula; Edward Van Sloan as Professor Van Helsing; Helen Chandler as Lucy; Dwight Frye as Renfield; David Manners as Jonathan Harker.

And Please Reverse the Charges

E.T. – THE EXTRA-TERRESTRIAL

An alien from a flying saucer is befriended by a small boy.

The truth is that I didn't much care for it, despite the fact that in 1982 it turned out to be commercially the most successful film of all time, and gave the world a new catch-phrase: 'E.T., call home.' In my disappointment I searched dutifully for guides to what I had missed. The popular press was pretty useless: predictably it had been hypnotized by the hype, and was on analysis only grateful to be shown, after so many months of sex and savagery, something with a 'U' certificate to which the entire family might safely be taken (though surprisingly it contains at least one 'shit' as well as a questionable joke about Uranus). Equally predictably the British Film Institute's *Monthly Film Bulletin* wasn't much help, with overwrought in-depth pronouncements such as the following:

> Its most striking feature is that adult males are never seen above the midriff till the end of the film . . . Spielberg's talent for fantasy is so complete – the liberty he takes with our vision and sense of identification – that one wants to call it something else, a graphic re-invention of the world. Here it amounts to what might be experienced by anthropomorphized cartoon characters – Tom and Jerry, perhaps – playing in a world occupied by headless, harrying people, who interfere with their (and Spielberg's) delight in knocking over the furniture.

More intelligibly, the *M.F.B.* suggested a Jesus Christ parallel: 'a mother called Mary, the resurrection of E.T., and then his revelation, robed in white, to his disciples (the kids on their bikes).' The posher papers had, of course, been equally sharp to spot the metaphors and the references to various myths. Tinkerbell was cited along with Christ as a character who died and was resurrected. The men who chase away the spaceship in the first place are, of course, our clumsy governments who never know what's best. The hygienic cocoon in which the house is shrouded must be a womb image. Teaching E.T.

30

E.T. The eccentric visitor is about to try flying home rather than calling home.

to speak English reminded several critics of both Eliza Dolittle and the Frankenstein monster, though he accomplishes it more easily than either. The ease with which E.T. stimulates jaded lives made it a partial rewrite of *The Passing of the Third Floor Back*. And, of course, the message that one should be kind to extra-terrestrials should equally apply to our less fortunate neighbours. Speaking of less fortunate beings, one might have thought that a race able to send space ships across the solar system would by the process of natural selection have provided itself with bodies capable of more graceful movement; but then, if the legs had been longer than the stumps we see it would have been impossible to hide a dwarf in them for the long shots. This is presumably why E.T. doesn't look much like the idealized space creature glimpsed at the end of *Close Encounters*, to which this film is a sort of sequel. By the way, when the ship descends through the dark, armed with what look like two sets of gleaming white teeth, are we not intended to think of the arch villain of another Spielberg film, namely *Jaws*?

The empathy between a space creature and the small boy who befriends and protects him is a pleasant conceit, especially since the boy's name is Elliott, which starts with an E and ends with a T. But the fact is that the film devotes most of its time to tantalizing us with glimpses of the creature, and this leaves little room for plot development. Nor are the trick shots, when they come, at all impressive: driving a Model T across the sky in 1961's *The Absent-Minded*

Professor was much more convincingly done than the aerial bicycle-riding here. Even E.T. himself is never much more than a random construction of pop eyes and plastic, which is why we are left for so long to get used to him in semi-darkness. Possibly for associated reasons, the colour and lighting tend towards the ugly, save for that one magical shot of the backyard with the crescent moon above and light blazing oddly from the garden shed in which E.T. is hiding. Incidentally, there is a chase from here into what seems to be a cornfield, but when we see the house in full daylight it is hemmed in on all sides by the mountain, on a shoulder of which it sits. Tut tut, Mr Spielberg.

The music carries the film along as well as, or better than, it deserves, and Spielberg himself has a way with a quick cut to a telling image which is most effective. But the script is surprisingly deficient in drive, clarity and even simple logic, and Elliott himself has no more personality than a doll boy in F.A.O. Schwarz. We are reminded too often that Spielberg likes untidiness: the house is quite appallingly cluttered, and people keep dropping messy things like milk and eggs, without stopping to mop them up. Finally, though I saw the film in the distributor's private screening room (with an audience of children, I might add) there was the usual trouble with audibility. There isn't *that* much dialogue, but I caught less than half of it, so plangent and sibilant is the recording.

I hate to be carping, I truly do, about a film which so many seem to have watched with wonder and satisfaction, especially one which sets itself so firmly on the side of benevolence and trust and family feeling and the hope of glory. But honestly, these things were more enjoyably and emotionally diffused many years ago in movies like *The Blue Bird* and *Pinocchio* and *The Wizard of Oz*. To wallow in E.T., perhaps, you have to be young enough not to have seen any of them.

E.T. US 1982; De Luxe Colour; 115 minutes. Produced by Steven Spielberg and Kathleen Kennedy for Universal. Written by Melissa Mathison. Directed by Steven Spielberg. Photographed by Allen Daviau. Music by John Williams. E.T. created by Carlo Rimbaldi. With Dee Wallace as Mary; Henry Thomas as Elliott; Peter Coyote as Keys; Robert MacNaughton as Michael; Drew Barrymore as Gertie.

Start Checking the Moniker File
THE ENFORCER

A district attorney accumulates evidence against a gang which murders for profit.

I refer not to the late seventies drek starring Clint Eastwood, but to the highly burnished little black-and-white thriller which in Britain in 1951, under the title *Murder Inc.*, received not only an 'X' certificate, which made it taboo to those under eighteen, but was subjected to extra public warnings as to its unprecedentedly shocking nature. They must have meant morally shocking, for physically this is a remarkably unviolent film, implying far more than it ever dares to show. Murder for profit was then a new concept, which the censor doubtless felt to be just as socially undesirable as the hoodlum motor cyclists who zoomed along three years later in *The Wild One*. Personally, I've always preferred the camera to avert its gaze when a nasty murder is looming up, but I suppose that in this case the easy treatment is inclined to make a fairy tale out of a very brutish and nasty business which involves bodies in a swamp, bodies in a furnace, violent mental patients, a razor murder and various stabbings by ice-pick.

The Enforcer is nevertheless a key film, forging a link between *film noir* and *The French Connection*. It also moved its ageing star (Humphrey Bogart) out of his Rick Blaine period into a role where his hairpiece showed and he wasn't even very tough, just a patient assistant district attorney who acted virtually as narrator and had no female involvements. (After this interregnum, he would return as a first-rate character actor.) All the more reason perhaps to hand the assignment to a director who could inject some well-shot action sequences; yet the man chosen was a new name from Broadway, Bretaigne Windust, who seems to have failed to the extent that most of the film was directed by Raoul Walsh, working incognito.

The story told is a totally fictitious account of the real *Murder Inc.* (Today's scriptwriters would at least have pretended to be sticking as closely to the facts as possible, but clearly the chief concern in 1950 was to tell a rattling good yarn.) The appeal which emerges, thirty-odd years after the film was made, is the appeal of a Chinese box: you fix one set of characters and situations, and they lead you back in time and introduce you to others; it is not until you have met them all that you can work out exactly how things happened. Or as a character puts it, you open one can of beans, and inside there's another. It all starts, and virtually ends, on a dark night at the DA's office. Robert Burks's brilliant day-for-night photography, while enabling some of us to recognize the outside of the Warner stages doubling for street buildings, instantly asserts its dramatic superiority to the murky blue hazes we would be offered nowadays. A key witness, a very nervous one, shark turned into blubber, is being guarded so that tomorrow he can testify against Mendoza, the head of the murder organization, who as a result is going to fry in the electric chair. Rico becomes so hysterical that he is taken down to see Mendoza in his cell, just to prove that the master criminal is only human. The tactic doesn't work, because Mendoza's evil eye unnerves the potential witness even more. (We don't see Mendoza again for seventy minutes, which increases our own awe of the satanic figure.) Despite the guards and the guns ('Don't leave him for anything,' Bogart cries) the now totally unbalanced Rico escapes through a toilet window, and after a hair-raising rescue attempt falls to his death. Now the cops, after years of work, have no case against Mendoza. 'There's nothing we could hold him on?' asks the mayor. 'I couldn't even give him thirty days,'

33

THE ENFORCER. A terrified suspect, Zero Mostel, raises all kinds of suspicions in the mind of Humphrey Bogart.

snarls Bogie. So the assistant DA spends the night feverishly going through the cabinets of evidence (flashback looming) in search of the one overlooked fact which is stuck at the back of his mind and which might still convict Mendoza. ('Ever have a tune running through your head and you can't remember the words?')

And so the report springs to life through the old familiar optical shimmer. It consists chiefly of the blubberings of small-time hoodlums who have gone spectacularly to pieces on discovering the exact nature of the outfit they are mixed up with. 'They made me kill my girl,' whines Duke Malloy when he turns himself in at a precinct house. Big Babe Lazich is rescued screaming from a church confessional. ('It always worries me when these hoodlums get religion,' mutters Bogie. 'Start checking the moniker file.') Philadelphia Tom Zaca, many times a murderer, is already in the nuthouse where he belongs. Gradually the assistant DA, after a maze of grisly discoveries based on unexpected information, learns to his amazement what is a hit, a contract and a troop. And when the truth begins to be fitted together, and a picture of the spider at the centre is built up, Mendoza's recourse is to order the wholesale slaughter of his own suspected men so that they can't turn him in. Only Rico

34

escapes the net, and he decides to squeal. Only he, it seems, can actually link Mendoza to a killing, and that was years ago when the master criminal's unusual service was a one-man show and he was obliged to give demonstrations. His dark deed was witnessed by a taxi driver, who was later eliminated because he saw and recognized Mendoza in the street. (The murder takes place under hot towels in a barber shop, and there is a nice shot when the hand of the barber stropping the razor is replaced by that of the hired killer.) The man's daughter has been murdered too, as a safety precaution . . . but hold it . . . at dawn the DA realizes what he should have realized long before. They got the wrong girl, the eyes are the wrong colour in the record. The girl now posing as the victim's flatmate is the real Angela Vetto, and she must be reached and protected at once. Needless to say, Mendoza's emissaries are on the same trail, and the film climaxes in a modestly tense sequence in a shopping street as police and killers close in, neither knowing what the girl they seek looks like. 'Get off the street, Angela Vetto, your life is in danger,' lisps Bogie through a loudspeaker. And there's a nervous moment when the would-be victim gives herself away and walks off the pavement right behind one of the assassins who is looking for her.

To be truthful, *The Enforcer* probably never aspired to a status lordlier than that of what *Variety* would call a 'nervous A', a cheaply if efficiently made programmer which might with luck become a money-maker because of its exploitation values. If it was a stunt, it happened to be a very slick one, and one which took the public's fancy, despite the hero's lack of characterization: he's just a public defender, like McGarrett in *Hawaii Five-O*. Even the picturesque hoodlums are no more than extravagant caricatures in familiar moulds, quite unlike the real human beings indulging in 'a left-handed form of human endeavour' in the contemporaneous *The Asphalt Jungle*. Even the splendid Everett Sloane is hard pressed to get a good cameo out of Mendoza when he is finally allowed to appear, enlisting the aid of the thug who has been sent to beat him up. ('I've been gone over by experts, but you're the best.') Yet for all its demerits, few watchers even in the sophisticated eighties will be able to take their eyes off the screen while this mordant thriller is playing.

The Enforcer (GB title: *Murder Inc.*). US 1950; black and white; 87 minutes. Produced by Milton Sperling for United States Pictures. Written by Martin Rackin. Directed by Bretaigne Windust (and Raoul Walsh). Photographed by Robert Burks. Music by David Buttolph. With Humphrey Bogart as Martin Ferguson; Zero Mostel as Big Babe Lazich; Ted de Corsia as Joseph Rico; Everett Sloane as Albert Mendoza; Roy Roberts as Captain Nelson; Lawrence Tolan as Duke Malloy; Adelaide Klein as Olga Kirshen; Jack Lambert as Philadelphia Tom Zaca; Patricia Joiner as Angela Vetto.

Flight from Veidt
ESCAPE

An American goes to pre-war Germany to get his mother out of a concentration camp.

Some films are not born great, but have greatness thrust upon them. My political consciousness has never reached any very awesome heights, but *Escape* is the movie which first caused it to germinate and bud. I saw it in 1940 at the Bolton Odeon, and we had to queue. As we did so, the sirens sounded for an air raid, which rather pleased my mother and me because it caused some chicken-hearted souls to forsake their places and head for the shelter, and that meant that we got into the sixpenny front stalls earlier than we expected. Just three minutes, in fact, before the first evening performance ended. Conrad Veidt, one of our favourite actors, and British by adoption, had gone to Hollywood to make the movie. (He never came back.) There he stood, six feet something of teutonic arrogance but looking ten times the height on the Odeon's giant luminescent screen, of which from the front stalls entrance we got a melodramatically distorted view. We groped open-mouthed for our seats; Mr Veidt could not be ignored for a second, his face and body being distorted by tremors of fury. Norma Shearer put out a hand in concern; then both were distracted by the sound of a plane overhead, and we got a shot of it against the night sky, which caused the audience (who knew the situation) to cheer. Back to Mr Veidt, plainly more ill than before; he had now assumed a horizontal position. He had a deathly pallor; his upper lip suffered a splendid twitch; and he was murmuring: 'Don't leave me.' Miss Shearer promised that she would not, and there was a fade to a distant shot of the plane, then finis. As the lights went up I puzzled as to what could have happened to the film's nominal hero Robert Taylor. Presumably he was in the plane, but that was odd; for at that time we were not used to movies which failed to end in a romantic clinch. I settled down with increased anticipation as Donald Duck came on. *Escape* had been posted as an important picture, and was clearly going to be different in all kinds of ways, notably in its reintroduction of a silent star, Nazimova, whose name we could not pronounce with confidence.

In fact what remains with me about *Escape* is its provision of my first knowledge about concentration camps in which German citizens of the mid-thirties could be imprisoned, forgotten, and later executed, simply for wanting to take their money out of the country. As we strolled home through the leather tannery, the air raid not having amounted to much, I asked about the Germans. We were fighting them, and Hitler was supposed to be a madman, but the film had indicated that not all Germans were bad Germans, that many might wish to show their hatred of the Nazi regime but were afraid to do so. Even the general as played by Conrad Veidt had been depicted in the first half of the picture as a man of taste and refinement; his nasty side came

ESCAPE. Conrad Veidt realizes that Norma Shearer has not been telling him the entire truth.

out only when, on a purely personal level, he became jealous of the American hero's interest in a luscious German-American countess who for years had been numbered among the general's own preserves. My mother said that there was good and bad in everybody, with a few exceptions, and next morning she whisked me off to the branch library for a book which would explain to me what had happened in Europe between the wars. *A Contemporary History*, it was called, and I found it rather hard going, but I remember hoping that the war would not go on until I was old enough to fight in it, for I found the Germans rather interesting and had no particular wish to kill any.

When on Channel Four in 1983 I ran a series of revivals under the heading 'The Gathering Storm', aiming to show various aspects of the run-up to World War II, *Escape* was naturally among them. I wish I could hail it as a better film than it is. It holds the interest, of course, as a top MGM production should, but it suffers from an unconvincing plot, turgid dialogue, a lack of action and some very variable acting. The negative, luckily, has been perfectly preserved, and Robert Planck's gleaming photography is as rich and wondrous to behold as it ever was; but there isn't a shot taken outside the sound stage, and the mountain backdrops are cardboard and the snow looks like cereal and Mervyn Le Roy's direction is already showing signs of the paralysis which was to overtake it twenty years later. What chiefly remains, apart from the superficial interest of the story, is the political importance. Here was Hollywood, a year and more before America came into the war, making its emotions perfectly plain, giving those with imagination a glimmering of what it must have been like for good Germans in Bavaria in 1936, when the only easy and comfortable way of living was to close one's eyes to what was going on behind the mountain.

Robert Taylor, alas, is a stick of a hero. He never suggests German ancestry, and his attempts at showing the man's fear and confusion only remind one of his very limited acting training. He isn't even theatrical like Nazimova, who from her concentration camp bed plays the ailing mother as Sarah Bernhardt must have played Hamlet, with tremulous defiance and with a soft open look to her face so that the wrinkles won't show. Mr Taylor's attempts to find her are not helped by the local villagers, who seem to have strayed from the Frankenstein set, performing frantic double-takes and doing everything but cross themselves at the mention of the Nazis. He is recommended at last to an old sick lawyer (the magnificent Albert Bassermann in his first English-speaking part) who can say only that we all have to face death, and he sooner than most. It seems rather petulant and tactless of Mr Taylor to spring up with the unlikely cry: 'Death? What's my mother got to do with death? She's the livest person you ever saw!'

Soon Mr Taylor is the picture of despair, for the local police chief threatens him and nobody else will talk to him; even an old family servant brandishes a horse-whip. As he rather clumsily expresses the situation: 'Every door looks like a door until you try to go through it. Every person looks like a human being until you talk to him.' His luck begins to change when halfway up the mountain he meets the half-American countess, who lives in one of those Tyrolean-style villas which seem to have been furnished for Deanna Durbin. Having been born on East 57th Street she is not unsympathetic, though nor is she about to rock her own comfortable little boat. However, later that evening she remarks to her lover Mr Veidt that she does sometimes feel she is living on a mountaintop high above the real cruel world. Since the conversation has moved into metaphors, Mr Veidt opines that everyone should keep his real self on a mountaintop, and Miss Shearer agrees that nobody can be unhappy all the time without a moment's relief. (Yes, the scriptwriters have much to regret.) The plot finally progresses only because Mr Veidt in his light clipped way remarks that if Mr Taylor keeps on asking questions he will be dealt with; Miss Shearer then feels impelled to warn Mr Taylor, which leads to his meeting a sympathetic camp doctor, who evolves a scheme for slipping mother a mickey which will give her the appearance of death for long enough for her to be taken over the border in a coffin.

Everyone, in fact, is left with some sort of honour, the real villains being kept off screen. Even the old servant turns up trumps, which is nice as he's played by Felix Bressart, and the film tightens its grip on our pulse when the escape plan is carried through with only a few near misses, then aborted when snow forces all concerned to take refuge by night in Miss Shearer's château. The final act, as it were, has Mr Veidt slowly waking up to what is going on under his adopted roof, while the refugees prepare to make it to the airport. Will the countess, with tears in her eyes and her eyes on Mr Taylor, head for the new world with her new friends? No, for all his faults she still loves her German general, heart condition and all. (Yes, of course it's a plot point.) Mr Taylor can't waste time arguing: 'The plane's at nine. It's twenty-one minutes to, and it takes fifteen minutes to the airport. We'd better leave.' He better had, unless clearances were quicker then, which with all those Nazis about we can hardly believe.

And so, with Mr Veidt fatally stricken at the realization of his own blindness, to where we came in.

Escape. US 1940; black and white; 104 minutes. Produced by Lawrence Weingarten for MGM. Written by Arch Oboler and Marguerite Roberts from the novel by Ethel Vance. Directed by Mervyn Le Roy. Photographed by Robert Planck. Music by Franz Waxman. With Robert Taylor as Mark Pressing; Norma Shearer as Countess von Teck; Conrad Veidt as General Kurt von Kolb; Alla Nazimova as Emmy Ritter; Felix Bressart as Fritz Keller; Albert Bassermann as Dr Arthur Henning; Philip Dorn as Dr Ditten; Bonita Granville as Ursula; Blanche Yurka as the nurse.

A Villain of the Deepest Dye
THE FACE AT THE WINDOW

A villain uses his moronic half-brother to distract his victims as he murders them.

The reissue in the seventies of Graham Greene's film reviews of the thirties caused a mild stirring of curiosity about this long-forgotten barnstormer, for in 1939 the melancholy sophisticate had called it 'one of the best English pictures I have seen'. He continued: 'Mr Tod Slaughter is certainly one of our finest living actors: we see in this picture at whose feet Mr Laughton must have sat – that dancing sinister step, the raised shoulder and the flickering eyelid.' Well, well, Mr Slaughter must have been pleased, though the review did not prevent him from ending his days in twice-nightly reach-me-down tourers. Modern viewers taking the chance to reassess *The Face at the Window* may well conclude that Mr Greene had gone slightly potty, though they are likely to concede that the piece possessed some unexpected merit for a horror quickie.

It certainly has competence. It is adequately set, very creditably lit, sharply edited, quite excitingly scored, and even on occasion fairly enterprisingly directed if one allows for a tendency to show too much of each set at first glance, thereby sending the sense of mystery packing: the film lacks unknown

THE FACE AT THE WINDOW. Tod Slaughter has Marjorie Taylor right in his clutches. She should try pulling at his beard.

recesses from which clutching hands might reach. The physical excesses of melodrama, in fact, are muted here: the 'face' is cut away from almost before it has been established, and one regrets the lack of a hiss track to stir us to heights of indignation at the villain's outlandish behaviour. For the only way to enjoy what the main title calls 'Brooke Warren's famous melodrama' is as a pantomime from which the songs and slapstick have been removed, and the wicked uncle given the star part.

Mr Slaughter behaves in any event like a man born to stardom. He never outstays his welcome in a scene, but while he's about he has a whale of a time, curling his lip and wiggling his crepe eyebrows. He can't help seeming more comic than sinister, not only because his rococo moustache changes its shape from scene to scene, but because even in the name of his art he has been unwilling or unable to reduce his rolling girth, and his massive stomach is held precariously in place by will-power and corseting. When Donald Wolfit played Hamlet, the line 'he's fat and scant o' breath' came into its own. When Slaughter grapples the protesting heroine in a half-Nelson, his imperfections must be eked out by our thoughts. But he can never be denied his seedy grandeur, and he enunciates his lines with a clarity which must have ensured no cries of 'speak up' from the back of the gallery.

It would be unfair any longer to withhold from the reader some of the piece's juicier conceits, starting with the nifty disclaimer which follows the credits:

> France, 1880. A series of unsolved murders – a country panic-stricken – fantastic stories of Le Loup – a wolf man. A wave of terror which inspired this melodrama of the old school – dear to the hearts of all who unashamedly enjoy a shudder or a laugh at the heights of villainy.

Now we are inside the bank of respectable old de Brisson, who seems to live on the premises with his virginal daughter Cecile, the honourably intended of his chief cashier Lucien. Enter, to thwart these happy motives, the Chevalier del Gardo, who whatever the hour sports a black opera cloak, and might be more respected were it not for an unfortunate tendency to order minions about. De Brisson is in a state. The bank has been robbed overnight, and an assistant murdered by the mysterious Le Loup, whose wolf-call was heard to chill the blood at the very moment of the robbery. It is already a familiar pattern, and before he died the victim had time, as usual, to say: 'The face! The face at the window!' A pretty puzzle indeed; the stolid police inspector has no clues (and Sherlock Holmes is not yet available for consultation). De Brisson does not expect del Gardo to continue his support, as his deposits have been stolen and 'he inquired most carefully what precautions we take against robbery'; but the Chevalier announces at once that his offer to continue as an investor remains firm, though he does have in mind a means by which the old banker can show proper gratitude.

DEL GARDO: You have a very charming daughter. So charming that I am no longer content to remain a bachelor.
DE BRISSON: But the disparity of age . . .
DEL GARDO: An experienced man of the world makes the best husband, you know.

Get out of that, de Brisson. Alas, the maiden when left alone with del Gardo rejects his advances, and tells him that she loves honest Lucien. Far from flummoxed, the Chevalier treats the audience to a crafty chuckle while stroking his curly beard and making further plans. Meanwhile Lucien visits his scientist friend, an old dodderer who by the use of dead rabbits has proved to his own satisfaction that electricity is life and can stimulate a corpse to complete the action dictated by the brain at the moment of death. With the help of a laboratory somewhat less elaborate than Dr Frankenstein's, he hopes to extract from the next victim of Le Loup the name of his murderer.

Del Gardo has retired to his unofficial headquarters, a demi-monde tavern-cum-brothel called The Blind Rat. Here low-life characters quiver at the sound of his name, and he brooks no familiarity from the hachet-faced madam: 'Bring me another absinthe, woman, and stop chattering.' (Another blot on his escutcheon: only the most dastardly villain would drink absinthe.)

Del Gardo's plot is to incriminate Lucien in the bank robbery; some of the stolen notes are to be found in the cashier's desk. It works, up to a point; but old de Brisson recognizes the seal on the wrapping as del Gardo's and is shocked when the Chevalier jauntily tosses the incriminating evidence into the fire:

DE BRISSON: You can't do that!
DEL GARDO: A piece of grease-marked paper? Of what value can that be? But any mention of this to the police would, I suggest, be . . . inadvisable.

De Brisson scarcely has the chance, for that night Le Loup pays his expected call. (Expected to the audience, that is.) De Brisson is alone. The wolf howls. The victim looks up. At the window is a grotesque, slobbering, half-human face. While thus distracted, de Brisson is stabbed in the back by the Chevalier, who nips out from behind a curtain for the purpose. (What is never explained is why, if the evil Chevalier is able to enter and leave other people's premises so silently and undetected, he needs the face at the window at all; except that as melodramas go it's an agreeably gruesome touch and makes a great title.)

In dashes our genteel heroine, to fall with a little scream beside the prone figure with the knife in its back. 'Father, speak to me!' Then: 'He knew who killed him: I can see it in his face!' Meanwhile del Gardo is taunting Lucien into an unfair duel, during which the cashier is seized by cut-throats and made to suffer del Gardo's sneers. 'Think of her in my arms, my lips upon hers, and you'll be pleased to die.' Lucien is bound and tossed into the Seine, but rescue is at hand: don't worry from whom, they're of the servant class. With an instant change of clothing and a full beard, Lucien materializes as Renard the Coiner in The Blind Rat, to which del Gardo has lured the innocent Cecile. Del Gardo, being an expert in beards, has Lucien's measure, but luckily the police chief turns up too, and is suspicious: 'I didn't expect to find Chevalier del Gardo in The Blind Rat.' But our elegant villain has an answer for everything. 'I came on an errand of mercy. I stayed in the interests of justice.' As for Cecile: 'I regard myself *in loco parentis*, as it were.'

Even the doltish policeman now begins to listen to our hero and heroine, and there is soon a move afoot to test the professor's theories on the corpse of de Brisson. Del Gardo, superstitious about things like that, is one step ahead: when the experimenters arrive, the professor has already undergone the face at the window treatment. There is only one way forward: Lucien must conduct the experiment himself. 'But you can't do it,' cries Cecile, 'you don't understand electricity!' He sweeps her aside: 'This is no time for questions.' Sure enough, when the entire remaining cast assembles to see the trick performed, a dead hand emerges from under the shroud to write the name of his murderer. Guess who. The arch villain, so easily tricked (for of course it isn't a dead man under there at all), escapes with a defiant cry: 'You have unmasked the wolf, but the secret of the face at the window still remains!'

Not for long. The Chevalier is tracked to the cellar of his house, where after a brief mad scene, while the goodies pound on the door, he reveals to the audience a cage containing his idiot brother, the face. In del Gardo's view (but not necessarily in mine) dim brother is the only proof of his crimes, and must therefore be pushed through a trick wall into the seething Seine below. It proves a bad idea, for just as he's about it the police break through, in time to see brother's hand stretch round the neck of the Chevalier, so that not one but two del Gardos disappear with a plop into the murky depths. *A bientôt*, perhaps.

The Face at the Window. GB 1939; black and white; 65 minutes. Produced by George King for Pennant/Ambassador. Written by A. R. Rawlinson and Randall Faye from the play by F. Brooke Warren. Directed by George King. With Tod Slaughter as Chevalier del Gardo; Majorie Taylor as Cecile de Brisson; John Warwick as Lucien Cortier; Aubrey Mallalieu as de Brisson; Leonard Henry as Gaston; Margaret Yarde as Le Pinan; Harry Terry as the Face.

Who's Got a Secret?
THE FALLEN IDOL

The small son of an ambassador nearly incriminates his butler friend in murder.

This is a film which cheered me up no end in 1948, during the darkest days of my National Service. I hastened to catch it at the Cosham ABC, across the water from Portsmouth, and I can see myself now, emerging from the brightly-lit foyer into the drabness of austerity Britain, filled with an elation which lasted easily until I got back to the barracks and wrote enthusiastically in my film notebook: 'After seeing so good a film, all comment seems superfluous. This is a miniature masterpiece, carefully proportioned and meticulously detailed . . . it will always be remembered by connoisseurs.'

Well, thirty-six years later *The Fallen Idol* still works up a fair lather of suspense, but its twists are heavily manufactured, and the film now seems to take an unconscionable time getting to them. I had forgotten the cold, chill feel of its embassy setting: all that marble works against audience sympathy for the humans trapped in it. Alwyn's music score now seems rather aimlessly upper class, and Reed's direction has a remoteness typified by the credits, Roman letters on yet more marble. The fact that we see the action through the eyes of the ambassador's lonely son, who eavesdrops over much of the plot, means that the adult characters are mostly observed from afar, a handicap from which only the rich full tones of Ralph Richardson emerge unscathed. In fact, more and more during my 1984 viewing I came to hate the embassy, with its multitude of physical traps for the unwary: slippery steps, low balconies, and an absurd window which if leaned upon tends to knock one's legs from a high and narrow parapet. One may argue that the romantic leads are lifelike characters, a butler and a typist, but the setting works its insidious way even with them: they are an utterly refined pair, especially when set against the true working-class characters who act as chorus: the detectives, the clock-mender, the footman who wants to know when Selfridge's should deliver the forty gilt chairs, the picture postcard charladies who saunter through the action like Shakespeare's cushion-laying officers. ('Watch it, Mrs Baines is on the warpath again.' 'Garn, these foreigners like a bit of dirt.') Mr Baines the butler, coping with his houseproud wife's threats of suicide, has an allied thought: 'When there's nothing but carbolic around, you hanker after rot.' His particular form of rot is a love affair with a girl from the typing pool; unconsummated and brave so far, but clearly the stiff upper lips must crack before long.

Baines has made the mistake of telling the ambassador's small French son a few tall stories about himself, which the lad believes implicitly, even if he doesn't understand them:

PHILIPPE: Baines, why did you come back from Africa?
BAINES: Oh, to get married, for one thing.
PHILIPPE: Was there no one to marry over there?
BAINES: Plenty, but they weren't white.
PHILIPPE: Must they be white?

In this picture the adults are so careless that a small boy can see quite a lot of things he shouldn't, and when young Philippe goes for a solitary stroll, who should he encounter in the local tea-room but Baines and the typist, who the butler clumsily passes off as his niece while indulging with her in a third person conversation so transparent that an intelligent baby could decipher it, especially since the girl has tears in her eyes throughout.

And so the film develops into a maze of secrets. The lovers were supposedly secret from Philippe; now Baines persuades him to keep their meeting secret from Mrs Baines. But Philippe inadvertently blurts it out under pressure, and Mrs Baines responds by urging him to keep *their* conversation a secret, for which service she will reward him with a 2A Meccano Set. Her somewhat inexplicable plan is to pretend to be visiting her aunt for several days, but all the time to be hiding in the near-empty house to spy on the lovers at their play. She is waiting for them when they return with Philippe from the zoo and have a picnic tea in the basement area, followed by hide-and-seek among the dust sheets. This sequence is made agreeably sinister by the camera's constant suggestion of Mrs Baines's unseen presence: a shadow, a shoe, a footfall. It is also made sombre by the boy's discovery that Mrs Baines has cruelly disposed of his pet snake, for whom he proposes an epitaph: 'McGregor. Killed by Mrs Baines. And the date.' But the evil presence does not make itself physically felt until night has come, and Philippe is awakened by a hairgrip falling on to his pillow. One wonders why Mrs Baines feels the need to hiss into the boy's ear 'where are they, where are they?' when it must be pretty plain to the audience that they are having it off in the guest bedroom, from which, when hysteria

44

THE FALLEN IDOL. Philippe (Bobby Henrey) at the teashop is drawn inexorably into the web of lies which Bates (Ralph Richardson) and Lucy (Michèle Morgan) have woven for themselves.

develops on the landing, Baines appears, impeccably dressed (as a good butler should be at all times).

Timing now becomes of the essence. Philippe, terrified of the ruthless matron, hides on the fire escape and sees Mr and Mrs Baines struggling on the top landing. While the boy is changing his vantage point, Baines thrusts the struggling woman from him and goes back to comfort his beloved. Mrs Baines rushes to the fatal window, trying to look into the *chambre d'amour*, and falls to her death at the foot of the stairs. Philippe, seeing the result, assumes that Baines has done the deed and rushes blindly into the night, in an overdone sequence afflicted by what Hitchcock would have called the wet pavement syndrome. When he is taken to the police station some ill-timed comic relief is offered by Dora Bryan as a tart in a shiny mac. When asked by the desk sergeant to comfort the boy she can only manage: 'Hello, dearie, can I take you home?' And when she learns that the boy is the French ambassador's son, she makes the unlikely comment: 'Oh, I know your daddy!'

Back at the now-swarming embassy the tired and confused boy, out to protect his idol, only gets him in deeper with remarks like 'Was it self-defence like in Africa?'; and, to the police: 'You're not angry with Baines, are you?

You're not going to put him in prison?' Neither of them mentions the typist, the boy following Baines's lead that Mrs Baines had the third place at tea. But Philippe can't keep up with the lies, and finally Baines has to tell him that his efforts are only making things worse and they must all now tell exactly what happened as they know it. 'No, no!' cries Philippe, 'we've got to think of lies and tell them all the time, and stop them finding out the truth!' It takes the girl – who returns to the scene by the stretching of coincidence's long arm – to put a stop to all this and admit that Baines was with her and that Mrs Baines must have fallen down the stairs. But the injuries to Mrs Baines are not consistent with such an explanation, and only a last minute discovery of new evidence – the victim's footprint in soil on the high narrow landing by the trick window – seems to stop Baines from shooting himself. As the police leave, with sighs of relief all round, the boy is still trying to tell the truth as instructed, but nobody listens, which is just as well since his version of it would have caused even more problems.

   The Fallen Idol, a title at odds with the film's main thrust (Graham Greene says it was chosen by the distributor), was based on a sombre little story called 'The Basement Room' in which the butler was considerably more guilty. This being unthinkable in a British film of the forties – even one with a vaguely French atmosphere – the emphasis was shifted to the tangle of deceit, and at the time of release the publicity almost entirely concerned the performance elicited by Carol Reed from the boy, half-French Bobby Henrey. The direction now seems rather bloodless, and as for the boy's acting, it always did leave much to be desired in terms of intelligibility. The performance can now be seen as a jigsaw puzzle of separate shots, some hitting the mark but others quite a long way from it. Richardson, of course, is brilliant as always, but his is a totally constrained role which does not linger sympathetically in the memory. Only Michèle Morgan as the girlfriend has the chance for a stab at honesty. When asked by the police where she and Baines were at the time of Mrs Baines's scream, she shrugs, points defiantly at the bed, and says: 'There!' In 1948 that took some doing.

The Fallen Idol. GB 1948; black and white; 94 minutes. Produced by Alexander Korda for London Films and British Lion. Written by Graham Greene from his story 'The Basement Room'. Directed by Carol Reed. Photographed by Georges Périnal. Music by William Alwyn. With Ralph Richardson as Bates; Bobby Henrey as Philippe; Michèle Morgan as Julie; Jack Hawkins as Detective Lake; Denis O'Dea as Detective Crowe; Dora Bryan as Rose; Sonia Dresdel as Mrs Bates.

Forgotten Man
FATHER OF THE BRIDE
A businessman surveys the cost and chaos of his daughter's marriage.

Some books simply don't work as films, and this is usually because their style is more important than their story. I first encountered Edward Streeter's very mild comic classic at college, and it made me laugh a lot, mainly because the foibles of its central character were so accurately represented in the drawings by Gluyas Williams. It is a deceptively simple account of the trials and tribulations endured by a well-to-do banker when his daughter, the apple of his eye, decides to get married. Families, rich and poor, doubtless found in it something to respond to. Its humour, however, was of the chuckling rather than the belly-laugh variety, and depended to a large extent on the reader imagining how he would personally respond in a similar situation.

The fact that Gluyas Williams also illustrated most of the books of Robert Benchley, who took as jaundiced and helpless a view of the world as Mr Banks, and was so often left similarly behind the eight ball, would seem to have made Benchley the ideal star of any film version of *Father of the Bride*. So he would have been, but sadly he died five years before the project was considered. MGM, who bought the rights, never had much sense of humour anyway, and ordained that so expensive a property must have a star of the first magnitude. Spencer Tracy was under contract, and somehow he came to be settled upon, but it was a mistake. While I am second to none in my admiration for Tracy, he is first and foremost an actor, and the man selected to play Mr Banks should be first and foremost a reactor, a sympathetic comic with a perfect sense of timing and the ability to do double-takes. Besides, the Tracy personality is so strong that one cannot imagine him being less than master of any given situation. In real life, one feels, he would have taken all the professional parasites who try Mr Banks so sorely, tied them in a sack and booted them into the ocean. So Tracy is flummoxed throughout by having to hold himself in to such an extent that his character pretty well fails to convince; nor is he helped by the fact that his wife and daughter are strictly one-dimensional figures, played by Joan Bennett and Elizabeth Taylor. To my recollection neither has a single big scene without him; they are used solely as foils to point up his own problems. Only when one gets down to the minor eccentrics, with Melville Cooper as the verger and Leo G. Carroll as the caterer, does there seem much hope of real comedy; but both these superior humorists are hamstrung by thin material and by Vincente Minnelli's tentative direction. One might well have preferred to see the whole subject treated as outright farce in the freewheeling manner of Preston Sturges.

It would be churlish to deny that there are enjoyable sequences, but the movie does take its time about them. One suspects that it will from the opening scene, which has more about it of tragedy than of comedy. Tracy is discovered by twilight, amid the debris of the wedding party at his own home. He has apparently been deserted even by the caterers who should be clearing up. Painfully he removes his too tight shoes and addresses the camera. (Tracy probably learned to enjoy this technique in *Edward My Son* two years earlier, but the effect is less than it might be: his eyes seem pale and he looks somehow dishonest.) 'I would like to say a few words about weddings,' he tells us. 'I have just been through one. You fathers will understand.' We wait for the jokes, but they too are a long time coming. Instead we segue into the evening domestic scene when, after a long hard day at the office, the well-heeled Mr Banks first becomes aware of the impending disruption to his family unit: the daughter he has worshipped for so many years announces that she is to be ripped away from the family circle by someone called Buckley, who 'won't be pinned down'. We can all understand something of Mr Banks's horror and incredulity, but he seems to blunder too far in questioning his future son-in-law's antecedents, after which he finds his daughter positively fighting him. 'They live in Westbridge. I guess you'll have heard of Westbridge. It's just as good a place as Fairbridge Manor.' The scene needs a clincher, but doesn't get one, and Mr Banks's narrative continues heavily: 'From now on her love would be doled out like a farmer's wife tossing scraps to the family rooster.'

For a professional man Mr Banks begins to show surprising errors of judgement. Edgily he accepts dinner from his impeccably mannered in-laws-to-be, but gets sleepily drunk on their aperitifs. He persuades Buckley into his study for a talk about the young couple's finances, but exhausts the available time in summarizing his own. These things would have been funny if exaggerated by Benchley; but Tracy can only play for real, like one of us. Luckily we come shortly to a big scene. Mr Banks: 'It is the duty of the bride's father to give a party to announce the engagement. Apparently this is done only after everybody knows about it.' The humour here stems from Mr Banks's unlikely decision that he alone will serve the drinks and that everybody will want martinis. In fact nobody asks for a single martini and he is stuck all evening in the kitchen mixing mint juleps and old-fashioneds. After this débâcle he is determined on success in limiting the invitations to the reception. He even tries to persuade his daughter to elope, but how can she disappoint her friends and relations? Reluctantly Mr Banks calls in professional help and finds at once that 'an experienced caterer can make you ashamed of your home in fifteen minutes'. A marquee on the lawn is required, in view of the high degree of acceptance: 'Apparently Kay had picked a day for her wedding when nobody within four hundred miles had anything else to do.' There are the usual appalling gifts: Aunt Hattie sends a naked statue with a clock embedded in its stomach. And there is the usual emotional hitch when Kay calls off the whole thing because she discovers that Buckley has booked a honeymoon in Nova Scotia so that he can fish. (All is well again when she finds that she has inadvertently slammed the car door on his hand.)

Mr Banks now suffers a conventional nightmare of being unable to make the right responses in church, indeed of being unable to reach the altar along an

FATHER OF THE BRIDE. The end of an imperfect day. Spencer Tracy and Joan Bennett survey the debris.

aisle which has turned to soft rubber. But the event (despite its curious timing at 4.30 P.M.) passes off well enough, and 'the race is now on to get back to the house and the free champagne'. The only remaining hitches are that Aunt Hattie has been left at the railroad depot all day waiting for someone to pick her up, and that the crowds in the house are so great as to prevent Mr Banks from wishing his own daughter goodbye.

This tribute to a forgotten man may be very small beer, but it had a strong appeal for women the world over, and was certainly received with more enthusiasm than politeness when I saw it on my first London visit to the old London Empire (price one shilling anywhere in the house if you got in before noon). Thrown into the bargain package, in addition to the obligatory Tom and Jerry cartoon (for this was an MGM-owned theatre), was a fifty-minute stage show called *Spangles* or *Stardust* or some such thing, in which the chorus, during the final Egyptian scena, formed themselves memorably into a pyramid. At the time it seemed to provide me with more stimulating entertainment than *Father of the Bride*, but over the years Mr Banks has been more vivid in the memory, perhaps because one can't help feeling sorry for him. However, I never bothered to catch up with the sequel which appeared a

49

year later. Title, *Father's Little Dividend*; subject obvious. My own daughter, I am happy to say, chose to get married in Northern Ireland where her father-in-law was the village priest; so that apart from turning up as a befuddled guest (they drink a lot of Old Bushmills in that part of the world) I had none of the responsibilities and felt little of the chagrin of Mr Stanley Banks.

Father of the Bride. US 1950; black and white; 93 minutes. Produced by Pandro S. Berman for MGM. Written by Frances Goodrich and Albert Hackett from the novel by Edward Streeter. Directed by Vincente Minnelli. Photographed by John Alton. Music by Adolph Deutsch. With Spencer Tracy as Stanley T. Banks; Joan Bennett as Mrs Banks; Elizabeth Taylor as Kay Banks; Don Taylor as Buckley Dunstan: Billie Burke as Doris Dunstan; Moroni Olson as Herbert Dunstan; Leo G. Carroll as Mr Massoula; Melville Cooper as Verger.

Doing it for Defence
FIRE OVER ENGLAND

A young courtier of Elizabeth I goes to Spain on a secret mission, and deflects the invasion plans of Philip II.

It was released in 1936, and met all requirements: excitement, romance, fine acting, history, patriotism. Then it was reissued during World War II, and apart from the Queen's Churchillian call to arms at Tilbury it looked 100 years out of date (which is worse than 400). It was subsequently unavailable, or at least unshown, for the best part of thirty years; and although the negative had not disintegrated, as I sometimes suspected, it was not in the most responsible of hands. When it did turn up on the BBC one afternoon in the late seventies, it had the rained–upon look of something from the back shelf of the archive. I watched it idly, prepared to be derisive, and realized only halfway through that I was in the presence of a movie of some quality, at least the equal of Korda's other, more celebrated historical epics. Then in 1982 London Weekend, of all commercially-minded stations, played it at 10.30 p.m. because they were stuck for a short season to introduce their two-part biography of Lord Olivier; and apart from some printing wobbles at the beginning it came up as fresh as paint.

It does start rather lamely, with too many introductory titles, but then Korda wanted to get across that in the guise of a historical adventure he was really warning about the danger from Hitler. 'How small we are, how wretched, how defenceless,' says Lord Burleigh in the splendid person of Morton Selten; the scene in which the aged, bedridden statesman is fed soup by his queen is most affecting. Meanwhile, the personages of the drama are

50

being cleverly introduced on the run, as it were, for this is a very fluent film which ought to have established William K. Howard as a director of real standing. At court, the Spanish ambassador is being more than a little impertinent and the voice of Queen Elizabeth I begins to boom. But we don't see her until the line 'I *am* England', spoken with all the magnificence Flora Robson can muster. Then she brushes aside Mr Henry Oscar like a troublesome fly. '*Must* is not a word to use with princes. *Little* man! Our council shall confer with you. Meanwhile go home, and be quiet.'

The audience has had time by now to delight in Richard Addinsell's lilting music, in James Wong Howe's dazzling camera work, and in Lazare Meerson's superb white sets with their long shadows. Are they in fact real sets, or photographs blown up for use with the magic lantern technique which made *Le Million* so memorable? There is a church scene, used twice as though to emphasize its oddness. No doors, just a huge arched doorway, while at the altar end there seems to be neither wall nor window, just air. This is a film to be seen time and time again for the look of it alone.

At last the young Olivier takes over the thrust of the plot, in his ripest Errol Flynn manner. (Flynn's 1940 *The Sea Hawk*, again with Robson as Elizabeth, can be seen as a partial remake.) Escaping through Spain after his father's death by inquisition and burning at the stake, he finds time for romantic badinage when a Spanish lady offers him a newly-discovered delicacy:

They call it a potato. It's a kind of fruit. It is very rare.
– Is it safe to eat?
My father ate a whole one. He said he never felt better in his life.

Olivier gives a spirited if always actorish performance, adding extra dimensions to a Lyceum-like script which he treats as solemnly as if it were Shakespeare. There is in fact to be no fire over England, only the threat of it; but there is plenty of fire in Olivier's performance, and fire in a way is the film's theme: the young man getting over his horror of it after his father's gruesome death, until he is able to use it to burn and sink the ships of the Armada. Meanwhile he has the job of a Pimpernel to do for his queen, impersonating a dead spy (James Mason, uncredited, as Sir Hilary Vane) at the court of the Spanish king. As Philip II, Raymond Massey sits brooding magnificently in his Escorial:

> I am always cold.
> – A cordial?
> No wine warms me.
> – Is it not time to rest?
> Not in this world.

He does find time, however, to jest with the newcomer: 'An Englishman. I lived a year with Englishmen. I hated every one of them. And how it rained!'

By the time Olivier has been discovered, and arrested, and has escaped à la Fairbanks, we have been allowed to consider other matters. Leicester's unrequited love for his queen. The queen's premature baldness. The lady-in-

FIRE OVER ENGLAND. Vivien Leigh and Laurence Olivier are surveyed rather sternly by their queen, Flora Robson.

waiting's love for Olivier, which makes her careless in the temperamental royal presence. ('Crooked answers, crooked answers!' 'Yes, madam, to cross questions.') We have shared the queen's fears of age, and heard her stirring address to the troops at Tilbury: 'I have the body of a weak and feeble woman, but I have the heart and valour of a king, and a king of England too!'

Then Olivier returns with the names of the conspirators, who all rather absurdly change sides (shades of Sheridan's *The Critic*) and help him defeat the Armada. It couldn't possibly be more inspiring; and there's barely space to raise an eyebrow at Robert Newton's casting as a refined and sensitive Spanish gentleman, a masterpiece of mental corseting which is in itself worth the price of admission.

Fire over England. GB 1936; black and white; 92 minutes. Produced by Erich Pommer for Alexander Korda/London Films. Written by Clemence Dane and Sergei Nolbandov from the novel by A. E. W. Mason. Directed by William K. Howard. Photographed by James Wong Howe. Music by Richard Addinsell. With Flora Robson as Elizabeth I; Leslie Banks as Leicester; Raymond Massey as Philip II; Morton Selten as Burleigh; Laurence Olivier as Michael; Vivien Leigh as Cynthia; Tamara Desni as Elena; Robert Newton as Don Pedro; Lyn Harding as Sir Richard; Donald Calthrop as Don Escobal; James Mason as Hilary Vane.

Why Must the Show Go On?
FOOTLIGHT PARADE

A determined cine-variety producer gets his show going despite all obstacles.

The real fascination of this brash musical is that it is set so completely within its period. Not only does it feature most of the Warner contract players of the early thirties, each of them charmingly introduced in a cameo during the opening credits, but it deals with an intriguing problem, which, if it ever was historically pressing, must have been very quickly resolved, for it has not passed into any of the history books. Mr Cagney is introduced as a producer of slick Broadway musical comedies who has fallen on hard times because movie musicals have stolen all his thunder. 'Talkies are a fact,' say his erstwhile backers, who are so delighted that they have gone over to the enemy and opened a cinema chain. 'They deliver the show in tin cans and we got nothing to worry about.' Well, that's not exactly true, for they do worry about being beaten at the box office by better movies across the street, and Mr Cagney soon devises an infallible lure for the cash customers which will also help him out of his financial embarrassment. 'Give 'em prologues with live performers, if possible keyed into the theme of the film but full of live music and professional bounce, using up all the cheap unemployed theatrical talent of New York.' 'It might work,' admits Guy Kibbee, scratching his head, and of course it does: before you can say Nijinsky the boys have a nation-wide chain of performing units, all trained and operated from a slickly styled modern building proudly labelled FRASER AND GOULD STUDIOS, HOME OF CHESTER KENT PROLOGUES. And when the first thrust slackens, Mr Cagney goes one better: why not buy up all the unproduced musical comedies that are milling around and reduce them to forty minutes, thus giving the customers a plot as well as new tunes to whistle? And talking about plot, that's all there is in Footlight Parade, unless you count some stuff about a spy from the rival camp and a last minute panic when they need a guarantee from a dyspeptic backer who demands to see three new numbers at three theatres next Saturday night. Of course they oblige, amid wild applause, and the backer signs the necessary cheque with one hand while comforting his stomach with the other.

This being a Warner musical, all the big numbers are reserved for the finale, and we are treated meanwhile only to snatches from rehearsal, as hundreds of participants crowd into a rabbit warren of rehearsal rooms which they are not allowed to leave for three days because of the fear that some of Mr Cagney's ideas might be stolen. Other wisps of story involve Ruby Keeler as the secretary who by simply discarding her glasses turns out to be the swellest looker and the niftiest dancer of all; and Dick Powell as the amateur protégé of the impresario's wife. (He turns out to be a great guy and a swell tenor.) Hobart Cavanagh appears occasionally as a little man who considers himself an

FOOTLIGHT PARADE. Frank McHugh looks doubtful, but Ruby Keeler, James Cagney, Joan Blondell and Dick Powell are certain that the show must go on.

ace title-thinker-upper. Frank McHugh, cigar perpetually in mouth, is the world's least likely dance director, frantically thinking up movements that cats might perform. Herman Bing plays a musical director who stutters in German; Busby Berkeley himself turns up briefly as a protesting choreographer. Joan Blondell, as the loyal secretary watching her beloved boss dally with a treacherous blonde, suffers mainly in silence but gives out with a few wisecracks. Cagney himself, as a man near the end of his tether, takes briefly to drink, which isn't surprising since he spends his waking hours dreaming up ideas for ballets based on ghosts, voodoo, baby dolls and the French Revolution. Especially if he has watched the results of his own cat idea, which features Miss Keeler as a demure alley cat failing to respond to the tenor pussy's urgent plea:

> Come on, come on, come on and get your lovin',
> Don't you leave me in suspense.
> Come on, come on, we'll do some turtle dovin',
> Sitting on the backyard fence.

Mr Cagney recovers himself in time to take the place in the 'Shanghai Lil' number of the scheduled leading man, who is unforgivably drunk on opening night. This gives us a glimpse, though a limited one, of Mr Cagney's terpischorean abilities, which we would gladly have allowed to dazzle us for the film's entire running time.

These rehearsal scenes are told through a scintillating display of wipes, mixes and assorted opticals which suggest that they were originally shot at much greater length, that their lack of real merit was belatedly recognized, and that amid general agreement the brothers Warner decided to cut a swathe through them and get the audience as quickly as possible to the triple-decker finale. I don't think anybody watching would argue with that decision.

It is with the finale that *Footlight Parade* moves from a simulation of realism into a fantasy heaven; just as *Mystery of the Wax Museum*, made the same year, did in a different way when its action moved for the climax into an impossibly high, wide, elaborately furnished and gadget-ridden cellar. The footlight fantasy begins with shots of buses speeding round Manhattan from theatre to theatre, each filled with scantily-clad chorines changing costume en route. These are shots which would have delighted the eye of Salvador Dali; the Hays Office must have been looking the other way. But it is when the numbers start that the mind boggles, for while allegedly presented to a live audience in a cinema they quickly develop into multi-episode spectaculars incapable of accommodation on any known stage. 'Honeymoon Hotel', the first, promptly reminds us that we are in 1933, the year *before* the Legion of Decency was founded. It consists from beginning to end of leer and innuendo, based on the arrival of a honeymoon couple at a hostelry where every member of staff greets them with a wink and a nudge. Down a wide corridor the eager bridegrooms march to a communal bathroom (a curious anomaly, for surely even in the late twenties private bathrooms were *de rigueur* in God's own country?), and during their absence that wicked little boy so familiar in Warner musicals changes the numbers on the bedroom doors and causes a predictable sexual mix-up, at the end of which he is nearly brained by a chamberpot. Never again did Hollywood come so close to the land of Carry On: the fadeout, when husband and wife finally snuggle down together and turn the light out, closes in on a magazine whose pages ripple in the breeze to settle on the picture of a smiling baby. Busby Berkeley in this sequence handles his camera with great precision, but really comes into his own with 'By a Waterfall', a cinematographer's nightmare in which scores of scantily-clad females dive from rocks, or slide down them, into a limpid woodland pool which miraculously transforms itself into the kind of ornate romanesque bath which would have delighted the eye of William Randolph Hearst. Here they group and regroup to form those kaleidoscopic effects which Mr Berkeley so loved to photograph from above, with just the occasional venture underwater to register a few crotch shots as his camera glides and swoops among fish-like schools of nubile swimmers. This number may well be the apogee of his dubious but highly spectacular art, and of course none of its effects, all created within the camera or on the editing bench, could possibly have been appreciated by that dinner-jacketed audience periodically shown applauding inanely from the stalls. This absurdity scarcely matters any more, not when we are asked to believe that the girls who a minute ago were indisputably wet from head to toe are now back on the bus, hurriedly transforming themselves into Chinese prostitutes (yes, in 1933 they could) for 'Shanghai Lil'. The title suggests a vague back-reference to *Shanghai Express*, in which Dietrich so memorably intoned: 'It took more than one man to change my name to Shanghai Lily.' But Ruby Keeler is no Dietrich, just a good natured hoofer in a black wig. In fact there is very little real dancing. The number is a matter of sailor-boy Cagney finding his lost love Lil in a bar (or rather, curiouser and oddlier, in a box *behind* the bar), then changing into uniform, joining the troops and waving bye-bye. Recitative is amusingly employed, and there's a brief tap duet, but for the most part the screen is filled with vast numbers of men, grouping and regrouping on the march. At one point they become the American eagle, firing guns in all directions; then, with the aid of roller flags, they present a vertical picture of the Stars and Stripes and a horizontal one of President Roosevelt, whose New Deal clearly had the approval of the Warner hierarchy. It is all enough to send audiences home in a delirium; and if anyone chooses to deny its brilliance, well, that's his bad luck.

Footlight Parade. US 1933; black and white; 104 minutes. Produced by Robert Lord for Warners. Written by Manuel Seff and James Seymour. Directed by Lloyd Bacon. Dance numbers directed by Busby Berkeley. Songs by Sammy Fain and Irving Kahal, Harry Warren and Al Dubin. Photographed by George Barnes. Music director Leo Forbstein. With James Cagney as Chester Kent; Joan Blondell as Nan Prescott; Ruby Keeler as Bea Thorn; Dick Powell as Scotty Blair; Guy Kibbee as Silas Gould; Ruth Donnelly as Harriet Gould; Hugh Herbert as Charlie Bowers; Frank McHugh as Francis; Paul Porcasi as Appolinaris; Claire Dodd as Vivian Rich.

Windmills in Amsterdam

FOREIGN CORRESPONDENT

An American journalist is sent to Europe shortly before the outbreak of World War II, and uncovers a Fascist plot.

No Hitchcock film, perhaps, should be taken entirely seriously. But this one, because it was made with the serious purpose of bringing America into World War II, is particularly disconcerting (though by no means uninteresting) to watch forty-five years later. Like Mitchell Leisen's *Arise my Love*, released within two months of it, it depicts a Europe safe for showing only to persons who have never been there. It moves like a dream, in which Nazis are not named as Nazis and the national identity of the villains is mentioned only once, when the perfect English gentleman running the peace organization reveals himself as a Prussian coated with an English accent ('a thin coat'). The topical

FOREIGN CORRESPONDENT. The villain gets away after the famous assassination in the rain. Stars don't have to get wet: the victim on the ground for this shot is Albert Bassermann's stand-in.

background swims in and out of focus, then finally disappears; but always in sharp definition are the elaborate suspense set-ups, and they are what one goes away remembering: the assassination, the windmill, the cathedral, the plane. This was always Hitchcock's way: he never cared about the meaning or the detail of his plots, reducing them if he could into something almost abstract, something both sides want and can't quite get, the famous McGuffin which is briefly described and then ignored, lest it get in the way of the action. Even when, at the climax, old Van Meer begins to recite the contents of the secret clause which he alone has memorized, Hitchcock cuts away, just as he did twenty years later when Leo G. Carroll began to explain the plot of *North by Northwest*. Thus his famous propaganda film boils down into a series of attempts by the baddies to kidnap an old man and beat the hell out of him, also to eliminate an American correspondent who has not only stumbled on the plot but fallen in love with the chief baddie's daughter. Only Hitch would dare treat the run-up to World War II in this way; but probably his audiences were so grateful not to be jawed at that they listened the more intently to the propaganda pitch at the end.

As an instance of the film's two-mindedness, a pretentious foreword is set against music suggesting a light western of the *Destry Rides Again* type, perhaps appropriate to the concept of a total innocent blundering in and winning where professionals fear to tread. We home in on Mr Powers, editor-in-chief of the New York *Globe*, who is frustrated by the lack of hard news from Europe. His long-time London man can only report feebly that 'there is no chance of war this year because of late crops'. Powers and his news editor know better: when the latter is called upstairs he tells his minions at their earphones, 'Don't declare war for five minutes'. Powers wants to send a new man over to London, and the news editor offers himself; but he is the eminent author of a book called *The Twilight of Feudalism*, and Powers doesn't want an intellectual. He wants a crime reporter, because 'there's a crime brewing on that bedevilled continent'. A hunch summons one Johnny Jones, a reporter who has just been suspended for socking a policeman (the good old American way). When asked his opinion of the impending European crisis he asks: 'What crisis?' That makes him the man for Mr Powers, and he is willing enough: 'Just give me an expense account and I'll cover anything.' Powers packs him off with the merest word of explanation about someone called Van Meer: 'Holland's strong man. If he stays in office another three months, war may be averted.'

It is August 1939, and one of the first jobs for Mr Jones (who for by-line purposes has been renamed Huntley Haverstock) is to attend a Savoy Hotel luncheon at which Van Meer will be the chief speaker. Here Hitch expects us rather too soon to suspend our disbelief. Haverstock just happens to share a taxi with the affable Van Meer (who would surely not be travelling alone) then loses him in the Savoy cloakroom amid a bustling throng of bowler hats. Five minutes later the host announces that Van Meer has sent a telegram of regret: he can't attend. Shades of *The Lady Vanishes*: yet the device seems clumsy. Van Meer has clearly been kidnapped, but surely a hundred people must have recognized him on the way in and so queried the phoney telegram? They do not, and the sudden introduction of the romantic element allows us too much time to simmer with annoyance: but soon we are in Amsterdam for a meeting of the Peace Corps headed by Herbert Marshall at his suavest. This is one of Hitch's most famous set-ups, though a good deal of the credit should probably go to the famous production designer William Cameron Menzies, who is credited with 'special sequences'. It's the one with the steps, the rain, the umbrellas and the tramcars, and when Van Meer is shot in the face by an apparent photographer and tumbles down the steps, we may well suspect some influence from Eisenstein's Odessa. The assassin gets away, and Haverstock leads the car chase, which would be even more exciting if Hitch had concentrated on getting the background plates right and tossed out the joke about the old peasant being unable to cross the road for all the rumpus. He would probably say that it helps to distract attention from the quite incredible suddenness with which the villains' car turns a corner and vanishes, almost into a puff of smoke. Or could it just possibly, we idly wonder while our heroes are looking confused, have been driven into that windmill whose sails are turning so serenely? It could: someone notices that the sails are going against the wind, probably as a signal to the plane circling above. Naturally Haverstock determines on a lone intrusion, and discovers the mill to be a nest of Nazis (well, it's a safe assumption) who have the drugged Van Meer (the real one, not the dead decoy) and are about fly him back to London. If you ask why, and why did they kidnap him in London in the first place, and why did they shoot the decoy anyway, since if the world thinks Van Meer dead then his clause can have no significance, then you're a poor student of the man whose prime dictum was, 'Don't ask questions, just sit back and enjoy it.'

The sequence inside the mill is a genuine *tour de force*, carefully designed and lit to look less like reality than like a fragment of *Die Dreigroschenoper*, all creaking cog-wheels and shafts of sunlight and shadowed groupings spied on through frames of wooden beams. Its visual richness is not matched elsewhere in the film, and if the hero's successful outcome seems more by good luck than good management, well, that's Hitchcock again, though as far as suspense goes one certainly can't fault the moment when HH gets his mackintosh sleeve caught in a cog-wheel. He manages not only to wriggle out of the garment just a second before his arm must be crushed but also to retrieve it moments later as it is about to fall by the side of a conspirator. In all, a splendid justification of another Hitch dictum, that the location must be put to work: in Switzerland a chocolate factory, in North Dakota Mount Rushmore, in Holland (of course) a windmill.

Rather similarly, the next sequence takes place in the Hotel Europe, and as soon as we see the name spelled out in neon between the top floor balconies we should know that as part of the action the sign will be damaged, no doubt symbolizing the lights going out all over the continent. Simplistic stuff, but it gets the message across. The London sequence, which follows, very convincingly uses Westminster Cathedral (by a sad coincidence the scene of Hitch's requiem mass forty years later). Edmund Gwenn has a splendid five minutes here, cast against type as a hired assassin (watch the way he keeps flexing his hands) who takes the high fall intended for his victim; but the plot then stalls again for the romantic interest, and gives an amusingly dated motivation to the heroine, who lets the right side down by dashing back to father just because she hears Haverstock innocently booking a bedroom for her at the hotel where he is hiding out. This section has some odd technical slip-ups, especially considering that Hitch was such a recent emigré from London. Charlotte Street is said to be off the Tottenham Court Road instead of parallel with it; a signpost suggests that Cambridge is sixty-five miles from London; a butler comes in to draw the blackout curtains at 10.40, long after it has gone dark. Soon, however, we are drawn to another splendidly impressionist set, that of the Soho hideout where the drugged Van Meer is being brainwashed. Actually the Nazi swine are fairly restrained in their beastliness, which consists of playing a jazz record too loud and shining lights in the old man's eyes, and he is not too far gone to sneak in a propaganda point: 'When the beasts like you have devoured each other, the world will belong again to the little people who give crumbs to birds.' That piece of cheek, of course, might have earned him a touch of the mailed fist were not rescue at hand. The sequence ends in a fine old rugger scrum, but despite the evidence of three fairly reputable chaps, one of them called Scott-ffolliott and played by jolly George Sanders, Scotland Yard still refuses to act against the elegant Mr Marshall, who on the very eve of war is allowed to book seats on the transatlantic clipper for himself and his still only vaguely suspecting daughter. And all our heroes can do is get themselves on the same plane, Scott-ffolliott remembering in the nick of time to cancel his rumba lesson.

The design of the 1939 flying ship is presumably accurate; it seems unconvincingly nostalgic. Fourteen hours to New York; as our heroine remarks, her hand on Daddy's arm, if would be nice if they could keep flying for a long time, live in the clouds. But of course they can't, for a German destroyer treacherously fires on the plane, and an elderly lady has only time to cry 'I shall see the British Consul as soon as we land' before she is shot dead. It remains only to stage the famous sea crash, in which Hitch spectacularly coincided the moment of impact, viewed from the cockpit, with the inrush of hundreds of gallons of water through a paper screen, then separated the various fragments of the plane by having them attached to a railway on the base of the studio tank which stood in so convincingly for the Atlantic. The ruse by which Haverstock gets his story through from a neutral ship is slightly tedious, especially as it holds up his climactic Ed-Murrow-like broadcast from London during the blitz, in a subterranean studio:

> Hello, America . . . I've been watching a part of the world blown to pieces . . . I can't read the rest of my speech because the lights have gone out. Yours are the only lights left burning. Cover them with steel, ring them with guns. Hang on to your lights, America, they're the only lights left in the world!

And as the scene fades out and the credits fade up, what should be playing on the sound track but 'Home of the Brave, Land of the Free'. Franklin Roosevelt must have been delighted.

Foreign Correspondent. US 1940; black and white; 120 minutes. Produced by Walter Wanger. Written by Charles Bennett and Joan Harrison; additional dialogue by James Hilton and Robert Benchley. Directed by Alfred Hitchcock. Photographed by Rudolph Maté. Music by Alfred Newman. With Joel McCrea as Huntley Haverstock; Herbert Marshall as Stephen Fisher; Laraine Day as Carol Fisher; George Sanders as Scott-ffolliott; Albert Bassermann as Van Meer; Robert Benchley as Stebbins; Harry Davenport as Mr Powers; Eduardo Ciannelli as Krug; Edmund Gwenn as Rowley.

A Rose by Any Other Name
G MEN

A young lawyer becomes a government agent in order to avenge his best friend's murder.

Although *G Men*, released in 1935, comes well within the parameters of my filmgoing career, I somehow never manged to see it until it was revived on television in the sixties. By then it had acquired a curious little late forties prologue, in which a 'modern' FBI man, played briefly by David Brian, proposed to show it to his new recruits as an example of heroism from the days when government agents (that's what the 'G' stands for, government) were not allowed to carry guns even when they walked into a hail of machine-gun bullets. Looking straight at the reissue audience rather than the recruits, Mr Brian apologizes for the dated appearance of the fourteen-year-old picture: 'You won't see women wearing the new look.' Well, thirty-five years have passed since 1949, and who remembers the new look? *G Men* on the other hand still comes up fresh as paint, probably because that 1949 revival caused a new 35mm negative to be struck. As for the ladies' costumes, who knows what's fashionable in these days of anything goes? What remains is a punchy little movie which, although no blood is seen to be spilt, might still earn a censor restriction for the cold-eyed way it goes about its business, finally leaving all but three of its twelve main players dead on the sidewalk.

Ironically, what *G Men* was *supposed* to be on its first release was Warners' token act of repentance for having concentrated so frequently on films of violent crime as to have made a significant contribution, in official eyes, to the nation-wide increase in juvenile delinquency. *The Public Enemy* and *Little Caesar* had both been told from the gangster's point of view, and even though the protagonist in each case, and in the case of the dozens of semi-sequels, had ended up full of bullets, the impression left with the viewer was seldom that crime does not pay. There were clouds of glory attached to strutting through city streets while shooting from the hip, and wisps from these clouds had in their turn attached themselves to frustrated adolescents through the land. As early as 1932 the heat was on. Howard Hughes was forced to keep *Scarface* off the screens for a year while he fought various censorship battles, and at last had to release it under the apologetic title *The Shame of a Nation*. Even so, the watchdogs fumed as they saw him make a fortune from it by milking dry every suggestive possibility that could cause a publicity sensation. By 1934, however, the Legion of Decency held sway, and studio heads were virtually under orders from Roosevelt himself not to make heroes out of hoodlums. Jack L. Warner's pocket, and powers of invention, were hit hardest of all, since stories of low life on the New York backlot were what his studio thrived on: the same actors, the same sets, even the same menacing shadows were capable of a dozen variations a year.

G MEN. James Cagney leads the fight against crime as keenly as he once led the fight against the law. Robert Armstrong, the man who tamed King Kong, can only look on.

The solution which came to Mr Warner, or for which at any rate he assumed full responsibility, was brilliantly simple. He would continue to remake the same stories, more or less; but this time the gangsters would be shown up unmistakably as the punks they were, because the dauntless cops would be the heroes instead of the distant targets. A change in perspective was all that was required, and the result was something with which nobody could possibly argue. John Q Public minded not at all, provided he got his pound of violence. He accepted lines like 'I've been in rackets all my life, and they don't pay off – except in dough'; and 'I spent too much time in back alleys to want to go back to them.'

On whichever side of the law, Cagney was still a star. Even when asked only to walk down a corridor, he does so as though about to go into a dance. He is first seen as a struggling young lawyer, refusing to defend a hood who beat up his old lady with the butt end of a revolver. Cagney's secret is that his own career has been financed by an amiable racketeer now about to retire, and although loyally he defends his mentor against other more violent criminals, he has no intention of becoming a shyster. In fact, when a G-man friend is machine-gunned in the street, he applies to join the Department of Justice. His girlfriend is starry-eyed at the prospect: 'Gee, Brick, I think it's great, getting into work like that.' Yes, that's the level of the dialogue: girls are swell kids, men are great guys (or lousy punks), and the villain-in-hiding gives himself away by buying every morning a gardenia for his buttonhole. In between come 'Calling all cars', 'Let's go', and 'Give 'em the tear gas'; and at the end the modest hero shrugs away congratulations with: 'It wasn't much, I had a lucky break, that's all.' But forget the dialogue: the action sequences, and the editing technique, are brilliant. Any slack in between is taken up with scientific crime-solving, training sessions in the gym, the violent deaths of a few of the good guys, and half a dozen screaming montages of gang warfare, through which the regulation newspaper headlines zoom into close-up: 'THE COUNTRY DEMANDS ACTION', 'CONGRESS TO ARM G-MEN'. That sort of thing. Cagney finds time to fall for his boss's sister, who spurns him until he saves the life of her G-man brother, who was daft enough to escort a top public enemy single-handedly to jail. He's also not very bright at tracking down the criminals' hide-out. 'They're in that circle somewhere,' he announces, making a vague sweep round a wall map. Cagney's retort sounds as though written by the cocky star himself. 'Only six states. We've got 'em covered.'

G Men is an assured grade A product of the Warner film factory, which, as Cagney learned when two years later he left it for independent production, added to any project a tremendous amount of the professional backing which even the greatest star needs. Music, photography, art direction and a score of other skills provide the kind of expertise which sends an audience home poleaxed with delight at having enjoyed the ballet of violence from a comfortable seat. The contemporary publicists knew exactly what they were selling: star appeal, screeching tyres, and crescendos of bullets. The presidential seal of approval took a back seat:

> The producers of *The Public Enemy* have trained their cameras on the men who trained their guns on the craftiest killers of this gang-ridden day and age . . . It's all here! Every graphic detail of how the deadly trap was set and sprung on the Mad Dog of the Mobs . . . and of how the Big Shot no jail could hold kept his rendezvous with death!

Those still in doubt as to the purpose of the picture need only consult the cast of characters, which includes such figures as Man Shot at Lodge, Gangster, Accomplice, Ballistics Expert, Cop, Bank Cashier, Henchman, Congressman, Police Broadcaster, Moll, Deputy Sheriff, Announcer, Nurse, Prison Guard and Machine Gunners. Armed with that list, any self-respecting filmgoer should be able to write his own script.

G-Men. US 1935; black and white; 85 minutes. Produced by Lou Edelman for Warners. Written by Seton I. Miller from the book *Public Enemy Number One* by Gregory Rogers. Directed by William Keighley. Photographed by Sol Polito. Music director Leo Forbstein. With James Cagney as Brick Davis; Ann Dvorak as Jean Morgan; Margaret Lindsay as Kay McCord; Robert Armstrong as Jeff McCord; Lloyd Nolan as Hugh Farrell; Barton MacLane as Brad Collins; William Harrigan as McKay; Regis Toomey as Eddie Buchanan; Russell Hopton as Gerard; Edward Pawley as Danny Leggett.

Something for the Boys
THE GANG'S ALL HERE
Club entertainers give a charity benefit.

In 1943, when I first saw this modish musical extravaganza at the Manchester Odeon, it was called *The Girls He Left Behind* because there had already been a minor British film called *The Gang's All Here*. Come to think of it, I have no idea why the boys at Fox thought *The Gang's All Here* a good title, for it doesn't reflect a song, and plotwise it could fit several other musicals better than this one. What we have under examination is one of those putting-on-a-show affairs, modernized to fit the mood of wartime New York, with the second half set in the sort of Long Island estate that was burlesqued in *Hellzapoppin*. The initial locale is a Manhattan nightclub, the management of which is invited, for various unimportant reasons, to put on a charity show to sell war bonds at a millionaire's home. The top chanteuse falls for the rich man's uniformed son, who for even more complicated reasons doesn't tell her who he is and goes back to war. When they meet again at the house she discovers that he is supposed to be marrying the girl next door, but plans during his embarkation leave to tell her that he has eyes for but one woman. She naturally doesn't believe him, but luckily, between the second act and the finale the other girl informs her that so far as she is concerned it was only a childhood thing and she has other plans. I came in during the brief tying up of this wisp of a plot, and had no idea that so much of the preceding two hours had been so tediously devoted to it. But I did sense at once that I was in the presence of a transitional entertainment, that after this musicals were going to be brasher and more expensive and probably less witty, because the new post-war talents would cut themselves off from what had served so well in the past. The big finale, in fact, had the air of a grandiose farewell to old styles. I'm sure that at the time I did not know the name Busby Berkeley, but the rhythmic gyrations and optical effects of the 'Polka Dot Polka', with its long curving lines of even more curving chorines, each brandishing a neon circle and all coming together in multiple kaleidoscopic groupings, did remind me vividly of a long-ago infancy spent watching Warner musicals with much the same plot values, very similar finales, but more zest and rather less posh production.

During the forty years which passed before I caught up again with *The Gang's All Here*, it had achieved minor cult status as an exercise in phallic symbolism, for the things it did with bananas in 'The Lady in the Tutti Frutti Hat'. It now struck me, as I watched it on Channel Four on Christmas Day 1983, glorying in the astonishingly colour-faithful print which Fox had magically produced, as being rather more dated in feel than, say, *Gold Diggers of 1935*, with which in black and white it would seem contemporaneous were it not that the actors so familiar in the thirties had mostly been replaced by new faces with equal talent but less empathy. Instead of Ruby Keeler and Dick Powell we have Alice Faye and James Ellison, though the first doesn't dance and the second doesn't sing. The producer character, who might once have been played by Warner Baxter or James Cagney, is in the less endearing hands of Phil Baker. The bossy rich man once essayed by Guy Kibbee is now Eugene Pallette; the nervous partner is not Hugh Herbert but Edward Everett Horton (who after so many busy years was losing some of his bounce); while as the suspicious wife Charlotte Greenwood had replaced Ruth Donnelly. To add a little forties class there is also Benny Goodman's band, and for a smattering of the new brashness in full colour, not to mention a whiff of the good neighbour policy, there is the skyscraper-hatted Carmen Miranda, billed as the Brazilian Bombshell but in fact Portuguese. (Was her unlikely popularity worldwide due to the well-floated rumour that under her garish gowns she never wore any panties?)

The 3-strip Technicolor varies from acid to metallic but is seldom unbearable; the wisecracks are rarely wise but always relentlessly topical, with a tendency to home in on wartime shortages. 'You try to get a piece of butter and you discover you're in New York' is an actual line from the first number, at the end of which Mr Baker sidles up to Miss Miranda and asks: 'Got any coffee on you?' The soldiers and sailors are obsessed with 'making it'; even the older generation feels obliged to pander to the new morality, or lack of same. 'Don't be a square from Delaware, get hep to yourself,' advises Mr Pallette. 'What kind of talk is that?' asks the surprised Mr Horton. 'I heard it on the juke-box,' is the answer. (Students of forties sub-cultures need look no further.) Mr Horton, however, stoutly stands up for the old puritan values: 'My wife expects me to be home by midnight. I expect her to, and she expects me to expect it.' But he can't resist being grabbed by a chorine who wants to teach him the Uncle Samba, and, oh dear, his picture appears in the tabloids. He should have left earlier, then he would not have had to endure a truly awful song called 'Minnie's in the Money', about a lady who became a welder for the war effort:

> She's helping Uncle Sam to keep his people free;
> She's OK, hey hey hey, Minnie's in the dough re mi.

Mr Ellison sweeps Miss Faye off her feet with lines like: 'When I saw you, I said target for tonight.' Well, she does raise an eyebrow at that, but later when he saves her from a wolfish marine she explains her philosophy: 'They're a long way from home, a long way from their girls. You can't blame them if they get off the beam once in a while.' No, the script isn't exactly witty, but it does rise to a couple of in-jokes. When he says he hopes she doesn't mind that he has told the doorman they're sweethearts, her retort is: 'Stop acting like Don Ameche and get me a taxi.' Then there's the quiet moment by the night ferry when she starts to sing. 'Hear the orchestra?' she asks. 'Yeah, where's it coming from?' 'Where's your imagination?' Mr Ellison goes off to war by train (from Track 29, we notice: would that be to Chattanooga?), and Miss Faye sings the torch song which the whole nation, and especially the forces abroad, wanted very much to hear:

65

THE GANG'S ALL HERE. Sheila Ryan drives Carmen Miranda, Phil Baker and Alice Faye out to Long Island for the charity show.

No love, no nothin',
Until my baby comes home.
No, sir, no nothin',
As long as baby must roam.
I promised him I'd care for him
Till even Hades froze.
I'm lonesome, heaven knows,
But what I said still goes.

No love, no nothin',
And that's a promise I'll keep.
No fun, with no one,
I'm getting plenty of sleep.
My heart's on strike and feels just like
An empty honeycomb.
No love, no sir, no nothin'
Till my baby comes home.

Me, I prefer the honesty of Bette Davis' contemporaneous lament in *Thank Your Lucky Stars*. They're either too young or too old, she says; there isn't any gravy, the gravy's in the navy.

On Long Island the fun becomes a little strained. Tony di Marco swears in his native language and is told: 'If you don't cut that out, the censors will.' Mr Baker discovers that he and Miss Greenwood were once entertainers together in Paris, and addresses her lovingly: 'Come along, you old tenderized ham.' 'At least I'm worth something,' she twinkles. Meanwhile Mr Horton is being playfully seduced by Miss Miranda: 'You have the *busiest* hands,' he tells her. But she arouses the beast in him, and his wife finds him with his face full of lipstick, which he insists is ketchup. 'Ketchup,' she sneers, 'and from a Brazilian tomato!' Miss Miranda of course was only doing it for a friend (don't ask why, you wouldn't believe it anyway) and now declares: 'I wash my face of the whole business.' And so to the finale.

It must be the budget that keeps Berkeley in trim for the first two-thirds of the three decker. 'Paducah' is a patter song involving an uncertain Benny Goodman; 'Journey to a Star' reprises the evening's chief love theme; both are economically presented between curtains of dancing waters, which once installed cost nothing to run. But in 'Polka Dot Polka' he goes bananas again, even though it is madness without wit, saved for me by the final engaging naivety of having each and every star emerge at last in a coloured neon circle, as though in a pantomime finale, to sing a line of the farewell song. As Miss Miranda has said, 'Nice works if you can get them'; and it must be Eugene Pallette's finest moment. For me back in 1943 it certainly justified the management's decision that the free list must be entirely suspended for the duration of the engagement.

The Gang's All Here (GB title: *The Girls He Left Behind*). US 1943; Technicolor; 103 minutes. Produced by William Le Baron for Twentieth Century-Fox. Written by Walter Bullock. Directed by Busby Berkeley. Songs by Leo Robin and Harry Warren. Photographed by Edward Cronjager. Music director Alfred Newman. With Alice Faye as Eadie; Carmen Miranda as Rosita; Phil Baker as himself; Benny Goodman and his band as themselves; Eugene Pallette as Mr Mason; Charlotte Greenwood as Mrs Peyton Potter; Edward Everett Horton as Mr Peyton Potter; James Ellison as Andy Mason; Sheila Ryan as Vivian.

They're in the Money
GOLD DIGGERS OF 1933
Three Broadway chorus girls seek rich husbands.

It isn't easy now to imagine oneself a cinema patron in the key year of the great American depression. It isn't possible to conceive how in that year Warners could get away with the opening number in this glittery, hard-boiled musical. Lines of chorus girls come at you wearing (apparently) nothing but gold coins and singing 'We're in the Money', a lyric containing such lines as:

> You never see a headline
> About a breadline
> Today . . .

In 1933 you certainly did see headlines about breadlines – it was the year of *Hallelujah I'm a Bum*, with *Man's Castle* and *Our Daily Bread* to follow – and to aver that you didn't, even in the name of popular entertainment, took a lot of gall, a commodity of which the Brothers Warner always had plenty. To put it more kindly, in words from the same song, 'we've got a lot of what it takes to get along'. Did the public notice that these girls who had succeeded were boasting of being cheap chisellers? That's what this movie is about, and one can't imagine that it was the kind of success President Roosevelt had envisaged in his New Deal.

The big production number which climaxes this nostalgic entertainment must also have been conceived with tongue firmly in cheek. Called 'Remember My Forgotten Man', it's basically a blues scena in which war veterans of 1918 are shown as having descended through unemployment to the level of street beggars. Finally they are reduced to the stature of a musical comedy chorus as they march, slightly out of time, over three illuminated bridges which arch across the rear stage as Busby Berkeley's mini-opera comes to its climax. Divorced from its arresting subject it isn't a very good number at all, despite the insistent throb of its music, and one might think it could have been justified only if collecting boxes had been promptly passed around the theatre in aid of veterans' relief. Needless to say that never happened: all the profits from the picture went straight into Jack L. Warner's bank account.

Fitting between these off-key musical extremities is a brisk revamp of a mildly saucy play about three mercenary chorines who, with varying levels of apprehension and remorse, blackmail a stuffy Bostonian into thinking he's slept with one of them. This they accomplish by getting him drunk, taking off his clothes, and slipping him neatly between the bed sheets of their youngest member. Even though she demurely sleeps on the sofa, it's a ruse they'd never have got away with after 1933, for within months of this film's release the Legion of Decency was asserting over Hollywood that moral stranglehold which lasted for thirty years. Indeed, *Gold Diggers* was very likely one of the straws that broke the camel's back, especially for the morning-after scene when the toughest of the girls demands from their victim a fat cheque. When he asks what for, she nods at the bed and wisecracks: 'Call it payment for a night's lodging if you like.'

This saucy style is echoed in the other big production number 'Pettin' in the Park', which has a precocious male infant ringing up the curtains on the girls' changing rooms. Silhouette effects have previously allowed us to ogle the ladies as they disrobe to the buff after a rain shower; but they finally emerge in cast-iron scanties, which annoys the hell out of their legion of boyfriends. The

GOLD DIGGERS OF 1933. The spectacular 'Remember My Forgotten Man' number which closes the show.

grinning infant even has an answer for this problem: he sells the chaps tin openers.

In 1933 all these sexual innuendoes were clearly taken by patrons in their stride. They had endured twelve years of prohibition and felt no further need for censorship of their enjoyment. They got it, in spades, but *Gold Diggers of 1933* is perhaps the finest flowering of Hollywood's moral abandon. And when it isn't raising eyebrows, it's an enjoyable hard-nosed comedy of the type which could come only from Warners, the studio where the girls were always more than a match for the men, somebody in the cast was bound to be friendly with the mob, anyone in an opera hat was due for a fall, and the unendearing male singer was bound to be struck down by lumbago so that the shy young composer would have to replace him five minutes before curtain up – even though it meant revealing his true identity and being disowned by his millionaire father, who strongly disapproved of what everybody in sight quaintly called 'the show business'.

Sex appeal and wisecracks flow thick and fast, most of the latter coming from Trixie, mother hen of the harem, who steals milk from next door and excuses herself by saying that the dairy company stole it from the cow anyway. 'Excuse me while I fix up the old sex appeal,' she says, 'the way I feel this morning I'll need a steam shovel.' And when a friend sets off in a filmy dress to audition, she has the wisest words of advice: 'Don't forget to stand in the light when you're talking to a producer.' Trixie is played by Aline MacMahon, a respected actress for whom this was a rare venture into smart-alecry. Her later career was a little disappointing, though I remember seeing her on the New York stage when she was eighty, playing a grandmother in *Trelawny of the Wells*. Nice to catch her here, getting depth as well as fun out of a sketchily written part.

The plot takes too long, but the movie is full of nice character bits as well as splendiferous spectacle. There's gloomy Ned Sparks as the producer, who tells Dick Powell after hearing four bars of his first song: 'Cancel my contract with Warren and Dubin, they're out; *you* write the words and the music!' And while we're on in-jokes, the call-boy is played by Busby Berkeley himself. There's a character rather belatedly selling illicit hooch: 'Straight off the boat – just as good for a liniment as it is to drink.' But if the movie were remade, Powell might have to find a new lyric for his hit tune: 'I couldn't sing a gay song, it wouldn't be sincere.' The way he sings it, it looks rather as if it would.

Gold Diggers of 1933. US 1933; black and white; 96 minutes. Produced by Robert Lord for Warners. Written by Erwin Gelsey and James Seymour from the play *Gold Diggers of Broadway* by Avery Hopwood. Directed by Mervyn Le Roy. Dance direction by Busby Berkeley. Photographed by Sol Polito. Music and lyrics by Harry Warren and Al Dubin. With Warren William as J. Lawrence Bradford; Joan Blondell as Carol King; Aline MacMahon as Trixie Lorraine; Ruby Keeler as Polly Parker; Dick Powell as Brad Roberts; Guy Kibbee as F. H. Peabody; Ned Sparks as Barney Hopkins; Ginger Rogers as Fay Fortune; Clarence Nordstrom as Gordon.

Thank You, Mr Woollcott

GOODBYE, MR CHIPS

A shy schoolmaster becomes more popular as he grows older.

I had a schoolmaster who looked rather like Mr Chips. He taught English, in a very unassuming way, and he directed the annual school play without much sense of style but in a manner directly calculated to accentuate the natural talents of the boys rather than any theory of stagecraft. He had a blithe enough wit, and ran school camps with efficiency and aplomb, though when he wasn't actually talking he had a tendency to fade into the wallpaper. He hated Mr Chips. Sentimental nonsense, he called the book, and wild horses would never have dragged him to see the film. A schoolmaster's life was never like that, he said, all wise words and a tear in the eye: it was a damned hard grind.

Yet *Goodbye, Mr Chips* does, I suspect, present a picture of our schooldays as we would all have liked them to be. It has much the same ambience as Frank Richards's still-cherished Greyfriars stories, which were once rather waspishly described by George Orwell:

> The year is 1910 – or 1940, but it is all the same. You are at Greyfriars, a rosy-cheeked boy of fourteen in posh tailor-made clothes, sitting down to tea in your study in the Remove passage, after an exciting game of football which was won by an odd goal in the last half-minute. There is a cosy fire in the study and outside the wind is whistling. The ivy clusters thickly round the old grey stones. The king is on his throne and a pound is worth a pound . . . Lord Mauleverer has just got another fiver and we are settling down to a tremendous tea of sausages, sardines, crumpets, potted meat, jam and doughnuts. After tea we shall sit round the study fire having a good laugh at Billy Bunter and discussing the team for next week's match against Rookwood. Everything is safe, solid and unquestionable. Everything will be the same for ever and ever.

Goodbye, Mr Chips, book and film, even has a Billy Bunter-type character called Bullock, and it's full of clean-limbed young Harry Whartons, who talk about letting down the side. The only difference is that generations do pass, and old pupils are reported as being killed at the front; but at Brookwood the crumpets and cake are always ready for tea, and there are roses round the door of Mrs Wicket's cottage. I never read the book without some misgiving – it is sometimes as though the author of *Lost Horizon*, the discoverer of Shangri-la, had ironically lapsed into doddering senility – but the film despite its artificial sets does have a steel-like spirit and a ready wit, and if it can be accused of sentimentality, then that lies in the unavoidable contrivance of the leading character, who has to age by the use of crepe whiskers from twenty-two to eighty-three, and in the later stages inevitably seems more like an impersonation than a man. It's a great impersonation, though, done chiefly by means of a heightened voice, sucked-in cheeks and an increasingly shambling step; and it was enough to win Robert Donat a well-deserved Academy Award at the time when the Britons really were conquering Hollywood.

We meet him first in the 'present', i.e. 1939, when the film-makers could not be sure that yet another generation was about to be killed off in Europe. The headmaster has been welcoming a new college graduate to the staff, and both have been making rather desperate John o'Gaunt speeches about age and tradition and the heart of England, when the whistle is heard of the train bringing hundreds of 'stinkers' (new boys) for the start of term. 'In fifteen minutes,' says the head with a welcome touch of asperity, 'the heart of England is going to have slight palpitations.' At assembly he has to announce that old Mr Chipping will miss prayers for the first time in fifty-eight years and is 'now sitting under violent protest by his own fireside'; but we are privileged next to see the old boy skipping along like a jack rabbit, holding on

GOODBYE, MR CHIPS. Robert Donat as the young schoolmaster who has a rough time with his first class.

his mortar board with his walking stick as he mounts the stone steps to Hall, where he and a solitary stinker find the doors closed against latecomers. Old Chips passes the time by impressing the boy with the tablets to famous Old Boys:

BOY: Sir Francis Drake? Was he here?
CHIPS: Yes.
BOY: Was he a stinker too?
CHIPS: He was, but he grew out of it.

This piping octogenarian, one must admit, is unlike any old man of one's acquaintance, but the camera shot that evening when he lies asleep full of memory, and we dissolve to the young Donat arriving at school in the eighties, still provokes incredulity that the same actor can possibly have encompassed both images. These Victorian scenes, indeed, are a little like musical comedy, with a bearded headmaster perpetually on the move and a rowdy first prep reminiscent of a Will Hay sketch ('Who was Cadiz?'). But by the time the callow young classics master, concerned about noun declension, has developed into a dry moustachioed fellow on the young side of middle age, we are thoroughly on his side, especially when he is passed over for the housemastership because he has no warmth and no vision. ('H. G. Wells, he'll never come to anything, too fantastic.') On a holiday in Austria he meets and marries a twinkling young bicyclist who before long dies in childbirth; but not before she has taught him to invite boys to tea and to make dry little classroom jokes about the Lex Canuleia. By now the film is well into its stride as an accomplished mingler of laughter and tears, a huge success for MGM's short-lived British studio, which clearly, with *A Yank at Oxford* and *The Citadel* as the other strings to its bow, got things exactly right for the world's audiences as well as its own local ones.

The interesting thing is that the book might never have been bought for filming, never indeed been a great success, had it not been for its enthusiastic promotion over the American radio by the famous columnist Alexander Woollcott, the petulant original of *The Man Who Came to Dinner*. Woollcott loved a good cry even more than he loved cream cakes, but a cynical modern observer might just wonder whether his enthusiasm was due to a misunderstanding of Chips's last line. As the old boy lies dying, he rallies briefly when he hears the doctor say what a pity that he never had any children. 'Oh, but I did. Thousands of them. And all boys . . .' Could the curl of the lip on the last words possibly have been construed as a pederast's leer?

Goodbye, Mr Chips. GB 1939; black and white; 114 minutes. Produced by Victor Saville for MGM. Written by R. C. Sherriff, Claudine West and Eric Maschwitz from the novel by James Hilton. Directed by Sam Wood. Photographed by Frederick A. Young. Music by Richard Addinsell. With Robert Donat as Mr Chipping; Greer Garson as Mrs Chipping; Paul Henreid as Staefel; John Mills as Colley (adult); Terry Kilburn as Colley (boy); Lyn Harding as Wetherby; Austin Trevor as Ralston; Louise Hampton as Mrs Wickett.

Just Plain Folks
GRAND HOTEL

In a Berlin hotel, the lives of various guests become dramatically intertwined.

Despite being Oscar's best film of 1932, it survives less well as an entertainment than as an historical artefact. Like most big MGM films of the thirties, it still has the silvery box office gleam, but its script lacks humour, and its scenes are choppily edited, as though someone was screaming that it had to come in under two hours or there wouldn't be enough turnover for profit. It may also be the most overacted talkie of all time, with five stars striving to out-do each other in the art which is nowadays called mugging. But then, the outsize allure and celebrity of these people was what *Grand Hotel* chiefly had to sell, for the production itself is a kind of confidence trick. Apart from one clever but oft-repeated 'special effect' looking down past infinitely receding circular balconies, this hotel exists for the cinema audience only as one reception area, one bar, a couple of short corridors and five bedrooms.

The rule of Hollywood at the time was that two stars to a picture was more than enough, and Louis B. Mayer was assured by his shocked competitors that if he dared to give his public five, plus two expensive contract players, that was what they would henceforth demand every time. Mayer gambled and won, establishing no precedent but setting MGM even more firmly on its pedestal as the prime purveyor of celestial talent. The strength of his convictions may be judged by the fact that he ordered no attempt to simplify or Americanize the material. Berlin is still the scene, and all the difficult German names are kept; the scenario, moreover, comes not from the novel but from the multi-faceted Broadway adaptation, which was thought so sophisticated at the time. The only concession made is a clever one: all the interweaving plots are set up in the first couple of minutes by the simple device of having most of the main characters on the phone and cutting from one to the other. The hotel receptionist, Senf, is in frantic touch with the hospital where his wife is expecting a baby. The doddering old clerk Otto Kringelein is telling his lawyer to tear up his will because he hasn't long to live and is in Berlin for one last expensive fling. Herr Direktor Preysing, a bullying businessman on the point of closing a deal, stresses to his mother and father the importance of a telegram from Manchester which will clinch it. The confidante of ballerina Grusinskaya is telling the theatre that her mistress is too exhausted to dance tonight. The dapper Baron von Gaigern explains to a friend that he needs money desperately if he is to stay at the hotel much longer. And the cynical old doctor, whose badly blotched face is a result of the war, mutters to himself: 'People coming, going. Nothing ever happens.'

To the strains of 'The Blue Danube' (Dr William Axt's idea of a musical score was to play one popular classic after another) the characters begin to mingle. 'I'm ill,' Kringelein confides to the doctor. 'I know. When a man's collar is an inch too big for him, I know he's ill.' The dying man, overjoyed at the opulence of his new surroundings, encounters a temporary typist, Flaemmchen, who has been hired by Preysing, and invites her to share his caviare. She winces: 'Have caviare if you like, but it tastes like herring to me.' He is not put off: 'I wonder if you'd like to see my bathroom? I can have a bath any time I like.' And the Baron, though he has more pressing things on his mind, can't resist a little flirtation with Flaemmchen on the landing: 'So you're a little stenographist. I don't suppose you'd take dictation from me sometime?'

All is now ready for the entrance of the star of stars, Greta Garbo, who is playing Grusinskaya. In fact she does not enter in the normal sense. She rises, swan-like, from a tumble of bedclothes, and says in her deep Swedish accent: 'I think I have never been so tired in my life.'

By now, the viewer of the eighties may reasonably complain that he is watching no more than an extended variation on some such television series as

GRAND HOTEL. Greta Garbo decides that she does want to be alone – with John Barrymore.

Hotel or *Love Boat*, as produced by Aaron Spelling in his patented cut-and-shuffle manner, which is to say that anecdotes are filmed separately and then intercut to look like a slice of life, or in Spelling's case a slice of hokum melodrama. One might also think back to Arthur Hailey's novel called *Hotel*, filmed in the sixties; it too had a character who, like the Baron, was a jewel thief. As far back as 1945 MGM had tried to revamp *Grand Hotel* as *Weekend at the Waldorf*, with a second team cast, and it flopped; while in the same year Vicki Baum wrote and Warner Brothers filmed *Hotel Berlin*, which applied the same technique to Berlin at the end of the war. There is not much new under the sun, but in 1932 *Grand Hotel* was arguably the first of its breed; which is why, somehow, and despite its deficiencies, it retains a vestige of its original glamour. It has the self-confidence of an original. The audiences of that day were hypnotized into not minding that any character seems to be able to walk into any other character's room, or that Garbo is too tall for a ballerina and walks like an ostrich. They were sold on the stars and the concept, and nothing else mattered.

There is also a dog, owned by the Baron, who is now seen lecturing it: 'Adolphus, I have something very serious to discuss with you. When you meet lady dogs on the street who are not dachshunds, you must exercise self-control.' Thief or no, the Baron is by far the most sympathetic character we have met, so by the natural reversal of drama we know that he is bound to lose out. This evening is his, though. By some acrobatic balcony-leaping he enters Grusinskaya's guarded room and steals her pearls, only to be trapped in the wardrobe when she unexpectedly returns in her tutu, having walked out on her own indifferent performance. At the door she wafts away all criticism from her entourage: 'I want to be alone,' she says. She really does say it; in fact she says it three times. Then, secure from prying eyes and perhaps near suicide, she encounters the escaping but inventive Baron.

GRUSINSKAYA: Who are you?
BARON: Someone who happened to be in your room.
GRUSINSKAYA: Why?
BARON: I often come here when you are at the theatre. Just to be in your room. Just to breathe the air you breathe.
GRUSINSKAYA: Who are you?
BARON: Someone who loves you, that's all. Someone who's forgotten everything else.
GRUSINSKAYA: You must go now. I want to be alone.
BARON: That isn't true. You don't want to be alone. You were in despair just now. Please let me stay.

As romantic dialogue goes, this must have been fairly leaden even in 1932, but Grusinskaya succumbs to it and asks no more questions. Even though next morning both are still fully dressed, something has happened to transform the jaded Grusinskaya, and the Baron, lulled into believing his own pretty speeches, is genuinely in love with her.

We pass on to the *thé dansant*, at five o'clock in the bar. Kringelein, who has spent the previous night getting drunk with the doctor, is now learning the delights of Louisiana Flip. Flaemmchen presently joins them, having escaped an hour of dictation by the nervous and bad-tempered Preysing (Wallace Beery by now is clearly modelling his performance on Sig Rumann, who entered America by playing the role on Broadway). She casts eyes at the dapper Baron, whose thoughts are all for Grusinskaya, and has eyes cast at her in her turn by Kringelein. The doctor observes wryly: 'You are right, Mr Kringelein: a man who is not with a woman is a dead man.' The Baron asks Flaemmchen if she wants to make a man happy, and she eagerly agrees; but he only wants her to 'dance with old Kringelein.' 'You're not a bit like you were yesterday,' she complains. 'Perhaps not,' he replies a shade ungallantly, 'but you see, I fell in love last night. The real thing.'

Meanwhile Kringelein is having a stand-up row with his old boss Preysing, who has come in search of his stenographist, and displays a contemptuous attitude for the old sick man. 'You can't discharge me,' croaks the ex-clerk. 'I'm my own master for the first time in my life. I'm going to die, and nobody can do anything to me any more.'

At seven, poor Senf is still waiting for news from the maternity ward.

'Things drag when you're tired. I was at the hospital all night.' And by now the unattractive Preysing has become the centre of three dramas. Kringelein knows he's incompetent, Flaemmchen knows he's a crook, and the Baron is after his fat wallet. But first the Baron borrows gambling money from Kringelein, only to lose it all while the old man wins a fortune. Putting the drunken clerk to bed, the Baron is tempted to steal *his* wallet instead of Preysing's, a fact silently noted by the doctor; but he can't bring himself to do it. Meanwhile Flaemmchen, fancying life as a rich mistress, has finally given in to Preysing's innuendoes:

PREYSING: Are you going to be nice to me?
FLAEMMCHEN: Yes.
PREYSING: Very nice?
FLAEMMCHEN: That's what you expect, isn't it?

But she is saved in the nick of time from a fate worse than death, for when they go to Preysing's room they disturb the Baron in his felt-footed search for ill-gotten gains. In the ensuing struggle, the thieving nobleman is struck and killed by the hot-tempered businessman. The body is discreetly removed, just as Grusinskaya returns from a triumphant evening at the theatre. Finding the Baron waiting for her would make things perfect. Without him she can only murmur: 'The music has stopped . . .'

It is 6.30 the following morning. Grusinskaya and entourage have to catch their train, and only the thought that the Baron may be meeting her on it persuades her to leave the hotel. Next, Preysing is led away, ashamed and shrunken, in handcuffs; and that little procession is astonishingly followed by a smiling Kringelein and Flaemmchen; for having taken refuge in his room after the fight, she has found him to be the most worthwhile man in sight (and possibly the richest). Together they will scour Europe for a specialist who can cure his ailment; but first, he informs the clerk with a grandiloquent gesture, he wants to book a room at the Grand Hotel in Paris. 'How do you know there is one?' she asks. Resplendent in top hat and cutaway, he smiles. 'My dear, there's a grand hotel everywhere in the world.' Now, there's a moral to top all the clichés which have been piling up; but perhaps through this mesh of melodrama most of us have been able to glimpse something of ourselves. Only the doctor remains blind to the human drama. As the camera backs away through the doors, he is left muttering to himself: 'People come. People go. Nothing ever happens.'

Grand Hotel. US 1932; black and white; 115 minutes. Produced by Irving Thalberg for MGM. Written by William A. Drake, from the novel and play by Vicki Baum. Directed by Edmund Goulding. Photographed by William Daniels. Music by Dr William Axt. With Greta Garbo as Grusinskaya; Joan Crawford as Flaemmchen; John Barrymore as Baron von Gaigern; Wallace Beery as Preysing; Lionel Barrymore as Kringelein; Jean Hersholt as Senf; Lewis Stone as doctor.

Baby Mine
THE GREAT LIE

A determined girl takes over the baby which her husband's ex-wife does not want.

This is a film set among the well-to-do of America's sophisticated east coast: concert pianists, explorers, plantation owners. I first saw it in Bolton, Lancashire, in a suburban cinema which smelled of cottonseed oil from the clothes of the spinners at the local mills. I next came across it fifteen years later in a Norwegian coastal town called Molde. The cinema there had a tin roof, and the rain pattered down so heavily during the performance that most of the dialogue was drowned; this scarcely mattered to the local audience, who were reading the Norwegian subtitles anyway. *The Great Lie* has since then cropped up several times on television, usually during the doldrums of Sunday afternoon, or so late at night that one's eyelids have to be propped open with matchsticks. I watch it avidly every time I can, for with all its many and obvious faults it is a curiosity to be cherished. Its storyline is totally daft, emanating from the heyday of *Peg's Paper* or even *East Lynne*; yet for much of its length it is told with assurance as bitchy comedy, and acted with many a wink and a nudge by two high-powered female stars of the golden age, who should have come together more often in order to cleanse our jaded palates.

Like *A Night at the Opera* it begins abruptly, as though something has been lost. My guess is that something was, some more conventional introduction to all three characters. Perhaps we were meant to see them preserving their previous status quo, before the irresponsible Peter ditched his childhood sweetheart Maggie for an impulsive marriage, during a drunken spree in New York, with a tigress of a concert pianist called Sandra Kovak. Whole reels of such scene setting may have ended on the cutting-room floor, but the film as we have it begins on a closeup of Sandra's maid clearing up debris on the morning after the wedding party, and fifteen minutes of screen time are to pass before we see Sandra (Mary Astor) as more than a slumbering figure on her bridal bed. We see plenty of the hangover-ridden Peter, shrugging off Sandra's impatient concert manager and staggering eventually into the offices of his own long-suffering lawyer, who tells him the marriage wasn't legal because Sandra's divorce wasn't final: he will have to do it again. But something stirs in his sobering thoughts. Still lounge-suited, he pops into his private plane and flies straight down to Maryland, where his arrival is greeted with the sort of remark black servants used to make in Hollywood pictures of those days: 'Dere's Massa Peter, coming down from de sky like de angel of de lord,' and so on. He is less enthusiastically received by Mammy (Hattie McDaniel in a reprise of her *Gone with the Wind* role), and not at all well by his former love, who for some reason not dictated by the plot Bette Davis chooses to portray in this scene with a streaming cold.

Massa Peter is clearly nosing around the old homestead to find out whether, if he were free, he'd be welcome. His curious sense of honour, however, prevents him from saying so. Instead, having picked up a few pointers he zooms back (offscreen, for this is a film of talking heads rather than cockpit set-ups) to inform his supposed new wife of the delicate situation in which they find themselves, and to suggest that he will marry her again in New York on her first legally free day, which is Tuesday. She is testy about the whole thing, and has just given her masseur a bad time. Won't another day do, she reasonably asks, since on Tuesday she is booked to give a concert in Philadelphia? If he can't wait a day, he can't be so keen on the idea.

'I'm asking you to marry me,' he replies, neither confirming nor denying.

'You were much more amusing the first time.'

'Well, I'm sober now.'

Not the way to win friends and influence people, and Sandra tells him so. But according to Peter it has to be Tuesday in New York or nothing, and we suspect he hopes for the latter. Which is what it turns out to be, for Sandra goes to Philadelphia and plays her heart out in a magnificent silken cape for which nothing but Tchaikovsky will do. Backstage her heart is not gladdened by a visit from Maggie, who, not knowing the new situation, sees no reason why the three of them should not continue to be friends. She simply wants Sandra to treat Peter right and not selfishly to prevent him from offering to the government his expertise in maps and navigation – which come to think of it is a pretty vague expertise. Sandra has never enjoyed being told what to do, especially not by a rival who, though she has got over her cold, still looks pretty dowdy. 'Supposing you go,' she suggests icily. 'If I didn't think you meant so well, I'd feel like slapping your face.' It's been something of a wasted journey for Maggie, but when she gets back to Maryland, the intrepid Peter is waiting with the good news that he's free, despite Mammy's having 'tried every way but witchcraft to keep him out of the house'.

Next, it's honeymoon time among the apple blossom. The haze of happiness lingers even when Peter is called away to fly for the government over the Brazilian jungle. To do precisely what is never explained, but military gentlemen are involved in the phone call which sets it up. 'This is Colonel Harriston.' 'Not *the* Colonel Harriston?' Maggie, smoking incessantly but now immaculately coiffed, goes to New York and accidentally meets her former rival in the Palm Lounge. Their silly hats cancel each other out, but Sandra has a trump card:

SANDRA: I'm going to have a baby.
MAGGIE: But you wouldn't.
SANDRA: I can and I will. And I'm going to get him back.

Are you surprised, dear reader, to hear that fate steps in, that Peter is reported missing after a forced landing in the Brazilian jungle? Of course you are not surprised: you have seen too many movies. The news gives Maggie opportunities for several scenes with highly glycerined eyes, but she's a quick recoverer. Soon she is marching defiantly into Sandra's lair with a direct

THE GREAT LIE. Mary Astor and Bette Davis, in echt forties headgear, hear some distressing news.

question: 'Were you lying when you told me you were going to have Peter's child?' Sandra was not lying, as her bad temper quickly shows, and so Maggie has a proposition which gives rise to the film's title: 'You have Peter's child. I have Peter's money. Let me insure your future. Give me your child; and I'll make you secure financially always.' Though the picture doesn't exactly come out with it, Sandra was clearly thinking of an abortion, for the prospect of a nine-month pregnancy repels and scares her: 'I'd be alone, I'd be afraid.' But Maggie is persuasive, and without so much as a title card the film whisks us westward, some months later, to a dusty desert full of joshua trees, and in particular to a log cabin where the two women propose to get on each other's nerves in secrecy for as long as it takes. 'Cologne . . . talc . . . bath salts . . . no pickles?' screams Sandra as she frantically unpacks Maggie's shopping bag. 'And why don't you tell me I'm smoking too much?'

MAGGIE: If it takes your mind off the weather . . .
SANDRA: That's right, humour me! Maggie the martyr! You make me sick!

Maggie remains determinedly bright, through gritted teeth, throughout the ordeal, forcing Sandra to take long walks in the desert and uttering only mild reproof when she catches her at the larder in the middle of the night:

80

MAGGIE: Ham – onions – butter – pickles. Everything the doctor said you shouldn't have.

SANDRA: I love food. That's the way I'm made.

Maggie balks only at attending the actual birth, though she does oblige with the pacing and chain-smoking normally expected of the father. Luckily the local doctor has dextrous hands and comes complete with rural philosophy: 'Woman without a child, is like a man without a right arm.'

Back at the old plantation some while later, junior is at the receiving end of a lot of fuss and Mammy gets her best line in the picture ('I's a-coming, telephone, I's a-coming'). But guess who's on the phone after ten months, 'just like the grave opened up and spoke'? Yes, it's good old Peter, who's meanwhile been accepting native hospitality somewhere upstream from Manaos. We never do find out what he was up to in Brazil, but despite make-up pouches under the old eyes, he has clearly lost none of his skills, since he seems able to land his monoplane in a nearby field at night without lights. But maybe he'll soon wish he'd stayed in the jungle, for the reunion is scarcely over when Sandra shows up with a gleam in her eye: 'When I heard you were alive I drank a bottle of champagne and played Chopin's funeral march in swingtime.' Maggie is out with the dogs at the time, but she knows what's afoot the moment she hears Tchaikovsky being played in the house. And there is her old friend Sandra, looking like the cat that swallowed the canary and remarking none too subtly: 'How I love to do things I shouldn't.' As she says to Maggie in an aside, it was never part of their bargain that Peter should be alive: 'I'd be too proud to hold a man with another woman's child.' She even offers to give the money back, but of course Maggie's love for Pete (and Pete Jnr) is above rubies. The only contribution made by the bewildered Pete is to order 'three mint juleps, nice and cold and frosty'. The frost is quite unnecessary when these two ladies are around.

Eventually, rather lamely, Maggie is forced to confess the truth, and all Pete can say is, 'I thought there was something funny.' But in two shakes he gathers his wits about him in a way one would never have thought possible from his previous performance, and announces to Sandra that she is welcome to the baby but she can't have him. This offer, predictably, evokes from Sandra no more than a pout and a request for a drink before she makes her final exit, whereupon Maggie can't resist taking Pete Jnr for his rest, with the instruction: 'Kiss your mammy and your pappy and say bye-bye to the lady.'

Yes, it's all the creamiest of nonsense, but it's good for the blood and there's quite a tang to most of it. George Brent attempts the role of Peter in several tentative ways, but generally behaves, as well he might, like a man with a lighted firecracker stuck to each hand. The fireworks come mostly from Miss Astor, who seized this chance with sufficient style and flavour to win herself an Academy Award; Bette Davis was gallant enough to let her, yet in her immodest way steals enough scenes to let the audience know who's really boss. There never was anyone like Miss Davis for acting with her whole body: the involuntary cry, the grin, the shrug, the turn of the head, the hand to the cheek, the collapse. And the whole romantic delirium is soaked in Tchaikovsky soup and lit with that dazzling Warner photography which is never quite out of focus nor absolutely in it. Besides, it can't have cost a bomb to make, so Jack Warner as well as the audience must have gone home very happy indeed.

The Great Lie. US 1941; black and white; 107 minutes. Produced by Hal B. Wallis and Henry Blanke for Warners. Written by Lenore Coffee from the novel by Polan Banks. Directed by Edmund Goulding. Photographed by Tony Gaudio. Music by Max Steiner. With Bette Davis as Maggie; Mary Astor as Sandra; George Brent as Peter Van Allen; Lucile Watson as Aunt Ada; Hattie McDaniel as Violet, Jerome Cowan as Jock Thomson.

Rosencrantz and Guildenstern are Missing
HAMLET

A Danish prince is slow to make up his mind about avenging his father's murder.

In the middle of 1948, one of the *New Statesman's* popular if rather academic literary competitions invited readers to compose a sonnet as though written by the statue of William Shakespeare which stands at the centre of the Leicester Square garden; it was to give the bard's opinion of the film of *Hamlet* then running a few yards to the statue's right, at the Odeon. The setter expressly forbade use of the line: 'O this offence is Rank . . .'

In fact, J. Arthur Rank, not yet ennobled, could afford to smile at such brickbats. Unlike *Henry V*, which emptied a few cinemas in its time, Olivier's less expensive black-and-white *Hamlet* ran for months at Leicester Square's flagship cinema, and became the fashionable thing for Londoners to see. It went on to win in Hollywood the Academy Awards for best film, best actor, best art director and best costume design, with nominations for Olivier as director, Jean Simmons as supporting actress, and William Walton's music. Financially it rapidly went into the black, and seemed set for a self-supporting reissue career. Yet over the last thirty-odd years it has seldom been shown, apart from occasional airings on television.

Is it possible that even at the time it was admired rather than liked? It is certainly a cold film, but that is to be expected in a medieval setting of winter gloom, with a theme of murder and retribution. Olivier himself saw it as an experiment, an attempt to bring Shakespeare to the people by paring down his greatest play to its barest melodramatic essentials. So Hamlet's foils were first to disappear, the characters to whose more natural actions we may compare his moody procrastination. Horatio in this version is a mere stick; Rosencrantz, Guildenstern and Fortinbras are nowhere at all. Olivier took care to explain in a book of the film that all had been done on the best possible advice:

HAMLET. Laurence Olivier leads Felix Aylmer around one of Elsinore's very unlikely sets.

This is not the place to indulge in a recital of the technical difficulties of merging, sequence, montage and other features of film-making, and their difference from production on the stage. But suffice it to say . . . that the same basic problems remain, of reducing the length, elucidating the plot, unravelling irrelevancies, and relating the result to the type of audience . . .

The cinema can, and must, nose into corners and magnify details that escape notice on the stage . . . It is not to be imagined that the Shakespeare who wrote parts for opposing armies, and tried to turn his little riverside stage into the scenes of Antony's fall and Prospero's island, would not have eagerly welcomed the means to show these places more realistically, if they had been to his hand. Nothing that we know of Shakespeare suggests that he enjoyed being 'cabin'd, cribb'd, confined' by the rudimentary conditions of the stage for which he wrote.

All very true: Hamlet takes up to five hours to play on the stage in full, and Olivier was taking a chance with a film as long as two hours and thirty-five minutes. But sadly, the time saved on cutting the text is then wasted on aimless camera-tracking around the corridors and battlements of a very stagey castle. Despite the small gain of deep focus, it is a method which by eliminating editing is the antithesis of cinema excitement, as Hitchcock found when he tried in *Rope* to make a whole film without a cut. Some of the textual changes, too, are clumsy: one does not mind 'hinders' for 'lets', for the latter word has come to have the opposite meaning to that which is meant, but the metre is ruined when an actor stops halfway through a blank verse line, as Olivier does on 'leave her to heaven', and even to those who know nothing of blank verse it sounds like an unintended hiccup. Nor are the soliloquies well used. The device of making them unspoken thoughts, on the soundtrack only, becomes boring in a film, and the audience's attention is caught somewhere between what is seen and what is heard; this is especially distracting when what is seen is waves crashing on the battlements of Elsinore.

The battlements in fact occupy too much time altogether, perhaps because it was thought that the ghost would grab the attention of the audience; but it is not a good ghost, and the result of dallying with it is that the court scenes which follow have to be cut to almost nothing, and probably *mean* nothing to an audience still dizzy from the swirling mists and magnified heartbeats which have previously afflicted the eye and ear. The king's part in particular is drastically cut, so that he becomes the poorest of adversaries; yet all this emphasis on Hamlet himself seems absurd when in a cut version such as this the advice to the players is retained. (It was in the original no more than a satirical interlude for habitués of the Globe.) The text might have been more carefully watched at this point, for what Hamlet clearly promises as 'a speech of some ten or fourteen lines' turns out to be not a speech at all, but a mime.

It does seem that Olivier as director was too concerned with economy of technique, hoping that massive sets and deep focus would enable him to direct the action theatrically, in groups of people rather than close-ups. So the increasingly stagey scenes seem to take place in a solemn fairy tale castle with no doors or exterior walls, just endless open spaces through which the camera can track interminably in search of the actor next required. The rooms are by Olivier's rule bare of furniture except that needed for specific use in a scene. The grandiose settings seldom please the eye, reminding one rather of a Victorian production by Irving or Wolfit; while despite its superb definition the photography is dark and gritty, suggesting a climate in which the only background elements available are night and fog. There is no zest to any of these people or places. The whole production has been so carefully story-boarded that the baby was thrown out with the bath water.

Nor is the acting on the highest level. Olivier's central performance is, alas, one of his least interesting, and only people unfamiliar with Shakespeare could have given him an award for it. He is too old, too stiff, too careful with his words to suggest either vacillation or hypocrisy. We don't feel that this Hamlet needs to be urged to make up his mind, rather that he will never do it under any circumstances. When he finally does stab the king, we receive it as an Olivier stage trick rather than a development of character.

Perhaps it is television which works now against Olivier's concept, but where else in this day and age, apart from the National Film Theatre, will we ever be able to see Hamlet again on the big screen in its correct ratio? The wide screen, which came in in 1952 and casually lopped off the top and bottom of the image, made it impossible to enjoy earlier films in any commercial cinema. I am certainly unable to rekindle the glow in which I emerged from the Leicester Square Odeon in 1948, having queued to get in and even sat part of the film through again in order to decide how the ghost was manipulated. When the credit 'A J. Arthur Rank Enterprise' came up, I felt that the enterprise was more than justified. But then, I came fresh from having played the king in a school production of Hamlet, with Irving Wardle (later dramatic critic of *The Times*) as the gloomy Dane; and I knew every line of the play and revelled in its glory.

Hamlet. GB 1948; black and white; 155 minutes. Produced by Laurence Olivier for Two Cities Films and Rank. Written by Laurence Olivier and Alan Dent from the play by William Shakespeare. Directed by Laurence Olivier. Photographed by Desmond Dickinson. Music by William Walton. Designed by Roger Furse. Art director Carmen Dillon. With Laurence Olivier as Hamlet; Basil Sydney as Claudius; Felix Aylmer as Polonius; Jean Simmons as Ophelia; Eileen Herlie as Gertrude; Terence Morgan as Laertes; Norman Wooland as Horatio; Peter Cushing as Osric; Stanley Holloway as the gravedigger; John Laurie as Francisco; Esmond Knight as Bernardo; Anthony Quayle as Marcellus; Harcourt Williams as First Player.

Period Piece

HEAVEN CAN WAIT

On arrival in Hades, an elderly playboy recounts to Satan his small sins.

Heaven Can Wait was the original title of a play filmed by Hollywood in 1941 as *Here Comes Mr Jordan* (qv), and again in 1978 under the original title. But the *Heaven Can Wait* I am thinking of is not this supernatural fantasy but a period domestic comedy made by Lubitsch in 1943, from an original screenplay by his favourite writer Samson Raphaelson, who was to him what I. A. L. Diamond became to Billy Wilder. The supernatural elements of this *Heaven Can Wait* are confined to its bookends, and they are in the nature of a joke which, although diverting, seems to be at cross-purposes with the main burden of the story, which concerns a man who goes through life thinking he's quite a roué, and isn't.

Even while one watches and enjoys it, it is rather surprising that this film should have turned out so satisfactorily. All the while one is conscious that it has nowhere very definite to go, yet it contrives to dawdle on its way there.

HEAVEN CAN WAIT. Don Ameche gets an idea that he wants to see Gene Tierney again.

Lubitsch fans may regret the lack of visual cleverness, and admirers of Raphaelson's wit may feel it to be mainly absent. No two comedies, in fact, could be more different in texture than this one and the masterpiece on which these two talents had collaborated eleven years earlier, namely *Trouble in Paradise*. That had the sharpness of steel, the elegance of artificial manners; this is at best a sentimental romance of a bygone age.

I saw it three times: oddly enough in 1944, 1964 and 1984. On each occasion a few other people enthused about it; but to the great mass of filmgoers and even historians it remains largely unknown, and now suffers from confusion with the Warren Beatty remake of the other film. But at least its niche in history is now a little more secure because in 1983, shortly before his death, Raphaelson published his original script with some added notes. He does not say why he and Lubitsch favoured this particular property at that particular point in their careers, but one may guess that its Hungarian source may have clinched the matter, for Hungarian originals had served them well before. Raphaelson does call the making of it 'a blithe experience', and one can understand that. The notices were favourable too, if a little puzzled; what did these two ageing sophisticates think they were doing with such a mild piece?

The humour of the opening title is typical of the whole film:

As Henry Van Cleeve's soul passed over the Great Divide, he realized that it was extremely unlikely that the next stop would be Heaven, and so, philosophically, he presented himself where quite a few people had told him to go . . .

There follows a few minutes of pastel-shaded comedy in an ante-room of Hades, with Laird Cregar monstrously urbane as His Excellency but given very little meat to chew on. His most amusing moment comes in disposing of a pushy female interloper (who else but Florence Bates?) by pressing a button and consigning her through a trapdoor into billowing flames. Mr Van Cleeve, naturally nervous after witnessing this, is then asked for a few personal particulars, including a description of his own death: 'I ate everything the doctor forbade. And then . . . shall we say I fell asleep without realizing it? When I awakened, there were my relatives, saying nothing but the kindest things about me. And then I knew I was dead.'

His Excellency, making notes, goes on to ask for a list of Mr Van Cleeve's crimes. His guest can't think of any: 'but I can safely say that my whole life has been one continuous misdemeanour.' 'My dear Mr Van Cleeve,' answers the Devil in a state of shock, 'a passport to Hell is not issued on generalities!'

There is nothing for it: our hero must detail his peccadilloes. And what they add up to, over the next hour and a half, is no more than a roving eye for the ladies, pictured against luxurious turn-of-the-century backdrops. At nine he wins his first girlfriend by giving her his beetle in a matchbox. At sixteen, encouraged by his mischievous grandfather, he is taught a few tricks by the French maid. At twenty-six he steals his cousin's fiancée, which must be a Good Thing since the official swain had taken her to Grant's Tomb for a romantic time. She is the beautiful daughter of a loud-mouthed Kansas City meat-packer whose creation Mabel the cow appears on every one of his cans:

> To the world my name is Mabel,
> Which you'll find on every label.
> I am packed by E. F. Strabel
> For the pleasure of your table.

(The fact that the senior Strabels are played by Eugene Pallette and Marjorie Main gives experienced filmgoers a pretty good idea of *them*.) The girl, played by Gene Tierney at her most innocent, has mistaken the pursuing Henry for a book salesman, which he is honest enough to deny:

> I'm not employed here. I took one look at you and followed you into this store. If you had gone into a restaurant, I would have become a waiter. If you had gone into a burning building, I would have become a fireman. If you had stepped into an elevator, I would have stopped it between two floors and we'd have stayed there the rest of our lives.

Martha finds this approach irresistible, and feels bound to explain how she came to be engaged to the stuffy Albert:

> Whenever a young man came and asked for my hand, if my mother said

yes, my father said no. And when my father said yes, my mother said no. But Albert came in one of the rare moments when they were both on speaking terms. If I hadn't said yes, who knows when it might have happened again? I might have spent the rest of my life in Kansas. Don't misunderstand me. I love Kansas. I just don't like living there. And besides, I didn't want to be an old maid – not in Kansas!

Henry and Martha marry happily, but not ever after. Ten years later she goes home to mother because of suspicions which may or may not be justified: all she saw was her husband having tea with another woman at the Plaza Hotel. Since she refuses his explanations, we never get them either, except that there was 'nothing to it'. But when Henry and his grandfather chase her to Kansas, she elopes again with him happily enough, and the old man's gleeful last lines in the film are:

> And so farewell, dear E. F. Strabel:
> We take Martha, you keep Mabel.

Amazingly, two-thirds of a longish film have now passed in these mildly sparkling scenes; but pace is now required, and we begin to move through Henry's birthdays in a montage. He is forty-five and getting advice about his arteries; fifty and saving his son from a gold-digger; fifty-five and receiving the first premonitions of his wife's fatal illness; sixty and trying to persuade his son to give him a bonus, but getting instead a lecture on the costs of his night life. At seventy, he is bewildered by the extent of his medicine cabinet; and he attributes his death at seventy-five to over-excitement at the charms of the night nurse.

His Excellency is perplexed. How could he be otherwise at the thought of the extra accommodation required if such mild sinners as Henry were to be admitted? He coughs: 'I hope you will not consider me inhospitable if I say sorry, Mr Van Cleeve, we don't cater to your class of people. Please make your reservations somewhere else.'

Henry takes some convincing, but is eventually awakened to the possibility that his dear wife may be waiting for him on a higher plane, and steps willingly into the elevator. 'Down?' asks the boy. 'No, up,' says His Excellency.

An odd, fluffy mixture, it doesn't sound like the material of a two-hour film, and in many ways it isn't. But with the help of subtle Technicolor, and a pleasantly understated performance from Don Ameche, Lubitsch makes it glow like a Currier and Ives print, so that it can be watched again and again with quiet pleasure. It just doesn't seem likely that he made it immediately after finishing the mordant, fast and funny black comedy *To Be or Not to Be*. But he did.

Heaven Can Wait. US 1943; Technicolor; 113 minutes. Produced by Ernst Lubitsch for Twentieth Century-Fox. Written by Samson Raphaelson from the play *Birthday* by Lazlo Bus-Fekete. Directed by Ernst Lubitsch. Photographed by Edward Cronjager. Music by Alfred Newman. Art direction by James Basevi and Leland Fuller. With Don Ameche as

Henry Van Cleeve; Gene Tierney as Martha; Charles Coburn as Grandpa; Marjorie Main as Mrs Strabel; Eugene Pallette as Mr Strabel; Allyn Joslyn as Albert; Laird Cregar as His Excellency; Spring Byington as Mrs Van Cleeve; Louis Calhern as Mr Van Cleeve; Signe Hasso as Mademoiselle.

Heaven Can't Wait

HERE COMES MR JORDAN

A prize fighter crashes his plane and is prematurely taken to heaven.

> It is obvious that the producers of this film hoped much from the novelty of the story. They have cast it strongly and the standard of production on the technical side is fairly high. It is doubtful however whether it will have a very strong appeal to British audiences. There appear to be certain kinds of fantasy to which the American genius is in general so ill-suited that it handles them with extreme clumsiness. This is a case in point. Moreover, the central idea never quite loses a slightly unpleasant tinge . . . Within these limitations the members of the cast do their best to give some vitality to the film, and are the principal source of the sparing measure of entertainment which it contains.

This is the rather schoolmasterish 1941 verdict of one E.H.L. in the British Film Institute's Monthly Film Bulletin on a movie which must have taken a lot of people equally by surprise. It certainly came right out of the blue, and its casual attitude to death may well have seemed incompatible with what was going on in Western Europe at the time. However, *Here Comes Mr Jordan* must have had some merit, or at least some significance in the history of cinema, for on both sides of the Atlantic it spawned a whole host of derivatives, and thirty-seven years later was itself the subject of a smash hit remake starring Warren Beatty.

One can imagine E.H.L.'s distaste for a tall story in which death seems less painful than a pinprick, and on the other side of the great divide stands the warmly smiling and immaculately suited Claude Rains, as a heavenly official of indeterminate authority, waiting to welcome you with patience and courtesy (mixed with his own rather twisted ideas of fair play). But very soon, as the war progressed, another attitude became paramount: amid so much real bereavement people had need of reassurance, and even the rather empty afterlife presided over by the serene Mr Jordan went some way towards providing it. After all, there were plenty of precedents: even if one excludes the Bible from consideration, angels and devils are as old in our popular literature at least as the medieval miracle plays, and the Faust legend has had new interpretations by the score in every century since it was first written down. Perhaps the supposed tastelessness of *Here Comes Mr Jordan* was only that its highway to heaven seems to be devoid of religious fulfilment, let alone comfort. There is nowhere even to sit, just limitless vistas of dry-ice cloud, and a small plane waiting to take new recruits heaven knows where. (The uncredited pilot, with one line, is Lloyd Bridges.)

Despite its negative qualities this image of the hereafter must have satisfied a lot of people, for it was instantly repeated with variations, time out of number. *The Horn Blows at Midnight, Cabin in the Sky, Heaven only Knows, Carousel, A Guy Named Joe, That's the Spirit* and *You Never Can Tell* were just a few of the Hollywood retreads, and Powell and Pressburger were obviously influenced by it in fashioning their British fantasy *A Matter of Life and Death*. Yet for all Mr Jordan's influence, which surfaced yet again in a popular Michael Landon television series of 1984, it must be admitted that there is something cold and unsympathetic about his pioneering appearance: a substitution of busy antics for character study, of surface liveliness for wit. One smiles *at* it, but never laughs *with* it. All the same, it lodged strongly enough in the public mind for Bob Hope to make a gag of it in *Road to Morocco* a year later.

The main titles don't help to set a mood. They are set against a vaguely clouded sky, to the accompaniment of nondescript music; but as always in the forties they are mercifully brief. Alas, they are followed by the kind of self-conscious double disclaimer which makes an audience instantly suspicious:

> We heard a story the other day – from a fellow named Max Corkle – as fantastic a yarn as was ever spun. You'll say it couldn't have happened. Anyway, this one was so fascinating, we thought we would pass it on to you.
>
> It begins in Pleasant Valley – where all is peace – and harmony – and love – and where two men are beating each other's brains out.

We are at the training camp of Joe Pendleton, an untutored, saxophone-playing, plane-flying prizefighter, the Flying Pug as he's known in the trade. Robert Montgomery, who plays Joe in a thick Brooklyn accent, always liked putting himself in character, but (like Clark Gable before him at the time of *It Happened One Night*) he resisted this role because being lent out by MGM to Columbia was a comedown. (In fact it brought him an Academy Award nomination, which must have annoyed the hell out of Louis B. Mayer who in agreeing to the loan-out was putting Montgomery down for getting his own way about *Night Must Fall*. Such are the complexities of show business.)

Joe is happily manipulating the plane and the saxophone at the same time, in defiance of his trainer (the aforesaid Max Corkle, played with intuitive skill by James Gleason), when an aileron snaps and down he plunges. He can scarcely believe it when within the instant he and his sax are trailing clouds in the sky, being hurried along by a nervous messenger who wanted to spare him the agony of crashing, and so 'collected' him a moment or two before his time. Messenger 7013, played with familiar fussiness by Edward Everett Horton, is already losing patience with Joe's pleas that he could have brought the plane safely to earth; but the suavely unfathomable Mr Jordan, who is checking off new arrivals at the heavenly aircraft, confirms that according to the register Joe is not expected on the higher plane for another fifty years. A reprimand is due to 7013:

HERE COMES MR JORDAN. Robert Montgomery, having disbelieved Edward Everett Horton, has some distressing news confirmed by Claude Rains.

JORDAN: Unpardonable presumption. What territory do you cover?
7013: It's a place called New Jersey, and if it can be arranged, sir, I should very much like to be transferred.
JORDAN: You're new, aren't you?
7013: I am, yes sir, first trip. I was put on only this morning.
JORDAN: I thought so. Over-zealousness, out for record collections. This happens right along with the inexperienced.

Mr Jordan concludes that it is only right and proper for him to correct the error personally, but when he takes Joe back to the crash site, the boxer finds with horror that his body is missing. The answer must lie in Manhattan with Max, and Joe is impressed by their rapid transit:

JOE: Boy, we sure get around. Zip, we're at the crash. Bam, we're in New York. How do you do it?
JORDAN: I'm going to ask you not to pry into trade secrets, Mr Pendleton.

Indeed the film positively avoids disclosure of how heaven works, and provides almost no characterization for Mr Jordan. It eschews cinematic

91

trickery: only a couple of times does Jordan even walk through a closed door. But he faces a knotty problem when Max is heard explaining to a friend (the heavenly intruders being invisible and inaudible to both) that Joe's body has been cremated. (The other-worldly red tape must have taken an unconscionable time.) Joe is aghast:

JOE: I put in ten years getting that body in the pink.
JORDAN: But it's gone. Your body doesn't exist any more. You shall have your choice of a thousand bodies, all excellent specimens.
JOE: I warn you, you may be just wasting your time.
JORDAN: I have a lot of that.

The pair of them set off on their curious quest for a suitable fresh corpse, but, by courtesy of a couple of fast cinematic wipes, they soon find themselves back on a Manhattan street (every studio had one):

JORDAN: Russia, Australia, South Africa, and now New York. We've made a hundred and thirty stops. I know how you feel about a perfect body, but I've shown you the cream of this year's crop, and you've turned up your nose at the lot.
JOE: Mr Jordan, you can't palm off a second-rater on me. You've gotta remember that I was in the pink.
JORDAN: That is becoming a most obnoxious colour, Joe. Please don't mention it again.

Silently and unnoticed they arrive in the mansion of Bruce Farnsworth, millionaire industrialist, who according to Mr Jordan is a choice Joe can't possibly resist, though 'in slightly rundown condition'.

JOE: Fine body you want to make me a present of. He's gonna die, anyway.
JORDAN: He's being murdered, Joe.
JOE: Murdered? Who did it?
JORDAN: His wife and his confidential secretary.

Embarrassed, Joe is all for a discreet withdrawal, but the entry of one Bette Logan, pleading with the murderers for mercy for the father Farnsworth has ruined, inspires in the bodiless soul a romantic desire to help. Now he willingly enters the body in the bathtub (just like putting on a new overcoat, says Jordan), and is only slightly disconcerted to find that in the mirror he still looks like Joe Pendleton.

JOE: Hey, it's still me.
JORDAN: Inwardly you haven't changed. You're still Joe Pendleton, and that's what we'll see. Outwardly you're Bruce Farnsworth, and that's what they'll see.

(That's convenient for Montgomery, who was promised a star part, but it confused a lot of audiences.) Joe is assured also that the outsiders will hear the cultured voice of Farnsworth, instantaneously translated from Joe's deze-dem-and-doze tones. His obvious bewilderment – and ours – is calmed to some extent by Jordan's reassurance: 'If there were no mystery left to explain, life would be rather dull, wouldn't it?'

The would-be widow is naturally astonished to find that not only is her recently drowned hubby still alive and chirpy, but he has emerged from the bathroom with a hitherto unsuspected addiction to the saxophone and the square ring, not to mention an uncharacteristic predilection for righting wrongs, especially those he has committed himself. In so doing he naturally inspires something like love in the equally dazed Miss Logan. As for his new guise as a financial wizard, he has no trouble with that: as Mr Jordan remarks, rather too glibly this time, 'Finance is merely a matter of the heart being in the right place.' But Joe grows nostalgic for the ring, and especially for an opportunity to fight his old opponent Murdock. So he trains Farnsworth's body until it is quite undeniably in the pink, and earns a new reputation as 'the fighting financier'. In order to do so he must enlist the aid of the bewildered Max, who in a scene filled with frantic double-takes finds it hard to believe what he's hearing until Farnsworth plays 'The Last Rose of Summer' and hits the same sour note that always troubled his dead friend.

All concerned might have guessed – but don't seem to – that the murderers will have another go. Jordan fails to explain why he can't stop them as he did before: perhaps there's a rule about only one soul transplant per body. This time Joe/Bruce finishes up dead as a doornail on the library carpet, just about the time that boxer Murdock is shot in the ring by crooked promoters. The switch is obvious: Joe's soul steps into Murdock and triumphantly finishes the bout. Meanwhile a police inspector (Donald MacBride at his most explosive) has been assigned to the case of Farnsworth's disappearance, but you wouldn't expect him to solve it, not with Max Corkle wandering around with the jitters, wondering whose body Joe is inhabiting at present. (He even suspects a Pekinese.)

Jordan by this time is clearly impatient to return to other pressing matters. 'You made Murdock very happy,' he tells Joe, 'he was told how the fight came out.' But now, with both sets of murderers about to be rounded up, Jordan decides he must wipe out the memory of Joe Pendleton, who will henceforth become Murdock body and soul. Even so, the writers contrive not only a just and proper ending, with the body of Farnsworth discovered in the basement refrigerator, but a happy romantic ending in the true Hollywood tradition. For in the stadium corridor, with a new life before him, Pendleton/Farnsworth/Murdock bumps into sweet little Bette Logan, distraught from her lover's death but with a strange feeling when she looks into the boxer's eyes:

BETTE: I felt I was standing high up . . . looking out at the sea . . . and someone came swimming towards me shouting something . . . something I felt I'd heard long ago. People are always thinking they knew someone before, in another existence.

This is a plane of vague mysticism on which Hollywood has always felt secure – its apogee was the later *Portrait of Jennie* – and as Jordan calls 'So long, champ' to the departing couple, the film fades out quickly before any awkward questions can be asked.

Here Comes Mr Jordan made millions, and six years later a staff writer confronted Harry Cohn, the monstrous head of Columbia, with an idea for another heavenly whimsy he had written. Cohn was unresponsive, even negative. 'Fantasies don't make money,' he grumbled. 'But Harry,' said the writer, 'think of *Here Comes Mr Jordan*. That was a fantasy, and it made a lot of money.'

Cohn's eyes brightened, and as usual he had the last word. 'Yeah,' he agreed. 'But think of how much more it would have made if it *hadn't* been a fantasy!'

Here Comes Mr Jordan. US 1941; black and white; 93 minutes. Produced by Everett Riskin for Columbia. Written by Seton I. Miller and Sidney Buchman from the play *Halfway to Heaven* by Harry Segal. Directed by Alexander Hall. Photographed by Joseph Walker. Music by Frederick Hollander. With Robert Montgomery as Joe Pendleton; Claude Rains as Mr Jordan; Evelyn Keyes as Bette Logan; Edward Everett Horton as Messenger 7013; James Gleason as Max Corkle; Donald MacBride as Insp. Williams; Rita Johnson as Julia Farnsworth; John Emery as Tony Abbott; Halliwell Hobbes as Sisk.

I Spy

THE HOUSE ON 92nd STREET

During World War II, the FBI routs Nazi spies after the atom bomb formula.

Even as a teenager, when the typewriter excitingly tapped out the main title at me and I snuggled comfortably into my seat at the Bolton Odeon, I think I suspected that this 'new kind of movie' might prove just a shade too melodramatic to be as factual as the publicity said it was. That business about the atom spy getting his secrets out by memorizing them – it was straight out of *The Thirty-nine Steps*. Nor did there seem any good reason why the top German agent 'Mr Christopher', who was really a woman and as such ran a business open to anybody, should take the trouble to dress up rather unconvincingly as a man for contact and getaway purposes. Still, the photography of New York was marvellously clearcut, and with my cineaste's hat on I enjoyed the show for its speed and precision, perhaps especially for the impression it gave of having discovered a new cinema form, something rediscovered by television in the seventies and then called faction, or drama documentary. What producer Louis de Rochemont had done was to take the newsreel editing techniques of his *March of Time* series – a close forerunner of our World in Action – and apply them to an exciting spy story, parts of which might well be more or less true. He brought with him the linking device of the stentorian commentator, though Reed Hadley was far less over the top than Westbrook van Voorhis used to be. And perhaps he consciously borrowed a little, in the imaginary scenes of the furtive spies working out their plans, and in the ease with which they were routed by the Federal Bureau of Investigation, from *Crime Does Not Pay*, the series of two-reelers which MGM used as a training ground through the mid-thirties for such stars as Robert Taylor and such directors as Fred Zinnemann.

The Naked City claimed in 1948 to be the first thriller filmed on location in New York, but *The House on 92nd Street* clearly predates it. Between them they set in train a whole host of films which brought documentary techniques and some heavy fictionalizing to bear on 'real' cases which, so far as the final film synopsis was concerned, could have been compressed into one short sentence. *Kiss of Death*, *The Street with no Name*, *Walk East on Beacon* and *Boomerang* (qv) were among them, and together they comprise a very tolerable sub-genre of the American thriller; but they should all be taken with several grains of salt. A tip-off is a name in the credits of this first among them: Barre Lyndon, creator of such crime fantasies as *The Amazing Dr Clitterhouse* and *The Man in Half Moon Street*. Even in a supposedly realistic story, how could such a man possibly resist a few *coups de théâtre*?

The title sequence fades in on the words Federal Bureau of Investigation, and we are shortly leafing through an apparently official report, the contents of which, we are told, 'could not be made public until the first atomic bomb was dropped on Japan'. The note continues: 'Wherever possible, the actual locations have been used, and apart from the main actors, supporting roles will be played by genuine FBI personnel.' This promise swiftly proves to have the texture of piecrust when we spot the well-known actor E. G. Marshall, not a name in 1945, in a one-sentence role as a fingerprint expert.

'Now it can be told,' the voice booms on: the FBI trained 15,000 special agents to rout out spies, for 'Germany was recruiting American Nazis for its US espionage service, to build up a fifth column within the motherland.' In what was once a sequence of great fascination, but now seems as old hat as the baggy pants worn by the men, we are shown some of the spies' techniques: two-way mirrors, invisible writing, hidden cameras. In fact what we are watching now is a subtle mixture of re-enacted scenes and old newsreel, the latter chiefly of suspects entering the German embassy. It is a transitional mixture only: actors having once been established, we can now zoom into a file marked The Christopher Case, which the initiated may take as a signal that from now on no fictional holds will be barred. A man is killed in a traffic accident; someone in pointed shoes steals his briefcase; the dying man's last word is 'Christopher'. (Really? Who said so? And if the witness saw the shoes, wouldn't he also look up to see the face?) Our G-man hero is an American spy in Berlin, pretending to be a German agent. The Nazis send him back to New

THE HOUSE ON 92ND STREET. William Eythe watches master spy Leo G. Carroll get suspicious.

York with a fresh set of papers (though, as a professed American, it is not clear why he should need these). His instructions are that Mr Christopher will concentrate on process 97, the secret ingredient of the atom bomb. He stops to make contacts in Lisbon, 'the communications centre for international espionage'. On arrival in New York he establishes himself as instructed with one Elsa Gebhardt in East 92nd Street, where she pretends to be a dress designer in a nicely-chosen, evil-looking house with five floors and a plethora of fire escapes. Elsa seems to have few customers; instead she spends a lot of time in the back room with her thuggish Nazi cronies, including a lady Gestapo agent who never takes off her black leather coat and has to deal with such lines as: 'I don't trust that guy – he knows too much.'

It all sounds like the most dreadful ragbag of clichés, but in 1945 it was fresher; and cinematically it's a most enjoyable ride to the shoot-out finale, though the Nazis seem a remarkably ineffective bunch. Most interesting of them is the careful traitor Colonel Hammersohn, very stylishly played by Leo G. Carroll in a black homburg and an astrakhan collar. And so finally to the voice again, as Elsa Gebhardt Christopher (didn't you guess?) lies riddled with bullets and the FBI can report the arrest of '16,000 enemy agents of whom six were executed'. Crime does not pay, not in J. Edgar Hoover's ever-vigilant America.

The House on 92nd Street. US 1945; black and white; 88 minutes. Produced by Louis de Rochemont for Twentieth Century-Fox. Written by Barre Lyndon, Charles G. Booth and John Monks Jnr. Directed by Henry Hathaway. Photographed by Norbert Brodine. Music by David Buttolph. With Signe Hasso as Elsa Gebhardt; William Eythe as Bill Dietrich; Leo G. Carroll as Colonel Hammersohn; Gene Lockhart as Roper; Lloyd Nolan as Inspector Briggs.

Medieval Panorama

THE HUNCHBACK OF NOTRE DAME

A deformed bell-ringer rescues a gypsy girl from the evil intentions of a frustrated priest.

There isn't much doubt, really, that in Hollywood in 1939 somebody concerned with the remaking of this old warhorse thought it might make a useful comment on the plight of the German Jews, who are here represented by the gypsies of fifteenth-century Paris. 'Get out of here,' they are told, 'you have no place in France, you're foreigners.' 'All you mean,' comes the answer, 'is that you got here before we did.' There is a thought for the times also in the villainous Frollo's intention to protect France from the horrors of the printing press: free speech by the populace, and the general dissemination of knowledge, are to be resisted at all costs. But it is hard to see Goebbels in the superb frozen-lipped performance of Cedric Hardwicke, whose best film role this was, his cold eyes surveying Esmeralda's cleavage while his words purport to save her soul. Since he can't possess her, he murders her lover and has Esmeralda condemned for the crime. There is a fine modern plot here, something on the lines of *Double Indemnity*; but it all stems, more or less, from Victor Hugo, whose sprawling medieval canvas has been broken down and reconstructed to provide a texture very much like that of *Casablanca*, with a wide range of characters interacting in one set – in this case a vast one taking in the Nôtre Dame square and the courtyards and garrets which surround it. An opening roller title tells us that the film is all about dreams of progress being held back by superstition and prejudice, though at the time, of course, what the paying customers came to see was Charles Laughton's grotesque make-up, with its one eye two inches below the other.

Not a single still is supposed to exist of that make-up, for the makers insisted that in order to experience it you had to buy a ticket. It would probably have looked unconvincing in repose, but at twenty-four frames a second it worked pretty well, from the opening thrust of the head through the crown of fools to the final track back from the cathedral roof as Quasimodo hugs a gargoyle as big as himself and moans: 'Why could I not be made of stone like you?' But when one considers that he gets a whole frame to himself in the credits, and everyone else is squeezed in after the title, Mr Laughton is applied to this film very sparingly indeed. His appearances during the first hour total little more than five minutes, most of them brief glimpses to show off his one rolling eye. He comes into his own, of course, when he quite implausibly swings Tarzan-like across the square to rescue Esmeralda from hanging and spirit her away in an upward backswing to the belfry, where he has a fine old time toppling oak beams on to the rebellious crowd below, and even spraying molten bell metal through the mouths of gargoyles. To Esmeralda, however, he is considerate enough to inform her in his hollowest tones that he is leaving the room 'so that you don't have to see my ugly face while you're eating'. It is indeed a splendid performance while it lasts, even though it smacks of the Lyceum: Quasimodo the half-human becomes a thoroughly sympathetic character, and we are delighted that in this version he is allowed to survive at the end, even though he can't very well get the girl.

But this is not really a film for a star; the star is top of the bill, that's all. It survives so much better than the subsequent versions because of its intricate structure. The saturnine Frollo is balanced not only against the innocent beauty of the girl but against the well-intentioned half-wisdom of the king, a rich performance by Harry Davenport; against the misplaced heroism of Gringoire, an incredibly slim Edmond O'Brien; even against the superstitious unwisdom of the mutinous crowd, every member of which crosses himself when the hunchback passes, and against the aged doctor who keeps on muttering that the world isn't round, it's flat. The king sharply senses that 'the ugly is very appealing to man', but he is slow to recognize the evil in Frollo, which is plain enough for the audience to see, at times making the archdeacon like Iago to the hunchback's Othello. 'I am what I wish to be,' he enunciates, and the audience shivers because it knows that behind his façade of haughty correctness he wants to be something very nasty indeed.

So the film fascinates by its distillation of medieval attitudes; but it fascinates too as a superb example of Hollywood craftsmanship, a dazzling show of technical magic. If one excuses a wobble or two when the painted glass shot of the cathedral's upper reaches don't quite match the lower storeys which were built life-size, it is never less than absorbing to look at, apparently shot in deep focus so that every unpleasant detail of medieval life can imprint itself on the memory. The result is a rich Breughel-like canvas, even in the night scenes which do not in the modern manner mistake impenetrable blackness for realism. In this film one sees everything, and almost smells everything, while at the same time one is swept forward by sharp editing which keeps the multi-faceted drama constantly reclarified. A generous word, too, for William Dieterle's masterly direction and for the script by Sonya Levien and Bruno Frank, which takes in its stride such vigorous exchanges as this one between the poet and the king of the beggars:

THE HUNCHBACK OF NOTRE DAME. An impression of the immense set for the Feast of Fools.

POET: Being a poet, I'm already a vagabond and can quickly learn to be a thief.
KING OF BEGGARS: Good intentions aren't enough. They never put an onion in the soup yet.

P.S. Sharp eyes will spot George Tobias playing two small but quite separate parts in the crowd scenes; and buffs will relish the appearance of George Zucco as the prosecutor who complains: 'My lord, surely it's time to use the tortures on this stubborn wench?'

The Hunchback of Notre Dame. US 1939; black and white; 117 minutes. Produced by Pandro S. Berman for RKO. Written by Sonya Levien and Bruno Frank from the novel by Victor Hugo. Directed by William Dieterle. Photographed by Joseph August. Music by Alfred Newman. With Charles Laughton as Quasimodo; Maureen O'Hara as Esmeralda; Cedric Hardwicke as Frollo; Harry Davenport as Louis XI; Thomas Mitchell as Clopin; Edmond O'Brien as Gringoire; Alan Marshal as Phoebus; Walter Hampden as Claude; George Zucco as Procurator; Etienne Girardot as Physician.

Mountaintop in Bedlam
IDIOT'S DELIGHT

Just before the outbreak of World War II, an assortment of people find themselves stranded in a hotel on the Swiss border.

Through the credits are filtered the familiar strains of 'Over There' and 'Pack Up Your Troubles', which might well lead one to expect a jingoistic war movie. But this is 1939, before even Britain had declared war. Metro-Goldwyn-Mayer had bought a contemporary Broadway smash without knowing what to do with it. For once the blame must be shared by the playwright, for he gets sole screenplay credit. The first half of this film version shifts the focus away from his 'mountaintop in Bedlam', back to 1918 America and 'that certain day', as a caption facetiously calls the Armistice. Desultorily we follow the fortunes of a character caled Harry Van, described in the play script as 'a wan, thoughtful, lonely vaudevillian promoter, press agent, book agent, crooner, hoofer, broker of shill, who has undertaken all sorts of jobs in his time, all of them capitalizing his powers of salesmanship, and none of them entirely honest'. (Yes, Sherwood's plays were all equally overwritten; and no, we don't know what shill is.) The role seems hardly suited to a romantic star, yet here is Clark Gable playing it with all his might, exploiting his moustache, his dimple and that boyish mischief which for so many years melted the hearts of female audiences. He even has to escape from four admiring nurses at the veterans' hospital. We are soon invited to read an ad which states that he is 'available for engagements, outdoors or in'. We watch him as half of a grotesque comedy double-act. We see him in the chorus; touting encyclo-paedias; selling medicine on the sidewalk; and acting as audience stooge to a drunken mentalist for one week in Omaha. Here he meets and falls for a mysterious fellow trouper, an ex-Russian trapeze artiste with a vivid imagin-ation; she is in fact an incorrigible liar, first cousin to Brigid O'Shaughnessy in *The Maltese Falcon*. He doubts her biographical details, but she has an airy way of concealment:

HARRY: From the University of Vienna to the Embassy Theatre in Omaha?
IRENE: Today the mountaintops, tomorrow the Dead Sea.

Harry is entranced, merely remarking that she has 'a very remarkable way of talking for a girl who earns her living swinging by her teeth'. She can't be silenced. When he takes her for a cheap supper in a dive labelled 'Daka's Place: Eats' she goes into foreign-sounding ecstasies: 'What beautiful simplicity in those words! They tell the whole story!' 'You're so beautifully phoney,' he informs her half-admiringly. Like all facile liars she is quick to defend herself: 'Maybe we are the only ones in this crazy world who are real.'

There is no time for the cementing of this curious relationship, for their bookings take them in different directions, which doubtless relieved the Hays

Office. By courtesy of another of those montages which used to provide more fun in ninety seconds than the rest of the film in ninety minutes, we watch Harry's further progress, from supporting Sappho the educated penguin to solo eccentric dancing. Then, bingo, though he looks no older it is 1938 and he is leading a troupe of six chorus girls through the apprehensive cities of Europe. They are heading for home via Geneva, and the play proper now begins with them stranded overnight at a glossy chromium-plated hotel in the Alps, prevented by the local soldiery (who look like Nazis though nobody says they are) from travelling any further. According to the railway station the spot is called Pakajevo, and another sign reading Autonuso leads one to suspect that someone at MGM thought no country could be offended if the signs were in Esperanto. Luckily the hotel affords every comfort, though the other characters stranded in it are a motley crew such as you would expect to find in any Hollywood film purporting to represent the human race. They include a Nobel-prize-winning doctor about to find a cure for cancer, an American pacifist who won't be silenced, and an international munitions millionaire who has brought along his mistress, a phoney-looking Russian countess complete with blonde wig and diamond-studded cigarette-holder.

The shiny, anonymous hotel sets may remind movie veterans of the ship in *Outward Bound*. These people clearly don't know it, but perhaps they are all dead, emotionally and intellectually if not literally. Or could we be heading for a spy thriller on the lines of *The Lady Vanishes*? Alas, no. What Mr Sherwood has in mind is a work more akin to the talk pieces of Bernard Shaw, who might even recognize the characters as first cousins of his own brain children, for each of them expresses himself in long speeches replete with epigram and paradox. The difference is that Mr Shaw used to get a laugh out of us now and then: Mr Sherwood is heavy going with his clichés. His doctor: 'Why should I save people who don't want to be saved, so that they can go out and exterminate each other?' His army commandant: 'My colleagues wish to know respectfully if the young ladies will join them in a little drink?' His pacifist: 'I preach the brotherhood of man.' His munitions manufacturer: 'There will be no war. They are all much too well prepared.' And when they all excitedly get through to England on short wave, the news is predictably of a football match.

Mr Gable raises an eyebrow at all this and makes his own comment: 'Everybody would be much happier in Europe if they knew how to make decent coffee.' He keeps looking askance at the countess, she who thinks that the hotel 'suggests an amusing kind of horror. It is like somebody's tomb.' In her sequin-studded evening gown she is given to wide-armed gestures and such unanswerable statements as: 'I think the whole world should be covered in snow: it would be so much more clean.' Yes, of course, she is the girl Harry knew in Omaha, except that the years have made her even more of a liar, which presumably is her way of retreating from reality into illusion: and she won't admit the truth even to Harry until the bombs start to fall just before the final curtain. The trouble is that we don't care, because the character is woodenly written and even more woodenly played. You need to be a considerable actress to get away with Irene (or as Miss Norma Shearer

IDIOT'S DELIGHT. Clark Gable is still not quite sure that the countess (Norma Shearer) can be the acrobat he once knew back home.

pronounces it, Ee Ray Nah); and Miss Shearer is not that much of an actress even when one gets out of the beam of her slightly crossed eyes. She is game, we must give her that, but all her speeches come out with the same emphasis, as though she were encountering them for the first time, on autocue.

The talk ends only when the bombs fall, though it is never clear who is bombing whom. Everyone else deserts the hotel; the erstwhile lovers sit at the piano singing 'Abide with Me'. (In the play it was 'Onward Christian Soldiers', but perhaps that was felt to exclude too many paying customers.) Can Hollywood stomach the ending of the play, a suicidal defiance of fate? Of course not. The bombing stops. Irene looks through the window and says: 'Oh, look, Harry, they've gone away.' Fade up cheerful music; Leo the Lion, take your bow. Would that it had been so easy in real life.

Idiot's Delight is remembered, if at all, by patrons intrigued to watch Mr Gable do a little hoofing, which he gets through with a good-natured lack of skill. Physically, owing to MGM's excellent care of its negatives, it survives magnificently, looking just as good forty-five years later as it did on the day of its première. But what would have been worthier of preservation, and cannot now be recaptured, is the performance of the Lunts in the original Broadway production, which by the way also featured Richard Whorf, Thomas Gomez,

Bretaigne Windust and Sydney Greenstreet. The play for all its creakiness had an urgent anti-isolationist message; the film has no idea what it's about, though for historians of all kinds it's still a field day, and despite its chill, uninvolved feel it has passages which do evoke a wan smile:

IRENE: Did I ever tell you about my escapes from the Soviets?
HARRY: About eleven times. And each time it was different.
IRENE: I made several escapes. I was always making escapes.

But the best laugh is achieved by the hotel handyman going off to war. You will enjoy being a soldier, he is told. Oh yes, he says, if I'm taken prisoner soon enough.

Idiot's Delight. US 1939; black and white; 105 minutes. Produced by Hunt Stromberg for MGM. Written by Robert E. Sherwood from his play. Directed by Clarence Brown. Photographed by William Daniels. Music by Herbert Stothart. With Norma Shearer as Irene; Clark Gable as Harry Van; Edward Arnold as Achille Weber; Charles Coburn as Dr Waldersee; Joseph Schildkraut as Captain Kurvline; Burgess Meredith as Quillery; Pat Paterson as Mrs Cherry; Skeets Gallagher as Donald Navadel; Peter Willes as Mr Cherry; Fritz Feld as Pittatek.

Even the Moon is Frightened
THE INVISIBLE MAN

A scientist discovers an invisibility drug which turns him into a raving megalomaniac.

'Ow can I 'andcuff a bloomin' shirt?

Though it belonged to the middle generation of the family tree of monsters spawned by Universal Studios in the thirties, and though its sequels explored every angle from outright horror to spy burlesque, *The Invisible Man* presents itself unequivocally as a black comedy, which is what you might expect from the director of *The Old Dark House*. James Whale was in search of more elegant grotesqueries which would appeal to his macabre sense of humour; and the way in which the H. G. Wells novel was adapted for the screen for him must have made him smile a good deal.

Whale had gone to Hollywood following the immense success of his London and Broadway staging of *Journey's End*, a stark little play about trench warfare written more than ten years after the event by a mild insurance agent and ex-conscript called R. C. Sherriff. Whale fell rather accidentally into *Frankenstein*, which although it doesn't contain many laughs constantly suggests their presence lurking in the shadows; but *The Old Dark House* is clearly the work of a man who enjoys what he is doing, with its mixture of cynics, frightened ladies, religious fanatics, drunks and pyromaniacs. The Wells novel occurred to him to be an admirable follow-up in similar vein; the studio was in a mood to agree to his every suggestion; and it seemed to Whale that Sherriff, with his quintessential Englishness and feeling for words, might be just the man to adapt it for the screen and to resist any Hollywood interference except Whale's; so he sent him a wire and a generous offer for sixteen weeks' work on the other side of the Atlantic. Sherriff, aglow in his new-found world of wealth and leisure, was on the point of enrolling as a somewhat elderly Oxford undergraduate; but the warden understandingly agreed to a postponement, adding that Sherriff had better make a good job of the film since Wells was a friend of his. Easier said than done. After escorting his mother on a 6000-mile journey by sea and land, Sherriff found Whale still preoccupied by other projects. There had been a casting problem on *The Invisible Man*: Boris Karloff had turned down the role because he would not be seen, and a rich-voiced newcomer called Claude Rains had only just been signed. Meanwhile the impatient studio had set a whole barrage of contract writers to work on the story, and Sherriff was now expected only to make a final draft from the best elements of their scripts. He uncomplainingly accepted the foot-high stack of paper; but when he asked to refresh his memory with a copy of Wells's book, the story editor looked blank. There probably had been a copy once, but someone had lost it. Sherriff was not to worry. 'Everything worth using in that old book has gone into these scripts, and a great deal more besides, because these chaps are swell writers and they worked up a lot of stuff that Mr H. G. Wells never thought of.' Sherriff took the accumulation of words back to his suite at the Château Elysée, where he found that one version was set in the Russian Revolution, another made the invisible man a Martian, and so on. The charm, the intricate treatment of the main character, and the English rustic setting had been thrown out by all of them. Sherriff was certain that Whale would prefer a version closer to the original tone and narrative, which were presumably what had attracted him in the first place. But where could he get a copy of the book? Why indeed had he forgotten to bring his own? In his little hired car he made a tour of Los Angeles's limited range of bookshops, all in vain: Wells was out of print. Finally, when hope had been abandoned, he saw a box of old books among a pile of cabbages outside a Chinese grocery. Instinct impelled him to investigate, and there hidden away was an old copy of *The Invisible Man*, which he promptly acquired for fifteen cents.

It is an amusing story, which Sherriff relates in his autobiography *No Leading Lady*, though it has to be said that his finished screenplay, with its blackening of the character of Dr Kemp, and its Gilbert-and-Sullivan-style chorus of comic policemen, is closer to Wells in spirit than in detail. Moreover, the straight scenes featuring the mad hero's distraught fiancée are fumbled just as Whale fumbled the straight romantic scenes in *The Old Dark House*. But at a spare seventy minutes *The Invisible Man*, edited with

THE INVISIBLE MAN. Claude Rains is desperately short of a good idea.

tremendous pace, is for the most part not only packed with fun, thrills and bewildering photographic tricks; it is a work of true eccentricity, and Hollywood did not allow many of those through its net.

A great deal of the fun lies in Whale's observation of characters' faces, even in the tiniest parts: the gaunt cheeks of a darts player in the Lion's Head; the bowler-hatted pianist who takes so long to acknowledge applause that the player-piano starts again without him; the five old ladies in the snug who don't allow the violent fracas caused by the invisible one to distract them from their glasses of stout; the brief snatch of Walter Brennan with a cockney accent; the persistent reporter essayed by Dwight Frye, Whale's mad hunchback from *Frankenstein*; the droopily moustachioed police constable who dutifully listens to his super's combat plan and comments without enthusiasm, 'Oh, I see. Pretty good.' A pity that Whale didn't order the removal from the Lion's Head set of the vat of rye whiskey; but perhaps he wasn't a drinking man.

The whole thing starts with the heavily-bandaged stranger struggling at night through a splendidly ominous snowstorm; snow is indeed a continuing motif and the element which finally traps Dr Griffin, and the only really painful aspect of the narrative is the thought of a man, invisible but necessarily naked, braving the rigours of an English winter in order to achieve his dubious ends. He is not of course a bad man at heart: he simply wants to extend the boundaries of science. But the drug leads to megalomania. As he is finally provoked into explaining to the gawping rustics:

A few chemicals mixed together, that's all, and flesh and blood and bone just fade away. A little of this injected under the skin of the arm every day for a month. An invisible man can rule the world. Nobody will see him come, nobody will see him go. He can hear every secret. He can rob, rape and kill . . .

When in his mad exultation he takes off his bandages the crowd is staggered: 'Look, 'e's all eaten away!' But when P.C. Jaffers (''Ere, what's all this?') reports as much to his superintendent, he is met with disbelief: 'Where are you speaking from? The Lion's Head? Well, put more water in it next time.'
  The audience knows better than to be cynical, for it has heard from the lips of Griffin's old mentor the awful physical effects of the specific Griffin has stumbled upon:

Monocaine. A terrible drug made from a flower that's grown in India. It draws colour from everything it touches. Years ago they used it for bleaching cloth: they gave up because it destroyed the material. They tried it on a dog: it turned it dead white and sent it raving mad.

And soon we can fully calculate the effect on Griffin himself, who invades Kemp's house and sets himself stylishly up in dressing gown and white gloves, with a new-styled facial bandage which really does make him look like the master of the world:

The drugs I took seemed to light up my brain. Soon I realized the power I held – the power to rule. We'll begin with a reign of terror – a few murders here and there – murders of big men, murders of little men, just to show that we make no distinction. We might even wreck a train or two – just these fingers round a signalman's throat – that's all. Then sometimes I'll make *you* invisible, Kemp, it will give me a rest.

Even his wide-eyed fiancée Flora is aghast at the enormity of his ambition, which bursts through his protestations of love:

Power to walk into the gold vaults of the nations – into the secrets of kings – into the holy of holies. Power to make multitudes run screaming in terror at the touch of my little invisible finger. Even the moon's frightened of me – frightened to death. The whole world is frightened to death.

This is not the usual Hollywood hokum output, and the entire speech, delivered in bandaged close-up, with just one stretch of Griffin's white-gloved hand, is a Whale master-stroke.

Kemp has been foolish enough to blab to the police, so his number is clearly up. The rest of the film is devoted to Griffin's successful stalking of him ('At ten o'clock tomorrow night I shall kill you') and to the final successful police trap laid for the invisible one after an aged rustic in a smock has incredulously reported: 'There's breathing in me barn!' It is a pity that the naked fugitive's last tracks in the snow are of invisible shoes rather than invisible feet, but the film is over by now anyway: the audience waits only for the promised glimpse of its new star as Griffin dies and the effects of the drug very unscientifically wear off.

The Invisible Man is a film of many wonders and innumerable delights. Una O'Connor in a role which consists chiefly of piercing screams. An apparently unsupported policeman being swung round by the feet. A pair of trousers dancing up the road, singing 'Nuts In May'. Books tidying themselves up and transporting themselves to a window ledge. A bicycle riding itself down the street. And, above all, perhaps, that vibrant, insistent voice, which implants every word of a long part more clearly in our brain than if we could see the speaker. Yes, Hollywood had cause to be grateful for Claude Rains . . . and for James Whale and R. C. Sherriff too.

The Invisible Man. US 1933; black and white; 71 minutes. Produced by Carl Laemmle Jnr for Universal. Written by R. C. Sherriff from the novel by H. G. Wells. Directed by James Whale. Photographed by Arthur Edeson. Trick photography by John P. Fulton. With Claude Rains as Dr Griffin; Gloria Stuart as Flora; William Harrigan as Dr Kemp; Henry Travers as Dr Cranley; Una O'Connor as Mrs Hall; Forrester Harvey as Mr Hall; E. E. Clive as P.C. Jaffers; Dudley Digges as Chief of Detectives.

Radio Revellers
IT'S IN THE BAG

The owner of a flea circus seeks a legacy which has been hidden in one of five chairs.

When it first emerged in Great Britain towards the end of the war it was called *The Fifth Chair*, a title which made more sense; but the British publicists had clearly been too busy to see it, for on its opening at the London Pavilion it was billed as 'the funniest, the most horrific comedy-thriller ever made'. Since the ad was built round a shot of Fred Allen apparently scared to death, the mistake was perhaps forgivable, but those who see the film quickly realize that the expression merely connotes surprise on the face of the baggy-eyed radio comedian best known in Britain for his running feud with Jack Benny, which

107

was carefully nurtured throughout the forties. In fact, those with first-hand experience of American radio comedy will certainly get more out of the picture than the rest of us, who see only a modestly amusing, rambling, cheaply-made farce, shot on the barest minimum of sets, with the apparent aim of rivalling *Hellzapoppin* in its assembly of old burlesque gags and topical wisecracks. The story, such as it is, serves only as a casual peg on which to hang cameo appearances by media celebrities of the time, and on television in the eighties, with no audience response to fill in the cracks, the mixture does seem on occasion a bit leaden. The movie waits too obviously for laughs; it leaps too irrelevantly from one set-up to the next; many of its gags fall flat (and always did). But a unique curiosity it certainly is, one which with just a little more work all round might have become a comedy classic.

It begins with a credit-kidding sequence in which Mr Allen talks to the audience while the names are fading in and out:

Ladies and gentlemen, this is Fred Allen. Who knows who these people are? Who cares? You can find names like this in any phone book. Jack Benny. Who needs Jack Benny? A little radio actor. 'With sincere thanks for the contribution of Morrie Ryskind.' Ryskind's contribution! In one scene four people are eating dinner. Ryskind loaned us half a pound of butter so that the bread would look yellow in the close-ups. Now look at that one: associate producer. He's the only guy who would associate with the producer. Director? That's the producer's father-in-law, another relative.

If anyone bothered about the plot, which they don't, it would be a steal from *The Twelve Chairs*, or if you like from George Formby's *Keep Your Seats Please*. This version starts with one of those cranky old millionaires being shot just as he has hidden his fortune in the stuffing of a chair and bequeathed the set to his long-lost heir Frederick Floogle Trumble. (Photo of an eight-month-old child with a bald pate and baggy eyes.) We find the adult heir running a flea circus. He has a daughter whose boyfriend's father makes it clear that he doesn't care to associate with fleas. 'If that's the way your family feels about my father,' says the girl spiritedly, 'I'll go and have my own baby'; and there follows a brief sketch in a lift, from which none of the absorbed passengers will emerge until they learn how the spat comes out. There is also a bespectacled twelve-year-old called Homer on whom the family calls for any information required. His verbal wit deflects physical abuse: 'Striking your own child, father, denotes a fundamental weakness of character.'

Father-in-law-to-be naturally rallies round when he hears of Floogle's windfall, and seeks a loan to finance his own son's new patent mousetrap, which involves the mouse in climbing up steps so as to fall into a tub of water and drown. 'It seems rather complicated,' says Mrs Floogle. 'I thought you'd see it my way,' he glibly replies. Father-in-law has in fact a secret of his own, getting free room and board in return for acting as hotel rat-catcher, and there is a splendid little moment when he assembles his requirements for the evening's work. 'Ant paste . . . termite's delight . . . roach powder . . .

IT'S IN THE BAG. The barber shop quartet: Fred Allen, Rudy Vallee, Victor Moore, Don Ameche.

vitamins, for me . . . saw . . . that's for snakes . . . and lunch.' Mr Robert Benchley plays this role with his accustomed *sang froid*.

Floogle's wife has been dreaming of the travel which their new life will bring: 'Easthampton . . . Tijuana . . . maybe Coney Island.' And he has been playing up to her: 'Now I can get you what you always wanted: mink underwear and a chinchilla sarong.' (If that was one of Ryskind's lines, they *should* have cut out his credit.) But all is changed when cadaverous John Carradine, an organ-playing lawyer in an office with stained-glass windows, explains that there is no fortune, just a billiard table (in trust) and five chairs. Next day a delivery man brings the chairs and only shrugs when he is roundly abused by the frantic Floogle: 'What else can you expect from a bum still in his pyjamas at ten in the morning?' By the time Floogle learns the secret of the chairs they have been sold at an antique store, and he must set about tracking them down. (So must the bad guys, who have an ear to every wall.) First purchaser is a character called Mrs Nussbaum, a Jewish malaprop artist from Allen's radio show; she might well have been eliminated except that she has already sold her chair to Jack Benny, who, since Allen for the occasion is impersonating a founder fan-club member, receives him courteously but charges him for everything: there is a cigarette machine in the parlour and a hat-check girl in the closet. Benny explains his scriptwriting technique: 'I laugh first, then think back to the joke. Of course, sometimes I can't think of a joke, but nobody can say I don't have laughs on my programme.' When Allen, hoping for the chair, requests a personal memento for the fans, Benny whips off the tie he is wearing, neatly wraps it, and sells it to Allen for two dollars fifty. ('The same as I paid for it five years ago.') But he does agree to rent the chair for ten dollars a day. It proves of course to be the wrong one.

There is now a pause for an irrelevant but amusing routine reminiscent of old time burlesque. The Floogles decide to go to the movies, the attraction being *Zombie in the Attic*. 'Immediate seating,' calls the uniformed commissionaire on the street, but inside all seats are taken, and they find themselves shunted from aisle to aisle until they end up back on the pavement in an argument with an uncooperative usher. 'I'd sure like to see this picture through just once without interruption,' he tells them.

When they do find an official to listen to their complaint about the announcement outside, he replies with a laugh 'Oh, that's Joe, always looks on the bright side of things,' and they are sent upstairs, where the procedure is repeated. There are no seats, and even the elevator attendant roars with laughter at the mention of Joe. So does the assistant manager ('Your money back? I never heard of such a thing!') and the jovial manager himself, just back from a hunting trip in Ohio but a man for standing on his rights ('You understand, sir, we don't make these pictures. We just show them!') Finally, since a seat is what Floogle wants, he gives him one from the cupboard . . . and of course it turns out to be one of the required set. But not the right one . . .

Floogle Jnr has lost his memory from shock, and to retrieve the names of the other purchasers a psychiatrist is hired and willingly makes himself at home. ('That guy eats like a relative.') The trail now leads to a nightclub where Floogle wangles himself a job as a singing waiter. His three companions seem oddly familiar. They are Don Ameche, who sighs, 'I ran out of inventions'; Rudy Vallee ('I ran out of megaphones'); and Victor Moore ('After fifty years of chasing women I ran out of breath'). Through the ensuing riot he is followed by Carradine and Co., who are followed by detective Sidney Toler (more often seen as Charlie Chan), who is followed by Floogle's genius son. The trail finally takes them all to the suite of a gangster (William Bendix) who is apparently rubbed out by his devoted boys but makes a surprising comeback thanks to a bullet-proof vest. He's just an old softie really: the gang was bequeathed to him by his mother, Machine-gun Molly, and he never had the heart to disband it.

Everybody turns up for the final inconsequential mayhem; even the villains are not too proud to look into the camera and ask the audience which way. And when Floogle finds his fortune, the entire cast celebrates in his apartment for a wedding finale achieving the genuine *Hellzapoppin* touch, with Jerry Colonna (the shrink) yelling 'Where's the maraschino?', Robert Benchley (the father-in-law) wearing a light-up tuxedo reading 'Parker's Pisto Kills Fleas', and the police bringing along their glee club. 'My only daughter,' sighs Mrs

110

Floogle, 'and am I glad to get rid of her.' To which Mr Floogle responds: 'All we need is a brass band.' And of course he gets one. This film may not have class, but you can't say it doesn't try everything.

It's in the Bag (GB title: *The Fifth Chair*). US 1945; black and white; 87 minutes. Produced by Jack H. Skirball for Manhattan Productions. Written by Jay Dratler and Alma Reville. Directed by Richard Wallace. Photographed by Russell Metty. Music by Werner Heymann. With Fred Allen as Floogle; Binnie Barnes as Mrs Floogle; Robert Benchley as the father-in-law; Jerry Colonna as the psychiatrist; Victor Moore, Don Ameche, Rudy Vallee as the barber shop trio; William Bendix as the gangster; John Carradine as the lawyer.

Getting the Girl
KEEP FIT

A barber is mistaken for an athlete.

It isn't just that I have a soft spot for George Formby, though I have. It isn't just that his comedies filled northern cinemas when I was at an impressionable age, though they did. It is that he was first and foremost a star, and once they got going his films were never less than highly professional jobs which knew the most direct and fruitful way through a simple story. *Keep Fit* may not be the best of them, but it will serve; and at least it was founded in the social history of its time, for in 1937 the powers that were did have an official keep fit policy. (I remember in a magazine called *The Humorist* seeing a cartoon in which a motor car driver, approaching a double bend sign, gazed quizzically at his wife as she remarked: 'I do think the government is overdoing this keep fit campaign.')

George, the amiable goof, was inevitably the underdog at the beginning, but by the final fadeout he had always, incredibly, won the girl, thus demonstrating that there is hope for us all. No wonder we queued to see him; but we had to assume that the damsel had been hypnotized by his ukulele playing rather than by his gormless grin or his coy gesticulations. In this case he is an assistant hairdresser in a department store, and his rival for the hand of Kay Walsh is the dastardly head of sportswear, played by Guy Middleton with plenty of *savoir faire* but rather too fat a stomach to justify his claim that he is kingpin of every sport and 'all man'. George is stung to defend himself.

GEORGE: I was once second in an egg and spoon race.
HECTOR: How many runners?
GEORGE: Two.

But he gets his confidence back when he sings to himself, oddly enough in his braces in the men's washroom:

KEEP FIT. George Formby happily serenades Kay Walsh, but he's bound to have chosen a field with a bull in it.

> The nation's got an A1 plan,
> And I might turn in*to* a man
> If I'd biceps, muscle and brawn.
>
> The girls would all love *my* physique;
> I'd let them see it twice a week
> If I'd biceps, muscle and brawn.

'If that's the result of physical exercise,' comments a passer-by, 'thank God I had a misspent youth.' But the humour is less a matter of wisecracks than of the familiar Formby catch-phrases. 'Mother!' 'Go on, you daft thing!' 'Ha ha, never touched me!' Regulars will have welcomed them as old friends, drawing cheer the while from George's oddly angular physical assembly: surely nobody can be as misshapen as that. Predictably too his gym shorts are twice as long and twice as baggy as anybody else's, and the dialogue given to him is a concatenation of confusions, though in the following case the observation could have been designed for Oliver Hardy: 'Nice weather we're having. Lots of nice weather to come, too – all next week's not been touched yet.'

George the character has no sense. When at the staff dance he accidentally interrupts his boss having a quick cuddle behind a potted palm, he is shrewd enough to excuse himself but daft enough to go back and ask for instructions. It is possible that he was just as dense in real life. Certainly he must have been afraid of women, for it is a known fact that he never stood up to his redoubtable wife Beryl. I remember attending a function in Bolton Town Hall during the war. George turned up because he was appearing at the Theatre Royal that week, and a labour councillor called Alf Booth took him to task. 'How is it, George,' he asked, 'that when you come to't Theatre, all't prices goo up?' George looked blank for just a moment, then remembered the reason. 'Beryl says . . . if they want to see me, they mun *pay*.' Certainly Beryl made a rule that he must never kiss a girl on screen, and she stayed around the studio throughout all shooting days to make sure that he didn't. Perhaps she need have worried least of all about the heroine of *Keep Fit*, for she is played by Kay Walsh with an ultra-refined accent and such a repertoire of girlish simperings as have seldom been seen outside a Victorian parlour, and perhaps not even there. The performance fully deserves a prize for archness, and sparks the wrong kind of laughter when she is asked by the leering Middleton to take a stroll in the moonlight, and replies with pursed lips: 'I prefair dahncing.'

The plot complexities of this little comedy are satisfactorily carpentered, with George's stuntman brought on to do the comic exits from each scene, whether on a backfiring motor bike or the back of a bull. But it's the small jokes that get the big laughs, and the way George tells them. 'Ten shillings or seven days,' says the magistrate. 'I'll have the ten shillings,' offers George. It takes nerve to get away with a line like that. And it takes showmanship to keep audiences happy by filling the screen so frequently with close-ups of George strumming his uke and singing his mildly saucy ditties:

> Keep fit: don't bend the knees,
> Don't sit: be careful please,
> You'll split your do-ray-mees,
>   Whatever you do, keep fit.

I See Ice, made in the same year, is not one of George's best, either, though perfectly competent on a technical level and providing its star with some good googly lines such as: 'You wouldn't talk to me like that if me mother was 'ere.' The trouble is that the plot has neither logic nor common sense. After a promising northern beginning with dear old Ernest Sefton as an old-fashioned photographer, it puts George on a train to London with no luggage and no money, and mixes him up with ice-skaters. No attempt is made to explain how he eats or where he sleeps, as he earns nothing throughout the film and is not the type to cadge. The film also goes wildly wrong in assuming that a leading man in a stage ice show can easily double as an ice-hockey star, and in casting Cyril Ritchard as either. Kay Walsh's accent is slightly less irritating this time, though she does once say she's been *secked* and makes it sound like a synonym for being raped. Still, she does condescend to sit down with George and eat a pig's trotter, and not many well-brought-up young ladies from the south could manage that.

The best song this time is 'In My Little Snapshot Album,' with verses like this:

> I've got a photograph of old Grand-dad
> In my little snapshot album.
> He's over eighty but a real bad lad
> In my little snapshot album.
>> Although he's just an old antique
>> He thinks he's still the village sheik;
>> I've got him dancing cheek to cheek
> In my little snapshot album.

> I've got a picture of the vicar's wife
> In my little snapshot album,
> Chasing the curate with a carving knife,
> In my little snapshot album.
>> What he did was all in fun
>> But it's not the kind of thing that's done;
>> I think he pinched her hot cross bun,
> In my little snapshot album.

Then there's the nudist camp verse:

>> There's Uncle Dick without a care
>> Discarding all his underwear
>> But his watch and chain still dangle there,
> In my little snapshot album.

Such innuendoes blend smoothly with the Carry On type humour of a dour policewoman marching into a ladies' toilet and informing two of the occupants (one of whom is George in a feather boa): 'Owing to information received I must satisfy myself as to your sex. I shall have to take down your particulars.' But my own favourite moment is George being assaulted by crooks *en masse* and crying out in desperation: 'Ho ho, mother, they're taking me trousers off!'

Keep Fit. GB 1937; black and white; 82 minutes. Produced by Basil Dean for Associated Talking Pictures. Written by Anthony Kimmins and Austin Melford. Directed by Anthony Kimmins. Photographed by Ronald Neame and Gordon Dines. With George Formby as George Green; Kay Walsh as Joan Allen; Guy Middleton as Hector Kent; Gus McNaughton as publicity man: Edmund Breon as Sir Augustus Marks; George Benson as Ernie Gill; C. Denier Warren as Editor.

Hooray for Topic A!
THE LADY EVE

A lady cardsharp plans an elaborate revenge on the millionaire simpleton who once outsmarted her.

The Lady Eve was a smash success which established Preston Sturges, after a couple of good tries, as a top writer-director capable of getting the best out of expensive stars and his own scripts. The studio in this case had to take a chance on his earlier promise, for Sturges did not finish the script of *The Lady Eve* until he was well into production, and even then he was prone regularly to produce a day's shooting which bore no relation at all to the typed pages. When a harassed production type asked him politely what the movie was really about, Sturges smiled serenely and said 'Topic A'. If the executive had known that by Topic A Sturges meant sex – which was always Topic A to him – he would have been even more worried. But Sturges was clever with his innuendo, and no critic ever called him a dirty old man, not even when *The Miracle of Morgan's Creek* came out and James Agee observed: 'The Hays Office has been raped in its sleep.' The cleverness in *The Lady Eve* is that it's the lady who's on the make, and she always smiles when she's being most suggestive. The film in fact had the luck to star Barbara Stanwyck as thousands of men of the forties liked to imagine her: sultry, witty, dangerous, available, and ready to make the first move. And after so many stereotyped romances the film itself was an unexpected delight: smouldering along in an inconsequential way, like an indoor firework to whose blue touch paper someone has just applied a light. It even has an explosive finish; but along the way it dazzles with bouts of romance, character comedy, witty dialogue and outrageous farce (the latter always a Sturges speciality).

In retrospect *The Lady Eve* has a curious structure: a longish first act leading to a climax of friction; a second act paralleling the first but with the boot on the other foot; then two reconciliations separated by a wham-bang five minute guffaw sequence. It's a unique formula, and even more surprisingly Sturges, after a snake has wiggled its animated way through the credit titles, starts his sophisticated show with a prologue up the Amazon. Henry Fonda, as the shy heir to Pike's Pale Ale ('the ale that won for Yale') has spent a year in seclusion with an expedition financed by his father. On the riverbank he takes his leave of the chief scientist: 'I want you to know how much I've enjoyed it. If I had my way, I'll tell you, this is how I'd like to spend all of my time – in the company of men like you in pursuit of knowledge.' These lofty sentiments are somewhat cut through by shots of young Pike's bodyguard Mugsy (William Demarest), taking his rough leave of a local girl. 'So long, Lulu,' he says. 'I'll send you a postcard.'

The travel plan is for Pike's tiny steamer to rendezvous with a luxury liner, and, when it does, the top first-class deck is filled with eligible females, all a-quiver with excitement at the smell of millions. 'Go put on your pink-a-poos,' says a mother somewhat inexplicably to her chubby daughter. But taking a more relaxed view is Miss Stanwyck as Jean, née Eugenia, in conversation with her cardsharp father Colonel Harrington (Charles Coburn):

JEAN: Gee, I hope he's rich. I hope he thinks he's a wizard at cards. But I hope he doesn't dance. I don't know why it is, a sucker always stands on your feet.

COLONEL: A sucker is a sucker in any language.

JEAN: I don't see why I should have to do all the dirty work. There must be plenty of rich old dames for you to push around.

COLONEL: You find 'em, I'll push 'em.

JEAN: Boy, would I like to see you give some old harpy the 301.

COLONEL: Don't be vulgar, Jean. Let us be crooked, but never common.

We cut to the dining lounge that evening. The sucker, the rich one, is alone, reading a book called *Are Snakes Necessary?* Every female in the room tries to catch his eye, one by such an old ruse as a dropped handkerchief. Jean alone seems to turn her back, but she is disdainfully watching these attempts through a purse mirror. She becomes particularly sarcastic when a well-stacked contestant enters the fray: 'Won't do you any good, dear, but swing 'em anyway.' Her own method is more direct. She trips the sucker on his way out, then accuses him of breaking her heel and insists on using him for support while she hobbles to her cabin. When he introduces himself she acts bored: everyone on the ship knows he's a millionaire, so what else is new? In his confusion he gets off to a bad start: they arrive at his cabin by mistake, and he asks a question which is easy to misinterpret:

PIKE: Would you care to come inside and see Emma?

JEAN: That's a new one, isn't it?

But when she finds that Emma is a snake, she is able to compromise her man by screaming and running . . . and so they arrive in *her* cabin, all soft lights, sweet music, and satin and scent. She invites him to choose a new pair of shoes from her collection, and drapes herself in front of it with the query: 'See anything you like?' His gentlemanly modesty is very nearly subdued by this: he excuses himself. 'When you've been up the Amazon for a year . . . that perfume!' 'Why, Hoppy,' she responds gaily, 'you ought to be kept in a cage . . .' Later she gets him down to her level for some heavy petting. But she doesn't want him to misunderstand her motives:

JEAN: I was just flirting with you.

PIKE: Oh.

JEAN: You're not going to faint, are you?

PIKE: No. Do you think they're dancing anywhere on board?

JEAN: Don't you think we ought to go to bed?

PIKE: You're a funny girl to meet for a man who's just been up the Amazon for a year.

JEAN: Good thing it wasn't two years.

116

THE LADY EVE. Henry Fonda is surprised by his own good luck. Charles Coburn isn't.

Since this is 1941, nothing happens that night except a card game which she and the colonel allow their victim to win handsomely, thus ensuring a return match. But by the time of this planned revenge, Jean has inevitably fallen in love with her poor chump, whom her father regards as 'the finest example of the sucker sapiens I've ever seen.' Hey, hands off, she tells him. The colonel sighs. 'The trouble with people who reform is that they always want to rain on everyone else's parade. Children don't have respect for their parents any more.'

How it all comes out, and how Eve comes in, and who Sir Alfred McGlennan Keith is, and why Pike senior bangs the covers of his silver service together like cymbals, and why the sucker sapiens keeps falling over things, is a collection of goodies which should not be described for fear of spoiling the pleasure of newcomers. Ah, to be young again, and seeing *The Lady Eve* for the first time on a Sunday night at the Arts Cinema, Cambridge, during the autumn of 1949. It was the last performance, and tickets were like gold dust, but to have secured one was a mark of glory.

The Lady Eve. US 1941; black and white; 97 minutes. Produced by Paul Jones for Paramount. Written and directed by Preston Sturges from a story by Monckton Hoffe. Photographed by Victor Milner. Music directed by Sigmund Krumgold. With Barbara Stanwyck as Jean Harrington; Henry Fonda as Charles Pike; Charles Coburn as Col.

Harrington; Eugene Pallette as Mr Pike; William Demarest as Mugsy; Eric Blore as Sir Alfred McGlennan Keith; Melville Cooper as Gerald; Martha O'Driscoll as Martha; Janet Beecher as Mrs Pike; Robert Greig as Burrows.

Broth of a Boy

LADY KILLER

A cinema usher turns to crime but later becomes a movie star.

This is a film with a meaningless title and the clumsiest of plots but plenty of box office appeal, most of it wrapped up in its star. In 1933, one might reasonably guess, not too much thought was given to its making: it came straight off the production line and most of it was probably made up by the writers as they went along. But apart from its sociological interest and the easy-going entertainment it provides, it does mark a watershed in the career of Jimmy Cagney. He had risen to fame in *The Public Enemy* as a gangster, a gangster with just a few redeeming features. He loved his mother, for one thing; but he ended up riddled with bullets and bandaged like a mummy on her doorstep. Still, he had such a lot of fun coming to that end, including pushing a grapefruit in Mae Clarke's face, and so many other movie gangsters imitated him that the forces of law and order began to get worried. After seeing what a high old time the criminals had, would the whole nation take to crime? The Hays Office began to wield its whip; the Legion of Decency was forming. The eventual answer for Cagney in the mid-thirties was to make him a G-man instead of a gangster, so that he could take part in the same blood sports while remaining on the lawful side of the fence; and something similar happened to Edward G. (*Little Caesar*) Robinson, who actually starred in a movie called *I am the Law*. But at the halfway stage, just three years after they first shot to evil fame, both actors played in movies which kidded their gangster images, and neither was terribly popular because in America, as elsewhere, satire is often defined as what closes Saturday night. *The Little Giant*, with Robinson as a crime boss trying to move into society, seems a terribly dull and dated entertainment now. But *Lady Killer*, which casts Cagney as a movie house usher who becomes involved in murder but winds up a Hollywood star, had a better balance even though its parts work more smoothly than its whole.

It begins with the manager's daily parade of white-gloved ushers on the roof of a Broadway movie house (which is naturally showing a Warner film, *Wild Boys of the Road*). Cagney is the usher who cheeks the manager, and chews gum when it is strictly forbidden. He isn't much with the customers either: when one asks him 'Why no Mickey Mouse?', he answers with a wisecrack:

118

LADY KILLER. Margaret Lindsay and James Cagney are a long way from the happy ending.

'Because he's making a poisonal appearance in Joisey City.' He is tough with his women, too. He asks one what kind of fur coat she'd like, and when she says mink, he snarls: 'You'll take rabbit and like it.' The plot proper gets going when he falls for a con trick, returning a lady's purse and getting drawn into a crooked poker game. Before you can blink, Cagney has taken over the racket, and in the next scene we find him in charge of a glass and chromium nightclub, being invited by his henchmen to take a gander at the rich bejewelled matron who has just come in. 'Did you say gander?' asks Cagney. 'I wonder how she'd go for a goose?' (In 1933 the Legion of Decency was still waiting in the wings.)

Wheeze number two is of Cagney's own devising. Just outside the matron's house he contrives to be almost run down by her limousine, and when carried inside to recover he takes careful note of the window fixings and the position of the safe. The same ruse works well enough for a whole series of robberies until someone is killed in the process and Cagney has to flee to the state of sunshine and grapefruit. Grapefruit? Yes, there are several in-references to his previous assault on Mae Clarke, all followed by double-takes, for in this picture nothing is quite what it seems: even the sinister figure following our

119

hero down a California street turns out to be a bum who only wants a cup of coffee. And of course when the train pulls into sunny Los Angeles it's pouring with rain.

The next man meaningfully to follow our hero is revealed at last to be a Hollywood talent scout who wants to sign on 'gangster types' for three bucks a day and a box lunch. The director soon picks him out from the crowd: 'Say, did you ever hit a guy on the chin?' (Knowing laughter from audience.) Soon he is promoted to Indian chief, and gets a sore behind from riding the prop horse. But after writing himself hundreds of fan letters, most of them signed Peggy Kelly, he is recognized as a potential star and is presently to be found indulging in riotous Hollywood parties, replete with live monkeys in the trifle. Amid the spoofing, ways are found for him to behave like the Cagney of old. He makes a critic eat his own bad notice; and when his old moll turns up as large as life after failing to bail him out from a police cell, he drags her by the hair into the corridor and dumps her. She is sore but not surprised. 'I suppose,' she says, 'you been rubbing noses with all the big female stars in the movie business.' 'Call it noses if you like,' he retorts.

The thing has to end in a chase. Cagney's old gang reassembles for a share in the rich pickings, and the next thing we see is a newspaper headline: GAY FILM PARTY ROBBED. For a while Cagney is suspected, but he clears himself by routing the robbers, and shares the fadeout with a reasonably pure leading lady he has met along the way. All this has happened in seventy-five minutes, which means that nobody can possibly be bored; and on the whole this is a fun picture which deserves its niche in the social history of Hollywood, as well as in the annals of screen gangsterdom.

Lady Killer. US 1933; black and white; 76 minutes. Produced by Henry Blanke for Warners. Written by Ben Markson and Lillie Hayward from the story 'The Finger Man' by Rosalind Keating Shaffer. Directed by Roy del Ruth. Photographed by Tony Gaudio. Music directed by Leo Forbstein. With James Cagney as Dan Quigley; Mae Clarke as Myra Gale; Leslie Fenton as Duke; Margaret Lindsay as Lois Underwood; Henry O'Neill as Ramick; Douglas Dumbrille as Spade Maddock; Russell Hopton as Smiley.

A Pair of Spanish Earrings

THE LAST FLIGHT

Four shattered flyers stay on in Paris after World War I.

Life and the movies are full of surprises. To any film buff who thinks he knows the hard-boiled, eye-to-the-main-chance style of Warner Brothers product in the thirties, nothing can be more surprising than this wry, allusive, dreamlike anecdote from the first year of the decade.

It is as though *The Sun Also Rises* had been rewritten by Lewis Carroll. It is slight, and short, and it leaves you just as you are becoming most interested, but being the way it is seems right for it, an accentuation of character. If a film can have a personality, this is an Elwood P. Dowd, a Kaspar Gutman, a C. K. Dexter Haven. It obeys no known rules, and it addresses the world in extraordinary language: you can bet it got by the front office without Jack L. Warner seeing the script. *The Last Flight* is a forgettable and even an irrelevant title, likely to confuse. But the film does at least convey an air of doom, of finality, an impression that the characters might as well give up if they have not done so already. The elegant fatalism is at once reminiscent of the classic German silents of the twenties, and it is not surprising that the director came from Ufa and was a leading actor in *Das Wachsfigurenkabinett* (*Waxworks*).

The Last Flight seems to have slipped past most of the critics of its day. Perhaps it was never shown to them: the publicists may have taken one look and decided that a press show would be a waste of effort. Presumably the few who paid to see it knew vaguely what they were in for: a study of the 'lost generation' which survived World War I, but they must certainly have expected more in the way of plot and action. The picture begins in lively enough fashion, with a montage of fighting scenes: trenches, tanks and (courtesy of *The Dawn Patrol* outtakes) an aerial dogfight. In a sense *The Last Flight*, which is by the same author as *The Dawn Patrol* (qv), can be seen as a sequel to it, except that these men are no longer hysterical: they are deadened by the horrors they have seen and have lost contact with the world. A man we shall know as Shep falls from the air to a crash landing, and as he lies in hospital the clock ticks its way towards 11 A.M. It is Armistice Day. When everything possible has been done for Shep, his old friend Cary is waiting for him:

SHEP: Well, the old war is fini.
CARY: What are you going to do now, Shep?
SHEP: Get tight.
CARY: And then what?
SHEP: Stay tight.

Shep knows instinctively that for him there is no future back home. Apart from a facial tic his body has been more or less preserved, but his mind can't make sense of what has happened to him or relate to conventional reality. The doctor knows it too as the two friends, demobbed, walk away:

DOCTOR: Well, there they go to face life. And their training was to face death. They fell six thousand metres. Like dropping a fine Swiss watch on the pavement. Their nervous systems are shattered.

Cary, though outwardly less withdrawn than Shep, is an oddly touchy individual, polite and quietly spoken but given to unpredictable moods. A year goes by, and they are still in Paris, afraid to go home, drowning their afflictions in alcohol. They have accumulated two other Americans of like disposition, and the quartet seems to have enough money from home for

121

THE LAST FLIGHT. Johnny Mack Brown, Elliott Nugent, David Manners and Richard Barthelmess look to see whether Helen Chandler really does have a set of false teeth in that glass.

smart suits and an unlimited supply of booze in elegant bars. It is in one of the latter that they meet the girl, Nikki, the 'single lady' of the author's original title and the character corresponding to Hemingway's Lady Brett Ashley. Her background is never explained, but she acts as a fairy godmother to the group from the moment they spot her standing alone by a pillar, holding a cocktail glass with a set of false teeth in it. She happily responds to Cary's bemused inquiry:

NIKKI: I was just standing here and a nice gentleman came along and begged my pardon and asked if I'd mind holding his teeth for him. I think he was going to slug somebody.

She is as uneasy with convention as they are, and she completes their world. It is this world we inhabit from now on, with no 'normal' people for comparison. Serious thought and direct answers are to be avoided:

Where are you going?
To take a Chinese singing lesson.

Where's he gone?
He's gone off to shave a horse.

What's she crying about?
She's crying because they didn't wash her strawberries this morning.

We all make mistakes. Michelangelo painted Adam with a navel.

Nikki is especially fascinated by Francis, whose face is a blank as though his thoughts were hidden very remotely within his brain. Cary explains:

CARY: He carries a chiming watch because he's always falling asleep in the daytime.
NIKKI: What kind of chimes?
CARY: Oh, Westminster, Canterbury, Whittington.
NIKKI: I'll take vanilla.

The other men are satirical about Cary's attentions to Nikki and he springs to her defence:

Hey, what kind of girl do you think she is?
I think she's the kind that sits down on phonograph records.
Well, people shouldn't leave those records lying about.

She grows on them all, especially when she allows them to spend the night in her ritzy apartment and have prairie oysters for breakfast (also the favourite reviver of Sally Bowles). They take her fully into their circle, without reservations: 'Despite your practically innumerable flaws, we have decided to adopt you.' They follow her everywhere, even to the beauty salon:

Why are you having your toenails painted?
I don't know, it seemed like a good idea at the time.

One day when the others go off 'to play billiards and drink beer', she follows the lonely Cary, first changing her footwear 'on account of I can run faster in red shoes'. They walk in the rain to the cemetery, where he feels like communing with his dead friends. At an ornate tomb, Cary tells her the story of Eloise and Abelard, and they find themselves picking up the heart-shaped pebbles which mean 'that no harm can ever come to you or your true love'. Cary seems on the point of proposing. But as usual Nikki can't resist a flip remark ('at least you've found a name for my turtles') and he sets off in a huff. She doesn't mend matters by telling him that he is behaving 'like an old Easter egg'. Cary goes to Portugal by train; the others, concerned, follow him. They have nothing better to do. They find themselves in a Lisbon bar, responding to an elderly Englishman who questions their motives:

We're here to investigate conditions. Drinking conditions, mostly. The drinking conditions are very bad here. The beer's so full of cinders, it makes you lay hardboiled eggs.

Naturally they go to a bullfight, but the once-tough westerner among them gets over-excited and jumps into the ring, where he is promptly gored. He dies in hospital, and outside Cary is asked: 'The reporters would like to know why your friend descended into the bullring.' He smiles wanly and looks away: 'Tell them . . . that it seemed a good idea at the time.'

Within hours of this first tragedy the rest of the group falls apart. At a shooting gallery there is an argument, and Francis shoots dead a heavy who is trying to kill Cary. Then Francis lopes off into the black night. 'We'll never see him again,' muses Cary, 'maybe he'll forget to wind his watch.' Not until the three remaining are inside a taxi does Shep reveal that he too was mortally wounded in the affray. 'You may not believe it,' he says, dying, 'but this is the best thing that ever happened to me.'

And so we fade out with Cary and Nikki, on a train to God knows where. 'Comradeship,' he muses, 'was all we had left; and now that's gone.'

She sees her chance. 'Cary, you're alone now. I don't want to be alone. Let me be with you.'

He smiles and takes her hand. 'I want to help you. What can I do for you? What do you want?'

Having already got him, she can't resist being flip again. 'Well . . . I've always wanted . . . a pair of Spanish earrings.'

In other words, they are on the same plane at last; for them only the trivial is important. And that, believe it or not, is the fadeout. When you see the film, it feels right; we are left as stranded as the characters, beached on an inhospitable shore. Or perhaps where they are is on cloud nine, which is where the film seems to have been made. Hard indeed to imagine it as the product of beautiful downtown Burbank. Perhaps the trick was that for once the author of the original material was allowed to write the screen play; and that he too was a disoriented war veteran.

The Last Flight. US 1931; black and white; 80 minutes. Produced by Warners. Written by John Monk Saunders from his story 'Single Lady'. Directed by William Dieterle. Photographed by Sid Hickox. With Richard Barthelmess as Cary Lockwood; Helen Chandler as Nikki; John Mack Brown as Bill Talbot; Elliott Nugent as Francis; Walter Byron as The Outsider; David Manners as Shep Lambert.

The World's Oldest Orphan
LAURA

A beautiful girl is murdered. Or is she?

It had a reputation, in the hokum-filled days of 1944, as a new kind of thriller: a sophisticated *film noir* in which the people were convincingly real, but disillusioned and cynical. A mystery of character rather than of plot, in a world

LAURA. Suspicion breaks through the smiles on the faces of Clifton Webb, Gene Tierney, Vincent Price and Judith Anderson.

in which the war did not impinge. Jean Gabin and Michèle Morgan, we thought, would not have been ashamed to play in it, with Michel Simon or Louis Jouvet in the Clifton Webb part. Its reputation as a trail-blazer survived well into the sixties, and only after forty years does *Laura* begin to look something of a sham. Its *film noir* elements are half-baked: the writers filled one character with *bon mots* and gave another a silver plate in his leg and a perpetual cigarette hanging from his lip. As a thriller it only just passes muster, for having seen Gene Tierney at the top of the cast we know for sure that she can't have been blasted into pulp by a shotgun, as the first two reels would have us believe; nor can she be the murderess, not in 1944 when they liked their ideas of good and evil well defined. Two of the other three possible suspects are devious without being in the least interesting; and so we are left with the growing suspicion that it was the suave but venomous columnist Waldo Lydecker who shot what he thought was his mistress through a half-open door in a fit of pique at being passed over. This inevitably proves to be the case; and although the role of Waldo turned Clifton Webb into the most unlikely star of the forties, it was essentially unsuitable for him because it flaunted his homosexuality rather than covered it. (In real life he was mother-fixated and wept uncontrollably when his parent died in his seventy-second year; Noel

125

Coward called him 'the world's oldest orphan'.) True, he paces the dialogue superbly; but one wishes sometimes that Coward himself had taken the part. He would have stood a better chance of bringing to real life such lines as: 'Laura considered me the wisest, the wittiest, the most understanding man she ever met. I was in complete accord with her on that point.' Still, Mr Webb does present one of the cinema's more memorable images, when he is first discovered typing in his bath in that elegant penthouse suite, telling the unimpressed detective that he is 'the most widely misquoted man in America'; and his stage technique comes to bear when he is seen in action, moving through a scene like an immaculately suited knife with a serrated edge, or withdrawing from the sight of a lovers' embrace with a bitter farewell: 'I hope you'll never regret what promises to be a disgustingly earthy relationship.'

Despite Mr Webb's superficial effectiveness, what once in *Laura* seemed like low-key style now seems like an absence of any kind of style. What once was thought to be Preminger's best film by miles (even allowing for the fact that Rouben Mamoulian started it) can now be seen as not far ahead of his others, ponderously shot and lacking rhythm in the editing. Only the plot business with the twin clocks is at all visual, and that now seems inadequately explained. Perhaps if Mamoulian had continued, we would have still had in *Laura* a highly pictorial film, something to treasure as a piece of art. Or if Darryl F. Zanuck had not thrown away the dream ending which he wrote and half-filmed. Most of the characters in *Laura* look half-asleep anyway, especially Judith Anderson who never has a line to help her rise to the occasion, and Vincent Price who doesn't seem to know whether or not he's supposed to be sympathetic. He makes do with lines like: 'I'm a natural born suspect. It's because I'm not the conventional type.' This was what passed for wit in the mid-forties, and Clifton Webb must have winced every time he was handed a script in which Waldo Lydecker was reincarnated, such as *The Dark Corner*, in which he is an art criminal more world-weary than Coward ever knew how to be. 'I hate the dawn,' he complains. 'The grass always looks as though it's been left out all night.' Still, he made a satisfactory second career out of waspishness, and when they did let him retire from service, as a kindly priest in *Satan Never Sleeps*, the robes of that office did not suit him.

Laura. US 1944; black and white; 88 minutes. Produced by Otto Preminger for Twentieth Century-Fox. Written by Jay Dratler, Samuel Hoffenstein and Betty Reinhardt from the novel by Vera Caspary. Directed by Otto Preminger and Rouben Mamoulian. Photographed by Joseph La Shelle. Music by David Raksin. With Gene Tierney as Laura; Clifton Webb as Waldo Lydecker; Dana Andrews as Mark McPherson; Vincent Price as Shelby Carpenter; Judith Anderson as Mrs Treadwell; Dorothy Adams as Bessie.

Spoiling the Vine
THE LITTLE FOXES
Members of a scheming family stop at nothing to outwit each other.

Although in *Halliwell's Hundred* I tossed a few words of commendation in the direction of this splendid old theatrical warhorse of a movie, I am impelled to return to it because of several more recent encounters with the material. In 1980 in San Francisco I enjoyed a solidly carpentered repertory revival of the play, with a non-star cast functioning efficiently in an extremely pleasing and solid set. In 1982 Elizabeth Taylor chose to inflict on London her own rather pitiful touring version, in which the set would have disgraced a summer stock company in Perranporth (presumably the star's percentage left little scope for any other expenditure), and the rest of the cast had to dance like moths round Miss Taylor's flickering flame, even to the extent of blackening the character of Horace Giddens so that Regina by contrast might appear less wholly evil. Later in 1982, Channel Four set as one of its opening film series Samuel Goldwyn Presents, in which most of the master mogul's celebrated movies were ably introduced by Sam Goldwyn Jnr. He especially recalled the painstaking methods adoped by William Wyler on *The Little Foxes*. Certain scenes suffered as many as fifty takes, Wyler's aim being not merely to achieve technical perfection but to discover comedy asides even in this wryest of melodramas.

At this time I had not seen the film for several years, and in some ways it fell short of my expectations. After the stunning credit roll (with Goldwyn himself as usual pre-empting the director for final place) there is a quite unnecessary card saying that little foxes (the ones which spoil the vine, according to the Song of Solomon) are to be found in all places and at all times, but that this particular breed existed in America's deep south in 1900. This superfluous gloss, a kind of apology for making a period picture, is followed by a newly added and quite irrelevant breakfast sequence which introduces all the characters far less dramatically than was accomplished in the play, where we met them after dinner on the point of consummating their deal with the northern mill-owner. Breakfast also brings in one extra character in the shape of the handsome if rather spineless David, who is clearly intended as a happy ending for Regina's daughter, in stark contrast to all the other men, who are either weak or downright villainous. There are other bits of obvious opening-out and padding at which one is surprised that Miss Hellman connived, even for the sake of the box office. All are designed to underline the new love interest; all dissipate the initial tension of the play and make Regina's role, never long in number of words, seem even shorter than usual.

In the face of such obstacles it takes an actress of consummate skill to send you home feeling that you have been watching a tragedy of which she is the protagonist. Bette Davis is such an actress, and her Regina has more the force of a Macbeth than of his lady. One hears that during shooting she did not get

127

THE LITTLE FOXES. Hatching a family plot: Bette Davis, Dan Duryea, Carl Benton Reid,
Charles Dingle.

on with Wyler, even that she was on the rebound from a passionate affair with
him; that she never felt she had the measure of Regina, that she was sure she
got the make-up wrong, that she was too young. She may have had the right
instincts, but I defy any watcher to remain unmoved by her final close-up
when the selfish villainess, outsmarted by her brothers despite her supreme
effort in allowing her own husband to die, is herself deserted by the daughter
she loves, and moves back alone and afraid into the shadows. It is quite an
achievement, confronted as she has been by a platoon of scene-stealers.
Herbert Marshall, wearily underplaying every line to maximum effect, and
having a heart attack in close-up. Charles Dingle as the self-confessed old
rascal, Ben, who knows when he's beaten and chews his way through some of
the play's best lines: 'Cynicism is an unpleasant way of telling the truth,' and 'I
don't believe the Lord means for the strong to parade their strength, but I
don't mind doing it if it has to be done.' Patricia Collinge as Aunt Birdie, the
one aristocrat of the family, married for her rank by the unimaginatively
unpleasant Oscar (Carl Benton Reid). She takes to drink because the others
despise her so, but she has their number: 'I don't like Leo. My own son and I
don't like him. Isn't that funny? I even like Oscar better than Leo.' Dan

Duryea as the moronic Leo, who doesn't even understand the duplicity required of him. Miss Davis caps them all, even gaining our sympathy when she realizes so much faster than her brothers that they are alienating the guest they have been at such pains to impress. Soon however she is shocking us when she hisses venom at her too-upright spouse: 'I hope you die. I hope you die soon. I'll be waiting for you to die!'

For all the extra scenes in the first half, *The Little Foxes* remains a photographed play; but never was any play so luxuriantly translated to the screen. Wyler and his brilliant photographer worked in deep focus to achieve some memorably breathtaking compositions, often with a three-dimensional effect and usually involving the staircase, which symbolizes the play's two levels of living and which we come to know so well as the story unfolds. Wyler was a great one for staircases, and sets as many scenes as he can on this one; but the whole house becomes like our own in our knowledge of its intimate details. Rugs, wallpaper, furniture, doors, mirrors, all are displayed before us as though for an ideal home exhibition of the nineties; except that we never for a moment think of this house as anything but real. Surely, we feel, it existed somewhere in life, breathing in the moist heat from the quiet southern streets which surround it, and exhaling the evil which is planned within it. Two cunningly constructed scenes especially stand out. First, the bathroom scene in which Oscar and Leo stand back to back shaving themselves, the one only dimly comprehending the nefarious scheme which the other obscurely suggests. Then, a wonderful moment when the invalid Horace, surrounded by impatient greed, realizes that he has been brought home from the sanatorium only because his money is required: his head jerks round to face the taunting Regina, and nothing at all is said for several seconds. And of course no one who saw it can forget the chilling climax, when the stricken man staggers upstairs for his medicine while in huge close-up we watch the cold unblinking eyes of the rice-powdered woman who is counting the seconds until she can call for help in the sure knowledge that it will be too late. Such moments are rare in the cinema. They should be cherished.

The Little Foxes. US 1941; black and white; 115 minutes. Produced by Samuel Goldwyn. Written by Lillian Hellman from her play; additional dialogue by Arthur Kober, Dorothy Parker and Alan Campbell. Directed by William Wyler. Photographed by Gregg Toland. Music by Meredith Willson. With Bette Davis as Regina Giddens; Herbert Marshall as Horace Giddens; Teresa Wright as Alexandra Giddens; Richard Carlson as David Hewitt; Patricia Collinge as Birdie Hubbard; Charles Dingle as Ben Hubbard; Dan Duryea as Leo Hubbard; Carl Benton Reid as Oscar Hubbard.

THE LODGER

The man upstairs is suspected of being Jack the Ripper . . .

In 1944 I took little enough notice of it, because its defects were obvious and its merits seemed routine. Forty years later, however, one can no longer take for granted excellence of set design, photography and direction; and in these respects *The Lodger* is something of a revelation. Its lustrous black-and-white photography by Lucien Ballard, for instance, with every other shot tip-tilted for impressionist effect, reminds us vividly of better-remembered melodramas, most of them starring Orson Welles, whom in many shots Laird Cregar strikingly resembles.

Cregar must be one of Hollywood's great regrets. During the first four years of the forties he made a series of indelible impressions, as the psychopath in *Hot Spot*, as Morgan the pirate in *The Black Swan*, as Spettigue in *Charley's Aunt*. Difficult to believe, when one absorbs his vast bulk and apparent maturity, that he was only twenty-eight when he died, in the same year as *The Lodger* was released. It was the film which at last convinced the studio to give him star status, though they insisted that for his next role in *Hangover Square* he should be considerably slimmer. The dieting proved a strain on his heart, and he collapsed and died just as shooting was completed. *Hangover Square* is not at all a happy film; *The Lodger* therefore contains Cregar's last full-blooded performance, and he is mesmerizing. Although the role is underwritten, and he is third-billed, there is no doubt whose name should be above the title. No audience could lift its eyes from his as he gazes bemused into the mid-distance, muttering a biblical text as he braces himself to seek yet another victim from among the actresses who have been responsible, in his view, for the death of his brother. (Yes, it's another fictional explanation of the Ripper murders, but it will do as well as any other.) We hang on his every gesture, whereas the nominal star, Merle Oberon, is a fish out of water as soon as she appears, fifteen minutes in; but then the poor girl has to fill out a thin role with two ill-performed music-hall numbers, including something called 'The Parisian Trot'. As for George Sanders, his first scene is even further delayed, and throughout the film he makes only token appearances, though at least he proves that he can play a stalwart hero without his familiar sneer.

In the silent version of Mrs Belloc-Lowndes's story, the ending was twisted so that all the suspicions directed at the mysterious lodger were ill-founded. Here we are left in no doubt whatever as to his guilt from the moment when Cregar looms out of the darkness and pauses by a lamppost which illuminates a street sign, Slade Walk. When he seeks rooms at a house round the corner, Slade is the name he gives. We have already been witness to a Ripper murder, in a studio night street full of dry ice and patches of indirect light; the whole mood is reminiscent of German melodramas of the twenties, which is not

THE LODGER. Laird Cregar makes a characteristic entrance.

surprising when we remember that the director is John Brahm, formerly Hans, one of the most brilliant technicians in his field. What we see may not look much like Whitechapel in the eighties, but it is a brilliantly handled sequence, beginning with a blind man having read to him a notice implying that vigilantes will take over if the police don't identify and capture the Ripper. Meanwhile at the pub on the corner pearly kings and queens are having a party, from which an elderly ginpot detaches herself to stagger home. 'Have you got far to go?' asks a friendly copper. 'No, dear, only round the next corner.' The well-trained audience knows, of course, that she will never make it; but, this being 1944, details of her demise are limited to a scream behind a gateway from which a bulky figure dashes. Suddenly the street is filled with galloping horses, shot from overhead. ''E's done 'er, same way as the others . . .'

Cregar has applied for rooms at the very proper home of Sara Allgood and Cedric Hardwicke, who are taking in gentlemen only because of the master's ill-health following a misjudgement in the city. Impressed by Mr Cregar, they are blind to his curious habits, such as turning to the wall all pictures of famous actresses, or his reaction to the family Bible with records of dates on the front endpaper: 'Mine too are the problems of life and death.' He is a pathologist, he says, and the gas-rings in the attic suit him perfectly: 'Occasionally I require great heat.' He is pleased that the house is near the Thames, because 'deep water is dark and restful and full of peace'. His every scene is cunningly and eccentrically lit to suggest madness; yet all his landlord can say of him, and that cheerfully, is 'a curious fellow, a very curious fellow'. When smoke billows from the attic on the following evening, every member of the family instinctively heeds the lodger's vague warning: 'Don't come up here, there is something I have to burn.' And even when the incinerated object turns out to be a small black bag such as the Ripper has been seen to carry on that same night's murder jaunt, Hardwicke merely shrugs that the burning is very sensible, as any man seen in London with such a bag is likely to be lynched.

Miss Oberon, as Hardwicke's supposedly provocative niece, invites the strange lodger to see her performance at the Whitechapel Palace of Varieties. But he disapproves of theatres and therefore can't come. The lady, tantalized by this, follows him to his alleged place of work, but he surprises her before she can find out anything:

SLADE: You followed me.
KITTY: Do you expect to be followed?
SLADE: No: but I know I arouse curiosity.

In fact Miss Oberon's curiosity is oddly diminished; from now on she takes Cregar's side even when the first twinges of suspicion creep somewhat belatedly across the faces of others. Even when she finds Cregar busily burning a bloodstained ulster on the night after another murder, she accepts his explanation that it became contaminated in an experiment. She is not even put off when he quotes Solomon at her:

A strange woman lyeth in wait for her prey. She increases transgressions among men. It was the evil of woman that led my brother to his destruction. There is evil in beauty, but if the evil is cut out . . .

And her comment on this moody musing? 'Mr Slade is quite a philosopher,' she tells her aunt.

Mr Sanders, as the Scotland Yard inspector investigating the murders, now turns his thoughts away from the alluring Miss Oberon for long enough to utter: 'There is a strange periodicity to these crimes.' In fact we have witnessed one on every night depicted; whenever a faded flower says goodnight and totters home, it's simply a matter of waiting for the darkness and the scream. The film must surely end with Miss Oberon in similar jeopardy, and of course she brings it on herself by finally persuading Cregar to witness a music-hall performance. Meanwhile Sanders has linked him with the Ripper by means of fingerprints (a good ten years before the system was invented). So his men search the theatre from top to bottom . . . everywhere but the star's dressing room. And the moment the star retires there, Cregar lopes out from behind the changing screen. She is saved only when her screams bring the entire police force backstage. Like all villains, Cregar climbs upward, in this case into the flies from which there is no escape. And so, perhaps remembering one of his earlier remarks ('I take my problems to the river') he hurls himself through a window and ends up a floating corpse, just south of Tower Bridge (also a good few years before its time). The dull young people look into each other's eyes, the organist prepares for the national anthem, and it's all been jolly good fun, if you like that kind of thing. Millions did.

The Lodger. US 1944; black and white; 84 minutes. Produced by Robert Bassler for Twentieth Century-Fox. Written by Barre Lyndon from the novel by Mrs Belloc-Lowndes. Directed by John Brahm. Photographed by Lucien Ballard. Music by Hugo Friedhofer. With Laird Cregar as the Lodger; Merle Oberon as Kitty; Cedric Hardwicke as Robert Burton; Sara Allgood as Ellen; George Sanders as John Garrick; Aubrey Mather as Superintendent Sutherland; Queenie Leonard as Daisy.

Conversation Piece
MAJOR BARBARA

The daughter of an armaments millionaire joins the Salvation Army.

At the time of writing, Bernard Shaw has been rediscovered only in terms of *My Fair Lady*. His other works tend to seem dated by his own cleverness: he is too concerned to invoke paradox in order to topple the unfavourite idols of his own period, to set society right by his own intellect without doing anything practical to improve it. A revival of *Major Barbara* at the National Theatre in 1982 emerged stiff and interminable. Yet the 1941 film had always seemed to blaze a trail as fresh as that of, say, *Things to Come*, and I had certainly never been bored by it. What I had not realized was how much of the original dialogue Bernard Shaw had allowed to be pared down and simplified. He even undertook most of the work himself, compressing and cutting like the very devil, while still claiming in the press that he would allow his work to be filmed only by those who did not tamper with it. He even added new scenes, and offered a roller preface in his own handwriting. Without ever talking down to the public, he easily assumed their level, knowing full well that he was the only 'educational' writer likely to be discussed in public bars of a Saturday night. To Britons at large he was a 'character', and they loved him even when he spoke a language they could not understand. 'Have I ever failed you?' he asks now. Their answer would be a resounding no.

133

MAJOR BARBARA. Robert Newton and Rex Harrison, caught on the brink of stardom.

Gabriel Pascal, a Hungarian and the one man to whom Shaw would listen in the matter of film versions of his plays, has been vilified by most critics, and no doubt shows a stiff hand on many occasions. But Shaw was no fool. He knew he would get no arguments from Pascal, who wanted only to sit at his feet, and that was fine by G.B.S. But he knew too that Pascal was devoted to the Shavian text, and that by his industry he was able not only to fight the government, which wanted to close down his studio during production (this was, after all, the height of the blitz), but also to gather together a cast which represents the cream of British acting talent at that time. Many of them, like poor Kathleen Harrison, were thrown away with one line to speak; others, like Edward Rigby who has a good little scene to himself, don't get credited at all; and Miles Malleson and Felix Aylmer have to make do with playing butlers. But they were all proud to be in *Major Barbara*.

The essential flaw in the play as a dramatic entity is that the title character is not really central to it; at least, she fades in importance as it proceeds. The story develops and climaxes not so much through her disillusionment with the compromises of religion as through the unexpected alliance, on friendly enemy terms, between Cusins the intellectual and Undershaft the munitions manufacturer. The only way in which they all come together is in their dissatisfaction with the life of the idle rich.

Still it is with the romance between the penniless Cusins and Barbara the heiress that the story begins. In the play it is already under way, but Shaw, who commercially was no fool, saw the need to draw in the romance-seeking crowds, and so added a new opening in which Cusins, speaking for the Workers' Educational Association, is outvoiced in the street by the redoubtable Barbara, speaking for the Salvation Army. There and then he declares himself devoted to a life of serfdom at her heels. When her long-lost father Andrew Undershaft turns up, rich as Croesus and anxious to find another foundling to replace him as head of Undershaft and Lazarus, not only is the plot established but the pillars of argument are clearly defined, as are the occasional jabs of comic relief from Barbara's mother Lady Brit, who tends to such Wildean remarks as 'You go on as though religion were a pleasant subject.' Barbara and the Army stand for Religion with a capital R: 'When all our money was gone we asked for more.' Cusins is intellectuality: 'I've swallowed twenty religions. It's my life's work.' Undershaft is commerce: 'My morality – my religion – must have a place for cannons and torpedoes in it.'

Incidentally, the real war which was raging at the time of the film's release is utterly ignored: Shaw is concerned with universal truths, not present problems. The play was written in 1905 and the film seems to be set in the mid-thirties, but nothing has had to be rewritten on that account. In some ways it is a pity that there aren't a few more historical reference points, for even in this shortened version Shaw's barrage of cynicism, paradox and punning does become tiresome when experienced in a vacuum. One simply can't keep up with his rapid changes of attitude.

The core of the play is the scene in the East End Salvation Army barracks, where three things happen. Barbara shows a waterfront thug, Bill Walker, that violence doesn't pay and that the only way to salvation is to turn the other cheek. She also reject's Undershaft's offer of financial backing as tainted money. But her general delightedly accepts his cheque for 50,000 pounds, and sets it beside that for a like amount from Bodger the whisky distiller. Barbara, her mind in a whirl and her father less converted than ever, resigns her Army commission and is taunted by Walker with the famous question: 'Wot prawce selvytion nah?' (Shaw in his play script thus sets it down phonetically, but the film softens it slightly in order to make it more intelligible.) The actor playing Walker is Robert Newton, not exactly a newcomer and indeed fresh from some very dud performances. In this film he found his thrust and caused some excitement: I remember vividly that *Picture Post* headlined him thus in a picture feature: 'British Studios Find a New Kind of Man.' There is no doubt that he was partly responsible for the film's rather surprising popularity in bomb-besieged Britain, for he helped to make Shaw palatable at a time when audiences might well have preferred easier entertainment.

Eventually the principals converge on Undershaft's colossal new industrial city at Perivale St Andrew, on the slopes of the South Downs. They are not only astonished by the god-like power of the steel smelting but impressed by the good taste of the domestic accommodation: even the reactionaries among them feel that something so well ordered must be spiritually acceptable. By now the question of whether Cusins will marry Barbara is decidedly secondary: as Undershaft remarks, 'Like most young men you greatly exaggerate the difference between one young woman and another.' (To this Barbara surprisingly chirps: 'Quite right, Dolly,' but one feels she is speaking only in Shaw's voice.) But, of course, Shaw knows the value of a happy ending. Cusins accepts Undershaft's offer of the succession even though it will mean harder work than he has been used to. ('Six o'clock tomorrow morning, Euripides.') Hard work is a religion in which both he and Barbara can believe, so they march off happily among the workers, to be joined (and this is one of Shaw's greater box office concessions) by a beaming and converted Bill Walker who has just time for a cheerful joke to Cusins ('Stop her jaw, mate, or you'll die afore your time') before William Walton's music reaches its climax and the three of them advance jauntily into the camera lens.

It may be said carpingly that what we are discussing here is not a film but a photographed play of ideas. True, but so was *The Philadelphia Story*; and Pascal's direction seems at least the equal of Cukor's. He gets his actors into the most photogenic spots, lights them to advantage, and gives full value to the lines. The composition within the frame, indeed, is startlingly good, and the film can still be seen at its full length in gleaming 35mm prints, which is more than can be said for its predecessor *Pygmalion* or for some even more distinguished contemporaries. So let us thank fate, and Gabriel Pascal, and Bernard Shaw for it, and marvel that so much talent was available both before and behind the camera at a time when British film-making still consisted mainly of George Formby and Gracie Fields and Will Hay, with the occasional Korda spectacular to offer a corrective.

Major Barbara. GB 1941; black and white; 131 minutes. Produced by Gabriel Pascal. Written by George Bernard Shaw from his play. Directed by Gabriel Pascal and Harold French. Photographed by Ronald Neame. Music by William Walton. With Wendy Hiller as Barbara Undershaft; Robert Morley as Andrew Undershaft; Rex Harrison as Adolphus Cusins; Marie Lohr as Lady Britomart Undershaft; Robert Newton as Bill Walker; Emlyn Williams as Snobby Price; Sybil Thorndike as the General; Deborah Kerr as Jenny Hill; Marie Ault as Rummy Mitchens; Donald Calthrop as Peter Shirley; Penelope Dudley Ward as Sarah Undershaft; David Tree as Charles Lomax.

Little Fellow

THE MAN WHO COULD WORK MIRACLES

Sportive gods give miraculous powers to a meek little man.

Or is it simply *Man Who Could Work Miracles*? According to H. G. Wells it is, but it sounds clumsy to me. I first caught up with this now somewhat obscure fantasy in the summer of 1937, when I was on holiday in the Isle of Man. One year previously in the same cinema I had been bowled over by the futuristic melodrama of H. G. Wells's *Things to Come*, and now here was an unheralded item purporting via its posters to wallow in the glory of that already classic masterwork, being a joint production of Wells and the same celebrated producer Alexander Korda, who to the British cinema at that time was God, even though a Hungarian. My mother, a film buff in her way, had thoroughly approved of Korda since *The Private Life of Henry VIII*, and my father, who liked to be known as a political thinker, found most of Wells's views very tenable for a working man. So we went to the new film *en famille*: and if either of my parents was disappointed in its political stature, they did not have time to say so, for they were too busy laughing. Besides, Roland Young had been a family pet ever since his Uriah Heep in *David Copperfield*.

What I liked about *The Man Who Could Work Miracles* was, of course, the magic. It began and ended against a background of stars at night, Mr Wells's key to the infinite and very probably the same illuminated backcloth before which Raymond Massey and Edward Chapman, in *Things to Come*, had tried to envision the future. All the way through the picture I feared some solemn message, but it turned out that this time Mr Wells was in playful mood, symbolized by the fact that for his starting point he had gone back to the gods of myth. At first they seem like naked ghosts, riding on horseback amid the galaxies; but at least they are in the shape of men. Finally, in close up, they speak. Says one, gazing offscreen: 'Yonder is our brother the giver of power, playing with his planet.' Comes the reply: 'That small queer planet with the live things upon it?' (Clearly these gods are related to Shakespeare's Cushion-Laying Gentlemen: they bring you up to date with the story so far.) The planet referred to has to be Earth, and we are next shown a third godlike presence, sitting crouched like Rodin's Thinker and gazing at some tiny object between his feet. He defends his little planet and the tiny creatures he has made in his own image: 'They are pitifully small and weak, but I like them. Their lives are so short and their efforts so feeble . . . but I am going to give them all the power I can. The will of God, released!' This intention is greeted with horror. 'Don't give power to all of them,' cries the first god, 'there would be an explosion. Try just one, and see what power there is in the human heart.

Someone commonplace. A fair sample.' This is agreed, and now the audience is allowed to come closer to Earth, with the three godlike heads peering down above it. Closer and closer, with a long finger pointing down, creating a column of light which relentlessly approaches the English village of De-whinton.

This heavenly opening was sufficiently apocalyptic to stun me into hypnotised silence. The comedy which followed was in fact on the thin side, and might have disappointed had not I too been entranced at the sight of the diffident actor around whom it was constructed. In Hollywood he would never figure as the name above the title, but back here on his native heath he was the undoubted star, his long immobile upper lip and his wide eyes turning him without much apparent effort into the very personification of Wells's little man, George McWhirter Fotheringay. I never required Roland Young to act: I had not myself much cared for his Uriah Heep, though I had gleefully imitated it at home on the hearthrug: 'I'm your very 'umble servant, Mr Copperfield.' But I adored him when he effortlessly played effete complaisant noblemen and henpecked middle-class husbands, and I was perfectly prepared to accept him here as the epitome of all browbeaten shop assistants. His finest hour, perhaps, would come later in 1937, when he played Cosmo Topper, beset by jovial ghosts in the first of a trio of heavenly comedies.

Fotheringay is a dryish bachelor on his way to the Long Dragon Inn, and he does not even notice the finger of light as it plunges down towards him and penetrates his bowler hat. The Long Dragon is a dark and dreary place, bare and ill-lit, more akin to previous Hollywood visions of English pubs, as in *The Invisible Man*, than to the reality. When he enters, Fotheringay very conveniently finds a discussion on miracles already in progress between the bar-room philosophers. Our hero, slowly imbibing, is ready with his own definition of same: something contrariwise to the usual course of nature, done by power of will. As, for instance, if he were to cause the paraffin lamp, which hangs from the ceiling, to turn upside down and still burn with safety. Needless to say, when he gives a brief examination of how he might phrase the command, the lamp instantly obeys, causing panic and consternation among the mild and bitter. Fotheringay is not at this early stage able to sustain his will power, so the lamp falls and smashes, leaving him with damages to pay. But he has been given a sign; and as he trudges home, bewildered by his sudden unpopularity, he vainly tries to work out how the miracle happened. Over his cocoa he plays increasingly sophisticated tricks with a candle and a kitten, and in bed, unable to sleep, gradually litters his counterpane with flowers, rabbits, watches, a walking stick, two china cats and a bunch of grapes (for miracle-making is thirsty work).

Within a few days, despite his caution, and in accordance with the British tradition of suspecting whatever is not understood, Fotheringay has become a public nuisance; and he is himself pretty nettled because he has not found a really useful way in which to exercise his power. In a temper, he tells a nosey policeman to go to Hades, but when the man vanishes thinks better of it and substitutes San Francisco. The officer finds himself in the middle of one of that

THE MAN WHO COULD WORK MIRACLES. Roland Young is about to turn the lamp – and his world – upside down. Mark Daly looks sceptical.

city's traffic jams and is taken away babbling incoherently. Eventually the Establishment becomes aware of Fotheringay's strange powers, and instantly tries to suppress them, just as fifteen years later a similar Establishment would try to suppress Alec Guinness's white suit. Indeed, an alcoholic military J.P., played somewhat unconvincingly by the young Ralph Richardson, voices pretty much the same argument: 'If you put an end to war, sir – as I believe you intend to do before teatime today – if you put an end to competition, make work unnecessary, give everybody more money than they can spend – then I ask you, what are people going to do, sir?'

There seems no answer to that: it is the one valid criticism of all Shangri-Las. Nor is Fotheringay much impressed by an evangelist's suggestion that people should go about loving each other, not even (as the miracle man muses) 'if you add art and science and making things'. The colonel seizes his advantage: 'Look here, won't you give this business a few days' consideration before you let rip? Here we all are. We've built up a sort of civilization. People fit into it, at any rate they get along. We've got the Empire. A kind of order.'

Fotheringay can only raise his eyebrows uncertainly. 'I think change may be a bit of a lark.'

This irresponsible statement spurs the colonel to secret action: Fotheringay must be put down like a mad dog. From the ensuing mayhem Fotheringay escapes without a single scratch, but his temper has suffered. From now on, 'to hell with doing good'; he will use his power to get 'exactly what I fancy'. To begin with, what he fancies is more height to his body, stronger eyes, dark eyebrows, a straighter nose and a good moustache. All these he gets instantly, so it is but a short step to fancying himself master of the world. He assembles his fearful acolytes and announces his plan to stop the present world and start a new one in the image of his own dreams. First he creates a vast court, and fills it with 5,000 world rulers prepared to do his bidding. He makes a speech which contains Mr Wells's principal statement, a negative one. 'Chaps like me have always had to trust you lot, willy-nilly. And what sort of deal did you give us?' Intoxicated by his own naïve argument, and defying advice that if he stops the earth rotating it will spin away into space, he petulantly stamps his foot and gives the order anyway, just to show who's boss.

Luckily the three gods we met at the beginning have given Fotheringay a charmed life, and amid the ensuing rush of flying people and objects he has time for one last frightened command: 'Let everything be just as it was, five minutes before I went into the Long Dragon.' And so it is. The gods retreat with a smile and a shrug: 'They were apes only yesterday. Give them time.' And Fotheringay, when he again tries his trick with the paraffin lamp, finds that it remains obstinately in the right place. He is left, an amnesiac, wondering what he would do if he *could* work miracles: not that he will ever get the chance. (Not again!)

The technical construction of this delightful fable was never of the best, and the negative has suffered through age and carelessness. Yet it has in it the stuff of popular success, and one wonders why nobody ever thought of remaking it. Perhaps the little man as hero, even if given delusions of grandeur, is simply out of fashion.

The Man Who Could Work Miracles. GB 1936; black and white; 82 minutes. Produced by Alexander Korda for London Films. Written by Lajos Biro from the story by H. G. Wells. Directed by Lothar Mendes. Photographed by Harold Rosson. Music by Mischa Spoliansky. With Roland Young as George Fotheringay; Ralph Richardson as Colonel Winstanley; Edward Chapman as Major Grigsby; Ernest Thesiger as Mr Maydig; Joan Gardner as Ada; Sophie Stewart as Maggie; George Zucco as Moody; George Sanders as Indifference; Torin Thatcher as Observer.

Trail of the Fox
THE MARK OF ZORRO

Oppressors in California are harassed by a masked avenger.

I don't know much, if anything, about Johnston McCulley, who wrote a comic strip called *The Curse of Capistrano* on which the Zorro legend is based, but I wager he'd admit to having read about Robin Hood and the Scarlet Pimpernel, on whose exploits his Zorro is firmly founded. He can hardly be accused of stealing from Batman or Superman or the Incredible Hulk – quite the reverse – but all these heroes are brothers under the skin, law-abiders stirred by injustice to adopt an alias and set things straight by means of violent action. The 1922 version of Zorro was chosen by Douglas Fairbanks as a vehicle for him to do his Spring-Heeled Jack routine, and though he performs some still-astonishing leaps the film itself is muddy in development and hard to tolerate. Not so the 1940 remake, which, though it forgets to mention that *zorro* is Spanish for fox, is blessed by the attentions of several great professionals from the golden age of Hollywood, which of course was, paradoxically, the age of black-and-white photography. Arthur Miller was behind the camera in this case, achieving limpid compositions of sunlight and shadow. Alfred Newman wrote a thumping Korngold-like score. Richard Day had a hand in the sets. And the piece was directed by Rouben Mamoulian, whose sensitive eye is evident in every frame of his reconstruction of a sleepy California of long ago: as somebody comments, 'a land of sleeping peons, gentle missions and everlasting boredom'. Certainly Los Angeles is unrecognizable, being presented as a few haciendas grouped round a dusty square.

By courtesy of a glass shot or two, the story starts in Spain:

MADRID: when the Spanish Empire encompassed the globe, and young
Spanish blades were taught the fine and fashionable art of killing . . .

In Hollywood's lavish tradition of spending much on a small effect, we are shown a field full of fifty duelling cadets, of whom one is our hero. The efforts to sketch in a romantic image for him are slightly risible now:

> You have an affair of the court, my lord?
> – No, of the heart.
> Have you forgotten that you cross swords
> with Lieutenant Cortez at three o'clock?
> – Santa Maria, it had slipped my mind!

Don Diego de Vega is, to be truthful, somewhat unsatisfactorily played by a chubby young Tyrone Power, who simply can't manage without unseemly grimaces the element of self-mockery which came so easily to Errol Flynn over at Warners. But the script wafts him along. His father orders him back to California, so he lodges his sword in the ceiling of the cadet school, not

THE MARK OF ZORRO. Tyrone Power has Basil Rathbone at a distinct disadvantage.

knowing how much he is going to need it. The moment he arrives on American soil, rather overdressed for the journey, he announces himself at an inn as the son of the Alcalde, and finds that all the locals walk out with a good deal of silent rhubarbing. The truth is that his noble father is no longer the Alcalde, having been deposed by a corrupt government. In his place is a conniving puppet, Don Luis Quintero (J. Edward Bromberg), backed by a military adjutant, Captain Esteban Pasquale (Basil Rathbone). These smirking villains are clearly modelled on *Robin Hood*'s Prince John and Sir Guy of Gisborne, so it is no surprise to find that in the latter case the same actor has been employed, though in this film he has to tart up his underwritten role by making dangerous thrusts and parries as he indulges in small talk: 'Most men have objects they play with. Churchmen have their beads; I toy with a sword.' As Don Diego says, when introduced to the upstart in a scene of cold politeness: 'How can I refuse anything to a man with a sword in his hand?' Answering a question with a question, Pasquale inquires: 'You fancy the weapon?'

Noting the undertones of relationship – Quintero is jealous of his wife's interest in Pasquale, she is jealous of her niece's beauty – Don Diego decides that the safest cover for him is to assume the guise of a fop. 'I love the

142

shimmer of satins and silks, the matching of scents and lotions. As to ornaments and jewels . . .' Thus he earns the contempt of all concerned, including his own father and the old priest, played by Eugene Pallette in yet another reprise from *Robin Hood*. 'What we need in California now,' says the friar guilelessly, 'is an angel with a flaming sword!' Well, of course they get one. Quintero may post up as many notices on the following lines as he wishes:

> RAW GRAPES will no longer be accepted in payment of taxes in this district. One bottle in five of the finished wine must be handed in by October 31st.

It is to no avail, for a masked figure on horseback comes riding pell mell into town and rips down the notices with his sword, inscribing instead a fancy Z and posting a notice of his own:

> Let it be known that Luis Quintero is a thief and an enemy of the people and cannot escape my vengeance! – Zorro.

Zorro also does a little robbing of the rich to give back to the poor, but on the whole it is hard to see why his rather modest exploits should strike such terror into the hearts of a military garrison. They don't even inspire his own father, who is a devotee of law and order even if the law is corrupt. But for the picture's purposes the masked rider thinks he can scare Quintero into resigning, which will apparently restore normalcy to California. So be it.

Zorro does a lot of bounding about, and when cornered on one occasion he even forces his horse to leap off a bridge into the foaming river below, but as a tactician he doesn't seem all that clever. Sometimes he wears an eye-mask, sometimes one which covers the lower part of his face, but either way he is pretty recognizable as Tyrone Power, though not to anybody in the picture. Certainly not to Linda Darnell, who has the boring task of playing the heroine; he courts her obliquely while disguised as a friar. Her confusion flushes her cheeks even more prettily, so that Aunt Inez (Gale Sondergaard, playing Quintero's flirtatious wife) suspects that the child is getting something her aunt isn't, which makes the lady even more of a martinet. 'Keep it cool, my girl,' she snarls, 'or I'll whisk you into a convent'; then, turning to flutter her eyelashes at Pasquale, she murmurs coyly: 'Let's fly, I'm dying for a canter!' As Pasquale, poor Rathbone, still looking for something to do, bad-temperedly attacks a melon at dinner. Diego comments: 'You seem to find that poor fruit an enemy.' 'No, sir,' replies Pasquale, 'a rival!' Mr Rathbone looks so resplendent in this film that some of us may be sorry that he is not given dialogue enabling him to polish off Zorro in double-quick time. Instead, he has to accept the foppish pretence, and nod civilly at a man who offers as an apology for lateness the fact that his bath was tepid. 'His bath was tepid!' Pasquale snorts *sotto voce*. 'Poor Lolita, I'm afraid her wedded life will be the same.'

Diego's methods are so amateur that even these blinkered villains recognize him at last, though one at a time. Pasquale is rash enough to challenge him to that famous duel, the one in which Pasquale with his sword slices the top off a candle; Diego in response seems to miss entirely, but is able to lift up half the candle by its wick. The duel itself is moderately exciting, with the usual pauses for exchanges between clenched teeth:

> Ah, the captain's blade is not so firm!
> – Firm enough to run you through!

We are surprised when Pasquale is suddenly dispatched, and even more so when the stupid Quintero turns into Sherlock Holmes and realizes, one, that Diego must have followed Zorro's known route through the cellars, and two, that he still has cellar mud on his boots. 'Third, you handle your sword like a devil from hell!' Such matters should have been left to Rathbone, who is unavoidably absent from the final action, when the caballeros get their courage back and storm the barricades. It's an adequate finale, but it relies rather too heavily on the corpulent friar hitting his enemies on the head and muttering 'God forgive me' to each. Like many another star vehicle *The Mark of Zorro* is good to look at but doesn't bear too much examination.

The Mark of Zorro. US 1940; black and white; 93 minutes. Produced by Darryl F. Zanuck for Twentieth Century-Fox. Written by John Tainton Foote, Bess Meredyth and Garrett Fort, from the story 'The Curse of Capistrano' by Johnston McCulley. Directed by Rouben Mamoulian. Photographed by Arthur Miller. Music by Alfred Newman. With Tyrone Power as Don Diego de Vega; Basil Rathbone as Captain Esteban Pasquale; J. Edward Bromberg as Don Luis Quintero; Linda Darnell as Lolita Quintero; Gale Sondergaard as Inez Quintero; Eugene Pallette as Fray Felipe; Montagu Love as Don Alejandro Vega; Janet Beecher as Dona Isabella Vega.

Digging up the Past

THE MASK OF DIMITRIOS

A mild Dutch novelist is drawn into a maze of European intrigue.

One of the most interesting aspects of this basically unsatisfactory film is that it should have been made at all in its present form, for it has no star role and its construction is decidedly of the Chinese box variety, a little taxing for the average fan. One welcomed it in the mid-forties for providing Peter Lorre with a leading role in an 'A' film, and it is therefore all the more surprising that he gets fourth billing (he must have had a poor agent) and that he fails so badly in the attempt. His familiar whimpers and petulant outbursts seem ill-suited to the role of a detective story writer so obsessed with the personality of a dead murderer as to risk dipping his own fingers into crime. (If the film were ever remade, one might think of casting Jeremy Irons in his *Brideshead Revisited* persona: watching, listening, wondering.)

THE MASK OF DIMITRIOS. Sydney Greenstreet assures Peter Lorre that there's nothing to fear, but neither of them knows who's waiting upstairs.

One can guess how it came about. Lorre and Greenstreet were both under Warner contract, and the latter was so popular after *The Maltese Falcon* that juicy variations on his Fat Man image were constantly sought. A try-out was needed for a new face, Zachary Scott, who was certainly not your common or garden hero; and there was a new European director called Jean Negulesco who might be expected to weave an attractive atmosphere round this convoluted yarn of thieves falling out in darkest Istanbul. And so the package took shape, picking up for its small female role another contractee named Faye Emerson, and also utilizing a number of exotic minor talents from Europe: Victor Francen (deliciously effete as a retired spy), Steve Geray (playing a variation on his Dirk Stroeve in *The Moon and Sixpence*), Eduardo Ciannelli (billed as Edward for the duration of the war), Kurt Katch (inheriting Orson Welles's *Journey into Fear* role as Colonel Haki of the Turkish Secret Service).

The result could have been a masterpiece: *Casablanca*, after all, was assembled by equally haphazard means. But one's impression of *The Mask of Dimitrios* is of several eminent actors stumbling around in search of a script, for Frank Gruber, who gets the writing credit, supplied neither unity nor wit. The ripest Gruyère was required; he offers only the stalest mousetrap. The film contains barely a quotable line, though Greenstreet is allowed to ramble on in sub-Kaspar Gutman vein about there being too little kindness in the world until Lorre is stung into a request: will he please not say it again?

So why is the film worth recalling and cherishing? Largely because of its splendid character actors; partly because of the intricately sustained story; and not least for the amusement it provides in showing how a Hollywood studio backlot could so easily provide the facilities for a yarn which takes in several European countries without a single actor being of the nationality required by the script.

A heavy-going foreword ('For money some men will allow the innocent to hang . . .') precedes a shot of a bloated body washed up on the shores of the Bosphorous. A label in the coat bears the name Dimitrios Makropoulos, and the mysterious social-climbing Colonel Haki breathes a sigh of relief that a scoundrel with a long history has breathed his last. That evening he cheerfully attends an evening of music given by Madame Elise Chauvez (Florence Bates with but a single line) in her mansion at 5 Road of the Golden Horn. It is 1938, the 25th of November, and the clouds of war do not yet seem to have blown towards Istanbul. Haki is introduced to Cornelius Leyden, a Dutch writer of detective stories, and in somewhat unlikely fashion begins to expand on his day's work, explaining in flashback how Dimitrios has finally been laid to rest after a trail of crime leading from Smyrna in 1922, when as a fig-packer he involved a colleague in theft and then left the man to be sentenced for a murder committed by himself. Leyden scents a story in so notorious a career, and persuades Haki to allow him to view the corpse. (With the customary good taste of the time, the dead man is seen only in shadow.) As they subsequently carouse in the hotel bar, we cut to the lobby, where the familiar waddling figure of Mr Greenstreet, as usual in a bowler hat, is shaken to read of the death of Dimitrios. He also hurries to the morgue; but by then the body has been disposed of.

Leyden continues his research in the Athens record office, which gives goggle-eyed John Abbott the chance for a good turn as the fussy librarian but doesn't advance the plot except by allowing Greenstreet (now calling himself 'Mr Peters' and spying at a distance) to guess at Leyden's mission, after which he scrapes up an acquaintance on the night train.

PETERS: Pardon me, sir, for disturbing you.
LEYDEN: That berth is not occupied.
PETERS: How kind of you to say so. How little kindness there is in the world today. How little thought for others.

Though we shall later be informed that Peters is in fact a Swede named Petersen, he introduces himself as 'an Englishman by birth, but I am really a citizen of the world'. He then settles down to read a book called *Pearls of Everyday Wisdom*. One can imagine just how much the actor was enjoying himself.

In Sofia, Leyden is introduced to a disillusioned brothel-keeper – Dimitrios's mistress in the days when he grew rich by blackmailing her previous lover. He then graduated to political assassination before running out on her; but she still weeps at the news of his death. Leyden returns to his hotel room only to find Peters in the act of searching it, without much regard for tidiness. He points a gun at Leyden's head. 'Would you mind closing the door? I think if you stretch out your left hand you can do it without moving your feet.' But five minutes later they are all buddy-buddy, with Leyden half asleep on the bed while Greenstreet deals with dialogue half remembered from his first and best picture *The Maltese Falcon*:

PETERS: Tell me frankly where you stand, sir. I am proposing an alliance, Mr Leyden, a pooling of resources. You have knowledge which I want, and in return I shall share with you a sum no less than one million francs, if you will meet me in Paris in a few days' time . . .

Meanwhile, Peters gives Leyden an introduction to a man who can throw light on another chapter in Dimitrios's villainous life. This is Grodek the international spy-master, who now lives with his Siamese cats in a vast mansion near Geneva, where he is intent on writing a life of St Francis, 'though I confidently expect to be dead before it is finished'. Dimitrios, it seems, once his smooth criminal instincts were appreciated, was employed on behalf of Italy as a spy, and asked to produce a copy of the Yugoslav minefield chart. He did so by landing a weak clerk with gambling debts, and then blackmailing him into a theft which led to his suicide. This mishap has no effect on Dimitrios's conscience: having delivered the plans, he steals them back for resale to another interested government.

Leyden, bemused and bewildered by Peters's interest in him, finally does move on to Paris, where the well-upholstered rogue remains sleekly full of chuckles. 'Let us cultivate at least an illusion of friendship.' Leyden is not outmatched in banter: 'Oh, you're knocking at doors now, quite an improvement.' At last the truth comes out. Peters was a member of an international gang organized by Dimitrios, and a glance at a picture of the group tells Leyden that the dead man he saw in the morgue was not Dimitrios, who is presumably still alive and may be susceptible to blackmail. A dangerous game, we may think, and we shall be right, especially as the odd couple go about the game so clumsily, Leyden doubtless convincing himself that it is all in the cause of literary research. They get the money they demand, and even deflect Dimitrios's hired assassin, but when they return to their hideout Dimitrios is waiting for them, as they should have expected. Peters is gunned down, but kills Dimitrios as he tries to strangle the frenzied, half-hysterical Leyden ('You shot my friend!'). Still able to stagger downstairs, Peters tries to help Leyden get away, but the police then arrive to round things off. They behave most oddly, ignoring Leyden completely but trundling Peters away without bothering to establish who killed Dimitrios or whether it was in self-defence (which in fact it was). Perhaps the long-anticipated remake will sort out these matters more satisfactorily, while, it is to be hoped, retaining the very splendid Grand Guignol staircase on which the finale takes place.

The Mask of Dimitrios. US 1944; black and white: 99 minutes. Produced by Henry Blanke for Warners. Written by Frank Gruber from the novel by Eric Ambler. Directed by Jean Negulesco. Photographed by Arthur Edeson. Music by Adolph Deutsch. With Sydney Greenstreet as Mr Peters; Peter Lorre as Cornelius Leyden; Zachary Scott as Dimitrios; Victor Francen as Grodek; Faye Emerson as Irena; Steve Geray as Bulic; John Abbott as Pappas; Kurt Katch as Colonel Haki; Eduardo Ciannelli as Marukakis.

A Touch of the Tortures
THE MASK OF FU MANCHU
A master oriental criminal seeks possession of Genghis Khan's treasures.

I was never an ardent fan of the Saturday morning serials. I resented the way in which the imprudent hero, at the beginning of each chapter, so easily escaped the inevitable doom which clearly faced him at the end of the last. But I never minded a serial-like story in a feature, if put over with style and speed. These are precisely the attractions of *The Mask of Fu Manchu*, an apparently quite expensive item in MGM's 'nervous A' category, which meant that with luck it might make a little money, and if it didn't no great harm was done. A clear forerunner of *Raiders of the Lost Ark*, and much more full-blooded than could have been the case two years later after the formation of the Legion of Decency, it suffers only from a static exposition, as though the mighty Metro, approaching such a subject for the first time since the demise of Lon Chaney, hoped to give it some quite unnecessary dignity.

It all begins one dark night in the British Museum, where Sir Lionel Barton, eminent archaeologist, is being asked by Nayland Smith of Scotland Yard to lead an expedition to the edge of the Gobi Desert and find the mask and scimitar of Genghis Khan before that dastardly arch villain Fu Manchu, the yellow peril himself, gets to them, which he is on the very point of doing. 'How do you know that?' asks Sir Lionel rather naïvely. 'It is my duty to know things,' responds Nayland Smith in his suavest Sherlock Holmes manner. 'And if Fu Manchu wields that gold scimitar and puts that golden mask across his face, he will declare himself Genghis Khan come to life again, and all Asia will rise.'

Stirring stuff: such an eventuality cannot be permitted. Sir Lionel strides out promptly to do as bid, but in the sombre corridors of the museum the Egyptian relics have darting eyes, and before you can say Tutankhamun Sir Lionel is on the other side of the world, struggling in the sinister grip of the smiling, slant-eyed yellow peril, whose face is first seen rather magnificently distorted in a convex mirror. We recognize under the make-up everybody's favourite, Mr Karloff himself, still cooing unctuously with the accent of

148

Cheltenham rather than Chungking, but sporting for this occasion a fine false set of Chinese gnashers. 'You fiend!' splutters his captive. Fu seems unperturbed, but his tone becomes even silkier. 'I am a doctor of philosophy from Edinburgh University. I am a doctor of law from Christchurch. I am a doctor of medicine from Harvard. My friends, out of courtesy, call me doctor.' Since the prisoner refuses, Fu sighs and has him strapped to a bench under a metal apparatus with a huge clapper. 'The torture of the bell. It never stops. You will be frantically thirsty. You will be unspeakably foul. But here you will lie, day by day, until you *tell* . . .'

Meanwhile, Sir Lionel's intrepid daughter, with her father's two assistants, has ventured as far as Gobi. It takes them barely two shakes to locate the great tomb, lost all those centuries, and break into it. It is guarded by the most splendidly grotesque artefacts, and when they remove the mask from the old warrior's skeleton, there is of course a tarantula popping through the eye socket. Alas, the undergrowth is full of Fu's men, so many that even a hero can't shoot them all, and Sheila is soon faced with an invitation she can hardly refuse, to a summit meeting in the Street of the Dragon, beneath the House of a Thousand Joys. We know, of course, that Fu is unlikely to stick to any bargain, for arrogance will not permit him to be any man's equal. We see him now apologizing to his followers for his lack of a male heir. 'Since I have no son, I must ask you to receive a message from my ugly and insignificant daughter.' This is the lustrous Myrna Loy in the last of many Chinese roles, not much more than a year away from her triumph in *The Thin Man*. For the nonce she expresses her disgusting oriental penchants by the wearing of a metallic teacosy hat with dangling chimes. 'The whips,' she cries, fondling the inert body of a captive in a way which has overtones of sado-masochism. 'He is not entirely unhandsome, is he, my father?' 'For a white man, no,' replies Fu, 'but I must suggest a short delay in your customary procedure.'

Fu is in a towering rage, for having stolen the sword he has tested it by deflecting towards it with his finger a crackling electrical discharge. The weapon melts; it is a fake. Fu's petulance knows no bounds, and next morning a dead captive turns up on Nayland Smith's doorstep. The Scotland Yard man sighs: 'In the east they have ways of shattering the strongest courage.' But there is now nothing for it but to take action himself. He presents himself at Fu's premises and brazenly asks for the opium department. 'What I want is a little comfort, a little rest. Pleasant dreams, perhaps?' Down there among the sleeping Orientals, he starts a small fire and follows the most sinister man he can spot through a secret exit which leads rather painfully to Fu's headquarters; for it involves a long drop through a trapdoor, and there at the bottom is Fu himself with his fingers lightly curled round the hilt of a slim revolver (though how, with six-inch fingernails, he could actually have fired the thing is a mystery).

Fu is not averse to explaining his next move. He will turn Sheila's boyfriend Terence into a zombie and send him for the real treasures. We thought Terence was pretty insensible throughout the preceding action, but making him completely malleable to Fu's requirements involves the preparation of an

THE MASK OF FU MANCHU. Boris Karloff may be asking Charles Starrett whether or not he needs to shave before accepting the hand of Myrna Loy.

exotic serum, which the fiend proceeds to mix in a splendidly decorated operating theatre guarded by four black slaves on pedestals. Juice is hypodermically extracted from the underbelly of a giant spider. Venom is extracted from a massive snake by the simple process of allowing it to sink its fangs into a slave, who promptly dies and is whisked away. These vital extracts are then mixed with 'the magic brew of the seven sacred herbs', and all is ready to be pumped into our hero.

Soon the same hero, recovering, is ashamed to find that he has led his remaining friends from the outside into a death trap. Smith's colleague Professor Von Berg keeps defying the fiend in the name of the British government, but frankly this hasn't much effect. He is strapped to a stool in the middle of a device which involves rows of metal spikes slowly closing in on him from both sides. Originally Nayland Smith himself was to have suffered this particular torture, but some power that was at MGM decided that a fatter man in the predicament would be more alarming. Smith himself is tied to an extremely unlikely seesaw which, when the sandbox at one end is empty, will bring his head down to exactly the right level for being snapped off by ravening crocodiles. Our heroine meanwhile has been clad in virginal white

150

(does she deserve it?) and is ready for sacrifice at the hands of Fu himself, wearing the ancient relics. 'You hideous yellow monster,' she screams rather rudely, 'do you mean to destroy us all?' 'Yes', he hisses as only Boris can hiss, 'and that is only the beginning!' (What *can* he mean?) But he has reckoned without the resources of Scotland Yard. With one bound Nayland Smith is free; he rescues the professor in the very nick of time; and together they turn Fu's death ray onto the assembled hordes of disposable Chinese, while dispatching their master himself with the sacred scimitar.

Sadly this climax is a little muffed, the recovery of the forces of evil too easy; while throughout the adventure Charles Brabin's camera has remained too often rooted to the spot instead of exploring the expensive and intricate MGM production design. But there has been much along the way to enjoy, which is not surprising when one considers the trio of writers involved: Edgar Allan Woolf, co-author of *The Wizard of Oz*; James Kevin McGuinness, co-author of *A Day at the Races*; John Willard, the playwright who scared audiences with *The Cat and the Canary*. They are well served by a cast which does all that could be required, and especially by Mr Karloff, who may have been a ham but a sweet and succulent one. All we lack, really, is the voice of Fu reverberating across the wide ocean at the end: 'The world shall hear from me again.' The world never did, not from Karloff or from MGM at any rate.

The Mask of Fu Manchu. US 1932; black and white; 67 minutes. Produced by MGM (no producer credited). Written by Edgar Allan Woolf, James Kevin McGuinness and John Willard from the novel by Sax Rohmer. Directed by Charles Brabin. Photographed by Tony Gaudio. With Boris Karloff as Fu Manchu; Lewis Stone as Nayland Smith; Jean Hersholt as Professor Von Berg; Charles Starrett as Terence Granville; Myrna Loy as Fah Lo See; Karen Morley as Sheila; Laurence Grant as Sir Lionel Barton.

Cinderella Story
MIDNIGHT

A girl stranded in Paris is hired by an aristocrat to deflect the attentions of his wife's lover.

The title refers to the midnight which every Cinderella has to face, and few Cinderellas have been in quite so much trouble by the time the clock strikes as Claudette Colbert finds herself in this comedic house of cards. The time of realization and truth, the time when all the lies have been elaborated to their fullest extent, leads inevitably to a dramatic letdown: and for this or some other reason *Midnight* never endeared itself to the mass audience, and even

151

among connoisseurs of Hollywood comedy it is less hallowed than in my view it deserves to be, as the best of its kind since *Trouble in Paradise*. No doubt by the time it came to be released, World War II had swept away all fond memory of the idle rich European society with which *Midnight* concerns itself, and the moment never seemed apt for revival; one year later the same star, Claudette Colbert, was having romantic adventures in a purportedly real Europe in *Arise My Love*, replete with executions and the sinking of the *Athenia*. Since I wrote briefly about *Midnight* in a previous volume, Channel Four played it at my own instigation in an excellent Sunday evening slot, and although this was its first exposure on British television, and probably its first exposure to the British public since 1939, it played to disappointing ratings. Perhaps the title is what lames it; to some people it just doesn't sound like a comedy.

Lying plays a large part in the plot, which is what you might expect from any script in which Billy Wilder had a hand. Eve Peabody, an American gold-digger, is lying from top to toe, except when first discovered asleep on a wooden-slatted seat in a train which has just arrived in Paris from Monte Carlo. (She has been deported.) The gold lamé gown which is her only asset, and that a more than slightly ridiculous one, completely belies her real status, which is that of penniless confidence trickster. Tibor Czerny, on the other hand, lies when he pretends to be a taxi driver; he is really the temporarily-embarrassed cousin of a Hungarian baron. Madame Flammarion is deceiving her husband. Flammarion is pretending he hasn't noticed. Madame's gigolo assumes the style of a nobleman. And as the plot thickens, so the deceptions proliferate: everybody has one. As Eve says to Flammarion, 'From the moment you looked at me, I had an idea you had an idea.' The idea is that she should pretend to be an aristocrat. And Czerny pretends to be the noble husband she doesn't have. And Flammarion pretends (on the phone) to be Eve's infant daughter. They both pretend that Czerny is mad.

Even the actors are lying. Claudette Colbert arranges to show only her favourite left profile to the camera. Barrymore pretends to be sober. Elaine Barrie, his real-life wife, given a small part only in the hope of controllng him, pretends she can act. Mary Astor, discreetly costumed, pretends she isn't pregnant. And so on. As Charles Laughton once said in a different context: 'Delicious debauchery!' And in this case the off-screen goings-on must have been almost as amusing as the ones designed by the writers. According to the director's memoirs, Barrymore (then very far gone, and looking it) used the bushes in the terrace set as toilets, and could not be dissuaded from reading his lines from idiot boards even when their use meant reconstructing the set.

It's a thoroughly immoral film, if only in the most sophisticated way. Nobody in it is concerned for the plight of the workers, or the future of mankind, and none of it could happen in real life; but then, neither could Cinderella. Could a girl in an evening dress, a girl with nothing in her handbag but a pawn ticket, really travel from Monte Carlo to Paris on a wooden seat and be ready without even a glance in the mirror to con her way into an elegant musical soiree? Might she possibly be invited by one guest to play bridge, and surreptitiously supplied by another with more than enough money

MIDNIGHT. There's no situation in which Claudette Colbert can't manage to show her left profile, even when she has Don Ameche on one side and John Barrymore on the other.

to cover her losses? Is it conceivable, having failed to escape being escorted back to the city's swankiest hotel, that she would find her alias welcomed to the extent of a luxurious suite, a trunkful of perfectly fitting clothes from a top couturier, and a car and chauffeur entirely at her disposal day and night? Certainly not; but then this is not Paris France but Paris Hollywood. And Ernst Lubitsch, who had been to both, said that he knew very well which he preferred.

Midnight. US 1939; black and white; 95 minutes. Produced by Arthur Hornblow Jnr for Paramount. Written by Billy Wilder and Charles Brackett from a story by Edwin Justus Mayer and Franz Schultz. Directed by Mitchell Leisen. Photographed by Charles Lang. Music by Frederick Hollander. With Claudette Colbert as Eve Peabody; Don Ameche as Tibor Czerny; John Barrymore as Georges Flammarion; Mary Astor as Helene Flammarion; Francis Lederer as Jacques; Rex O'Malley as Marcel; Elaine Barrie as Simone; Hedda Hopper as Stephanie.

MINISTRY OF FEAR

In England during World War II, an ex-mental patient finds himself caught up in a Nazi spy plot.

It isn't one of Fritz Lang's more deeply felt movies, and it's certainly a travesty of the Graham Greene novel on which it is based. In that the ministry of fear was the Gestapo, which is not even mentioned in the movie; and, if I remember correctly, the climax took place somewhat sordidly in a gentleman's lavatory (this, of course, would have been unthinkable for Hollywood in the forties). But the film is an oddity, never convincing us for a second yet seeming to have ideas above its station. I may even have liked it because of its defects, and especially because it treats the rules of logic and characterization with such cheerful contempt. All the people in it are absolute sticks, existing solely for the purpose of advancing a plot which holds no water but is compelled to move from one unexplained perplexity to another until enough reels have been assembled and the hero's problems can be shrugged off with a general shoot-out and a happy ending.

I liked it too because it began with a village fête. I have always been a sucker for these modest occasions, and in the movie, Ray Milland finds the fête especially attractive because he has just been released from a two-year stint in a mental hospital for the mercy killing of his wife. (According to the movie he didn't do it, but the book says he did.) Behind the credits is the swinging pendulum of a large clock which he watches while waiting for his release; the image is to be repeated even more pointlessly at a later stage of the story. It seems that in this country asylum, in the middle of World War II, patients are discharged at the curious hour of six P.M. Even odder, while waiting for a train he finds the fête still going on, under grey evening skies. The uniform half-light, in fact, smacks much more of a Hollywood sound stage than of an English summer evening, and one wonders whether the art director took his cue from *Random Harvest*, in which the asylum 'in the English Midlands' seemed to suffer equally dismal weather.

The fête is in aid of 'Mothers of the Free Nations', but the folk in charge seem a sinister lot. Our hero has a strange encounter with a fortune-teller, who in answer to his murmured remark 'Forget the past, tell me the future' (quite natural in his circumstances) becomes intensely conspiratorial, muttering: 'My instructions are these. You must win the cake. You must give the weight as four pounds fifteen ounces.' Well, with such help, how can he lose? But there has clearly been some error, for just as he is leaving, a nattily-suited Dan Duryea rolls up in a limo and gives the same password (yes, we all guessed it was a password) to the fortune-teller. Efforts are made to convince Mr Milland that he must hand back his prize, but he fancies the cake, which is allegedly made with real eggs, and carries it off to his train. Here he offers a slice to a stick-tapping blind man who, amid clouds of disconcerting steam, turns up at the last minute to share his compartment. We are not surprised to learn from a shifty close-up (reminiscent of that allotted to pyromaniac Saul Femm in *The Old Dark House*) that the blind man is not blind at all; and we are only mildly shocked when, after crumbling his cake very messily on the compartment floor, he takes advantage of an unscheduled air-raid stop to beat Mr Milland about the head with his white stick and escape with the remainder of the confectionery. The chase which follows is over a stunted no-man's-land more reminiscent of Transylvania than of English pastoral. Luckily, or unluckily, the air raid resumes and the fugitive is blown to bits by a bomb.

Mr Milland can think of nothing to do but nurse his wounded head and proceed to Hollywood's equally lunatic view of wartime London, where high society lives in houses above New Yorkish stoops on streets where children play. Mothers of the Free Nations proves to be run by an all-smiling brother and sister act of Austrian refugees. Carl Esmond can play this sort of part standing on his head, but Marjorie Reynolds has to concentrate so hard on her accent that her performance is a negative quantity. With their encouragement, Milland tracks down the fête's fortune-teller. But she isn't the same one (of course). Friendly-like, the imposter invites him quite irrelevantly to join her with some friends in a seance, in the middle of which a disembodied voice seems to know far too much about Milland's past, and a familiar latecomer (Dan Duryea in the second of three alarmingly brief appearances) seems to get shot and leave the finger of guilt pointing at our hero. Like Richard Hannay in *The Thirty-nine Steps*, Milland is now on the run from both police and what he suspects (at last) to be enemy agents; and his position is made even worse when someone stumbles over the corpse of a drunken detective he has unaccountably hired.

The police are personified by a stolid gentleman who wanders the streets after Milland and is forever trimming his finger nails with a penknife. At least Milland is in no danger from the Austrian girl, who loves him, and a note of topicality is attempted when they spend the night sheltering from bombs on a most unconvincing tube station platform. She takes him for protection to the premises of an old bookseller friend, who to practised eyes may seem just a little too friendly. He entrusts Milland with a suitcase of books for delivery, and Milland does not suspect that there might be a bomb inside until it explodes in his face. Luckily it seems to be of a most ineffective type, for he is only slightly marked when the police revive him. (No wonder the Nazis lost the war if they can't even kill off unsuspecting nuisances.) Scotland Yard proves surprisingly amenable too: it humours Milland by allowing him to take the police back to the railway bomb site, where although there isn't a fragment left of the blind man who wasn't blind, the cake he was carrying remains intact, three days later at least, on a nearby hillock. Inside it the investigators now discover microfilm (did you expect less?) depicting Britain's plans for the invasion of Europe. Pursuing the lead that one of the seance-sitters is an advisor to the Ministry of Home Security (and has written a book called *The Psychoanalysis of Nazidom*), it takes the man with the penknife no time at all to

MINISTRY OF FEAR. Ray Milland and Marjorie Reynolds prepare for the rooftop finale.

deduce that the recent leaks have all coincided with the visits by this uncivil servant to a tailor, Mr Travers of Travers and Braithwaite, whose premises are clearly the next port of call. Mr Travers turns out to be our old friend Dan Duryea, still very much alive but not for long, and coping less than magnificently with a supposed British accent which turns Braithwaite into Braathwaite. After ostentatiously using the points of his cutting-out scissors to phone a warning to Mr Big, he makes a dash for it and is found stabbed with the same implement.

At about this point even the less percipient watchers may begin to wonder why, if Duryea was the means of leaking the secrets from the Ministry, he had to turn up in the country in order to retrieve the said secrets from a cake? What indeed was the advantage of cake delivery over the official postal service, or even handing over the McGuffin personally to whoever was supposed to action it? The answer can only be that if it were not for such circumlocutions, the film might have been forced to stick to Graham Greene's original narrative, which would not do at all: the screenwriter might have been fired for being lazy. Anyway, plot is now abandoned in favour of action, and not before time. Mr Big, the smiling Austrian (did you guess?) is shot by his sister in a flood of tears, and the rest of the villains are variously dispatched on a rooftop in the rain. All that's left when the smoke subsides is an ill-advised fadeout joke:

156

Milland winces rather too melodramatically when his bride-to-be prattles on about the huge cake they're going to have at their wedding. In wartime?

The brothers Warner might have got away with the absurdities of this tale because no audience would have minded much if it had been photographed against Michael Curtiz's customary shadows and given the benefit of Warners' customary touch with action sequences. Mr Lang's handling is far too severe: it's as though Woodrow Wilson were directing an Aldwych farce. Lang himself remarked towards the end of his life that he had just seen the film on television and found that it sent him to sleep. But I don't know that I'd agree: it doesn't convince, and it isn't funny ha-ha, but it's certainly funny peculiar.

Ministry of Fear. US 1944; black and white; 85 minutes. Produced by Seton I. Miller for Paramount. Written by Seton I. Miller from the novel by Graham Greene. Directed by Fritz Lang. Photographed by Henry Sharp. Music by Victor Young. With Ray Milland as Stephen Neale; Marjorie Reynolds as Carla Hilfe; Carl Esmond as Willi Hilfe; Hillary Brooke as Mrs Bellaire; Dan Duryea as Cost; Percy Waram as Prentice; Alan Napier as Dr Forrester; Erskine Sanford as Mr Rennit.

Suiting You? Suiting Him!

MR MOTO'S LAST WARNING

A Japanese detective in Port Said prevents the deterioration of the Entente Cordiale.

I suppose one should not be too sentimental about a string of second features made to a rigid and parsimonious studio pattern, but the fact is that in most cities around the world the eight films in which Peter Lorre played John P. Marquand's Japanese detective Mr Moto were thought good enough to top the bill, and forty-five years later when revived on television they have enabled many people to recapture the simple charm of filmgoing at the end of the thirties. No doubt this is chiefly attributable to the appeal of their star, one of the best loved and most unassuming character actors of his day (his lisping voice is still a boon to impressionists); but there is also a pleasant expertise in the way these serial-like thrillers are assembled. The skill is unobtrusive, but even the layman may occasionally note how remarkable it is that the camera is always in exactly the right place, and the eye is never allowed to be bored. This is a good deal more than can be said for the Charlie Chan movies which were being ground out at the same time and in the same studio; only a handful of them have stood the test of time, for they depend almost entirely on talk, and all too often the players assemble in a line to be interrogated. At least the Motos are composed mainly of action, whether the action is relevant or not.

MR MOTO'S LAST WARNING. Peter Lorre was seldom quite so much in demand.

Indeed, the more patently absurd the premise, the better the actors seem to be enjoying themselves.

Mr Moto's Last Warning is a good one, though as usual the title has no relevance to the story. It takes place in a Port Said which is more of a cockney retreat than I ever imagined it to be, even in its days as a free port. Passing Jack Tars sing 'Knocked 'Em in the Old Kent Road', the Sultana Palace of Varieties looks suspiciously like a music hall I once knew in Camberwell, and the local bar is called Connie's Place. The main credits pass in a trice, but not before the background music has skilfully blended the twin themes of 'La Marseillaise' and 'Rule Britannia', after which we are briefly introduced to two senior service dignitaries who mutter about the Anglo-French training exercises in the Suez Canal. 'Last week one of our men in Egypt reported that he was on the verge of finding out something which might affect these joint manoeuvres by straining our good relations.' So there's the plot in a nutshell: meanwhile the French fleet is told to remain where it is until further orders, and our attention passes to a liner docking at Port Said. Passengers at the rail conveniently facing the camera include Rollo Venables, Erik Norvel and Mr Moto. Venables (Robert Coote) is such an English public school ass that we assume (quite wrongly as it happens) that he must be a master spy. 'What a sinister, brooding place,' he says in naïve anticipation of mystery ashore. 'And did you get the sinister, brooding smell of it?' asks the cynical Norvel (George Sanders), who has such a suave manner and so improbable an accent that he could be a merchant from Afghanistan (wrong, he's a real spy). As for Mr Moto, well, this rather nervous oriental simply isn't the wily Japanese we all know and love, for within five minutes of landing he has allowed himself to be kidnapped and bumped off by the baddies. (They include a speechless aide who oddly alternates between a smart fez and a beggar's outfit.) But we are not unduly worried, for by now we have glimpsed the real Mr Moto, who for his own good reasons has sent a double ahead and is travelling incognito; before long he turns up as Mr Kukori at the door of a back-street shop selling eastern antiques (English spoken).

The local music-hall, where all the principals assemble on a Friday night, is a cheerful place, but it has a mistake in both programme and main poster. Last day, the billing reads: *Charlie Chan in Honolulu* with Warner Oland. Now, as any good detective or film buff should know, Warner Oland was not to be seen in *Charlie Chan in Honolulu*, for he died during the early days of production and was replaced by Sidney Toler. *Mr Moto's Last Warning* must have been made just a little earlier, and no one thought the error worth correcting. (The next Moto film, *Mr Moto's Gamble*, was far more drastically affected, for most unsuitably it has a hastily refurbished Chan script, full of boring talk; definitely the poorest Moto extant.) Following Peter Gracias the knife-thrower on the stage of the Sultana is a ventriloquist named The Great Fabian (Ricardo Cortez), with his dummy Alf. The writers, even in 1938, could not resist a few suggestions of supernatural malevolence emanating from the wooden head; but Fabian is basically quite an ordinary master spy, and parrying the dummy's jokes is a sideline. ('Your laundry's back.' 'Already?' 'Yes, they rejected it.')

During the intermission all the villains congregate in Fabian's dressing room, according to a message received from the stage. 'There must be nothing to show which government is employing us,' he insists, no doubt echoing an instruction sent out by Darryl Zanuck (in 1938) to all studio personnel, for Germany was then still a lucrative market. Fabian is so secretive that nobody is allowed to know what his plans really are, so it is not clear why he needs assistants at all. But he has a little black book with particulars of all known agents, and with a sigh of relief he puts a thick black line through Moto. ('No photograph. Usually works alone. Has been known to use doubles.') But Moto, disguised as the clown next door, has been employing a listening device. Noting that the bearded villain is really a British agent named Danforth, he lures him to the antique shop for a conference.

DANFORTH: You really are Moto, then?

MOTO: That is my one permanent characteristic.

DANFORTH: How did you know me?

MOTO: You were in Nepal two years ago? Posing as a Buddist priest? You remember that extremely dirty mule driver who accompanied you to the border?

159

Alas, Danforth by this time has been rumbled, and Fabian, after taking him out to sea and revealing his plan (to sink the French fleet with explosives dropped from an old salvage vessel) has him neatly suffocated in a diving bell. (Picturesque, but wouldn't it have been less troublesome simply to heave him over the side?) Meanwhile, Moto is crossing an astonishingly well-populated street set (did they utilize a lunch break on the set where Ty Power was shooting *Suez*?) to visit the port commandant. This gentleman, rather surprisingly, is an army general, played by E. E. Clive in curly whiskers. ('How is that mare's nest they sent you to ferret out, what?')

Soon Fabian discovers that the slightly delectable English Connie, with whom he lodges, has been prying into his affairs, not to mention his doll. 'I thought I told you not to fool with Alf!' he yells (but only because his signed secret orders are hidden inside the dummy's head). Fabian has to admit that he is not exactly on the right side of the law: he confesses in fact to a spot of smuggling. This Connie swallows, but a dose of Movietone News at the local fleapit makes her uneasy. ('Only a spark is required to set off the tinder box of the world. But so long as Britain and France remain friends, war clouds are unlikely.') A moment of eavesdropping enables her to understand everything, but she is foolish enough to admit as much. 'You little fool!' snarls Fabian; then, to Alf, 'If it hadn't been for me she'd be rotting right now in Dartmoor prison.' (Funny: we didn't know ladies were admitted.)

I have omitted to describe a couple of street fights and a good deal of miscellaneous following, but time presses. Now an attempt is made to assassinate the real Moto by bombing, but our smart hero hears the ticking although his clock has stopped, and hurls the device through the back window just in time. Deduction leads him to the villains' lair, but he is foolish enough to send the idiotic Rollo for help. The Englishman promptly entrusts the message to the smirking Forvel, and in no time at all both Rollo and Moto are being trussed up in sacks and dropped into the dark waters of the bay, while Forvel, donning an absurd diving helmet, reluctantly undertakes the job of detonating the fatal charge from the seabed at Fabian's signal: three jerks on the line. Luckily, and predictably, Moto has concealed a sharp implement about his person, and the sacks are ripped open in good time for him to knock out Forvel and detonate the charges before the French fleet gets anywhere near them. Moto emerges from the murky depths to find Fabian's gun trained on him, but the half-strangled Connie turns patriot at last and shoots Fabian instead.

The Commandant returns in time to stress 'the vital importance of our knowing what country lies behind this outrage'. Moto extricates the secret orders. 'See, General,' he murmurs. 'Good God!' expostulates the old military dugout. 'Tell me,' pleads the dimwitted Rollo. But the dummy, abetted by Moto, has the last words: 'Don't talk, Mr Moto, or you may lose your job.'

A neat double meaning, but oddly enough it was just what happened. When hostilities finally broke out, there was no place on Allied screens for a Japanese detective.

160

Mr Moto's Last Warning. US 1939; black and white; 71 minutes. Produced by Sol M. Wurtzel for Twentieth Century Fox. Written by Philip MacDonald and Norman Foster from the character created by John P. Marquand. Directed by Norman Foster. Photographed by Virgil Miller. With Peter Lorre as Mr Moto; Ricardo Cortez as Fabian; Virginia Field as Connie; John Carradine as Danforth; George Sanders as Erik Norvel; Robert Coote as Rollo Venables; E. E. Clive as Commandant.

Cowardy Custard
MY FAVORITE BLONDE
A burlesque comic helps a lady spy in distress.

Hitchcock's *The Thirty-nine Steps* – and I do mean Hitchcock's rather than John Buchan's – has much to answer for. Bits of its peripatetic plot have turned up in a score of lesser movies: recently I came across a 1942 second feature called *Fly By Night* which preserves the whole central situation as well as much of the detail, and in a 1939 action filler called *Code of the Secret Service* our G-man hero (played by Ronald Reagan) having used up three standard plots in the first forty minutes, walks straight into *The Thirty-nine Steps* for his climactic exploit. The film was twice publicly remade by other hands, and Hitch himself adapted most of it into *North by Northwest*, which was itself plagiarized by *The Prize*. What I hadn't remembered until a recent revival, was that Bob Hope did his own version of *The Thirty-nine Steps* in what used to be thought of as one of his best vehicles, *My Favorite Blonde*. I suppose Madeleine Carroll as co-star ought to have been a tip-off.

I say 'what used to be thought of'. One would like to think that judgements once made are good for all time, but that would be to reckon without the effect of repetition, changes of taste, and in the case of cinema films the fact that after their first release they are nowadays seen at home on the box in the corner, with no audience to respond to their carefully timed laughs and thrills. We should not complain too much: without television as a commercial outlet, thousands of negatives would by now have been cut up for mandolin picks. But it is true that the box minimizes epics, muffles jokes, and prevents thrillers from thrilling, simply by virtue of the snug domestic comforts close at hand. Comedies which rendered us helpless with laughter in the cinema now tend to leave us stony-faced, because the timing is all wrong: at home one simply doesn't need the space which was deliberately left after a piece of slapstick for 3000 people to stop laughing. In the cinema even these spaces might be insufficient with a full house, so that one was frustrated at being unable to hear the next lines through the continuing uproar. But they do damage to the home viewing of a trifle like *My Favorite Blonde*, so that one comes to wonder

161

whether it ever had anything else to offer than topicality, a smart pace, and a star in his prime. Plus, of course, those echoes from an older and better movie.

It begins promisingly enough, on Paramount's favourite studio setting of the time: a passenger ship in fog, arriving in New York. A Nazi thug shoots an apparently innocent bystander, but fails to collect what he was after, a scorpion stickpin; for the victim has lived long enough to drag himself along the deck and hand the scorpion over to his associate, Miss Carroll, very fetchingly adorned. One would expect her to be in immediate danger but, this being a movie, the Nazi prefers to send a message, concealed in a flare, to be picked up by George Zucco and Gale Sondergaard in a waiting boat:

> Failed. British agent now has scorpion with flight plans. She wears raincoat with brown hat and feather.

Once in New York, our heroine changes clothes with a lookalike who is promptly killed; then, suspecting she is being followed, nips into the stage door of a vaudeville theatre where Haines and Percy are not far from the bottom of the bill. Haines collects the pay cheques but Percy is the star, for Percy is a performing penguin and deservedly receives all the applause. In fact, a cable has just arrived from Haines's agent in Hollywood:

> Have signed Percy for *Igloo Love* at 500 dollars per week. May be able to get you fifty dollars as trainer.

Haines is, of course, Mr Hope in his cowardy custard persona, always ready with a wisecrack but never with his fists. When he finds the lady agent hiding in his dressing room, the dialogue flows in this vein:

KAREN: My name's Karen Bentley, I can't tell you any more.
HAINES: My name's Larry Haines, there's no more to tell.
KAREN: I'm being followed by two men in black.
HAINES: You're sure you don't mean two men in white?
KAREN: Do you know how it feels to be followed and hounded and watched every second?
HAINES: I used to, but now I pay cash for everything.

By now the plot elements should be ringing a bell. The music-hall, the violent death, the men in black, the lady spy in need of help (but no breadknife in the back this time because she's the heroine; it was the double that got killed). Alas, *My Favorite Blonde* is high on energy but short on Hitchcock touches. It compensates with an abundance of Bob Hope throwaways. Try these for size.

> I gave up kissing strange women.
> – What made you stop?
> Strange women.

> I'm not getting mixed up in any murders, especially mine.

> If I'm not out of this door in two seconds my name's not Larry Haines.
> (*He opens the door; a knife thuds into it; he closes it.*)
> Meet John Doe.

MY FAVORITE BLONDE. Bob Hope tips Madeleine Carroll the wink that he's putting on an act for Esther Howard.

Those unseen flight plans in the scorpion keep the action moving, like any good Hitchcock McGuffin. They *must* be in Los Angeles by Thursday, so the rest of the movie's a chase, by train, bus and plane. Our fugitives also contrive to be trapped in an apartment with a body, and knife throwers waiting outside: they get out by pretending to be crazy, and thus obtaining a police escort. (Yes, that probably *was* the origin of the auction scene in *North by Northwest*.) By the way, should any member of the audience wonder why the plans can't be phoned through, Miss Carroll can tell you: 'They're in secret cipher, hieroglyphics, it would be like phoning a crossword puzzle.' (Wouldn't even *that* be easier than three days on the run? Yes, but the movie would become a two-reeler.)

At one point Haines and friend borrow a bus from a Teamsters' Annual Picnic in Chicago. All the teamsters seem to be Irish, especially the one who is briefly played, incognito, by Bing Crosby. Mr Hope, stepping out of character, does a double-take, looks at the audience, shakes his head, and says: 'Couldn't be.' In the mid-west they are arrested by a sheriff but escape (just like you know what), and Hope is welcomed by the Mothers of Glenby in

163

mistake for an expected speaker on obstetrics. (You know what again, but this time a suspense sequence is sacrificed for below par Hope patter.) By the time the gismo is handed over to a grateful Reginald Denny, our hero has stolen a truck and a bus, wrecked a plane and an apartment, and taken a ride on a freight train, all without getting so much as a parking ticket. He has also, somewhat inadvertently, trapped a gang of Nazis in a mortician's parlour; and at least that's a fresh note, for there was no mortician's parlour in *The Thirty-nine Steps*.

My Favorite Blonde. US 1942; black and white; 78 minutes. Produced by Paul Jones for Paramount. Written by Melvin Frank, Norman Panama, Don Hartman and Frank Butler. Directed by Sidney Lanfield. Photographed by William Mellor. Music by David Buttolph. With Bob Hope as Larry Haines; Madeleine Carroll as Karen Bentley; and Gale Sondergaard, George Zucco, Victor Varconi, Lionel Royce, Walter Kingsford, Esther Howard.

Comedy of Murders

MY LEARNED FRIEND

A mad ex-convict has a murder list of those who helped get him convicted.

It turned out to be Will Hay's last film, and when it came out the critics all wrote it off as a failure, partly, it seems, because they thought he looked so ill. He lived for another five years, but it's true that he looked older and more dyspeptic, and he handed over an uncharacteristically fair share of the comedy spotlight to his newish partner Claude Hulbert, whose best film this may be. It was in fact Hulbert's stupidity on which the fun mainly relied: Hay was closer to a straight man than he'd ever been before. As later happened to Tony Hancock when he 'outgrew' Sid James, the Hay boom had predictably tapered off when he discarded his old gang, Moore Marriott and Graham Moffatt (who went on to make Hay-type comedies with other stars), and he was no longer the draw he had been at the time of *Oh! Mr Porter*. At the Bolton Capitol it was difficult to tell whether *My Learned Friend* or *The Omaha Trail* was top feature in the double bill. *My Learned Friend* was billed first, but it also played first, so that in order to catch it you had to be seated by seven o'clock; a somewhat ignominious swan song for a great British star.

Hay's previous three Ealing films had all found him winning the war, one way or another. *My Learned Friend*, though it emerged in 1943, never mentioned the war at all, and seemed stuck in that pre-war haze of British stage farce, full of colonels and cockneys and comic postcard puns. The

164

difference was that it was a very black farce indeed; and that may be why the critics did not know what to make of it.

The quintessential Hay, incorrigibly seedy but game for any illicit enterprise, is on view only in the law court prologue. He is a disbarred barrister on trial for writing begging letters as a woman, under his ambiguous middle name of Evelyn. But the prosecuting counsel, Mr Hulbert, is unable to catch him out in an actual lie. Did he or did he not write the following? 'I have had three little tots and soon I shall be having another. A few pounds will enable me to have it in comfort.' Of course he did, nothing false there: the three little tots were tots of rum. But what about this? 'As I write, there is nothing between me and the workhouse?' By now the judge has Hay's measure: 'I suppose you wrote it on the workhouse door?' he asks drily. 'Oh, you know that one, do you?' says Mr Hay with a sniff and a slight double-take. 'It was the workhouse *wall*, as a matter of fact.'

The case is dismissed for lack of proof, and the dejected counsel makes for the pub next door. 'Ginger beer. No, dash it, make it a ginger ale.' But soon he finds himself buying a double brandy for the defendant who has outwitted him, and they are both joined by an amiably sinister little man with a March Hare laugh, one Arthur Grimshaw, just out of jug, and intent, he says, on murdering all those who put him there. Mr Hay was the defence counsel who made such a botch of his case, so he is being saved up as a final titbit. Grimshaw, a cheerful lunatic, proposes to keep the bemused Hay informed about his progress and even to challenge the ex-lawyer's deductive powers by offering in advance clues about his next crime. A duty to execute is what Grimshaw thinks he has; he fondles the words as he pronounces them. 'Six little dramas of retribution, all beautifully staged.' Within a moment of his leaving our stupefied heroes, a newsboy comes in with an evening paper for them. The headline announces that Lord Chelsfield, the judge presiding over Grimshaw's case, has been drowned in the Serpentine. But a marginal handwritten note asks: did he fall or was he pushed?

Mr Hulbert offers comfort on the way home. 'Don't worry, there's four before he gets to you.' 'Yes, but he may be a fast worker.' They are naturally alarmed to find Grimshaw in the rumble seat, listening to their conversation; but he only wants to offer 'a word to the wise . . . 'Safety Second'. It takes them no time at all to link this with Safety Wilson, a razor-wielding east end gangster whose evidence incriminated Grimshaw. He, Safety, splendidly overplayed by Charles Victor, is tracked down in a basement nightclub, and, while Hay tries in vain to warn him, Hulbert is robbed of his hat and umbrella, flirted and danced with by a local tart, and trampled all over by her giant boyfriend. The splendidly edited rumpus which follows has been engineered by Grimshaw, who all the while has been propping up the bar with only a moustache and bowler hat for disguise. (This brief characterization is borrowed from Mervyn Johns's own stage and screen role in *Saloon Bar*, complete with such motto-muttering as 'Hell hath no fury like a woman scorned.') Meanwhile the normally redoubtable Safety is so busy describing what he once did to somebody he didn't like ('they found 'is ear in 'oundsditch

MY LEARNED FRIEND. Claude Hulbert and Will Hay are shocked by the latest exploits of a mass murderer – especially as they fear they may be the next.

and 'is nose in Kensington Gore') that Grimshaw is easily able to slip in and finish him off, leaving only the next clue: 'Keep an eye on a lad in Bootle, nine o'clock tonight.'

From the depths of black comedy we rise for the next episode to backstage farce. Our heroes easily translate the clue as referring to a glamorous trial witness who is now playing principal boy in Aladdin, but after a frantic journey north-west the dour old stage door keeper won't let them in.

FITCH: But she's due to be murdered at nine!
DOOR KEEPER: Aye, and so is your Uncle John Willie.

Eventually they manage to impersonate two drunken actors, and find themselves catapulted through trapdoors onto the stage, as the Emperor of China and the Slave of the Lamp. Of course, they don't know the lines, which makes the doggerel even more curious than usual:

FITCH: I rub the lamp: transport me, slave, from here.
BABBINGTON: I'd rather not, I'm feeling very queer.

Aladdin is left screaming hysterically, but at least not murdered, as it is her sister, an old flame, whom Grimshaw has done in, and he himself is the lad in

Bootle they failed to keep an eye on. The next clue takes them to a mental home near Dorking, where Grimshaw has his eye on the proprietor. The victim finally falls into a patient's corridor tiger trap; but the comedy in this sequence gives us too much time to wonder about such questions as taste. Luckily the finale is a rouser.

Hay consults Hulbert's list of victims. 'Here, you've got me down already,' he complains. 'Yes, but only pencilled in.' His time approaches, for the next clue is found painted on Hulbert's ceiling:

> Your turn, Father William, soon,
> But first of all, tomorrow noon,
>   The Lords must die, the Lords know why,
>   No flop like 1605 when I'm the guy.

It may not scan, but it does make sense: Grimshaw's appeal was turned down by the House of Lords, which is now to be exploded. By a whim of the scriptwriter's pen, Hay and Hulbert are transformed into beefeaters searching the Houses of Parliament, but with typical stupidity they find themselves locked in the clock tower with a crate of dynamite and the ebullient Grimshaw, who explains that when Big Ben strikes the hour, the entire building, by 'a simple electrical connection', will be blown to smithereens. The resulting chase up and down the face of the famous clock, at one point with three people hanging from the minute hand in order to stop it striking, is a combination of art direction and special effects which seems never to have been equalled, certainly not when some thirty years later it was copied for the Robert Powell version of *The Thirty-nine Steps*. The whole of this modest film, in fact, is a splendid example of British farce comedy at a time when it was finding its way from the depths of music hall to the heights of Ealing. It stands as a particular tribute to the inventive craftsmanship of scriptwriter John Dighton, who later produced a true classic of the genre in *The Happiest Days of Your Life*; and it frames a very acceptable farewell appearance by one of our greatest comedians.

My Learned Friend. GB 1943; black and white; 74 minutes. Produced by S. C. Balcon for Ealing. Written by John Dighton and Angus Macphail. Directed by Will Hay and Basil Dearden. Photographed by Wilkie Cooper. Music by Ernest Irving. With Will Hay as William Fitch; Claude Hulbert as Claude Babbington; Mervyn Johns as Arthur Grimshaw; Charles Victor as Safety Wilson; G. H. Mulcaster as Dr Scudamore; Ernest Thesiger as Ferris; Lloyd Pearson as Colonel Chudleigh; Maudie Edwards as Aladdin.

Holding up the Building

A NIGHT IN CASABLANCA

Nazi refugees are routed in a North African hotel.

For a troupe which had such a major influence on film comedy, the Marx Brothers enjoyed a remarkably short hour of glory. An acquired taste in 1929; pretty big in 1930–31 with *Animal Crackers* and *Monkey Business*; commercially in decline by 1932, with *Horse Feathers*; declined by the time of 1933's brilliant *Duck Soup*, to the point at which they couldn't get another movie job. Rescued by Irving Thalberg who cast them in their two MGM biggies, *A Night at the Opera* and *A Day at the Races*, which brought them as close as they ever got to being household names; misguided in attempting to film a straight comedy, *Room Service*; let down by inferior scripts and production in *At the Circus*, *Go West* and *The Big Store*. When four years later they came back from the wilderness to announce a modest independent production, they were treated by the press like old men making a futile attempt to rescale their former heights. In fact their ages ranged between fifty-five and fifty-nine, though each claimed to be five years younger. They all professed to be tired, working only for the money, just one more time. But they were still in fine slangy form; the lines didn't show under the make-up; and this low budget production, with its shinily overlit sets which would be disdained by the cheapest of nightclubs, contains some of their funniest routines and most memorable attitudes. At the end, unfortunately, it descends into runaway aeroplane slapstick which sends the audience home with a ho-hum expression, and it does take an unconscionable while to set up its spy plot and its drearily forgettable boy-girl romance. But at least the romantic principals don't sing.

There is a sad lack of Margaret Dumont, but her male counterpart, Sig Rumann, is on hand as first villain to suffer various indignities, not least the removal of his toupé by a vacuum cleaner. We instantly guess his connection with the fact that the public rooms of the Hotel Casablanca are littered with dead managers, and, since Harpo and Chico are already on the sidelines (the latter as a camel taxi driver and the former featuring in the joke quoted by so many critics that it became a bore before anyone saw the picture), it is obvious that Groucho is to be the new manager, the patsy, the next victim. We ache for him to appear, to cast a disgusted eye at the sets and to make a quick pass at the nearest tall blonde. But twelve minutes elapse before his first appearance, a delay puzzling to all good Marxists. The explanation is that it was never intended to be thus. A 1946 book based on the film script reveals an early scene which may or may not have been shot but figured in none of the release prints. In it, Ronald Kornblow (Groucho) is seen, prior to his arrival in Casablanca, as manager of the dusty Desert View Motel, receiving by post the offer intended for the manager of the Desert View Hotel, a far grander establishment across the shifting sands. The motel is a fly-by-night sort of place even for a desert, and the manager is having an argument with his sole paying customer, a local sheikh, who is checking out. Was it twenty-eight wives for twenty-seven nights, or twenty-seven wives for twenty-eight nights? The sheikh opts for the lower cost, and Groucho shrugs. 'I'd have charged you for an extra wife if you hadn't been on your toes. And it takes quite a man to be on his toes after twenty-eight wives. I'd be on my heels.'

After the departure of the harem Groucho discovers an overlooked wife in tent number 2. He attempts to console her:

GROUCHO: I wouldn't worry. Men are ten cents a dozen. I wish women were.
WIFE: He'll come back for me.
GROUCHO: Well, he'd better hurry. The management is not responsible for wives left over thirty days. Don't be a fool, come away with me.
WIFE: I'll never leave here. I'm part of Africa, and Africa is part of me.
GROUCHO (*leering at her décolletage*): Well, I'm certainly seeing the best part of Africa.

At this tender moment the giant Arab returns, brandishing his suspicious nature. Groucho glances at the sands in the hour glass – 'Goodness, a quarter to eleven' – and remembers a pressing appointment. He dashes past the reception desk, where two brides and a groom are booking in. 'You can have number two, it's still warm,' he tells them. 'As a matter of fact it got too hot for me. It's a lovely tent with a fine view of the ocean.' The groom surveys the Sahara with a puzzled air: 'I see no ocean.' Groucho nods agreeably: 'So far all we got is the beach.'

At this moment a tornado demolishes the hotel and leaves him buried up to the neck in sand. So, on thinking things over, he decides on balance to accept the offer which came by the morning post.

Whether this scene was deleted because nobody thought it funny, or whether the Legion of Decency had a hand, its loss in terms of pacing is felt. But eventually Groucho does lope into the lobby of the Hotel Casablanca, having paid Chico 100 francs for the camel ride from the station. (The meter said fifty francs, but it's double for a camel with two humps.) 'We gotta speed things up,' he tells the assembled staff. 'From now on, if a customer orders a three-minute egg, give it to him in two minutes. If he orders a two-minute egg, give it to him in one minute. If he orders a one-minute egg, give him the chicken, let him work it out for himself.'

This sally is glumly received, but Groucho's next instruction causes shock: 'We're gonna change all the numbers on all the doors.'

'But, monsieur, think of the confusion!'

'Yeah,' says Groucho, wiggling his eyebrows, 'but think of the fun!'

It is not long before the new manager is being ogled by the Nazi villain's trained vamp, who blows smoke in his eyes. He blows it right back, but this doesn't faze her: 'I'm Beatrice Reiner, I stop at the hotel.' 'I'm Ronald Kornblow, I stop at nothing.' And watching her slinky rear view as she undulates away from him, he confides in the audience: 'That reminds me, I must get my watch fixed.'

In double quick time we are handed a reprise with variations of the cabin scene from *A Night at the Opera*. This time it's a dance floor getting smaller as Harpo and Chico bring more tables on and pocket the resulting tips. ('I'm not dancing,' says Groucho to the vamp, 'I'm trying to get my feet out of a champagne bucket.') Then there's Harpo's whistling routine, trying to tell Chico that Groucho will be compromised and shot if he goes to the vamp's room. 'Bee, twist, soup, rice, Beatrice is gonna give him a surprise!' There is the usual badinage between Groucho and Chico:

CHICO: I could keep you alive for fifty francs a week.
GROUCHO: It isn't worth it.
CHICO: You can't take it with you.
GROUCHO: Well, I'm not gonna leave it lying around here.
CHICO: If I'm your bodyguard, I'll watch you like a mother watches a baby.
GROUCHO: Is the mother pretty?
CHICO: Whats-a difference?
GROUCHO: There's a lot of difference. If the mother's pretty I'll watch the mother and you watch the baby.

When he finally realizes the danger he's in, Groucho can only shake his head and look scornfully at Chico: 'I don't mind being killed, but I resent hearing about it from a character whose head comes to a point.' But he's one up on everybody. He does accept the vamp's invitation –

BEATRICE: Won't you join me?
GROUCHO: Why, are you falling apart?

– but he keeps changing rooms, which is just as well, since Sig Rumann is after him with an outraged expression, a loaded gun, and cries of '*Schweinhund*'. Before the night is over, Groucho is dishevelled after shinning up a date tree to avoid a car with evil intent, but he still finds time to offer romantic advice to the hero and heroine. (Yes, they're still around.) 'Marriage is impossible,' sighs the handsome captain. 'Only *after* you're married,' snaps Groucho.

Daylight comes, and Groucho is back at the complaints desk. 'What's that, young lady,' he says into the phone, 'you were taking a shower and the water stopped running? Well, keep lathering yourself and I'll be up there with a wet sponge.' But he has a complaint of his own to voice to Chico: 'Do you know who came into my room at three o'clock this morning?' 'No, who?' 'Nobody. And that's my complaint.'

A little later, what passes for a plot requires the count to find the hidden loot and start packing. It is logical that Groucho and company should prevent him by hiding in his room and *un*packing, in ways so wildly mysterious, including a walk-through wardrobe and a drop-through table, that the count thinks he's going mad. This is the kind of scene you wait to sit through again, even if you miss the last bus. As the introduction to the 1946 paperback reminds us:

During the last few years we have done without many of the things that make life most worth while – nylon stockings, elastic sock suspenders,

A NIGHT IN CASABLANCA. Chico, Harpo and Groucho have a little fun.

bananas and the Marx Brothers. We have had nights in air raid shelters but not nights at the opera; days in queues but not days at the races. Now at long last we can have *A Night in Casablanca*.

Typically, Groucho found himself summoned to public defence of his work. Warner Brothers seemed to think that for anyone to make a film with the word Casablanca in the title was an infringement of their rights in the famous Bogart-Bergman hit of three years previously. This patently absurd proposition drew from Groucho a letter to Warners' legal department which was almost as funny as anything in the movie:

Dear Sirs,
Apparently there is more than one way of conquering a city and making it your own. For instance, up to the time we contemplated making this picture, I had no idea that the city of Casablanca belonged exclusively to Warner Brothers . . . It seems that in 1471 Ferdinand Balboa Warner, your great grandfather, while looking for a short cut to the city of Burbank, had stumbled on the shores of Africa and, raising his alpenstock, named it Casablanca.

   I don't understand your attitude. Even if you plan on re-releasing your picture, I am sure that the average movie fan could learn in time to distinguish between Ingrid Bergman and Harpo. I don't know whether *I* could, but I certainly would like to try.

171

There was more, and it puzzled the lawyers, who wrote a polite letter asking for some idea of what the story of Groucho's film was to be about. Groucho obliged:

> In it I play a doctor of divinity who ministers to the natives and, as a sideline, hawks can-openers and pea jackets to the savages along the gold coast of Africa. When I first meet Chico, he is working in a saloon, selling sponges to barflies who are unable to carry their liquor. Harpo is an Arabian caddie who lives in a small Grecian urn on the outskirts of the city.
>
> As the story opens, Porridge, a mealy-mouthed native girl, is sharpening some arrows for the hunt. Paul Hangover, our hero, is constantly lighting two cigarettes simultaneously. He apparently is unaware of the cigarette shortage . . .

Groucho was delighted when the attorneys wrote back for more detail. He gave it gladly:

> Dear Brothers,
> Since I last wrote you, I regret to say there have been changes in the plot. In the new version I play Bordello, the sweetheart of Humphrey Bogart. Harpo and Chico are itinerant drug peddlers who enter a monastery for a lark. This is a good joke on them, as there hasn't been a lark in the place for fifteen years.
>
> Across from the monastery is a waterfront hotel, chockful of apple-cheeked damsels, most of whom have been barred by the Hays Office for soliciting. In the fifth reel, Gladstone makes a speech that sets the House of Commons in an uproar, and the King promptly asks for his resignation. Harpo marries a hotel detective; Chico operates an ostrich farm. Humphrey Bogart's girl, Bordello, spends her last years in a Bacall house.
>
> This as you can see is a very skimpy outline. The only thing that can save us from extermination is a continuation of the film shortage.

The correspondence now ceased, and the film made lots of money, perhaps after all because of that Harpo joke which gets the picture's first laugh. The police chief's men are rounding up suspects and come across Harpo leaning against a wall. 'Hey, what're you doing,' one cries, 'holding up the building?' Harpo nods and grins insanely as he is led away. The building collapses. It would have been such a great beginning if the critics hadn't all blabbed.

A Night in Casablanca. US 1946; black and white; 85 minutes. Produced by David L. Loew. Written by Joseph Fields, Roland Kibbee and Frank Tashlin. Directed by Archie Mayo. Photographed by James Van Trees. Music by Werner Janssen. With Groucho Marx as Ronald Kornblow; Harpo Marx as Rusty; Chico Marx as Corbaccio; Lisette Verea as Beatrice; Sig Rumann as Heinrich Stubel; Lois Collier as Annette; Charles Drake as Lieutenant Pierre Delmar; Dan Seymour as Captain Brizzard.

Twilight Zone

THE NIGHT MY NUMBER CAME UP

A man dreams that a plane will crash and the dream begins to come true on a journey from Hong Kong to Tokyo.

One gives this late Ealing item a warm welcome despite its deficiencies, for it is one of the few movie equivalents of a smoking-room story, the kind that was traditionally told over brandy and cigars, with the click of billiard balls serving as occasional accompaniment. It entirely eschews romance. It pretty well eschews humour too, more's the pity, but then it is largely about people with stiff upper lips. Nor are its rather solemn opening titles conducive to the right mood, even though they end with the shadowy figure 13. Over this is superimposed the legend that the plane with which the story concerns itself had eight passengers and five crew. The title itself seems clumsy, for we are shown the story from no particular viewpoint, and never know to whose number the title refers. Besides, it doesn't come up anyway, not quite. And the crisis takes place not at night, but in the late afternoon, not long after twilight.

Although made well after the golden age of flashback, the piece begins retrospectively, and in doing so virtually gives away the end, for Air Marshal Hardie's Dakota is already missing, and Wing Commander Lindsay (Michael Hordern) calls to instigate, without saying why, a search along a part of the Japanese coastline that nobody else would have thought of. Now the flashback, to Hordern's own arrival in Hong Kong a few days earlier (on the tricky runway 13) and subsequently to a dinner party at the home of Robertson (Alexander Knox), a civil servant overdue for promotion and both nervous and bitter on that account. After a bit of local colour, with the Chinese celebrating a festival in which the honoured dead are supposed to return for a few hours in their own homes, someone remarks that the Chinese see dreams as a vision of what is to come. This impels Lindsay somewhat tactlessly to narrate an unfortunate dream which kept him awake on the previous night. In it Hardie (another guest), together with Robertson and six other people, plus a crew of five, were in a Dakota which crash-landed in a fishing village after travelling through cloud, storm and snow and dealing with a severe case of panic in the cockpit. Even though Hardie is flying on to Tokyo the next day, none of the detail seems to fit, since his plane is a Lancaster and the numbers are wrong. Only men will join the Air Marshal (there were women in the dream), and as for Robertson, the idea is absurd, as he has never flown and the prospect terrifies him. Hardie, being one of those top chaps who stifle any concern with a pipe, merely smiles politely at the story and changes the subject; but seasoned audiences will scarcely need telling that the pattern of events quickly changes to fit the dream.

First, Lord Wainwright (Ralph Truman) has to get to Tokyo in a hurry, and

173

THE NIGHT MY NUMBER CAME UP. It gets tenser later, but suspicions are already abounding. Ralph Truman, Denholm Elliott, Michael Redgrave, George Rose (with unidentified aide), Alexander Knox.

needs Robertson to translate for him, plus a girl secretary; then at the airport two soldiers successfully cadge a lift to Okinawa; and the plane is changed to a Dakota at the last minute. Robertson, who for the sake of possible advancement has agreed to fly, goes rapidly to pieces and behaves so badly that it would have been better for him to refuse the journey point blank. (When taxed with being a bit of an idiot, he snaps back that he has written a book proving the absurdity of superstition; but he is careful to step round a ladder as he says so.) Hardie is plainly disturbed, but sees no reason, no logical reason at least, not to take off, though he does thoughtfully recount the story of the old lady who said that she didn't believe in ghosts but was still afraid of them. As for Robertson, by the time they are airborne he is wondering whether anything in the world ever happens without somebody dreaming about it first.

Despite the storm they all arrive safely at Okinawa, the overnight stop. Over drinks in the mess they begin to pat themselves on the back, their numbers having been reduced to six plus crew and no loud flashy man, so prominent in the dream, having presented himself. Hardie even recovers his confidence to the extent of ordaining next day a two-hour detour so that Lord

174

Wainright can see Hiroshima and Nagasaki. Clearly none of them is listening to the band, which is ominously playing

> Everything in the dream was lovely . . .
> I hope it still will be
> When my dream I see
> Tonight

And lo and behold, here comes George Rose, than whom nobody can be louder or flashier, as businessman Bennett, with a bullying request for a lift for himself and his male secretary, so that he shall not miss an important deal in Tokyo. Hardie says no rather sharply, and the others find reasons to leave the room when approached, but when Lord Wainwright hears about the problem he poo-poohs such nonsense: 'If we left these men behind we should be putting ourselves back a thousand years. All the same, I wish this fellow Bennett were at the bottom of a coal mine; I shan't sleep a wink tonight.'

Next morning there is some fear (or possibly hope) that Robertson will be unfit to fly; but he appears on the tarmac, wan after a night of fear, having posted some last words to his wife. He is even sufficiently resigned to tell the whole story as a joke to the pilot, which the audience could have told him is a bad idea, for no actor cracks up under pressure like Nigel Stock. Oblivious to this possibility, the others all ask themselves what can possibly go wrong? After an enjoyable six-hour flight they will be in their private bedrooms in Tokyo in good time for dinner.

Events quickly conspire to prove them wrong. Hiroshima and Nagasaki are fogbound, so the extra flying time has been wasted. The radio burns out. To get above the fog they must climb to 19,000 feet, and they carry no oxygen; crosswinds up there drive them off course, and when icing forces them down again they have not the slightest idea where they are. After using up half their fuel in supposedly following the coast, they discover that they have in fact gone right around a remote island on the wrong side of Japan, and the only thing they can do now is ditch on a beach by a fishing village: 'We're going down for an emergency landing, but it's been done many times before so there's no need for undue alarm.' We know better than that, of course, and so does Bennett, for it is he rather than Robertson who has hysterics. Meanwhile there is a brainstorm in the cockpit, but luckily the pilot snaps out of it at the last minute and, finding the beach too short, makes a fine shot at landing nose down in a snowed-over paddy field. Redgrave's final remarks are an assertion of their correctness in defying the dream: 'Our duty to life is to live it to the utmost. We've been given a brain and we have to use it.'

Well, perhaps they didn't use it very intelligently, but back in Hong Kong word eventually comes through that the search has been successful and they're all safe. The operations man takes full credit for knowing where to look, and Lindsay seems not to mind until the ops man asks whether he often has dreams like that. Then he takes the last word. 'Yes, I do. Had rather a strange one last night. No, I won't tell you; but if you do disappear, I'll tell the authorities where to look for you.'

That's a touch worthy of Maugham; and incidentally the credits tell us that this always interesting if slightly sluggish flight of fancy was scripted by R. C. Sherriff, who not only started his career with a study of men under stress (*Journey's End*) and adapted one of the screen's finest fantasies (*The Invisible Man*, qv) but also translated into screen terms the Maugham ironies of *Quartet*. This slight essay in the semi-supernatural might be thought of as an amalgam of all three moods; though its actual source is probably the framing story of *Dead of Night*, in which the architect who thought he had been somewhere before ended up committing a murder, only to find himself trapped in an endless series of recurring dreams. A twist like that is what *The Night My Number Came Up* really needed!

The Night My Number Came Up. GB 1954; black and white; 94 minutes. Produced by Tom Morahan for Ealing. Written by R. C. Sherriff from a story by Air Vice-Marshal Sir Victor Goddard. Directed by Leslie Norman. Photographed by Lionel Banes. Music by Malcolm Arnold. With Michael Redgrave as Air Marshal John Hardie; Sheila Sim as Mary Campbell; Alexander Knox as Owen Robertson; Ursula Jeans as Mrs Robertson; Denholm Elliott as Flight Lieutenant Mackenzie; Michael Hordern as Wing Commander Lindsay; Ralph Truman as Lord Wainwright; Nigel Stock as Squadron Leader Walker; George Rose as Walter Bennett.

Frightful Fiend
NIGHT OF THE DEMON

An occultist dispatches his enemies by raising a medieval devil.

This is one of those movies that get more marks for trying than for actual achievement. Like *The Uninvited* (qv) it is one of the few popular films to treat the supernatural with a modicum of seriousness, and its tall tale is unfurled with the help of some intelligent dialogue, but despite brilliant scenes it does lack cinematic flow and is held back by poor acting from the leads. Critics used to blame the monster's appearances at beginning and end; these were allegedly added just before release because box office prospects were thought to be a trifle dim, and the pressure is supposed to show. All I can say is that a medieval demon can't be easy to animate, and this one scares me every time I see it. Besides, something to gawp at does no harm to a movie which otherwise sets its sights on the cerebral rather than the visual.

The credits are interesting: a script largely written by Charles Bennett, the British scenarist who contributed to most of Hitchcock's early successes (though referred to contemptuously by Hitch as a 'ball-tosser'); direction by Jacques Tourneur, whose *Cat People* in 1942 caused a complete turnaround in the history of the horror film (he repeats some of its tricks here); as story

176

basis, one of the best supernatural tales of M. R. James, scholar and provost of Eton, who in the forty years before his death in 1936 turned out thirty-odd of the world's most shiversome ghost stories. (He would not, incidentally, have been pleased to see himself billed on the film credits at Montague R. James, especially since his first name boasted no 'e'.)

The story has been quite intelligently expanded for the screen, though in the process it becomes a mite too complicated. James began with an exchange of letters establishing the antipathy of an alchemist named Karswell for anyone who disagreed with his published opinions. There followed an account of the unpleasant fate of one such critic, who found his own imminent and unexpected death being magically predicted, and of the help given by his brother to a second critic in passing back to Karswell the runic symbols which are the alchemist's means of drawing his victim to the attention of a very nasty monster summoned from hell. This was all too scholarly for Hollywood, whence came the finance for the production. The title was promptly changed from *Casting the Runes*, first to *The Haunted*, then to what we have (and in America to *Curse of the Demon*). Further a portentous spoken foreword was added, over quite irrelevant pictures of Stonehenge:

> It has been written since the beginning of time, even unto these ancient stones, that evil supernatural creatures exist in a world of darkness; and that man using the magic power of the ancient runic symbols can call forth these powers of darkness . . . the demons of hell.

In more striking style there follows a prologue in which, to the accompaniment of Clifton Parker's splendidly minatory music, the first victim drives frantically through the night to plead with Karswell to call off his demon, which is getting altogether too close for comfort. Smooth, elegant and fleshy, Karswell agrees, but we know from his eyes that he intends to stick to his original plan: 'Some things are more easily started than stopped.' The relieved Harrington makes it to his lonely home, but before he can leave the driver's seat the demon makes its appearance, luminescent against a dark avenue of trees. Police identification of the mangled body is hampered by the fact that in his panic Harrington has backed the car into a telegraph pole, causing electrocution as well as apparent animal savaging.

We are now introduced to our nominal hero, an American professor of paranormal psychology. He is played very stodgily by Dana Andrews, who is not only unprofessorial but slurs a great many of his words; and the part as written calls for him to be churlish and sceptical beyond all reason. He has a 'meeting cute' with the deceased's niece, who has read about Karswell in her uncle's diary and now assumes the role of official avenger. Rather off-handedly he invites her to 'come and see me tonight at my hotel'. He doesn't say which hotel, but she finds him all right, only to discover that he is feeling curiously cold in the middle of summer. The audience suspects that this may have something to do with his having been to the British Museum and 'accidentally' met Karswell, who on establishing the professor's antipathy has genially but surreptitiously dropped the runic symbols into a convenient file. Clearly the monster may make his full presence felt at any time now, though to begin with there is no more than buzzing music to addle the professor's brain. One might also count the mystery of Karswell's visiting card, which at first had the professor's death date on it, in ink which not only becomes invisible but leaves no chemical trace.

The niece persuades the professor to drive to Karswell's country seat, Lufford Abbey, which please note is in Warwickshire and therefore at least 130 miles from London. This is important if the film's various journeys to and from Lufford are to fit into any reasonable time scale, which in fact they won't. Karswell is discovered in a sinister clown costume, doing tricks of white magic for the local children, an annual Halloween treat. The pleasantness of this occasion does not stop him, when jeered at, from conjuring up a mighty wind, which disconcerts everyone present including his silly ice-cream-making mother (delightfully played by Athene Seyler). The professor is, or pretends to be, unimpressed, which angers Karswell even more. 'You think I'm mad,' he sneers, 'but you won't be able to explain away your death on the 28th of this month so easily.' (Since the month is given as October, his Halloween party must have been a trifle early.)

Karswell, as played by Niall MacGinnis, is undoubtedly one of filmdom's most splendid villains, and the script even tinges him with a little seriousness. He lives like a lord, but his real pride is in his supernatural discoveries, and when his frightened mother urges him to give up such research he replies: 'I can't, mother. My followers, who pay for all this, do so out of fear . . .' The professor, meanwhile, is still stubbornly describing as 'auto suggestion and mass hysteria' all the odd things that happened to Harrington and are beginning to happen to him. But all the pages of his diary which follow October 28th have been torn out . . . and Harrington's diary is found to contain a splendid quote from 'The Ancient Mariner':

> Like one that on a lonesome road
> Doth walk in fear and dread . . .
> Because he knows a frightful fiend
> Doth close behind him tread.

The British release version of this film, no longer available, was cut to accommodate a circuit co-feature called *Twenty Thousand Miles to Earth*. What remains, under the American title, is some six minutes longer, the extra time being allotted to a somewhat unsatisfactory sub-plot about a disciple of Karswell who has been forced to murder his own brother and now lies in a catatonic state in prison. We should be grateful, however, for the restoration of a scene formerly unseen by British audiences in which the professor visits the prisoner's family in the hope of obtaining permission for hypnosis and truth injections which might incriminate the alchemist. A splendid scene it is, since the family lives on a blasted heath which can't be far from Cold Comfort Farm, and is ruled by a matriarch prone to such pronouncements as 'He has been chosen' and 'Let no arm be raised to defend him'. It makes an agreeably lunatic low point before the build up of the final action.

NIGHT OF THE DEMON. Niall MacGinnis regretfully assures his mother (Athene Seyler) that black magic is the only way out.

The fluttery Mrs K, anxious if she can to save her son by warning off his pursuers, induces the niece to attend a suburban seance at which the voice of her deceased uncle materializes to instil a note of terror. The professor, perhaps put off by the choral rendition of 'Cherry Ripe' which summons the spirits, still won't take advice and walks out in disgust; yet once outside he contradictorily agrees with the girl that what he needs in order to rid himself of the demon is one of Karswell's magical tomes, which he proposes there and then to steal from Lufford. They drive off to Warwickshire, arriving in the small hours, and he duly breaks in; but Karswell has naturally set a demon to guard the book, and the professor gets some severe scratches from a black panther which obligingly changes back into a pussy cat when the lights are switched on by the pyjama-clad Karswell. (How he contrived to be home and undressed first, when we saw him pick up his mother from the seance after the others left, is unexplained.) The professor is not only an unrepentant burglar but a defiant danger-seeker, as having been playfully warned by Karswell not to stray from the paths on his way back to the car he does just that, and suffers a famous sequence in which hot footfalls are made by an invisible beast, and a fireball comes hurtling at him through the trees. Meanwhile Karswell in his

179

lobby smiles equivocally at Mum. 'A very obstinate young man. I told him not to go back through the woods.'

By the time he gets back to London the professor is disgusted with himself, 'a man who would always walk under ladders just to see if something would happen'. He intends to prove the case against Karswell through Hobart the supposed murderer. But that formal examination does not proceed as planned: once aroused from his coma, the prisoner goes mad at the memory of the horrors he experienced in Karswell's company; after revealing that a demon was set on him and he transferred it to his brother, he annoyingly precludes further questions by jumping out of a fifth-floor window.

Now comes the real logistical impossibility which we are supposed not to notice. It is the evening of the 28th, already dark. The niece is on the phone from London to Karswell in Warwickshire, pleading her case and that of the professor, who is now her loved one. The alchemist puts down the phone with murmured regrets; yet when the girl leaves the house a few minutes later, he is waiting in the bushes to abduct her to the continent; which seems rather odd because until now he has shown no sexual inclinations whatsoever. Meanwhile the professor learns by an unconvincing chance that Karswell is taking the 8.45 to Dover. His own predicament finally gets to him, and by a mad dash through traffic he is able to get to Clapham Junction by 9.45, and here he is remarkably fortunate, since it seems to have taken the crack train one hour to do the five-minute journey from Victoria. But Karswell is on it all right, with a hypnotized heroine, and after some subtle banter the professor is finally able to return to him the fatal paper. It flutters away from the alchemist despite a crazy chase up the railway line, where it suddenly spurts into flame and ashes. The time for retribution has come, and there in the distance, along the track, the demon approaches in search of a victim. Breathing fire and smoke, it reaches Karswell just as the express whistles by. There are a couple of splendidly exciting shots before the police reach the body and conclude, as police will, that he must have been run over by a passing train.

It would be pleasant if someone remade *Night of the Demon* with different romantic leads, a tauter and less flawed script, and a little more humour. But we could probably expect nothing better than Yorkshire TV's eighties version in which the action was updated to take place in a television studio and London airport, neither of them locations offering the right kind of shadows or moods. Best perhaps to be grateful for the good scenes in this lively little fifties version. At least it ventures part of the way down a path which few film-makers have trodden.

Night of the Demon (US title: *Curse of the Demon*). GB 1957; black and white; 87 minutes. Produced by Frank Bevis for Hal E. Chester/Columbia. Written by Charles Bennett and Hal E. Chester from the story 'Casting the Runes' by M. R. James. Directed by Jacques Tourneur. Photographed by Ted Scaife. Music by Clifton Parker. With Dana Andrews as John Holden; Niall MacGinnis as Karswell; Peggy Cummins as Joanna Harrington; Athene Seyler as Mrs Karswell; Brian Wilde as Hobart; Liam Redmond as O'Brien; Reginald Beckwith as Mr Meek; Maurice Denham as Harrington.

The Villain Has all the Fun

THE NIGHT OF THE HUNTER

A psychopathic preacher goes on the trail of hidden loot, the key to which is held by two children.

Nobody ever expected it to be popular, surely. Paul Gregory and Charles Laughton, who put the project together, were not at that time in the popularity business: they were arranging world tours of their rarefied all-star stage readings from 'John Brown's Body' and 'Don Juan in Hell', both well thought of, but certainly caviare to the general. Round about the same time, Davis Grubb's nasty little bad character study seems to have caught Laughton's attention, and the film, with Laughton at the megaphone, was set up without too much difficulty in an era when audiences could still be tempted to try something 'different'. Mitchum was reportedly astonished and flattered to find himself first choice for the part of the psychopathic preacher, and eagerly brushed aside considerations that it might damage his career. Mitchum was always a creature of impulse: if Laughton thought highly enough of his talents to ask him, then that was more important than what the men in the front office might say.

In fact, the preacher is remembered as one of his most stunning roles, though the film itself never broke even despite Laughton's efforts to enlighten it with stylized settings, furry animals, and biblical quotations from Lillian Gish. These efforts in the end prevented the film from being a unified whole, but what comes through is an eccentric morality play, played out by puppets under the direction of the voice of God and the whisper of Satan. There is a distinct literary flavour, but it is expressed in pictures as well as words, as though Grandma Moses were interpreting the Book of Isaiah. For me, when I first saw it one winter afternoon in a Wardour Street preview theatre, the entertainment came chiefly from the stunning pictorial compositions, mostly in moonlight and deep shadow, very studio-set and tending to over-use certain motifs, but adding up to a series of designs for elegant religious Christmas cards which Charles Addams might have designed. I didn't know what to make of the rest of it at all, for there was little in the story one could actually like, though one had to praise the way everything was done. I hastened to buy the book, and read it on a train journey, but it seemed to me to come from a cruder mind altogether: the film clearly had to stand or fall on its own merits. It was a problem for me, because I was coming to the end of my tenure of the Rex Cinema, Cambridge, where for several years George Webb and I had packed the place easily enough during university term and struggled in vain to keep it warm for the rest of the year. We had pleased the undergraduates chiefly by a diet of golden oldies, yet every now and then we would be offered a new film of cult significance which had been unwisely turned down by the ABC circuit (which had a stranglehold on Cambridge). *The Night of the Hunter*

THE NIGHT OF THE HUNTER. Robert Mitchum has no very tender designs on Shelley Winters.

was just such an instance. United Artists said we could have it if we would play it for seven days, with a re-run at the Kinema; otherwise it would vanish into the ABC hopper as a support. What I had to predict, with the national press show still a month ahead, was what the critical reaction might be. Thumbs up, and the Rex might do a burster; thumbs down, and George would curse me for leaving him with a wasted and unprofitable week. I had a couple of days to decide; and that night my sleep was filled with the disturbing silhouettes of Mitchum pursuing the children over land and water, alternating with Miss Gish encircled in a halo of stars, like the Paramount logo.

The film's basic flaw is that in order to flesh out the very simple plot the writers have recourse to spoken comment and moralizing, so that when the actors act they seem only to be repeating what we have already been told. Perhaps this is what gives the film its dreamlike quality. But Laughton does nothing quite as expected. His very first shot is of children's heads, oddly disposed about the night sky in little cameos. They are displaced by Miss Gish, who is reading to them from the Bible: 'Beware of false prophets who come to you in sheep's clothing, for they may be ravening wolves.' We don't see Miss Gish or the children again for forty-five minutes, but we are promptly introduced to our ravening wolf, Mr Mitchum, on whom we close in as he muses on his next victim: 'Well, Lord, what's it to be? Another widow?' This fake parson with the silver tongue has the word LOVE tattooed on the fingers of one hand, and HATE on the other, and he is fond of showing how they wrestle together; but what he really is is a sexual lunatic who murders women for their money and convinces himself that it is the Lord's work. The slightest jolt to his dignity, or the sight of sex being flaunted, is apt to bring on some nervous reaction such as the sudden clenching of his hand round a hidden knife which juts fiercely through the fabric of his coat. But he has a sharp eye for the main chance. Imprisoned for a minor offence, he says his prayers when he finds himself in the same cell as a condemned murderer who is known to have hidden his considerable loot: 'Lord, you sure knew what you was doing when you put me in this very cell at this very time. A man with 10,000 dollars, and a widow in the making.'

When the preacher gets out he makes short shrift of marrying and murdering the widow, dumping the body under water (a deservedly famous and eerily beautiful shot) and leaving her 'with a slit in her throat as though she had an extra mouth'. The rest of the movie is a chase. The madman decides that the secret must be held by the two children he has so casually orphaned, and he pursues them down the Mississippi. Even the river setting is fantasticated, to give the impression of a secluded locale where the presence of evil has seldom been felt. It is felt now, for the preacher's shadow is everywhere, over the children and over the house in which, after a few narrow escapes, they seek shelter with Miss Gish, who runs what seems to be an amateur orphan asylum. His figure menaces when he is no more than a speck on the horizon. Even the train in which he sometimes travels is black and satanic. Yet the evil fails, for the man blunders about like King Kong and the children find it easy enough to trap his fingers in a door. Up until now the mood has been that of *Gaslight*, the manner that of *All That Money Can Buy*; but now the quality of fable creeps in as Miss Gish exudes her goodness; during the last stage of their journey, gentle animals in close-up have contrasted with the limpid moonlit water over which the children's boat glides beneath a starry sky. And now in a final chapter we get a sense of *David Copperfield*, with Gish as Miss Trotwood, scrubbing the children and then dealing firmly with their pursuers. It is the resolution which is fumbled, the final battle not clear-cut; but eventually the preacher is led off to execution, Miss Gish proceeds to sing Christmas hymns, and the money is found in the flat-faced cloth doll which the little girl has clutched throughout her adventures. The film closes with many a mercy me from Miss Gish: 'I'm a strong tree with branches for many birds, and children are mankind at his strongest: they abide.'

I gave *The Night of the Hunter* the benefit of my doubt, and left. It opened in London, and the critical reaction ranged from enthusiasm through politeness to irritation; in general, one might say marks for trying rather than achievement. In all, the testimonial was probably insufficient to guarantee a good week at the Rex: I never dared inquire. But a few months later, while the course I was on obliged me to act as relief manager at various Odeon cinemas, it turned up on my beat in Radcliffe, Lancashire, and serve me right. That cinema may have been on its uppers, but seventeen pounds in three days was a low broken only by Laurence Olivier in *Richard III*.

The Night of the Hunter. US 1955; black and white; 93 minutes. Produced by Paul Gregory for United Artists. Written by James Agee from the novel by Davis Grubb. Directed by Charles Laughton. Photographed by Stanley Cortez. Music by Walter Schumann. With Robert Mitchum as Preacher; Shelley Winters as Willa Harper; Lillian Gish as Rachel; Don Beddoe as Walt; Evelyn Varden as Icey; Peter Graves as Ben Harper; James Gleason as Birdie; Billy Chapin as John; Sally Jane Bruce as Pearl.

Englishmen Abroad

NIGHT TRAIN TO MUNICH

A British agent poses as a Nazi in order to rescue a Czech inventor and his daughter.

By one of the awful ironies of show business, this pleasant, unimportant picture, probably because it was anti-Nazi in a cheerful way at a time when Americans wanted to show sympathy for terrorized Europe without getting involved themselves, won an Academy Award for best original story. Frank Launder and Sidney Gilliat, who wrote the screenplay in their own inimitable style, must have laughed like drains, for the story they were first handed occupies no more than the initial five minutes, within which it establishes the central idea of a scientist trying to escape from a Nazi-occupied country. Their own development, on which they were working when the war broke out, was a melodrama about the means by which the scientist and his daughter (their own invention) would eventually reach England and safety. With hostilities under way, and the future uncertain, a straight escape story seemed thoroughly tasteless, so they decided that the best insurance against failure would be to send it up in no uncertain terms. They found the exposition impossible to handle in this way, which is why the early reels seem forced and obvious; but as soon as they worked their way into the hare-brained rescue situations the jokes began to flow. Indeed, when two-thirds of the way through the adventure all the principals board the fateful train of the title, the centre of interest is quite deliberately switched to two English travellers whom we have not met before, not since *The Lady Vanishes* at any rate. Charters and Caldicott are still distrustful of foreigners and interested only in cricket, with perhaps a little golf on the side; but in this case at least, the climax of the story depends almost entirely on them, and we even find them uncharacteristically dressed as

NIGHT TRAIN TO MUNICH. Basil Radford and Naunton Wayne try to decide whether or not Rex Harrison did once play for the Gentlemen.

stormtroopers and firing rifles. This, you see, is a story in which almost anything goes, even a cable-car shoot-out finale which would not have disgraced James Bond thirty years later. To be fair to audiences of the time, they do seem to have recognized the movie's jocular qualities, and it was a smashing commercial success; but director Carol Reed got most of the credit, when all he really did, after that initial hesitation, was very meticulously to transmit a few Launder and Gilliat *jeux d'esprit* on to the screen.

A foreword states that the action takes place 'during the year preceding the war and on the night of September 3rd 1939'; but in fact all the essentials are crowded into the last few days of that period. Czech scientist Bomasch ('on no account is his armour plating to fall into Nazi hands') has got away safely to a secret English hide-out, but his daughter languishes in a Nazi concentration camp (not too uncomfortable an example). Soon, however, she is persuaded to join an escape plan devised by a fellow-prisoner, Karl Marsen. They get away so easily that she really should have suspected, especially on the last lap when they simply row a boat on to an English beach. On arrival in Hampstead Karl shows his true colours, to the audience at least. He visits an optician (Felix Aylmer), who clearly displays the steely offhand gaze of the covert Nazi. Karl takes the eye-test but instead of the second line gives his code number, which is easily confirmed from a card index before the two of them exchange Heil Hitlers. The optician suggests caution; if Miss Bomasch receives a message, Karl is not to follow her. And so when she is led to a singing room in Brightbourne, run by a cavalier young man called Gus Bennett, it is the optician who sees her reunited with Daddy on the pier. Father and daughter take refuge above the singing room, but on the very first night are politely abducted from it by two smart-looking naval officers; they are taken to a submarine which waits out in the bay, with duty-bound Karl in his Gestapo uniform waiting soulfully by the conning tower.

It is now, with the girl in presumably acute danger, that comedy begins to creep in. We have already heard a couple of chaps in the street exchanging opinions:

I see that fellow Ribbentrop's gone to Moscow.
– Mm. So did Napoleon.

– and now we are taken into an inner sanctum of the foreign office, with Big Ben striking in the background and everybody taking tea and looking despondent. Among them is Gus Bennett, and if anybody has a right to be despondent it is he, though with all that singing and salesmanship we couldn't see how he had time for secret service work in the first place. Conversation is glum, except when a newcomer remembers to ask a colleague: 'I say, Charles, the wife just phoned. I understand you're coming over to tea on Sunday. She wants you to remind Beryl to bring a recipe book, pickled walnuts or something.' But national pride dictates that a rescue has to be attempted, and Gus develops a daring plan. The Bomasches will have been taken to the Berlin war ministry; he will get them out. ('I was three years in Berlin, you know, sir.') The scheme evokes no more in the way of official sanction than a few admirably wry looks from Wyndham Goldie, of whom we should have liked to see more; but before you can say Lord Haw-Haw, dear old Gus, monocle in eye, is being driven down the Unter Den Linden in the splendid uniform of a German major in the Corps of Engineers, one Ulrich Herzog. His autocratic bearing even gets him into the war ministry, with the unexpected help of an elderly clerk who has grown petulant at having to show his identification so often: '*This* is a fine country to live in,' he says, and is quickly trundled upstairs to repent him of his sins before that old misery Raymond Huntley, who accuses him of uttering unpatriotic sentiments:

CLERK: But sir, what did I say?
KAMPENFELDT: You said, *this* is a fine country to live in.
CLERK: Oh no, sir, pardon me. What I said was, 'this is a *fine* country to live in.'

Mr Huntley's eyebrows are raised, and the clerk is dismissed with instructions not to make remarks that can be taken two ways. Alone, Mr Huntley tries it for himself: '*This* is a fine country to live in; this is a *fine* country to live in.' Then, direct to camera: 'This is a *bloody awful* country to live in.'

In order to imagine the roof-raising laughter which inevitably followed this moment, one has to cast oneself back to a time when 'bloody' was a really naughty word which had been previously used on the screen only once, by the incorrigible Bernard Shaw in *Pygmalion*. Even an undergraduate audience in Cambridge in 1954 cheered it on the first night and told their friends, who packed the house for the rest of the week. The joke serves also, to anyone watching the film at any period of history, as a signal that all attempts at plausibility have been abandoned, and that the rest of the film will be devoted to getting the principals out of their awkward situation with as much laughter and suspense as can be packed in before the happy ending.

Gus's impersonation of a Prussian is as near faultless as may be: he has an answer to every awkward question. Asked how are things at the Siegfried Line, he responds significantly and mysteriously: 'Pumping night and day.' Introduced to the astonished Bomasches, he blithely invents an old romance with Anna and obtains permission to court her through the night, much to the annoyance of the smitten Karl, who stands helplessly in attendance. In the middle of the night, however, with only half the champagne drunk, his plans are dashed when the Bomasches are ordered instantly to Munich for a conference with the Führer at Berchtesgaden. And this is where the film's calendar gets a little crazy, if anyone cares. It isn't so much a night train as one that starts at dawn, to judge from the light streaming through the station windows; which, since the date is later established as September 3rd, means that the war ministry scenes took place on a Saturday. And although Chamberlain did declare war at 11.15 A.M., nobody on the train is told about it until nightfall; and the English travellers are not arrested as enemy aliens. Launder and Gilliat got away with murder. Oh, and since the train arrives in Munich after dusk, and there follows an all-night drive preceding a daylight scene in the Alps, the film must end on September 4th despite what the prologue says.

It is at the railway bookstall that we encounter our unlikely *dei ex machina*, Charters and Caldicott. Astonished at the unavailability of *Punch* ('British magazine. Very humorous. You must have it.') they have to make do with *La Vie Parisienne*. Then there is a choice to be made between *Gone with the Wind* and *Mein Kampf*. They choose the latter:

CALDICOTT: I understand they give a copy to all the bridal couples over here.
CHARTERS: Oh, I don't think it's that kind of book, old man.

When Karl, Ulrich and the Bomasches commandeer their compartment, Caldicott is sure he recognizes one of them:

CALDICOTT: I'm sure that army officer is Dickie Randall. We were at Balliol together. Used to bowl slow leg breaks. Played for the Gentlemen once. Out for a duck, I remember.
CHARTERS: You don't think he's working for the Nazis?

187

CALDICOTT: Traitor? Hardly, old man. I told you, he played for the Gentlemen.

CHARTERS: Only once.

But at an unscheduled stop Charters hears Karl telephoning his suspicions of Major Herzog, whom the whole war ministry turns out to have accepted simply because he loudly demanded a 1935 committee report which didn't even exist. It must be Dickie Randall after all, and he must be warned, by the simple expedient of a note under the doughnut on the tea tray. ('He always liked doughnuts. Or was it rock cakes?') 'Will you take tea substitute or coffee substitute?' asks the waiter (that caused a roar, too, at a time when the Germans were a laughing stock for their ersatz food) and there follows a splendidly Hitchcockian sequence when the note nearly gets into the wrong hands (but not quite). Despite his peril Gus seems to be thoroughly enjoying himself, mouthing some splendidly over-the-top Nazi propaganda: 'Freedom in Germany is greatly advanced over elsewhere. It is organized and controlled by the state . . . unlike England, which is controlled by international Freemasons and the Jew Churchill.' Even when the jig seems to be up he is unperturbed, and when congratulated on his *sangfroid* he has time to reminisce: 'I *was* a member of the Foreign Office Operatic Society. Do you know I once played Pooh-Bah to the Foreign Secretary's Ko-Ko?' And who has the upper hand when the train steams into Munich? The right side, of course, which has no trouble at all in commandeering an army car and high-tailing it for the Swiss border. This unfortunately takes the shape of a chasm across which rather rickety cable cars provide a ferry service. It is fair to say that the film takes advantage of every dramatic possibility concerning the fear of falling and men with guns. Especially the guns: our hero's revolver seems to fire at least twenty-four bullets without reloading. It is an exciting sequence still, and the film is sensible enough to stop on the very second which ends it, with Karl ruefully licking his wounds and Gus having been more acrobatic in mid-air, despite a shot-up shoulder, than James Bond ever learned to be even with the help of his stuntmen. The mood was cannily judged: during England's first year of total war, *Night Train to Munich* made audiences more cheerful than any of the headlines warranted, and in the long run it's morale that wins wars.

Night Train to Munich. GB 1940; black and white; 95 minutes. Produced by Edward Black for Twentieth Century-Fox British. Written by Sidney Gilliat and Frank Launder from a story by Gordon Wellesley. Directed by Carol Reed. Photographed by Otto Kanturek. Music by Louis Levy. With Margaret Lockwood as Anna Bomasch; Rex Harrison as Gus Bennett; Paul Henreid as Karl Marsen; Basil Radford as Charters; Naunton Wayne as Caldicott; James Harcourt as Axel Bomasch; Felix Aylmer as Dr Fredericks; Raymond Huntley as Kampenfeldt; Keneth Kent as Controller; and Eliot Makeham, C. V. France, Wyndham Goldie, Roland Culver, Frederick Valk, Morland Graham.

Like an Elephant
NOTHING SACRED

A girl thought to be dying of a rare disease is built up by the press into a national heroine.

I saw it first when I was eight, and understood barely one word of it; but the audience was in stitches, so I enjoyed myself right along with them. I saw it again while in the army after the war; it was on a double bill with *Blithe Spirit* in an elegant Salisbury cinema called the Picture House, and I walked the five miles back to my barracks in utter bliss. When a few years later I controlled a Cambridge cinema I ran it on a double bill with *Wuthering Heights*, and the place was packed and responsive, though the print was poor.

I did not see *Nothing Sacred* again for thirty years. Although most of the other Selznick movies were readily available to a television buyer, this was one of four on which there was a flaw in the title so far as the United Kingdom was concerned: the pictures simply couldn't be cleared for sale, not without negotiations which nobody seemed willing to undertake. The others mattered rather less: *Little Lord Fauntleroy*, *Made for Each Other* and *The Young in Heart* (qv) (which eventually found its way to us when the world rights were bought out by another distributor). But *Nothing Sacred* nagged at me like a sore tooth, and eventually, when the distributors of the other Selznicks wanted a big deal from me, I said no way would it happen unless *Nothing Sacred* could be included. In my view, I said, they simply hadn't been trying. There was much delay and prevarication, but at last they said yes, but I would have to take my chances with the material, since a 1937 film in colour, and not the best colour at that, must be supposed to have deteriorated. A little later they announced that there was no decent negative from which they could print, and I would have to accept a tape from a very doubtful copy which the Germans had been holding on to for years. A year later nothing had happened, and when I pressed the matter word came back that the Germans didn't have a print after all; but a couple of months after that, with no further discussion, in from New York came a new and almost pristine 35mm print with excellent sound and all the original colour tones. In the spirit of not looking a gift horse in the mouth, I did not bother to ask by what form of magic it had been conjured from nowhere. I simply placed it gratefully, as the 'locomotive' in a Channel Four season of Hollywood comedy classics.

It has to be admitted that the second half of *Nothing Sacred* now seems a little stodgy: even that scriptwriting firework Ben Hecht had boxed himself into a comedy situation from which there was no spectacular exit. But so much that is memorable has gone before that no *aficionado* of thirties comedy (or of that much rarer commodity, satire) should dream of complaining. As for Wellman's direction, he seems curiously fond of masking off half the screen with foreground objects, usually vases of flowers, but otherwise does an admirable

NOTHING SACRED. The best-laid plans of Carole Lombard, Walter Connolly and Fredric March have clearly gang a-gley.

job of ensuring that we watch the actors' faces and hear the dialogue. In a raucous comedy like this it is essential to have pauses for the laughter of the mass audience; and if we watch the movie on television and don't need the pauses, then that's our bad luck.

The absurd tale is endearing from the first credits, which go to the trouble of showing us amusing puppets of the leading characters. In 1937, of course, the colour itself would be an excitement, especially when applied to a realistic subject rather than a musical or a western; and there in the first shot we see a panorama of Manhattan by night, with Hecht's first joke in the superimposed preface:

New York, where suckers and know-it-alls peddle gold bricks to each other, and where truth, crushed to earth, rises again more phony than a glass eye.

We are taken to a lavish dinner party, where the editor of the *Morning Star* is thanking the very black sultan of Mazupan for his committed gift to the city of a massive people's palace: 'Twenty-seven halls of beauty and culture, twenty-seven arenas of art.' The sultan was persuaded to this generous gesture, it seems, by one Wallace Cook, star reporter and 'pearl among journalists', who, looking decidedly blotto, sits next to editor Oliver Stone. But hold, who

190

comes down the marble stair? It is a black woman and her kids looking for their prodigal daddy. For the sultan is none other than an East Side bootblack, and the whole evening has been a publicity stunt; or, as other papers prefer to call it, 'the hoax of the century'.

So we have been warned against fakes; and so, for the last time, has Mr Cook. His contract runs five more years, so he can't be fired, but vengeful Mr Stone plans instead to 'remove him from the land of the living' by making him obituary editor. The sultan business, as we might guess, has done no good at all for Mr Stone's peptic ulcer: 'For the last three weeks I haven't been able to enter a café without the band playing Dixie.' But Mr Cook knows that Mr Stone knows that he really is a good reporter of sensational stories, and here is a clip in the paper about 'some poor little working girl up in Vermont, doomed to death of radium poisoning'. Wouldn't it be a great idea to bring her to the big city for a few last days of happiness? Wouldn't that really boost the *Star*'s circulation?

Mr Cook gets the go-ahead (otherwise there would be no story) but he hasn't reckoned with Vermont, and especially not with the little town of Warsaw, where all the taciturn natives say is 'yep' and 'nope'. 'Wouldn't have talked at all,' adds the stationmaster, 'if I'd known I was doin' it for nothin.' Mr Cook gets a similar response from the local druggist when he tries to locate the patient. 'How much do I owe you?' he asks in exasperation, having gained no information at all. 'Well,' she answers, 'you tooken up ma time . . .' And to cap it all, as Mr Cook strolls along a shady street, a small boy dashes out from behind a wicket gate and bites him in the leg.

Hazel Flagg is the name of the dying girl, and though Cook can't find her he finds her doctor, who has some trouble standing upright, a condition probably attributable to the various bottles from which he takes surreptitious swigs. Maintaining a hatred of newspapers because twenty-one years ago one of them failed to make him winner of a contest to name the six greatest Americans, he willingly transfers his disaffection to reporters and gets away with one of the best lines in the film: 'The hand of God, delving deep into the mire, could not elevate one of 'em to the depths of degradation.' As Mr Cook leaves, having got no further at all, he sees going in a girl he recognizes as Hazel Flagg, and lies in wait. When the girl comes out she is crying – as who wouldn't be when her end is near, thinks Mr Cook. But the audience knows the real reason: the doctor has admitted that in his befuddled state he mixed up the X-rays, and she isn't dying at all. He has spoiled her fun, she blurts out with confused indignation: she was going to blow all her savings on one last trip to New York. More soberly, she comments: 'It's kind of startling to be brought to life twice, and each time in Warsaw.' So when Cook waylays her with his proposition, she can't resist carrying on the deception, with the doctor's connivance (since he's included in the trip). 'And we're going on a plane?' she asks. 'Sure,' says the unfeeling Mr Cook, 'we haven't much time.'

On the plane she gets carried away with her enterprise. 'I'm not going to bed till I have convulsions and my teeth start falling out. That's the time to worry, isn't it?' 'It's as good a time as any,' mutters the doctor darkly. Cook warns her that she has yet to meet Oliver Stone, an encounter which may shorten her life still further because 'he's a cross between a ferris wheel and a werewolf, with a lovable streak if you care to blast for it'. At least Stone does his job: within three days Hazel Flagg is a national heroine. A crazy poet writes an elegy for her, and it is printed across the front page of the *Post* (but what we see is a fish being wrapped in it). In a delicatessen window a message is spelled out in sausages: MISS HAZEL FLAGG LUNCHED HERE TODAY, and underneath, ALL KINDS OF CHEESE AND BOLOGNA OUR SPECIALTY. At a wrestling match the referee recognizes her and calls for ten seconds of silence before the growlers start killing each other again. A nightclub sign in neon reads: CASINO MODERNE: HAZEL FLAGG NIGHT: TOOTSIES OF ALL NATIONS. Mr Cook is beginning to itch at the tastelessness of his self-imposed assignment, and comments that 'for good clean fun there's nothing like a wake'. 'Oh, please,' says the wacky Miss Flagg, 'let's not talk shop.' At one function she gets so drunk that when called up to the stage she collapses, and the worst is feared. 'Doctor,' says Stone nervously, 'I want to know the worst. I don't want you to spare our feelings. We go to press in fifteen minutes.'

Cook's last bright idea is a trip to Albany to persuade the governor to call a state funeral. He even tries to get the president but he's gone fishing; he gets a symphony orchestra instead. Meanwhile Mr Stone has over-reached himself. He calls in Dr Emil Egilhoffer, the world's greatest expert on radium poisoning, who happens to be visiting New York, and who tells Mr Stone positively that the girl is in blooming health and has no radium poisoning at all. The deception is naturally laid at the door of that proven faker Mr Cook, and when he returns in short-lived triumph it is to find Mr Stone positively quivering with rage: 'I am sitting here, Mr Cook, toying with the idea of cutting out your heart and stuffing it – like an olive!'

The rest of the story takes in a much publicized slugfest (as *Variety* would have it) between hero and heroine in dressing gowns, and is mainly concerned to extricate the characters from their surrounding morass of bad taste, without infuriating the newspaper owners and other millionaires who might be willing to finance Selznick's next picture. Hecht, who had written the script so far in thirty days, apparently threw up his hands (he probably wanted the girl to die) and what we see was knocked together by a committee and looks like it. Miss Flagg and Mr Cook naturally fall in love, and are last seen honeymooning at sea, reading an account of Miss Flagg's enormously successful New York memorial service, following the request expressed in her last letter that she be allowed to leave the city and face her end anonymous and alone – 'like an elephant'. It is left to the actors to get away with that – and they do, rather splendidly.

Nothing Sacred. US 1937; Technicolor; 75 minutes. Produced by David O. Selznick. Written by Ben Hecht. Directed by William Wellman. Photographed by W. Howard Greene. Music by Oscar Levant. With Fredric March as Wally Cook; Carole Lombard as Hazel Flagg; Charles Winninger as Dr Downer; Walter Connolly as Oliver Stone; Sig Rumann as Dr Emil Egilhoffer; Maxie Rosenbloom as Max.

The Moon and the Stars

NOW VOYAGER

A dowdy spinster is helped by a psychiatrist to blossom into a person of confidence.

On a cold Sunday night towards the end of 1983, my wife and I settled down before the fire at eleven and did not rise till after one, as this forty-odd-year-old four-handkerchief weepie unspooled for the umpteenth time on British television. It was, as always, compulsive viewing because of its star personalities and the sheer verve with which it is told; but it was not until we wondered over our cocoa why it had never been remade that we realized how much it differs from modern love stories.

The characters in it are too nice. In the cynical eighties they would be laughed off the screen. In this picture Bette Davis, Claude Rains and Paul Henreid would find it hard to come up with a moral blemish between them, and throughout the movie they are activated not by greed or by lust but by admiration, inspiration and duty. This alone would put the picture out of court with most audiences of the modern young, certainly with the one which on the very same evening had taken part in a studio discussion on the rights of the citizen. Yes, it was up to the government to feed and house them; no, they saw no reason to look for work; yes, stealing was OK because everybody had a right to be just as comfortable as everybody else. Such attitudes would have shocked even the villainess of *Now Voyager*, Charlotte Vale's mean old termagant of a mother (who remains for me a fairy tale witch figure because Gladys Cooper at the time was twenty years too young to play her, and the paint and powder do show).

When we first meet the rich, plain Charlotte she has barely recovered from a prolonged nervous collapse, induced by her mother's interference with a discreet shipboard romance. In Boston it isn't done to admit to a mental weakness, and Mum is thoroughly ashamed of her errant daughter; but luckily Charlotte's resourceful sister spirits into the house the warm, smiling Claude Rains as Dr Jaquith, for whom psychiatry comes in plain words and consists largely of common sense. By admiring Charlotte's ivory carvings (in these days of ecological awareness she would have a less reprehensible hobby) he overcomes her reserve, rides roughshod over mother, defiantly snaps her glasses in two (did Hollywood heroines never need them to see with, only to hide behind?), and transports her to his country retreat, which is poetically named Cascade. Within a few weeks, it seems, the ugly duckling is transformed into a sleek if somewhat unsteady swan. Dr Jaquith has also cured her of that unspeakable vice, secret smoking. Now she smokes in the open, as does almost everyone else in the picture. If they ever did remake it, the nicotine fog would seem the most unrealistic thing of all.

In her new guise Charlotte is sent off to negotiate her re-entry into the world

193

on a South American cruise, and here meets Paul Henreid as a smooth but soulfully romantic fellow called Jerry (he has other names too, but none of them explains his Viennese accent). What he does for a living is unclear, but his chief social accomplishment is the ability to light two cigarettes in his mouth and pass one to his guest. (Stars and director have wrangled in print as to who first had this brilliant idea, imitated the world over to the accompaniment of many torn lips. History tells us that George Brent first performed the service for Ruth Chatterton in a 1932 programmer called *The Rich are Always With Us*. In 1943 in *Let's Face It*, Bob Hope spoofed them all by lighting seven at a time and passing them around.) While the boat sails for Buenos Aires, a car accident keeps them in Rio for five potentially naughty nights, but if anything interesting does happen it never shows in their expressions. They don't even look back when they part, Charlotte on her way to Boston and Jerry to his ungrateful wife (never seen) and unbalanced daughter. Having taken a deep breath and some advice from Dr Jaquith, Charlotte is content for a while to run the family home, treating her now invalid mother with dutiful firmness and even keeping calm when the old dragon deliberately throws herself downstairs in search of more attention. Charlotte further encourages the attentions of Elliott, a staid Bostonian widower played by John Loder (than whom they don't come staider). But, Mr Loder being the Hollywood casting director's dream of a gallant loser, the audience simply waits for Jerry to happen through town and remind her of her mildly guilty past. It happens, and in two minutes flat, just as Elliott is musing about their wedding trip, she explains why it just isn't on, and shows him firmly out of the house.

Jerry being unattainable, Charlotte resigns herself to a life of spinsterish nobility, but when Mum's heart conks out during an inevitable quarrel she goes all of a guilty twitter again and makes a beeline for Cascade. And who is the scowling, bespectacled twelve-year-old she meets there, sobbing herself into a tizzy? Who else but the offspring of the said Jerry, who for all his talk of duty has had to hand her over to the doctors in the end. Cutting through a bale of red tape, Charlotte forgets her own problems and takes it upon herself to effect a cure. This she accomplishes, will you be surprised to hear, by throwing away the girl's glasses; when this cheers her up, she takes her on a camping trip. Jerry becomes a frequent visitor, but Charlotte has unwisely told Dr Jaquith her secret, and no way is he going to condone adultery in his sanatorium. Once or twice Jerry seems on the verge of making a sensible suggestion, such as his getting a divorce and providing a happy life for the two females he cares for (the ones without glasses). But Charlotte's measured tones prevent him from getting past his cigarette trick and a glance at the evening sky. Charlotte has the line that freezes. 'Oh, Jerry, don't let's ask for the moon: we have the stars.' Whatever that means. Personally I think it means that Charlotte is terrified of men at close quarters and likes to keep them on the run, lighting her cigarettes. But what audience can resist the fascinating wiles, however obscure, of Bette Davis? She plays this tormented leading lady like a frustrated pussy cat who settles for a saucer of milk. The performance confirmed her status as Hollywood's top female star; but as C. A. Lejeune said

NOW VOYAGER. How happy would I be with either, thinks Bette Davis; but John Loder is getting the brush-off, while Paul Henreid (right) waits smugly for the good news.

at the time, 'all she really has to do is dress well, look fresh and cured, and prevent us from noticing how long the film goes on.'

Clearly it once went on much longer. Mysterious stills exist of whole sections which were filmed and then edited out. Even a novice movie buff will notice the last-minute accommodations: awkward voice-over flashbacks, and a lot of aimless leafing through the book in double exposure. *Now Voyager* is also a signal revelation of how Warners could never resist economies even in their heyday, not even in a major movie. The back projection throughout tends not to be in focus, and on the approach to Rio it becomes quite risible. 'Oh, look,' says Charlotte, leaning over the rail, 'there's Rio.' It is hard to imagine how she can previously have failed to notice the famous sugarloaf mountain which we next see in central mid-shot over her shoulder. The view across the water is suddenly and absurdly succeeded by a close view of the surmounting statue, then a distant shot from quite a different angle. I think both my eyes and my logic would have been offended by that, even in 1942.

The title, by the way, comes from Walt Whitman. Claude Rains quotes two lines of poetry. I can never catch the first, but the second is: 'Now, voyager, sail thou forth to seek and find.' That accounts for the crudely drawn ship heading at us out of the credit titles; but the end title shows the ship sailing in the opposite direction. Perhaps the title card designer was a psychologist too.

Now Voyager. US 1942; black and white; 117 minutes. Produced by Hal B. Wallis for Warners. Written by Casey Robinson from the novel by Olive Higgins Prouty. Directed by Irving Rapper. Photographed by Sol Polito. Music by Max Steiner. With Bette Davis as Charlotte Vale; Paul Henreid as Jerry Durrance; Claude Rains as Dr Jaquith; Gladys Cooper as Mrs Vale; Bonita Granville as June; John Loder as Elliott; Ilka Chase as Lisa; Lee Patrick as Deb McIntyre.

Gobs and Gals

ON THE TOWN

Three sailors enjoy twenty-four hours in New York.

It was a sunny summer afternoon in Bolton, not the best time to see a Technicolor musical at the always inhospitable and by 1949 rather musty Capitol Cinema. I nearly didn't go at all, for the supporting feature was a justly forgotten B called *Skyliner*, with Tom Conway. I had heard and read some good things about *On the Town*, though, and this was my last chance that week to see it, since I was just back from holiday and that evening was booked to recite 'Albert and the Lion' at a church concert.

As so often happens when critics overpraise a movie (only one of them had complained there were no tunes he could go home whistling) I was a little disappointed with *On the Town*. Fewer than a hundred people were scattered around the Capitol, and none of them rose to the jokes; the sound amplification was too loud, and the sophisticated chords reverberated hollowly round the nicotine-stained walls, so I found the whole thing brash and rather empty. But the professionalism and the precision in every department were undeniable, even though it took me a couple of days to appreciate them; then I took a cycle ride round the Bolton districts to find out which of the lesser halls would be showing *On the Town* on its second run. How ungrateful I had been! Only three years earlier, a precocious teenager, I had written an article for *Picturegoer* complaining about intrusive plots in musicals. Well, here was a musical with almost no plot at all, or one that was simply a device to set down three guys and three girls in New York on a sunny day and allow them to let off steam. I was puzzled, I remember, by the end credit which said Made in Hollywood USA: I didn't know too much then about matte shots and back projection and studio New York streets. But what was that about the songs being unmemorable? Here was I, with no musical ear at all, humming them incessantly after only one viewing, and anxious to renew my acquaintance with the bouncy lyrics. Besides, the songs were almost of secondary importance to the dazzling footwork by a sextet of eager hoofers, and it's never easy to fit words and music to dance without seeming ragged. *On the Town* is never ragged, more usually a miracle of precision: however complex the movement, every performer is always exactly where he or she is supposed to be, and the wisecracks, sung or spoken, are snapped out with classic economy.

I saw *On the Town* half a dozen more times in cinemas: it became a popular reissue, often as half a bill with the Marx Brothers. (Bliss, pure bliss!) I played it at least three times myself, when I was managing the Cambridge Rex, and we always had a packed house for it on the Saturday night. Then I thought myself fortunate, as ITV film-buyer, to pick it up on a seven-year contract. Alas, I never managed to see it in all that time, for I lived in London and the London companies, first ATV and then LWT, thought musicals were bad for ratings and left it on a seven-year standby. I learned my lesson, and made sure that the BBC got it next time. When in 1982 Channel Four came along, I hastily reacquired it and programmed it in peak time on the following Easter Monday. It did not let me down. True, the first half is the best, and there is some tasteless business when Gene Kelly, deprived temporarily of his true love, reluctantly pairs off with an unattractive Jewish girl with a cold. Still, after thirty-five years, in a pristine print, the film's exhilaration is infectious, and there are no all-round talents around today to equal the ones it contains.

The credits are surrounded by a cartoon-like frieze of musical notation in which the notes constantly change colour. Then we see the Manhattan skyline at dawn, with a red sun behind the skyscraper tips; and along the dockside a burly man in an orange hard hat is strolling off to work at 5.57 A.M. (The times of the action, given frequently in white along the bottom of the screen, add something to the film's impression of perfect precision.) This man has the briefest of roles, but his three lines of song are unforgettable:

> I feel like I'm not out of bed yet.
> The sun is warm, but my bed is warmer.
> Sleep, sleep in your lady's arms . . .

We fear momentarily, perhaps, that we are in for a modern opera. But a whistle blows, and sailors in white uniforms pour off a nearby ship on twenty-four hours' leave, bellowing a song about having to see the town in just one day. Twenty-four hours, that is, until the following dawn, and none of them expects to need any sleep in that time. To find dates is their most pressing priority, but they are also mightily impressed by the Big Apple, in which most of them find themselves for the first time:

> New York, New York, it's a wonderful town.
> The Bronx is up, and the Battery's down.
> The people ride in a hole in the ground.
> New York, New York, it's a wonderful town.

They are, performer-wise, a curious trio. The brash acrobatic hoofer Gene Kelly, on the brink of his greatest period. Frank Sinatra, lean and wistful,

ON THE TOWN. The six principals put plenty of verve into the Empire State Building number. Betty Garrett, Frank Sinatra, Ann Miller, Jules Munshin, Vera-Ellen, Gene Kelly.

emerging from his bobbysox years and showing family audiences that he can be a reasonable light actor and dancer as well as a teenage heartthrob. Jules Munshin, a rubber-faced Jewish comic from the New York night clubs, not much heard from again by filmgoers. They had all had a trial run the previous year in *Take Me Out to the Ball Game*. Kelly and Sinatra had even played sailors on leave back in 1945, in *Anchors Aweigh*, but that was a slower and more sentimental affair which failed to take advantage of its Hollywood background. This time they knew what they were about. They were a team.

Perhaps the best part of the movie is the New York montage which follows their liberation. By the time 9.30 A.M. flashes across the screen it gets a laugh because they have already seen Chinatown, Wall Street, Central Park, the Statue of Liberty, the El, Rockefeller Plaza, Fifth Avenue and the Empire State Building, in a variety of different vehicles. There is even time for an in-joke: when Sinatra shrugs his shoulders at the passing female talent, the others josh him. 'Get him, Mr Particular. Who you got stashed at home, Ava Gardner?' (He did at the time: they were married.) Kelly is now entranced by a subway picture of Miss Turnstiles of the Month, whom he mistakes for a member of high society. His heart flutters even more when he comes across her being photographed and is asked to pose with her. ('Thanks, sailor, we're proud of our boys.') She steps on to a subway train and is lost, but Sinatra luckily finds a taxi driven by Betty Garrett who plays a lady named Brunhilde Esterhazy:

CHIP: What are you doing driving a cab, the war's over?
BRUNHILDE: I never give up anything I like. Come up to my place.

She doesn't even give up when she finds that this Sinatra is Mr Studious, who would rather see the Hippodrome, The Floradora Girl and the Woolworth Tower, none of which have been available for years:

CHIP: I've only got one day and I want to see all the famous landmarks of the city.
BRUNHILDE: Stick with me, kid, I'll show you plenty.

The search for Miss Turnstiles takes them to the Natural History Museum where they meet Ann Miller as a pulchritudinous female student writing a treatise on Modern Man, What is It? She immediately spots the similarity between Munshin and a model of Piceanthropus Erectus, and is discovered by the others holding him in a three-quarter Nelson.

CLAIRE: 'I was just doing a bit of research.'
BRUNHILDE: 'Dr Kinsey, I presume'.

The dance routine which follows is admirably composed of a number of short sharp tableaux:

> Modern man is not for me,
> The Wily Will and Dapper Dan.
> Give me a healthy Joe from ages ago,
> A prehistoric man.

Between them the happy wanderers contrive to collapse a model dinosaur, and the report confuses a policeman who receives it on his car radio: 'Gee, she's my favourite singer, that Dinah Shore.'

Miss Turnstiles is of course tracked down, and the six of them manage a rousing night on the town, in nightclubs which all seem to be singing variations of the same song. But just before midnight, like all good Cinderellas, Miss Turnstiles must vanish to avoid confiding that in order to pay for her ballet lessons she works as a cooch dancer on Coney Island. After the merest pause for a dream ballet recapitulating the day's activities, Kelly leads a madcap taxi chase through Brooklyn, and all ends reasonably happily when the errant sailors are bagged by shore patrol. The movie ends as it began, with the hardhat singing his familiar song and three new sailors singing about going on the town while their predecessors wave a sad farewell to the ladies on the dock.

On the Town. US 1949; Technicolor; 98 minutes. Produced by Arthur Freed for MGM. Written by Adolph Green and Betty Comden from their musical, with music by Leonard Bernstein. Directed by Gene Kelly and Stanley Donen. Photographed by Harold Rosson. Musical Director Lennie Hayton. With Gene Kelly as Gabey; Frank Sinatra as Chip; Betty Garrett as Brunhilde Esterhazy; Ann Miller as Claire Huddesen; Vera-Ellen as Ivy Smith; Jules Munshin as Ozzie; Alice Pearce as Lucy Schmeeler; Florence Bates as Madame Dilyovska.

ONE HOUR WITH YOU

A philandering Paris doctor gets himself in trouble.

This elegant trifle from 1932 did not première on British television until fifty-one years after it was made. I watched it from the comfort of my reclining chair, drooling with the kind of ecstasy experienced by a gourmet when he is offered a bottle of Moët et Chandon and one of Château d'Yquem to accompany a meal of Whitstable natives, salmon, trout and strawberries Romanoff. On the following morning I happened to walk to the station with a sixtyish neighbour, and asked him whether he had seen it and what he thought of it. I did not expect him to know about Lubitsch, or to enthuse about the gleaming mint quality of the brand new 35mm print with its angelically pure sound, obtained from negatives no doubt underused. But I did hope that, as a relief from this crass modern age, the style and subtlety of the narrative and the precision of the playing might have communicated themselves. 'Oh, I turned that off,' he said. 'It was in black and white. Besides, I never could stand that Jeanette MacDonald, simpering and wiggling her eyebrows. Didn't they overact in those days?'

Useless, they say, to explain sunlight to a blind man. Useless, too, to offer caviare to the general. Useless to explain that what he perceived as overacting is high comedy performance of a kind most cunningly judged to fit the film's brittle, artificial style, which itself was a form of satire on the society and pretensions of the early thirties. My neighbour would have walked out of Laurence Olivier in *The Way of the World* before the first act was over, and he would not have been alone. Best to leave him to his gardening and his Alistair MacLean, and to content myself with the thought that some great enjoyments simply can't be taken to the whole population, and that it is often the greatest satisfaction of all to be part of a minority. High comedy is not so very far behind opera as the most despised and misunderstood of art forms; which makes me wonder why I, who really can't take to opera and was brought up among the so-called working class, should have sat through *One Hour with You* in a positive paroxysm of delight, pondering only during the commercial breaks on what possible connection there can be between this serenely assured comedy of manners and the groping, yucky stuff which passes as comedy today.

To be sure, the story is thin, and its resolution is by no means the film's high point. But storylines were never the great strength of either Lubitsch or his favourite screenwriter Samson Raphaelson, who used them only as the basic necklace on which decorative jewels were to be strung. Both men delighted in milking situations for all the naughty nuances they could convey, and also in inventing little irrelevant comic doodles such as the scene in this film when an absurdly costumed gentleman around town (Charles Ruggles) telephones his inamorata (who is married to his best friend) to tell her that he is on the verge of departing for her costume party in the guise of Romeo. There is a pause for his face to fall at her unheard reply. Then he says: 'Oh. *Not* a costume party?' And the camera pulls back to emphasize again the full nature of his sartorial plight, which includes velvet doublet and silken hose. He replaces the phone and calls his butler (the bland Charles Coleman, whose sole appearance in the movie is this ten-second scene). 'Marcel, why did you tell me it was a costume party?' 'Oh sir,' says the man with just a hint of lasciviousness, 'I did so want to see you in tights.'

Some would call *One Hour with You* a musical, but although Oscar Straus's songs are delightful enough, they fit so closely into the narrative that one scarcely notices them as set pieces, especially when so much of the surrounding dialogue is in recitative. The tale begins obliquely with a superintendent of gendarmes giving the night's instructions to his officers:

> Now, listen to me, men, Spring is here,
> And Spring is a dangerous time of year,
> Especially in Paree . . .

The gendarmes leap into action with their torches, echoing the war cry: Cleaner Parks and More Prosperity! They scour the bushes and come across Maurice Chevalier on a dark bench with Jeanette MacDonald on his lap. 'You can't make love here,' they cry. 'I can make love anywhere,' he replies with a wink at the delighted audience, who know that he is only their wicked Maurice once again being funny and sexy at the same time. 'You see that moon?' he goes on. 'If that moon could speak French, do you know what he would say to you? Phooey.' But the gendarmes, on learning that Maurice is a doctor and Jeanette his legally wedded wife, have already lost interest: they send the couple home for using the park under false pretences.

Moments later we are in Lubitsch's favourite haunt, the bedroom, but while the lady is busy changing from one satin garment to another, Maurice slips outside to explain to the audience how much they love each other. 'Darling . . .' she calls from within. 'That's for me,' he explains, blushing. To her: 'Sweetheart!' To us: 'That's for her.' To her: 'I'll be with you in a minute . . .' And a final nod and wink to the camera: 'That's for both of us!' But before indulging in connubial bliss the couple find time for a song: 'What a little thing like a wedding ring will do.'

As musical comedies go, this is so intimate that it whispers, and the characterization is scaled accordingly. Chevalier is presented as a fashionable medic, but we are not supposed to believe that he ever opened *Gray's Anatomy*, especially since he resolutely wears his straw hat throughout. The plot now begins, and keep your eyes and ears open or you'll miss it. Madame expects a visit from her old friend Mitzi whom she hasn't seen for years but remembers as such a paragon of virtue that we suspect there must be some mistake. There is. Mitzi is a coquette, and her husband (Roland Young, delightfully dry as always) is having her followed. ('That's my wife,' he tells us, falling into the common habit of addressing the camera. 'When I married her she was a

ONE HOUR WITH YOU. High-society goings-on are superintended by Jeanette MacDonald and Maurice Chevalier.

brunette. Now you can't believe a word she says.') Alas for the good doctor, he is spotted having an apparent assignation with Mitzi when all he wants is to share her taxi in the rain. He is astonished when he gets home later to find the temptress being shown (by his wife) the top half of his rather splendid pyjamas. She is suitably impressed:

> Oh yes, they are stunning, as cute as cute can be.
> But where are the rest of them? Oh, pardon me.

He is further embarrassed when the girls whisper about him:

MADAME: He can . . . (*whisper, whisper*).
MITZI: He can?
MADAME: Yes, and he can . . . (*whisper, whisper*).
MITZI: I don't believe it. Let's see him do it.
MADAME: All right. Darling, look like an owl.

Mitzi loses no time in making her availability obvious, and soon the doctor is once again confiding to the audience:

202

My wife thinks I am a darling. My wife's best friend thinks I'm cute. It's a terrible situation. But I am determined not to weaken. (*He shrugs.*) We'll see.

This leads him into a musical description of his bedside manner, which seems to consist of recommending something or other three times a day, with *double entendres* falling thick and fast. Soon the jealous professor finds him holding Mitzi's hand, and is not fooled by the doctor's pretence of feeling her pulse:

DOCTOR: Your wife is in a very serious condition.
PROFESSOR: Why shouldn't she be? Conditions are bad everywhere.

How the doctor's white tie subsequently ends up round Mitzi's ankle is too long a tale to tell, but it sends his wife Colette flouncing off to bed in a tantrum, and the doctor once again seeks our advice in song:

> Should I be brave and misbehave, or not?
> I love Colette . . . I'm crazy for Colette,
> But ohhhh! that Mitzi!

The call of nature is too strong. Having pursued and presumably caught Mitzi, he returns at dawn, only slightly repentant:

> I ask you, what would you do?
> That's what I did too.

His absence, however, has let in the professor for an hour's self-justified dalliance with Colette: 'Any man who lets a woman like you take up on a night like this with a man like me . . . deserves it!' Thus Madame is not being entirely honest when she cries at Maurice: 'Our marriage is over: from now on you're nothing but a doctor to me!' The twinkle in her eye indicates that it is time for us to withdraw from this pre-Legion of Decency hothouse of innuendo, resplendent in glass and chromium sets by Hans Dreier. We have relished eighty minutes of the kind of high sophistication provided only by this star, this writer and this director. All, alas, are now dead, and seem to have left no successors, but since history usually proves to move in cycles, those of us with time to wait can only hope.

One Hour with You. US 1932; black and white; 80 minutes. Produced by Ernst Lubitsch for Paramount. Written by Samson Raphaelson from the play *Only a Dream* by Lothar Schmidt (and the silent film *The Marriage Circle*). Directed by George Cukor (and Ernst Lubitsch). Photographed by Victor Milner. Songs by Leo Robin, Oscar Straus and Richard Whiting. With Maurice Chevalier as Dr André Bertier; Jeanette MacDonald as Colette Bertier; Genevieve Tobin as Mitzi Olivier; Roland Young as Professor Olivier; Charles Ruggles as Adolph; George Barbier as the police commissioner.

Pest of the West
THE PALEFACE

Calamity Jane undertakes a secret government mission, and marries a timid dentist as a cover.

There are some films which should be seen only with an audience, and *The Paleface* is one of them. When one thinks of Bob Hope it is not the first title one remembers, because he does nothing new or unexpected in it. *The Cat and the Canary* and *Fancy Pants* and the *Road* films have better gags, and by 1948 Hope's amiable coward characterization, on which *The Paleface* entirely depends, was becoming just a shade wearisome. But the teaming of Hope with the then sensational Jane Russell put yet another spurt in a career which scarcely needed one; a lot of money had been spent on it. In Bolton it was booked, like all Paramount films, to the Odeon, but by some extraordinary arrangement the Theatre Royal was allowed to run it concurrently, so that all the expected crowds could be accommodated. It was to the Theatre Royal that I headed on a rainy Bank Holiday, not to the true matinée nor to the evening performances, but to the house in between. I still had to queue, and got in just as the feature hit the screen. The place was packed solid, and every joke threatened to raise the roof; I staggered home quite exhausted from laughter. It was not until I encountered *The Paleface* again many years later on television that I realized how thin the script really is, how all the gags one would expect turn up in the places where one would expect them, and how long are the pauses for audience reaction.

The Paleface is still a dandy production which, if one bears the foregoing in mind, can pass a pleasant ninety minutes as a cheerful package of western clichés. It has them all: it meant to; but so sure of themselves were its makers that they start the narrative with a straight face. We don't even see Hope for twelve minutes. Well, that's not quite true: the titles come on against the backing of a magnificent Red Indian headdress, which raises when Hope's name appears to reveal Hope's eyes underneath. That has to last us through the threadbare plot setting, something about renegades selling rifles to the Indians, and Calamity Jane being sprung from jail by the governor so that she can join a wagon train incognito and discover the identity of the villain. (The audience could have saved her the trouble; it's the governor's aide, the one who twitches a lot.) Needless to say, when she reaches the guy who is to pose as her husband she finds him dead at his desk, and is chased into a ladies' bath-house by the still-lurking gunmen. A gunbelt strapped to her combinations enables her to dispose of all three, and to escape from a balcony on to a wagon in which an incompetent dentist is making his escape from an irate gentleman whose gold tooth he has just extracted in mistake. Hope of course plays the said Painless Peter Potter. ('Is it safe? Safest thing in the world. Would you mind paying me now?') When a patient tries to help him locate the bad tooth, Hope snaps back

204

THE PALEFACE. Bob Hope subjects an attacking redman (Joe Vitale) to whiffs of laughing gas.

at him: 'Please! No clues!' But even with the anticipated help of laughing gas, the dentist scene could have been funnier, and the moment when Hope takes a hammer and chisel to a patient's teeth in order to sort out the sound ones would probably have been rejected even by Tom and Jerry as too cringe-making.

The plot proper begins next morning when Hope realizes what a beautiful bundle he has aboard his covered wagon. 'So that's what Horace Greeley meant!' he murmurs with his visual equivalent of a wolf whistle. To his extreme surprise, nay astonishment, Jane insists on marrying him, and this puts him in a stupor for the rest of the picture, since she means the relationship to be purely platonic. 'You promised to love and protect me,' she reminds him. 'Yeah,' he replies, 'let's do it in the order named!' But the writers have a predilection for Running Gag Number One: whenever the newlyweds look like making it to the sack, she knocks him out with the butt of her pistol, and he attributes his collapse to the way she kisses. Running Gag Number Two is even more familiar: every time he says 'giddyap', he gets dragged half a mile by the horses because he has forgotten to link up the wagon.

The other pioneers write him off after he introduces himself: 'We're Mr and

Mrs Peter Potter. I'm Mr.' But he sings a nifty little song called 'Buttons and Bows' (which won an Academy Award) and while doing so allows the horses to wander up the wrong trail, taking half the pioneers with them. The party is forced to hole up for the night at an abandoned camp threatened by marauding Indians. This leads to a smartly-handled scene in which Hope almost gets his wedding night with a brave who giggles in the dark because he has taken a whiff of laughing gas. Next morning, when the Indians attack, Hope is hiding in a barrel, but gets the credit for wiping out the whole hunting party: his bullets have actually hit the ground, and it is Jane who from an unseen vantage point has accounted for every redskin in sight. She gives Hope the credit, and he is acclaimed as a hero. (The same situation was taken seriously a few years later in John Ford's *The Man Who Shot Liberty Valance*; one wonders where the legend originated.)

Hope in his foolhardy character is naturally ready to take command.

POTTER: Ladies and gentlemen, at this time I'd like to say a few words.
MAN: Hey, let's get outa here before those Indians come back.
POTTER: Those are the words.

The scene shifts to the dangerous resort of Bottleneck, recognizable by all who have been there as the western street set at Paramount Studios. Here we find Robert Watson, who often played Hitler, making a good stab at the kind of villain who runs the Dirty Shame Saloon but paints murals on the side. He thinks it might be a good idea to arrange an accident for the unlikely-looking sharpshooter, so Hope is encouraged to make play with the saloon songstress ('Got a seegar on you, sister?') who just happens to be the girlfriend of the town's most gun-happy gunfighter. By now Hope believes his own legend, and even wisecracks with the heavy:

HEAVY: I don't like nobody foolin' around with my girl.
POTTER: Yeah, well, I got news for you. I ain't foolin'.

The inevitable duel is fixed for sundown, and while sustaining himself with four fingers of redeye (which nearly kill him) Hope receives three separate but confusing pieces of advice:

> He draws from the left, so lean to the right.
> There's a wind from the east, so aim to the west.
> He crouches when he shoots, so stand on your toes.

This routine, which served Eddie Cantor so well in *Roman Scandals* and was later perfected for Danny Kaye in *The Court Jester*, is rather thrown away here; perhaps Hope remembered having done something similar in his own *Never Say Die*.

Of course he wins the gunfight, with Jane's unseen help, and even has a cheery word for the waiting undertaker: 'Stick around, I'll make you wealthy.' He really thinks he may get his reward that night at last, and hangs on the bedroom door a sign reading: Beware, Mad Dog. ('That'll take care of the tourists.') But it is not to be. He finds himself instead hiding from the baddies in the undertakers, pretending to be a corpse on the slab and having his nose tickled by a fleeing cat. From here on, in fact, cartoon humour takes over. Jane is kidnapped by the Indians, and has to be rescued. Hope, sprung from a tree in a bungled attempt at execution, is catapulted a mile or more through the air and survives; he then fells a medicine man on the far horizon with a single stone (a gag also used by Laurel and Hardy to end *Swiss Miss*). But events come to a climax with dynamite being let off, after which there is only a runaway covered wagon to contend with. At last the newly weds can set off on their real honeymoon; but this time it is Jane's turn to take the reins and be dragged after the galloping horses. 'Well, what did you expect?' Hope asks us. 'A happy ending?'

The Paleface. US 1948; Technicolor; 91 minutes. Produced by Robert L. Welch for Paramount. Written by Edmund Hartmann and Frank Tashlin. Directed by Norman Z. McLeod. Photographed by Ray Rennahan. Music by Victor Young. Song 'Buttons and Bows' by Jay Livingston and Ray Evans. With Bob Hope as Painless Peter Potter; Jane Russell as Calamity Jane; Robert Armstrong as Terris; Iris Adrian as Pepper; Robert Watson as Toby Preston; Jackie Searl as Jasper Martin; Henry Brandon as Medicine Man.

An Absolute Shower
PRIVATE'S PROGRESS
An innocent in the army becomes a dupe for an art theft.

Some would claim this film as the first timorous step towards what later became known as 'the swinging sixties', for in it no man is admirable, most are irresponsible and even criminal behaviour is not necessarily punished. Its makers would probably have preferred to claim it as a satire on the bad old ways, the scrounging, spivving ways, which had become accepted in Britain during six years of total war. Both groups would certainly be surprised to remember that towards the end it turns into a wartime adventure story on the lines of *Where Eagles Dare*. But for the most part it is not much more than the hoariest kind of army farce, with jokes which have been used, and later scorned, by every film comedian from Charlie Chaplin to Goldie Hawn. Ah well, World War II has not been so thoroughly recorded on film that we can afford to give up even a belated comedy version of it, provided it is sharply observed – which *Private's Progress* for the most part is. I can personally vouch for the accuracy with which it depicts the inanity and boredom of army life, with everyone concerned to get away with as many wangles as possible. Only the language is bowdlerized.

PRIVATE'S PROGRESS. The officer (Terry-Thomas) views his new recruits with distaste. In the front rank: Richard Attenborough, Ian Carmichael and Victor Maddern.

The satirical element is what the Boultings put forward on the film's first release, for this was their idea of blazing a new trail in the British film industry, and what they had done for the army they later did, before inspiration totally failed, for the unions, the law and the church. However, probably aware of the show business definition of satire as 'what closes Saturday night', they decided not to make their aim too narrow. In the event they scattered their shots far too widely in all directions. This mattered not a jot at the box office, but it did mean that the reputations they had hoped for as national jesters were never sustained. Ian Carmichael on the other hand made a whole career out of playing their innocent abroad Stanley Windrush, the perpetual fall guy, snatched away from a Cambridge backwater to face a harsh and unreal world in which everyone either does him down or tries to blow him up. Stanley is given a great many foils on whom the spotlight shines in turn. There is Cox, the perennial spiv, who turns up always where you least expect him. There is Major Bertram Tracepurcel, Stanley's uncle and an upper-crust conman. There is the dim-witted company commander who thinks that everyone else is a positive shower. All these characters are to be found again in the sequel *I'm All Right*

Jack, along with Miles Malleson as Stanley's vaguely nudist father and John Le Mesurier as the psychologist who when confronted by Stanley rapidly develops a facial tic, but there they are all channelled into a strong comic story which superficially explores industrial relations. The trouble with *Private's Progress* is that the Boultings seem constantly to tire of whatever target they are aiming at and to train their sights on another.

Along the way one encounters plenty of simple pleasures. When I first succumbed to the film on a stormy evening in Clacton, having done my duty by *Richard III* in the afternoon, there was an enormous laugh when Stanley reluctantly dropped his trousers at the army medical, and the MO assured him after a cursory glance that he had nothing to be ashamed of. Nowadays, a simple reference to the private parts would be insufficient; a touch of wit would be required. The modern viewer may also find rather too many jokey captions at the start: 'The service caps issued for use in this film are intended to be used by imaginary personnel only.' And, with a background of service colonels adopting the attitudes of those famous three monkeys: 'The producers gratefully acknowledge the co-operation of absolutely nobody.'

We find poor Stanley quite bewildered by his call-up: 'I never felt less aggressive in my life.' He gets no help. Nobby, his college servant, says that what he learned in the first war was to look after number one. His father is too busy writing a history of the music hall to be much concerned. But Uncle Bertie, curling his moustache, thinks he might have a use for Stanley in Whitehall later on, and urges him to keep in touch: 'Nothing like having a friend at the War House. If he can't cut the red tape, at least he can pull the right strings.' Bertie is clearly a Bad Hat of the old school. But meanwhile Stanley has more mundane mysteries to solve at the ominously named Gravestone Barracks. William Hartnell (who else?) plays the archetypal sergeant who, when Stanley in bowler hat and dark suit apologizes for his late arrival on parade, remarks: 'You don't have to be sorry, son. It's *my* bleeding heart that's breaking.' We are shortly allowed to sit in on the usual fatuous lecture from the usual fatuous officer: 'The ultimate object of a trained soldier is to kill the enemy . . . the enemy does not play cricket . . . he does some pretty frightful things. We therefore have to show the enemy that when it comes to frightfulness we can be pretty frightful ourselves . . .'

One morning Stanley awakes feeling a little fragile and wants to get an aspirin from the MO. In a perfectly true yet quite appalling sequence he finds that in order to do so he must first report sick, which by the army's discouraging rules involves standing in half full pack outside the MO's office until called. The fact that it is pouring with rain worries nobody except Stanely, who catches pneumonia.

Stanley is sent to OCTU, but he simply isn't the officer type. He even manages to fail the word association test, when he answers 'coffin' with 'spittin' '. So he is sent to a holding unit, the army's synonym for inertia, where he is comforted by the ubiquitous Cox: 'If you failed a course, you're not fully trained. And if you're not trained you can't fight.'

Soon Stanley learns the truth of the army's famous dictum: 'If it moves, salute it. If it doesn't move, paint it.' And the only real training he gets is in tricking British Railways and never giving your right name to an officer. It is by an unhappy coincidence that the company commander is not above a little skiving himself, such as slipping off to see *In Which We Serve* at the local cinema, where he finds himself surrounded by the whole of Stanley's platoon. They are instantly dispersed by the most arduous postings that can be found, whereupon sly old Uncle Bertie takes a hand. Stanley is mysteriously commissioned and sent on a language course. By mistake what he gets is Chinese and not the intended German, for Bertie has in mind a little reconnaissance for art treasures behind enemy lines, and the mistake nearly costs them both dear. Operation Hatrack takes the second half of the movie on a very different course from the first, but the whole will still raise smiles on the faces of those who remember the forties, and can be recommended to those who can't as tolerably accurate history, while the final caption is calculated to send us all home wistfully happy: 'To all those who got away with it, this film is respectfully dedicated.'

Private's Progress. GB 1956; black and white; 102 minutes. Produced by the Boulting Brothers (Roy Boulting) for British Lion. Written by John Boulting and Frank Harvey from the novel by Alan Hackney. Directed by John Boulting. Photographed by Eric Cross. Music by John Addison. With Ian Carmichael as Stanley Windrush; Richard Attenborough as Cox; Terry-Thomas as Major Hitchcock; Dennis Price as Major Bertram Tracepurcel; Peter Jones as Egan; William Hartnell as Sergeant Sutton; Thorley Walters as Captain Bootle; Jill Adams as Prudence; Miles Malleson as Mr Windrush; John Le Mesurier as the psychiatrist; Kenneth Griffith as Private Jones; Victor Maddern as Private Blake.

Some Mothers Do Have 'Em; or, Just When you Thought It was Safe to Go Back in the Shower

PSYCHO

Vicious murders take place at a lonely motel.

A good many jokes have been made about *Psycho*, some of them by Hitchcock himself; the blood in the shower, he told the press, was really chocolate sauce, because it photographed better. Hitch was a close friend of the Bernsteins of Granada TV, for whom I worked (and still do). I well remember the air of gloom and bafflement which prevailed at a programme meeting when they sought ways of defending their old crony against the wave of hostile criticism which his tongue-in-cheek thriller had provoked in the national press. Try these reviews on for size:

A sad prostitution of talent. *Daily Express*

Hitch, old cock, this is the worst film you've made . . . it scrapes the bottom of the psychiatric barrel.   Fred Majdalany, *Daily Mail*

Generally overstrung, woefully overlong. I was bored to death.   Alexander Walker, *Evening Standard*

A Gothic absurdity.   *Spectator*

Many scenes inspire the wrong kind of laughter.   *The Times*

Nothing but depravity.   *Evening News*

I was so sick and tired of the whole beastly business that I didn't stay till the end.   C. A. Lejeune, *Observer*

It's sad to see a really big man make a fool of himself.   Derek Monsey, *Sunday Express*

There is not an ounce of decency or of genuine human artistry evident in front of or behind the cameras . . . this is the most miserable peepshow I have ever seen, and far more awful and suggestive than any pornographic film I have ever seen.   Clancy Sigal

Incredible, implausible and macabre.   Peter Burnup, *News of the World*

Fashionably unpleasant.   Paul Gibbs, *Daily Telegraph*

If you are lucky enough to arrive too late for the beginning, try missing the end and the middle too. It is almost worth the journey.   Paul Dehn, *News Chronicle*

A lascivious blood bath . . . he has become a caterer for cheap sniggers. *Sunday Dispatch*

If you've got a queasy stomach, stay away.   Margaret Hinxman, *Daily Mail*.

Perhaps they should all have noted that the Bates house seemed to have been modelled on the one created by *New Yorker* cartoonist Charles Addams for his family of vampires and ghouls. And to be quite fair, the spoofing in Hitch's mind should have been evident to anyone who saw the trailer; but then trailers are never shown to critics. In it the director took audiences on a conducted tour of the Bates place. 'This,' I remember him saying with ill-controlled glee, 'is where the first murder was committed. I wouldn't go in if I were you. All that blood. Horrible.'

At the programme meeting I was at a disadvantage, for I had seen neither film nor trailer. Being under the impression that Hitch had made a complex murder mystery with a diabolically twisty plot (a notion fostered by the posters, from which Hitch pleaded: 'Don't give away our ending, it's the only one we have'), I had determined to play absolutely fair both to him and to myself by postponing any further acquaintance with the movie until I had (I hoped) enjoyed it on my regular Monday date at the Kingston Granada. I had avoided the critics, too, in case they gave anything away, and could only suppose that the Granada reaction was exaggerated, born from disappointment that Hitch had done something different. Having been brought up in the belief that any publicity is good publicity, I rashly suggested that we take advantage of it by scheduling a season of Hitch's past hits. Victor Peers, our general manager, shuddered as though he had been shot. 'It's not good for our image to be associated with Hitch at the moment,' he said. 'He's gone far too far.' I was even instructed to withdraw with immediate effect *Alfred Hitchcock Presents*, that very mild series of television playlets; and the barricades were not raised again until *The Birds* came out three years later.

My wife had read the reviews, and so refused to accompany me. I went alone, and found that I had to queue, which made the occasion even more exciting. I settled into my seat with pleasurable anticipation of a deft mixture of thrills and laughter with just a touch of horror, something perhaps on the lines of *The Cat and the Canary*. I prepared myself to watch for clues. More than a thousand people sighed and shivered as the green light came up on the censor's certificate. Saul Bass's credits passed quickly, and we were zooming in on a cityscape: nothing to latch on to there. Then we were given the place, in little white letters; and the time. That must be significant; remember it.

One hundred and eight minutes later I left the cinema a disappointed man. *Psycho* the film has no humour at all, and that I suppose is Hitch's joke on the audience he had so carefully led up the garden in his promotion. It also has no plot to speak of, precious little mystery and no surprise ending, since what passes for one, and is so laboriously explained by a psychiatrist brought on for the purpose, is so obvious from Anthony Perkins's first sequence that I had instantly discarded it as a red herring. The first forty minutes of Marion Crane's crime and wanderings have no real connection with the rest of the picture, which might more suspensefully have begun with her appearance at the motel in the rain: clearly Hitch's idea was to be the first film-maker to butcher the heroine whose plight the audience had thus far been following with sympathy and interest. Certainly the tracking down of the murderous bird-fancier is tense enough in a cheap scary way – its high level of professional competence can most easily be judged by a glance at William Castle's poor imitation, *Homicidal* – and Hitch may have been right in claiming *Psycho* as a triumphant technical exercise: he had done what he set out to do, which was to tease, shock and stun a captive audience so audaciously that after the shower scene he could reduce the violence to almost nothing and still have them leave the theatre with sweaty hands. (Think about it: the next murder is shown from a distance, and in the frightened lady climax nobody gets hurt at all.)

Hitch never did understand why so few people, to start with, were willing to see his macabre joke. Even if he had taken any of the criticisms seriously, he must have been smiling behind his hand all the way to the bank, for by its crafty marketing *Psycho* had made him one of the richest men in America, with a personal profit of more than 5 million dollars in the first couple of months. All on account of a low-budget black-and-whiter made quickly by his television crew from a pulp horror novel. Not that Robert Bloch's original is entirely to be

212

PSYCHO. There's no such shot in the film, but it has become a trademark all the same. The house still exists, but it's by no means as big as you might think.

sneezed at: its opening chapter, with Bates apparently enjoying a conversation with his mad mother, does at least camouflage the obvious in a way which the film, using a revised structure, is never able to do.

When seen a second time *Psycho* is for the most part very boring, but at least a relaxed attitude enables one to give due credit to two seldom-sung people who worked on it. Bernard Herrmann's screechy score is a classic of its kind, and if you doubt that, next time the movie plays on television try turning down the sound on the shower scene: the effect is completely lost, for all the frissons are on the sound track. As Hitch was at pains to make clear, the girl was never nude and the knife never connects: it was all an optical and musical illusion. This is not to detract from the fiendishly clever editing of the brief sequence, which crams hundreds of images into a few seconds. The sequence has become the centre of a controversy: Hitch is celebrated for it, yet in recent years it has emerged that it was probably directed by Saul Bass on a day when Hitch was sick; either that, or Hitch simply couldn't be bothered with such a finicky job. Hitch in his last years brushed aside such claims: to him all collaborators were 'ball-tossers', on hand merely to convince the great man that his instincts in all cases were right. Bass has never pressed the matter; yet if he didn't make a contribution of some kind apart from his titles, why does he get a separate credit as 'consultant'? What is a

213

pictorial consultant, anyway? Perhaps it was he who determined that the old house on the hill should be built at two-thirds actual size. I have stood in its doorway and can vouch for this, and the reduced scale gives a curious air of unease, especially if you approach it quickly and try to enter. The interiors of course were full-scale studio sets, long dismantled, but the house itself remains, second only to the *Jaws* lake and the Parting of the Red Sea as a favourite stop on the Universal Studio tour of instantly recognizable Hollywoodiana. You can bet that Hitch's estate is still collecting royalties.

Psycho. US 1960; black and white; 109 minutes. Produced by Alfred Hitchcock for Paramount release. Written by Joseph Stefano from the novel by Robert Bloch. Directed by Alfred Hitchcock. Photographed by John L. Russell. Music by Bernard Herrmann; pictorial consultant Saul Bass. With Anthony Perkins as Norman Bates; Janet Leigh as Marion Crane; Vera Miles as Lila Crane; John Gavin as Sam Loomis; John McIntire as Sheriff Chambers; Martin Balsam as Milton Arbogast; Simon Oakland as Dr Richmond.

A Face from Space

THE QUATERMASS EXPERIMENT

When a rocketship returns from space, two of its crew members have disappeared and the third slowly turns into a walking fungus.

On its first British release this highly successful quickie, enabling Hammer Films to haul themselves up by the bootstraps from Poverty Row into the Big Time, was billed as *The Quatermass Xperiment*, thus underlining its suitability for the newish X certificate which indicated that it provided entertainment of a kind intended for adults only. The television prints available in the eighties restore the original label, though quite clearly from the change of grading the title card has been cut in from the negative used in America, where the movie was called *The Creeping Unknown* and cut very little ice at the box office. The changes of title may seem a little surprising in view of the fact that Nigel Kneale's original television serial cleared the streets of Britain on six Wednesday evenings in 1954, and that made it a highly marketable commodity. Movie moguls, however, always found it unthinkable that they could learn anything from television, and anything they bought from that medium had to be disguised just in case patrons refused to pay for something which had previously been available free. Well, the judgement of posterity is always unpredictable. The three Quatermass movies were made on gradually increasing budgets, and the last of them became something of a cult, but it is the original television scripts which were published by Penguin Books and have been selling very steadily for a couple of decades. (The fourth serial, called

214

simply *Quatermass*, emerged in the late seventies and was a dreary affair, despite a high budget and the star appeal of John Mills.)

The Quatermass Experiment, with or without the 'e', survives still as late-night entertainment and as a triumph of impudence over very modest means. It has the lean, single-minded qualities of an original, and part of the fun lies in spotting how thoroughly its theme has been plundered during the intervening years by even less worthy films; which is fair enough, since the film itself borrowed shamelessly from older models such as *Frankenstein* and *Werewolf of London*. These were not the inspirations of the television serial: Nigel Kneale's script had a hard visionary quality which the film totally discarded. If indeed you watch the film while holding the serial script ready for comparison, the first thing you notice is the ruthless pruning, the elimination of philosophy and even of adequate motive. All are sacrificed to the demands of the 'X' certificate, though the result today would probably get away with a 'U', since Val Guest positively shies away from showing the nasty moments. The second thing you notice is that the very testy, very British professor, whose brain admits none but scientific thoughts and who was played on television by the likes of Reginald Tate and André Morell, is here personified by the Irish-American Brian Donlevy, who clearly wouldn't know a space module from a telephone kiosk. The reason is that he might sell a few tickets in Pocatello, Idaho, and what does it matter if he barks his commands and trots flatfootedly through the action like a New York cop?

No attempt is made to define Quatermass's field of research. The film opens with night scenes at Bray, not far from the Hammer Studios (coffee and buns but no pay for the local extras). The Quatermass rocket has come down unexpectedly in a field. The director thinks (inaccurately) that it is too dark for us to notice that the rocket is made of cardboard or to worry about the crudely painted hillside backdrop, since he is zooming in on a canoodling couple in an oddly floodlit haystack. It's a clear case of coitus interruptus, for they have seen the thing descend from the night sky, and so has the local fire service. Within minutes the professor himself is on hand announcing that 'for the first time in the history of mankind man has sent a rocket fifteen hundred miles into space'. A Ministry of Defence spokesman has also arrived, but can only murmur softly: 'You launched it without official sanction.' (Since Quatermass's staff appears to be minimal, one is driven to conclude that he lit the blue touch paper and retired behind a tree during blast-off.) Quatermass announces authoritatively that it will take hours for the rocket to cool; but the movie can't wait that long, so within minutes, after a few inaccurate shots with hosepipes, he opens the door by remote control, whereupon one of the space-suited astronauts crawls out and collapses. It is Victor Carroon, and he is alive. But when Quatermass investigates the interior, he finds the other two space suits empty, and not even properly belted for landing. Can the heroes have been turned by some unknown force into the strange jelly which fills every crevice in the space vehicle? And if so, why wasn't Carroon so affected? Answer, because said evil force is using him as a carrier. But I anticipate.

The survivor seems not quite himself. Just like shaking hands with a piece of

THE QUATERMASS EXPERIMENT. Richard Wordsworth, turning by the hour into a walking cactus, puts the evil eye on Toke Townley.

ice, someone comments. Besides, he not only shivers and groans a lot but has lost the power to talk. Scotland Yard must be called in, in the comfortable person of Jack Warner, who is as flat-footed as Donlevy and raises many a laugh when they waddle out of a scene together. 'I don't read science fiction,' he says, 'I'm a plain simple Bible man.' It is the film's only concession to thoughtfulness, and it is not pursued. The suggestion is made that poor Carroon, already wrinkling unpleasantly like a very old orange, should be moved from the Quatermass lab to a proper hospital. Our hero scoffs somewhat unscientifically: 'Would a hospital know what's going on out there – on the other side of the air?' Even for Carroon's grieving wife he has a reason and a justification. 'There's no room for personal feelings in science, Judith: some of us have a mission.'

At least he shows more common sense than she does, for when he is outvoted and Carroon is sent to Ward 4B, she hires a detective to impersonate a male nurse and bring him home. It is at this point that the chief plot gimmick, never adequately explained, takes hold. Carroon spots a potted cactus, and is instantly attracted to it. He smashes it with his fist, which thereupon grows spines (described but not shown) and becomes a weapon of instant death, draining all life from its victims and leaving them a mass of crumbling chalk. The private eye is the first to get it; the second an innocent chemist, played by Toke Townley in the film industry's most unconvincing wig. By now it is clear that Richard Wordsworth who plays the monster (and who once on the west end stage was a memorable Coupler in *The Relapse*) is the only good actor in the film, despite a total absence of lines. His impact is comparable with that of Karloff in the first *Frankenstein*; and, perhaps realizing this, Mr Guest segues into a few sidetracking scenes of him on the run, showing signs of becoming more monstrous by the minute. Like the Frankenstein monster (and the Golem before him) he meets up with an unscarable little girl who invites him to play with her. Like *The Mummy* he drags his bandages along behind him, so that they can be followed by the camera. Like *Werewolf of London* he hides in the zoo by night and terrifies all the animals. (It is not explained how he gets through the bars of their cages, but next morning several of them are found dead.) Before long he has totally metamorphosed into a sort of jellyfish, and leaves behind him a snail-like track which remains a foot wide no matter how he grows. In some unexplained way he can also crawl up walls, and takes refuge in the rafters of Westminster Abbey, only to be spotted by Sir Vernon Dodds in the course of a lecture being given live for the television cameras of the BBC. It remains only for Quatermass to electrocute and ignite the now many-tentacled being by closing down London's electricity generators and sending their collective load through the abbey girders. Why this does not incinerate the entire abbey is left to our imagination, but for the film's purposes it is effective enough: it kills off the monster. Quatermass does not even wait to see the flames extinguished. He strides purposefully out into the darkness, and the entertainment ends abruptly with the launch of another rocket.

It isn't a masterpiece of any kind. What it is is an object lesson in mini-budget movie-making, proof that if you want to win an audience you don't need a lot of money, only a certain kind of opportunistic skill. It shows too that even in 1955 what wowed a BBC audience was thought too subtle for filmgoers; for in the serial the monster is killed not by electricity but by the recorded voice of Carroon's fellow astronauts, urged on by Quatermass, inspiring that part of themselves which is still part of the Thing to kill it from within. Quite a concept; and no film-maker has yet borrowed that.

The Quatermass Experiment. GB 1955; black and white; 82 minutes. Produced by Anthony Hinds for Hammer-Concanen-Exclusive. Written by Val Guest and Richard Landau from the television serial by Nigel Kneale. Directed by Val Guest. Photographed by Walter Harvey. Music by James Bernard. With Brian Donlevy as Professor Quatermass; Jack Warner as Inspector Lomax; Margia Dean as Judith Carroon; Richard Wordsworth as Victor Carroon; David King Wood as Dr Briscoe; Thora Hird as Rosie; Gordon Jackson as the television producer; Howard Lang as Christie.

Happy in the Jungle
RED DUST

On a Malayan rubber plantation, the overseer is torn between two women.

The impression historians give of Metro–Goldwyn–Mayer films in their heyday is of imitation European elegance, with dramatic chances missed in movie after movie because of the supposed need to refine and edit so as to exist on the highest level of good taste. It is therefore all the more to the credit of *Red Dust* that it is entirely lacking in good taste and has the feel throughout of a hard-hitting Warner melodrama. Most of the MGM films seem to be the product of a committee, with Irving Thalberg in the chair; *Red Dust* is clearly the work of one man, John Lee Mahin, whose script was niftily filmed by Jack Conway without any wasted minutes. Probably none of the studio heads thought well of it during production; but it made superstars of its two leads as well as drawing memorable performances from at least four other players. It is also remarkable for the amount of steamy sex one could get into a movie in pre-Legion of Decency days, without anybody having to appear in the buff or even in bed together. And it is fun from beginning to end, even fifty-odd years after it was made.

Whatever the precise significance of the title, somebody forgot to mention it in the movie, which begins with a shot of rubber draining from a tree into a bucket labelled North Cochin China Rubber Company. Within seconds, it seems, we have established Clark Gable as a virile plantation owner, tough with his coolies, demanding of his colleagues, and unsparing of himself. On returning to his primitive ranch house after a hard day he is displeased to find that the infrequent river boat has deposited on his landing a hard-as-nails young woman who makes no bones about herself or her motives: 'I got mixed up in a little trouble and I thought I'd stay out of town till the gendarmes forget about it.' Though she calls herself Pollyanna the glad girl, Fantine as played by Jean Harlow is clearly a prostitute who is prepared to pay for her board and lodging in kind. Gable's number two, a wise old bird played by Tully Marshall, tells him as they trek through the damp jungle that he ought to give the new arrival a tumble. 'You been smelling rubber and sweating to get it and you'll die that way.' Gable nods thoughtfully: 'Yeah, just so some old woman can take a hot water bottle to bed with her.' 'Yeah,' says Marshall, 'and so some baby can suck on a rubber nipple.' Gable is neither impressed nor inspired, and he decides too that he can do without Fantine's attractions: 'I been lookin' at her sort since my voice changed.'

But he proves not entirely immune to her well-used charms, especially when she walks into his room in a cloud of cheap satin and perfume. She can't sleep, she says: 'Not with that alley cat squawling out there. I'm not used to sleeping nights anyway.' For the sake of good discipline Gable manages to restrain himself, as in his turn does old Mr Marshall, who when asked by Fantine

RED DUST. The final moment of melodrama: Clark Gable, Gene Raymond, Jean Harlow, Mary Astor.

doesn't he know any games, replies: 'If this was the summer of 1894 I'd play games with you, sister. But life's much simpler now.' On the night before Harlow is placed firmly on the return boat, when it can't do much harm, Gable does succumb, but by now Harlow is in love with him and is offended to be offered money. 'It wasn't like that,' she says. Okay, answers Gable, he'll look her up in Singapore sometime.

Though we suspect we can't have seen the last of Harlow, she is temporarily replaced from the same boat by Gable's new assistant and his lady wife, to whom Gable takes an instant shine, and who can blame him as she's played by Mary Astor. 'My room,' he tells her, 'is that first one off the porch, if you should need me during the night.' This is not quite the proposition it might seem, as her callow young husband (Gene Raymond) has come off the boat with fever, and while he recovers there is plenty of time for illicit romance to bloom. But Harlow returns, her boat having been stranded on a mud bank, and she sizes up the situation the moment Gable enters as she has never seen him before: 'My, my, all shaved and dressed up fancy!' Gable's good behaviour, however, is reserved for Astor; when he retires and finds Harlow in his bed he gets rid of her very simply by starting to take his pants off in her presence, flinging them at her as she leaves the room. His main concern is that she should not let him down in front of Astor, such as by taking a bath in a rain barrel without letting down the blinds. 'Afraid I'll shock the duchess?' asks Harlow. 'Don't you suppose she's ever seen a French postcard?'

'That Fantine,' asks Astor later, very casually, 'is she a part of the life here?' 'Oh, very definitely,' Gable assures her equivocally, 'if a man wanted to be interested.' Astor is sufficiently encouraged to make her play:

BARBARA: Do you think *I* could be happy here?
CARSON: Do you mind if I make it my job to see that you are?

He does this by carrying her home during a tropical storm, all wet jodhpurs and heavy breathing, and we are left in no doubt that the relationship is consummated. Harlow, seeing him departing from the lady's room, yells after him: 'Be careful the rain doesn't wash the rouge off your mouth.' Next day Astor is apologetic to Harlow, as between girls: 'I don't know how it happened. I didn't do anything.' Harlow is cynical: 'I didn't hear you cry for help.'

Next day Raymond, recovered and eager, is sent out with the coolies for a month's surveying in a swamp infested by tigers. (One has heard of commanders in World War I finding comparable missions for men with attractive wives.) He's happy about the work but apprehensive about the coolies: 'The minute you turn your back they're trying to pull the wool over your eyes.' Three people exchange furtive glances of amusement at this. Despite Harlow's wisecracks the affair develops, and one day Gable takes it upon himself to journey out through a monsoon and reveal all to the unfortunate young man. Instead he sits in a tree with him and helps him shoot a tiger, then makes the six-hour trek back to tell the pulsating Astor that he can't do the dirty on her noble husband. 'I've deceived you,' he says. 'I'm not a one-woman man and I never have been. So if you want to take your turn . . .' She shoots him instead. Not seriously, just badly enough for Harlow to have some grisly fun cleaning up the wound. Raymond and Astor depart, sadder and wiser, having learned a little about this clammy land where men are men and woman are glad of it. And Harlow is left reading to the convalescent Gable, who has finally realized that she's the girl for him. The only reading matter is a children's book about Little Cottontail. 'A chipmunk and a rabbit,' she says incredulously. 'I wonder how that came out?'

Since the original play is credited to the author of the turgid *White Cargo*, which in structure it closely resembles, there is little to doubt that it began as a pretty starchy piece of work, which is why Mahin gets my vote as the only begetter of the raciest piece of big studio entertainment that ever ducked past the Hays Office. And it really did, despite Harlow's next film *Bombshell*, in which she plays an MGM movie star who has to return from her vacation to redo the bathtub scene from *Red Dust*. ('It seems the Hays Office censored something.') Though overlong, *Bombshell* is a fun picture, especially for addicts of studio in-jokes. 'Even Norma Shearer and Helen Hayes in their nicest pictures were never spoken to like that,' Harlow declares at one point;

and she is asked to report to the set in the 'white blouse and no brassiere' which was Harlow's own favourite attire. She gives an immensely likeable performance as the object of everyone else's dreams who is wakened at 6 A.M. from her own. ('Whaddya do that for? Something kinda cute was about to happen.') She is sorely tried by her staff and her sponging family, and it is Franchot Tone as an impossibly stuffy Bostonian who eventually gets the full force of her wrath: 'You can take your Bunker Hills and your bloodlines and stuff a codfish with 'em. And then you know what you can do with the codfish.'

If the style of invective sounds familiar . . . well, the co-writer was John Lee Mahin.

Red Dust. US 1932; black and white; 83 minutes. Produced by MGM. Written by John Lee Mahin from the play by Wilson Collison. Directed by Victor Fleming. Photographed by Harold Rosson. With Clark Gable as Dennis Carson; Jean Harlow as Fantine; Mary Astor as Barbara Willis; Gene Raymond as Gary Willis; Donald Crisp as Guidon; Tully Marshall as McQuarg.

Who Says Crime Doesn't Pay?

ROXIE HART

A twenties showgirl confesses to murder for the sake of the publicity.

Satire having been often defined by showbiz as 'what closes Saturday night', it is surprising how many attempts at the genre Hollywood has made. When *Roxie Hart* first appeared in the middle of World War II, nostalgia for a time when the people behind the guns were not Nazis may have had something to do with its popularity. It was in fact welcomed by most critics as on a par with the same director's *Nothing Sacred* (qv), which five years earlier had taken an equally sharp crack at newspapermen who will do anything for a story. *Roxie Hart* starts with all barrels blazing, and one still can't deny its amplitude of good lines and good moments. The trouble seems to be that they are just that: they don't in any way further the plot or the characterization, and by the time we get to the big courtoom scene, agreeably crazy as it is, the movie has quite simply run out of steam.

The need to apologize for America's naughty past may have something to do with it, for the impression given is that it couldn't happen today, that Chicago in 1942 is a lily-white city. This belief is scarcely borne out by the barrage of headlines with which the film begins:

NOT GUILTY VERDICT IN TRIAL OF BLONDE
WHO SHOT FRIEND SIX TIMES ACCIDENTALLY

HE REFUSED TO TAKE ME TO SEE VICTOR MATURE
CLAIMS WOMAN ON TRIAL FOR LIFE

NO RECOLLECTION OF PICKING UP AXE,
JILTED GIRL TESTIFIES

CROWD CHEERS AS JURY CLEARS REDHEAD OF DRIVING
CAR OVER ELECTRIC REFRIGERATOR SALESMAN

If you are a theatregoer and these lines seem vaguely familiar it may be because they were worked into one of the lyrics of *Chicago*, the seventies musical version of *Roxie Hart*. And that may be why the original *Roxie*, or at least the original talking *Roxie* (there was a silent version in 1928), now seems flatter than it did. One waits in vain for Billy Flynn to sing 'Razzle Dazzle,' for Amos Hart to appear as Mr Cellophane, for Roxie and Velma to tell us about class; but the inspiration for all these songs is to be found in the script, if only as faint hints of what they became. I can't listen now to Roxie's testimony about both grabbing for the gun without hearing the superlative precision of the chorus which belted it out on the Broadway stage.

For a seventy-three-minute film it takes quite a while to get through the present-day prologue into the flashback, which sets out the justification for the film's dedication 'to all the beautiful women in the world who have shot their men full of holes out of pique'. In a semi-tenement a man has been shot in Roxie's flat. Her husband is taking the blame: he thought the man was a burglar. But it transpires that the intruder was a theatrical agent present at Roxie's invitation while hubby was out. 'Let us say,' muses the dead man's partner, 'that Mrs Hart was ambitious – and a female.' 'A coquette?' asks a reporter. 'The word is nicely chosen.' This spurs hubby to tell the truth: she shot the man herself because he spurned her and thought it would sound better if the man took the blame. Such treachery causes the indignant Roxie to kick her way out of the cupboard where she has been hiding. 'Take it easy, honey,' says the cynical reporter as a shapely leg emerges, 'you don't want to damage your defence.' It seems that they have never yet hung a woman in Cook County, and the idea begins to bubble in Roxie's brain that she will confess to the truth for the sake of the publicity. All she needs is a crooked lawyer, and 'the streets of the city are congested with women whom Billy Flynn has saved from their just deserts.' Lynne Overman and Nigel Bruce, as reporter and seedy agent, tell her in an excited duologue: 'You'll be right up there with Peaches Browning, William Jennings Bryan, Queen Marie, Ma Ferguson, Mutt and Jeff, Red Grange, Ruth Snyder, Aimee Semple McPherson and Barney Google. Don't you realize, this is Chicago, the city of opportunity! And that city only awaits one word from you to be at your feet.'

The promise holds good for a while. In jail Roxie easily conquers another murderess who is fading from the limelight, even though the matron conquers them both by banging their heads together and leaving them in a heap on the floor. ('You girls have got to stop this squabbling.') Amos finds it easy to hire Billy Flynn, so long as the greenbacks keep coming. As the mouthpiece says testily: 'When you brought me this case, did I ask is she innocent or is she guilty? No. All I said was, have you got 5000 dollars?'

For weeks the women's jail is the centre of newspaper attention, with Roxie obligingly performing the Black Bottom for the photographers. But fashion changes, and in comes Two-Gun Gertie, on whom the spotlights are suddenly trained. 'Would you tell us, Miss Baxter,' coos Little Mary Sunshine the sob sister, 'how you happened to take up banditry? Was it an inferiority complex or would you call yourself a thrill slayer?' Roxie finds it hard to keep the attention even of the reporter who got her into the fix. 'Hey,' she tells him hopefully, 'I'm thinking of going on a hunger strike.' He waves back cheerily. 'Happy hiccups, kid.' Just one tenderfoot scribe, the one we met in the prologue, tells Roxie that justice will prevail since he is sure she is innocent. 'It's sweet of you to say that,' she nods, on the principle of never discarding a potentially useful contact, 'but if you print it I'll wrap a chair round your neck.'

Although Roxie doesn't see it, it seems that she is in some danger from reformers who want equal hanging rights for women. More money must be fuelled into Billy Flynn. Roxie's farmer father, somewhere out in middle

America, is appealed to but says no. He puts down the phone and shambles out to the porch where Ma is placidly knitting. 'They're going to hang Roxie,' he mutters as he sinks into his chair. And in the film's most famous line, Ma replies: 'What did I tell you?'

No movie could top that, and *Roxie Hart* doesn't. The courtoom scene is frenzied enough, with the judge making sure he appears in each and every flash photograph, but the device is overdone of having Roxie win by catching the eye of the foreman of the jury, especially when he turns out to be the disgruntled bartender to whom the story is being told by our innocent young reporter (now not so), who having told it dashes through the rain to be driven home by his wife (guess who). And if you want to know how in the middle of Hollywood's most censor-ridden age Roxie was allowed to get away with murder, the reaction must be sheer bewilderment, unless Ginger Rogers was then so popular that she could get away with anything. In this film her only comeuppance is that the car is packed with children, and all she has to say to Daddy is that they're going to need a bigger car next year. Chicago must have been full of good Catholics.

Roxie Hart. US 1942; black and white; 73 minutes. Produced by Nunnally Johnson for Twentieth Century-Fox. Written by Nunnally Johnson from a play by Maurine Watkins. Directed by William Wellman. Photographed by Leon Shamroy. Music by Alfred Newman. With Ginger Rogers as Roxie; Adolphe Menjou as Billy Flynn; George Montgomery as Walter Howard; William Frawley as O'Malley, the bartender; George Chandler as Amos Hart; Nigel Bruce as Benham; Lynne Overman as Callahan; Spring Byington as Little Mary Sunshine; Iris Adrian as Two-Gun Gertie; Phil Silvers as Babe; Sara Allgood as Wardress.

The Sad Song of J. Alfred Hitchcock
SABOTAGE

The proprietor of a small London cinema is a professional saboteur.

The reputation of this Hitchcock melodrama has suffered to some extent because of critical confusion as to exactly which film it is. Don't take it for *Saboteur*, which is Hitch's rather clumsy American retread of *The Thirty-Nine Steps*, made in 1942, in America for propaganda purposes, and leading sluggishly to the famous climax atop the Statue of Liberty. Nor, although it is based on a book called *The Secret Agent*, is it *The Secret Agent*: that's Hitch's 1936 British film based on Somerset Maugham's semi-autobiographical spy story *Ashenden*, with Peter Lorre as a sinister Mexican. No, *Sabotage* is the 1936 British film known in America as *A Woman Alone* (which, if a title change were needed, is certainly no improvement). And although probably nobody would name it as a favourite Hitchcock film, because of a central error in plotting which will be noted later, it is certainly to be counted among his most concentrated in atmosphere and cinematic in technique.

It is a film redolent of London. Not the real London, for Hitch built at Islington Studios a massive street set complete with trams and markets and traffic lights, but the imagined London of Max Miller and Gordon Harker and J. B. Priestley's *Angel Pavement*. In this film the background is the real star, with its constant rumbling of activity and its half-heard mutterings from passers-by: the actors are all perceived as part of this background, into which at the end they all seem to merge. In the entire Hitchcock canon *Sabotage* comes closest to the Russian and German styles which he so admired, for every incident of the story is told visually and there are long stretches without dialogue. Several minutes pass before the first spoken line. Behind the opening title is a dictionary definition of sabotage: 'A wilful destruction of buildings or machinery with the object of alarming a group of persons or inspiring public uneasiness.' The first image is of a lightbulb flickering, immediately prior to a total London blackout. Official heads crane forward as, in half-darkness, sand is discovered in an electric generator. Sand! Sabotage! Who did it? Next a shot of our chubby villain, Oscar Homolka, finding his way back in the dark to the busy suburban street which is his place of business as well as his home, for he lives behind the little cinema which he and his wife operate. Outside by gas flares the fruit and meat vendors are still in full cry, which helps him to get in unobserved by the back way. He pulls at the light switch, then smiles to himself. When his wife finds him he appears to have been asleep for some time, but we have seen the sand swirl from his hands as he washed them at the kitchen sink. 'What am I to do?' she wants to know, 'The patrons are clamouring for their money back.' 'Give it back,' he murmurs with playful irony, 'it doesn't pay to antagonize the public.'

The crowd in the foyer is getting nasty with the box office lady. 'I paid for my seat.' 'Yes, and what about the one you put your feet on?' Mrs Verloc comes out with permission to refund, and is immediately swamped; the handsome greengrocer's assistant from next door comes across to help her, clearly smitten. Hitchcock, having procured Sylvia Sidney from Hollywood to play Mrs Verloc, wanted Robert Donat for her swain with a cabbage in each hand, but for various reasons what he got was the amiable but dull John Loder. In particular, his cockney accent is so unconvincing that we instantly conclude, long before Hitch intends us to do so, that he is not at all what he seems, and so we are not in the least surprised when he leaves work and goes straight to Scotland Yard. The Yard is on to Verloc already (so why didn't they stop him tonight?). He isn't thought of as a bad man, only as an explosives expert who needs the money, and who will, they hope, lead Whitehall to the men at the top. Mrs Verloc and her young brother are certainly among the world's innocents, and their heavily built lady housekeeper, though last seen as the sinister organist in *The Man Who Knew Too Much*, is guilty in this picture of nothing more heinous than overboiling the greens.

Verloc seems to take no great interest in the running of the cinema, but next morning he announces himself as being off to a trade show. 'Make it a good one with plenty of murders,' says an acquaintance. Verloc's destination is in fact the Regent's Park Zoo aquarium, an ideal location for a director with Hitchcock's eye: the saboteur receives his orders from an aristocratic foreign agent against a background of swimming sharks and fleshy rays. As their plot thickens, so does the counterpoint of light relief from passers-by:

> What's the bubbles for, dad, have the fish got hiccups?
> – You'd have hiccups if you had to live on ants' eggs.

We don't hear Verloc's orders but we do hear him protesting: 'I'm not going to be associated with anything that involves loss of life.' But he is helpless in the clutches of his superiors. An outrage is planned for Saturday next, the day of the Lord Mayor's Show, and he must confer with the gang's master bomb-maker, a nervous, balding old man who lives behind a bird shop in rooms over-run by pets and children. Meanwhile our hero has abandoned his cabbages and blown his cover: he is recognized by members of the gang when he takes Mrs Verloc and her brother to lunch at Simpson's in the Strand. Then back at the cinema, while snooping, he practically falls into the middle of a group of plotters. The result of all this is that when the time bomb is delivered, Verloc is afraid to place it himself, and so disguises it in film cans ('Bartholomew the Strangler') and sends his wife's young brother across London with it by bus.

This is the bravura suspense sequence which Hitchcock later considered to be the greatest mistake of his career. The boy is told he must deliver the cans by 1.30. We know that the bomb will explode at 1.45. There should be no problem, Verloc thinks; but the boy is detained, chiefly by the Lord Mayor's Show itself, and when we reach the fatal time (it is brilliantly mirrored in a montage by traffic lights changing and clock hammers about to strike) he is still sitting on a bus making friends with a delightful puppy. Perhaps Hitch might have got away with it if the puppy at least had been saved? But no, the conception is wrong, for the nature of a story is to provide twists of plot, and after so many shots of the bomb on the seat beside the boy, the audience has to be expecting that something would happen to save him: there is simply no surprise when he is killed, only a dull sensation at the pit of the stomach. Alas, that is the plot Hitch is stuck with, its final interest lying in what the sister will do when she hears the tragic news. And what happens is that after the shock has worn off she realizes what her husband has been guilty of, and accuses him. He is sheepish, to say the least, but makes the mistake of reasoning out his actions, and finally suggests, rather absurdly, that they get on with dinner. She makes the preparations in a daze; then on her way through the cinema she briefly watches a Walt Disney cartoon, 'Who Killed Cock Robin?' And when she gets back into her little flat, she can't take her eyes off the carving knife. (Yes, Hitch is working up for a knife scene to top the one in *Blackmail*.) The scene is brilliantly constructed in sharp cuts, as though to suggest almost that the knife leaps into her hand and Verloc walks on to it: it is

SABOTAGE. Make the background work, was a Hitchcock maxim. And this scene shot in an aquarium emphasizes the sinister quality of villains Austin Trevor and Oscar Homolka.

a masterpiece of direction and editing. But as we see him lying dead, we wonder must the heroine pay for this crime? She staggers out into the arms of the hero, who tries to dissuade her from going to the police. And behold, there is no need, for the bird shop man, hearing that the police are on to Verloc, hurries over to collect another bomb which the expert has constructed within a bird cage. He finds himself surrounded and blows up the building, so that all the police can find in the way of evidence is his body next to Verloc's, as though the villains fell out and caused each other's deaths. Authority is left with only the slightest unprovable suspicion that everything is not what it seems.

The audience is left with an unsatisfactory entertainment but a brilliant technical exercise. There are fine moments of silent acting from Sidney and Homolka, and a number of uncredited cameos from faces which later became familiar: Martita Hunt, Charles Hawtrey, Peter Bull, Torin Thatcher, and so on. A pity that Loder was out of his class; but Hitch was often unlucky with casting, at least in the case of the films which need excuses.

Sabotage (US title: *A Woman Alone*). GB 1936; black and white; 76 minutes. Produced by Michael Balcon and Ivor Montagu for Gaumont British. Written by Charles Bennett, from the novel *The Secret Agent* by Joseph Conrad. Directed by Alfred Hitchcock. Photographed by Bernard Knowles. Music by Louis Levy. With Oscar Homolka as Verloc; Sylvia Sidney as Mrs Verloc; Desmond Tester as Mrs Verloc's brother; John Loder as Ted; Matthew Boulton as the superintendent.

American Dreamer

THE SECRET LIFE OF WALTER MITTY

A mother's boy dreams of derring-do, and eventually life catches up.

I was dismissive of this once-celebrated comedy on an earlier occasion, and each time it turns up on television I am conscious as it progresses of a sad falling off in its level of wit, which was not high in the first place. Nevertheless, there remains vivid in my memory the impression of a wet Saturday afternoon in Portsmouth in 1948 when, thoroughly disenchanted with the army, I fixed my sights on a good laugh and queued to see *Mitty* for over an hour outside the North End Odeon, only to find when I reached my seat in the back stalls that the distant screen was invisible through the steam rising from a thousand wet mackintoshes. The sightlines cleared, more or less, in time for the feature to start, and rarely can I have come so close to being deafened by laughter. It is true that Danny Kaye was then immensely fashionable in England, the idol of the London Palladium and the buddy of Bernard Shaw. It is equally true that in those austerity years the English would applaud almost any glamorous American movie, if only to take their minds off the endless queues and the empty shops, *Mitty* was welcome partly because the Goldwyn Girls could be seen lingering in the background in a succession of expensive though not very elegant costumes. But it still seems odd for a film to have dated so badly that we are now chiefly conscious of its faults when once we saw nothing but its virtues.

My own regrets are lodged chiefly in a sense of missed opportunity. It is well known that what Goldwyn and his script writers did to James Thurber's original story did not endear them to the short-sighted and short-tempered author, who left Hollywood muttering that the resultant film was 'more like the public life of Danny Kaye'. In fact as it originally stood the story would have been unfilmable, no more than a sketch about a mild little man whose daydreams are greater than his life. What the film does is to plunge its little man into an absurd real-life melodrama while expanding each of the daydreams into million-dollar production numbers, two of them with irrelevant patter songs to pad out the action to marathon length. All this might not have mattered if the action had had some spring to it, but the mood throughout is unsubtle to the point of vulgarity, which was in tune with late forties America and is underlined by the garish colour which sometimes looks as though you could scrape it off the screen. An eagerly awaited player like Boris Karloff is wasted as a villain who is not even in charge: after a fumbled first appearance in Mitty's office, we have to wait until the film is ninety minutes old before he is allowed to preside over a mildly amusing psychiatrist sketch, after which the story peters out in a knockabout finale.

Perhaps the key to the fading fortunes of this film is that Danny Kaye's own talent, which then shimmered so brightly, now looks decidedly overblown; in the eighties, when the fashion in humour is for the crude and insulting, a little of his gesticulating gibberish goes a long way. Still, he was always a performer of precision, and we instantly feel for him in the early scenes as he is leaned on by his selfish mother. 'Take a taxi from the station,' she tells him. 'Never mind the expense, I'll stop it from your allowance.' They live in Perth Amboy, and his irrepressible daydreams are doubtless a reaction to her endless prattling. On the way to the station a poster for Sea Drift Soap Chips is enough to send him off into a windblown fantasy in which he is the valiant skipper of a stricken vessel during a storm at sea, with hurricanes threatening and 'the straining pumps going topocka topocka topocka'. A sodden but still glamorous blonde implores him to leave the wheel:

> Captain Mitty, you're hurt.
> It's nothing, just a broken arm.

Mitty works as proofreader for the Pearce Publishing Company, which subsists on sensational magazines. As he enters the office he pauses to hear an artist musing on his design for a new cover: 'It's a bit mild, I think I ought to tear the dress off her other shoulder.' Mitty shrugs and points: 'You could use a little more blood on the axe.' Soon there is a heads-of-department conference at which the shameless Mr Pearce steals Mitty's idea for a new magazine called *Hospital Romances*. Mitty doesn't mind: he is off on another dream adventure with himself cast as Mitty the great surgeon, mending the great anaesthetizing machine – which of course goes topocka topocka topocka – with a propelling pencil, a repair which in his view 'will hold for ten minutes', just enough time. He dons the rubber gloves and proceeds to operate, though his demands for instruments somehow get mixed up with his mother's errands: 'Scalpel. Sock stretcher. Sprinkling can. Cheese grater. Floor wax. Needle and number two threads.' But soon the ordeal is over and he is again comforting the same glamorous blonde: 'There, there, Miss Cartwright. Your brother will play the violin again. I just sewed new fingers on him.'

The next daydream has him as a British air ace (with perfect enunciation), oblivious to the topocka topocka topocka of his failing engine. This time, having been congratulated by his commander (Reginald Denny precisely cast in a tiny role) he rather curiously pauses in a middle eastern café to give an impersonation of a European professor doing a comic song. (Nice to hear Kaye's musical fooling, but it rather cuts across the RAF joke.) Anything is preferable in Mitty's eyes – he has been sent to see to the furnace – to going

THE SECRET LIFE OF WALTER MITTY. Danny Kaye seems to sense the presence of Boris Karloff, but neither of them senses the humour of the situation.

back upstairs and facing his mother-in-law-to-be (the formidable Florence Bates) and her equally gorgon-like daughter, who keeps telling Mitty how many other young men have recently proposed to her. By now the writers are running out of absent-minded jokes, falling-over jokes and dream jokes, which is the signal for the plot proper to begin. (Lew Grade, when he was running ATV, once had the audacity to begin a transmission at this point, claiming that the story was easier to understand that way.) The mood is signalled by Mr Pearce in a second story conference: 'In the last issue Lord Cecil was only stabbed once. We've never stinted our readers in things like that. Have him stabbed front, and back, and side – and save the heart for last!'

Mitty's waking life is now astonishingly penetrated by the girl of his dreams, played by Virginia Mayo in a series of hideous hats, all totally encased within their period. She is innocently involved in some dastardly plot to do with the Dutch crown jewels; her smiling Uncle Peter is really the villainous Boot, and his aged friend (played by Frank Reicher, the captain from *King Kong*) has no sooner stepped off the boat than he is silently knifed by an actor from a file marked Villains, lean, unsmiling, moustached. Somehow the incriminating black book gets slipped into our hero's briefcase, and the pace quickens as the villains trail Mitty; while Mitty, discovering what they're after, keeps on hiding it and then having trouble recovering it. There is a good scene when he tracks a department store delivery van to a suburban home and then asks the burly householder who answers the bell: 'Do you mind if I look in your wife's corset?' But most of the shenanigans make little comedy sense, and least of all a scene in which Miss Mayo, on the run during a midnight thunderstorm, breaks into Mitty's cellar for protection and dries her dress before the kitchen stove, while the three grotesque Mitty females are in bed upstairs. It's a long run indeed to the splendid moment when Karloff, by the use of a little trickery, persuades our hero that he is mad enough to see women in their underwear even when they are fully dressed. When Mitty makes a confused exit it is to find that he can apparently apply the same technique to the picture of Whistler's mother in the hallway.

The Secret Life of Walter Mitty. US 1947; Technicolor; 110 minutes. Produced by Samuel Goldwyn. Written by Ken Englund and Everett Freeman from the story by James Thurber. Directed by Norman Z. McLeod. Photographed by Lee Garmes. Music by David Raksin. Songs by Sylvia Fine. With Danny Kaye as Walter Mitty; Virginia Mayo as Rosalind Van Hoorn; Boris Karloff as Dr Hugo Hollingshead; Thurston Hall as Bruce Pierce; Fay Bainter as Mrs Mitty; Ann Rutherford as Gertrude Griswold; Florence Bates as Mrs Griswold; Gordon Jones as Tubby Wadsworth; Konstantin Shayne as Peter Van Hoorn.

Freudian Gym Slip

THE SEVENTH VEIL

A concert pianist is torn between three men.

It was very much a film of its time, a combination of tolerably fresh elements which, taken at the flood, led on to fortune. James Mason, after ten years in the acting hinterlands, had been a box office sensation in *The Man in Grey* and *The Wicked Lady*, and it was agreed by all concerned that another opportunity for him to be the man everybody loved to hate would not come amiss. During the war classical music, like Sybil Thorndike in *The Trojan Women*, had risen to undreamed-of heights of popularity, and several films had already thrived on the fact, providing of course that the excerpts were tuneful and not too long: *A Song to Remember*, for instance, was Hollywood's current box office smash, driving misconceptions about the life of Chopin into the minds of untold millions who could not even pronounce his name. In the same year, Alfred Hitchcock in a film called *Spellbound* was making a huge romantic success out of a combination of psychiatry, mystery and romance.

231

All these elements came to fruition in *The Seventh Veil*, which also contrived to create a brand new star in the shape of Ann Todd, who like Mason had been in films for ten years and more without finding a role to suit her image, apart from a scene or two in *South Riding* as the mad wife who rides horses up the staircase. As popular films go, the new success was open to a lot of criticism and even scorn, but after six years of total war it was just what the public wanted. Everyone in it was rich. All the settings were elegant. And the distressed heroine finally clawed her weary way to the happiest of endings, if you call it a good idea to be married to a brooding megalomaniac. Astute observers of literary relationships might have commented that the story drew substantially on two enormously popular Victorian models: *Trilby*, about a young girl who can sing only when in the grip of a malevolent hypnotist, and *Jane Eyre*, about a timid girl in love with a sophisticated older man whose true personality is cloaked in mystery. The result of all these trends was a film which caused immense queues throughout the country. Even ten years later when it first played on television, it so emptied the cinemas as to provoke the formation by exhibitors of the Film Industry Defence Organization to keep films off television altogether.

A point which particularly enthused the industry was that *The Seventh Veil* had managed to beat Hollywood at its own game. Avoiding the understatement and low-key action so common to British films, it had a lush pictorial style, rapid editing, and a script unencumbered by any irrelevant details which might detract from the man/woman relationship at its core. The dialogue may be simplistic, the events contrived, and the production more economical than a first glance might suggest, but Orson Welles and Bette Davis would probably have given their eye-teeth to play Nicholas and Francesca because they are stereotypes as fresh and memorable forty years later as they were on the day when *The Seventh Veil* was first launched. Even I, who at sixteen probably claimed that it was not my kind of film at all, must have been more influenced than I cared to admit, for when I needed a pseudonym for my budding journalistic efforts Nicholas was part of it, while Francesca was the self-named heroine of a curiously memorable romantic dream which I experienced at about that time.

The film begins beguilingly. At night, a girl wakes up in a hospital bed, slips on a dressing gown, runs out of the building and throws herself from a bridge into the Thames. She is attended thereafter by what the film quaintly calls a hypnologist, Dr Larsen, played by Herbert Lom in an unlikely variety of hairstyles, all false. (The role almost certainly landed the soft-spoken, romantically foreign actor the star role in the subsequently popular television series *The Human Jungle*, for he is the psychiatrist on whose couch every female patient would wish to lie.) The bedside scenes are merely a flashback device so that the heroine, under sedation, can tell her story, with the benevolent Mr Lom zooming in and out of focus according to whether she is awake or asleep. Quite promptly and helpfully, he gives the film its title in an aside to an onlooker: 'The human mind is like Salome at the beginning of her dance. Salome, hidden from the world by seven veils. Veils of reserve,

THE SEVENTH VEIL. Ann Todd has her first inauspicious meeting with Uncle Nicholas (James Mason).

shyness, fear. With friends, the average person will drop first one veil, then another . . . maybe three or four altogether. With a lover she will take off five or even six. But never the seventh. Never.' This bunkum has little enough relevance to the plot, for with one minor exception Francesca tells all at first go. If there is a seventh veil in her mind it seems designed to keep covered the rather obvious fact that between her and Nicholas there exists a potentially nasty sado-masochistic love-hate relationship, which for obvious reasons the film does not delve into, beyond showing him rapping her knuckles with his cane so that she can't play the piano for anyone if she won't play it for him. Nor does it linger on the wisdom or otherwise of marrying your father's second cousin; but presumably worse things happened at sea, even in 1945.

Francesca is an orphan who has to live with Nicholas, her only relation, when she is unjustly expelled from school at the age of fourteen. He lives in a vast London mansion, which must be very draughty since nobody ever seems to close a door in it; and these days he would be a suspect homosexual rather than a macho figure. We are told very little about him except that he is moody, rich and hates his mother for having gone off with another fellow.

Every object about him has been selfishly chosen for its beauty or its intrinsic worth, so naturally he resents having to look after a gawky schoolgirl: 'This is a bachelor establishment. It means that I don't like women about the place. I promised myself that no woman should ever enter it.' He also adores cats (as Mason did in real life) and is even less friendly to Francesca when she says that they scare her.

Nicholas has had twelve years of this kind of life, and it changes only when he hears Francesca play the piano. He then devotes the next several years to making a great pianist of her. (Montage of applauding hands, concert programmes, keyboards.) Alas, along the way she falls for a Canadian clarinettist who plays in nightclubs. When she comes home and likes to play 'suburban shopgirl trash' Nicholas begins to suspect, and promptly locks her in so that she can't even say goodbye to Peter when she sets off on a long tour of Europe. Oddly enough, she seems to expect that when she finally returns Peter will still be waiting, even though she hasn't been able to send him so much as a postcard. He isn't waiting, so on the rebound she reluctantly falls for Max, the artist whom Nicholas has hired to paint her portrait; when she insists that she is determined on a life without love, Max murmurs suavely that without love one might as well be dead. This remark results in her giving in rather suddenly and barging into a row with Nicholas, who points out proudly that through all his years of self-sacrifice he has made no personal demands upon her. The unlucky girl, now beaten soundly for her honesty, escapes with Max and is driven straight into a road accident. What spurs her to suicide is fear that her injured hands will never play the piano again; but Dr Larsen believes that underneath is torment because she can't decide between the three men in her life (Peter being divorced and eager again). He calls them all together in the home of the now contrite Nicholas. Upstairs the patient lies in bed listening to a recording of a tune which had once meant a great deal to her and to Peter. One must assume that the playing of it has the effect of sweeping him from her mind and releasing her inhibitions, for within seconds she is at the piano performing the Sonata Pathetique, and Dr Larsen is at the stairhead informing his audience that they must prepare themselves for a new Francesca: 'The past for her is quite, quite over. Her mind is clear and the clouds have been swept away, and she is no longer afraid. She will want to be with the one she loves . . . or the one she has been happiest with . . . or the one she trusts.' Not hearing himself mentioned, Nicholas limps away into the library; but right on cue the music stops, and Francesca floats downstairs and runs to him as the door closes behind them. All this, and Eileen Joyce on the soundtrack too.

The Seventh Veil. GB 1945; black and white; 84 minutes. Produced by Sydney Box. Written by Muriel and Sydney Box. Directed by Compton Bennett. Photographed by Reginald H. Wyer. Music by Benjamin Frankel. With James Mason as Nicholas; Ann Todd as Francesca; Herbert Lom as Dr Larsen; Hugh McDermott as Peter; Albert Lieven as Maxwell Leyden; Yvonne Owen as Susan.

234

THE SHOP AROUND THE CORNER

In a Budapest gift shop, two assistants who dislike each other discover that they are pen pals.

This delightful comedy has been almost forgotten, even by Lubitsch's biographers. Perhaps they feel that it doesn't have the Lubitsch touch, that sly way of telling a risqué story by inserts of feet running upstairs, doorknobs turning, lights going out, and so on. That worked sensationally well in the likes of *Trouble in Paradise*, but towards the end of the thirties another Lubitsch was clearly struggling to get out, one which placed more reliance on first-rate actors doing their best with first-rate dialogue. This Lubitsch is well to the fore in *Ninotchka*. In his next film, *The Shop around the Corner*, though it is made with full awareness of all the production values possible at MGM, he concentrates on a small cast, on a minimum of sets, and on always having his camera in the right place at the right time. It makes a refreshing change even though it is not what one expects. One might almost call it a photographed play – as it stands, it would transfer with great ease to the stage – did we not have the word of the author, Samson Raphaelson, that of the original Hungarian play not one scene and not one line remain.

Although the story happens in Budapest, the signs are in Hungarian and the currency is the pengo, it could have been set anywhere in Europe, even in England, though in that case one would not expect the characters to be so witty. America is outside its gentle range, as was shown by the brash musical remake of ten years later: *In the Good Old Summertime* starred Judy Garland and Van Johnson, and although the plot still worked, the dialogue proved unspeakable. *The Shop around the Corner* is the work of exiles, a work of nostalgia for a Europe which was about to be erased from the face of the earth, a Europe which two years later Lubitsch showed us under the Nazi yoke in *To Be or Not to Be*.

Lubitsch's physical requirements could hardly have been simpler, yet even with a production cost of only half a million dollars the film still lost money. One medium-sized shop selling leather goods, with one office and one store room attached, is the arena for ninety per cent of the action. Otherwise there are brief visits to one café, one hospital and one bedroom, but these are accomplished with the minimum of establishing shots, as though the director was being careful not to break the unities any more than could be helped. We do once or twice venture out into the street, but that is just a small corner of the MGM backlot, and it is photographed from only one direction. We *start* in the street, in fact, after a prologue which has warned us in its way not to expect too much: 'This is the story of Matuschek and Company – of Mr Matuschek and the people who work for him. It is just around the corner from Andrassy Street – on Balto Street, in Budapest, Hungary.' The staff is

THE SHOP AROUND THE CORNER. Margaret Sullavan, James Stewart and Frank Morgan in the most charmingly subtle of light comedies.

gathering just before eight in the morning of an autumn day, waiting for the boss to come along and let them in. In five minutes, through brief snippets of dialogue, we feel that we know them all: Pirovitch, the downtrodden salesman, who is never to be found when Mr Matuschek wants an honest opinion (he has been caught that way once too often); his elegant, boastful colleague Vadas; Ilona the book-keeper who in her spare time does all right for fur coats; Pepi the Artful Dodger of an errand boy; and even the silent, smiling cashier Flora, who has almost no lines but for whom we can vividly imagine the spinster home life, taking care of an ailing mother and at least two cats. Then there is the honest, earnest young manager Kralik, the boss's favourite, and a frequent house guest at the Matuscheks'. He is well read, for he has ingratiated himself with the boss's wife by writing in her visitor's book a delightful poetic tribute which he later admits is: 'Half and half. Half me and half Shakespeare. I changed it a little to suit the occasion. I had the last line rhyme with Matuschek, that's all.' (The mind boggles.) Kralik's uprightness will be well expressed in a later scene by Klara, our heroine, who has yet to join the staff: 'When I worked at Foeldes Brothers and Sons, well, the sons were all right, but the *brothers*, Mr Kralik! And that's why I like it here so

236

much. When you say, "Miss Novak, let's go in the stock room and put some bags on the second shelf," you really *want* to put some bags on the second shelf. And that's my idea of a gentleman!'

James Stewart never gave a better performance than as this compound of determination and honour: the way the actor seems to fumble with dialogue while giving every syllable its full weight is a masterpiece of underplaying. It is through him that the film's two plots come together. The one about him and Klara hating each other at work yet being pen pals without knowing it is the only one generally remembered, but the film gives equal weight to Matuschek's suspicions of his wife's involvement with a member of his staff (who of course turns out to be not Kralik but Vadas).

The few jokes not related to these main themes are confined to the customers. There is a lovely throwaway bit which has come and gone in three lines and about six seconds:

WOMAN (*popping into shop*): How much is that belt in the window? The one that's marked 2.95?
KRALIK: Er . . . 2.95.
WOMAN (*disappearing*): Oh, no . . .

But the chief running gag is one which not only advances the plot but serves to reveal more character. It is the matter of the cigarette boxes which play 'Otchi Tchornya'. Mr Matuschek can get two dozen cheap, but are they a good buy? Kralik says no, the others temporize. It is the resourceful Klara, her patter selling one to a customer at 5.25, who clinches the matter and gets herself a job; but on the next fade-in we see a window full of the objects with a card reading:

SPECIAL CLEARANCE SALE
OTCHI TCHORNYA CIGARETTE BOXES
REDUCED FROM 4.25 to 2.29

So Klara has her job, but Kralik has once again been proved right.

We have talked about people and plotting, but attention should be paid to the abundance of soft golden dialogue in which this sad little comedy basks. It is the kind of self-consciously literary speech which is now respected in a Tom Stoppard or an Alan Bennett, but which in 1939 tended to get blue-pencilled out of Hollywood films unless a powerful creative controller capable of imposing his will was present. This function Lubitsch exercised with supreme suppleness even on his own creative off-days, and I suspect that it is to him that we should be grateful for the retention of the speech by the little waiter in the café who spots Klara's flower and her copy of *Anna Karenina*, and knows at once that she is waiting for a blind date:

Carnation, huh? A few nights ago we had a case with roses. Turned out very nice, very nice. But once, about three months ago, we had a very sad case – with gardenias. She waited all evening and nobody came, and when we cleaned the café, we found, underneath one of the other tables,

237

a gardenia. Well, you can imagine. The man must have come in, taken one look at her, said phooey, and threw away his gardenia . . . Listen, you have nothing to worry about, a pretty girl like you. If he doesn't come, I'll put on a carnation myself.

Only Lubitsch, one feels, would have given such a speech to a player we don't even see clearly, for the camera is busily favouring the star's reactions. But credit where credit is due: the waiter is played by one William Edmunds.

Finally, one must congratulate Raphaelson for the way in which the audience is allowed to guess early on that Klara is Kralik's secret lover, but she doesn't find out until the last few feet of film. It has been well established that their connection is through Post Office Box 237, and suddenly Kralik, having put the fear of God into Klara by suggesting that he has met her mysterious boyfriend who is fat and mercenary, suddenly takes pity on her and quotes phrases from her first letter to him: 'Dearest sweetheart Klara – I can't stand it any longer. Please get your key. Open postbox two thirty-seven. Take me out of my envelope and kiss me . . . dear friend.' Once she stares at him in sudden realization the film is over – or at least there are only nine lines to go before the final embrace. Filmgoers with long memories may be left with a fragrance of *Trouble in Paradise* and its repeated joke about Rooms two fifty-three, five, seven and nine; but of course that was a brittle comedy of manners. *The Shop around the Corner* is about honest people unversed in the ways of the world, and its creators, despite their own sophistication, never make the mistake of looking down on them.

The Shop around the Corner. US 1940; black and white; 97 minutes. Produced by Ernst Lubitsch for MGM. Written by Samson Raphaelson from a play by Nikolaus Laszlo. Directed by Ernst Lubitsch. Photographed by William Daniels. Music by Werner Heymann. With James Stewart as Alfred Kralik; Margaret Sullavan as Klara Novak; Frank Morgan as Matuschek; Felix Bressart as Pirovitch; Joseph Schildkraut as Vadas; Sara Haden as Flora; William Tracy as Pepi; Inez Courtney as Ilona; Charles Smith as Rudy.

Palmy Days
SHOW BUSINESS

The careers of four friends in vaudeville.

It's a small musical, made entirely within a small studio, and it concentrates more on talking heads than on vast sets, but it may just capture the flavour of old-time burlesque and vaudeville better than any other piece of celluloid extant. It never seemed to get much of a release in the UK. I remember reading in *Picturegoer* that it borrowed from Eddie Cantor's own reminiscences, and was originally to be called *Palmy Days*, a title he had used before; so when it turned up as *Show Business* at one of Bolton's second run houses, I had a hard time recognizing it. When I did so, I hurried off at once; and despite the many and varied discomforts of the Regal Cinema I came out bathed in that pleasant glow which comes from having discovered something refreshing and stimulating but not mentally taxing. *Show Business* revels in its own clichés; indeed, it is told so far as possible not so much in dialogue as in a series of corny old routines. And just to show that the writers did not take the story seriously (which is just as well, since we don't either) the five principals all play characters bearing their own real first names. Even the introductory blurb is facetious: 'In the era of belles, bloomers, and beer in buckets . . .' On the wings of show-business jargon we are transported to a low dive in the early years of the century. Here George Murphy, backed by six chorines in grass skirts, is dancing and singing a nifty ditty called 'They're Wearing 'Em Higher in Hawaii' (you have to pronounce it Haw-eye-yer), where

> All the maids are always full of pep,
> All the old men have to watch their step.

He interrupts the song to glance at the girls and ask the audience: 'Anybody here got a lawn mower?' This confidence ensures that after his final two-step he gets the hearty applause expected by Cheerful George Doan ('A Smile and a Song'). Joined by two chorus girls, he indulges in badinage with a burly audience plant who threatens to see him outside. George is unmoved. 'Ladies and gentlemen, this gentleman would like to meet me in the alley. So would these two pulchritudinous girls. Who do you think I could have more fun with?'

Friday night is amateur night, a money-saving device for the manager and a way of letting off steam for the audience, which has at the ready a barrage of rotten eggs and over-ripe tomatoes. In the wings George meets nervous Eddie Cantor, who since he is addressed throughout as 'the kid' is clearly meant to be playing himself at one third of his age when he made the film (fifty-one). George tries to show interest.

MURPHY: Have you any experience?
CANTOR: I sang last week at Coney Island.
MURPHY: How did you make out?
CANTOR: You see this bruise on my left temple?
MURPHY: Oh. Yeah. What's the one on the other side?
CANTOR: I dance a little too.

George winces when Eddie shuffles shyly on to the stage and begins to sing 'The Curse of an Aching Heart' in double slow time, narrowly escaping the hook used by the manager to drag off by the neck turns of which the audience clearly disapproves. 'Faster, Eddie, faster,' he yells, and Cantor takes the cue, hopping, skipping, clapping his hands, lightening his tone and sharpening his pace in order to avoid the cascade of flying objects. Thus, we are led to

239

believe, the Cantor technique was born, for naturally the new improved Eddie, burlesquing sentiment instead of wallowing in it, is a tremendous hit and is immediately offered a regular booking.

Of course George and Eddie team up, and equally of course they meet an out-of-work sister act played by Constance Moore (for George) and rubber-faced Joan Davis (for Eddie). 'The last stage we were on,' says Joan, 'was held up by Jesse James.' She is the one with the wisecracks. 'Watch it with George,' she tells Connie, 'they won't let him pass the old ladies' home unless he's on a leash.' And after a spell of Eddie's attentions she makes a firm statement: 'Now that I've met you I feel I've lived a full life. I think I'll go home and kill myself.' Even between this odd couple romance blossoms, but Joan gives Eddie some strange looks for the benefit of the audience. 'Looks like an owl, talks like a parrot,' she decides.

A quartet is the next step, establishing 'It Had to Be You' as the film's theme tune. For light relief they do an act on bicycles, singing 'I Want a Girl, Just Like the Girl That Married Dear Old Dad'. And at about this point there are quite a few of those old familiar train montages full of label stickers and names like Pocatello, Idaho, all to the beat of dancing feet. But even success doesn't make Eddie the marrying kind, to Joan's despair:

JOAN: I'll give you one last chance. Will you marry me?
CANTOR: No.
JOAN: Let's make it two out of three.

And she starts a running joke with the camera: 'I love that boy. Love him, I tell you.' Soon we see the quartet as living statues, as knife-throwers, as Cleopatra and Mr Antony:

> Let me run my fingers through your hair.
> – Because my hair is so silky?
> No, there are no towels in the washroom.

They become the Metropolitan Four, and borrow 10,000 dollars in order to present a classier act with six chorus girls. (Classier? When Eddie sings 'Dinah', they're all in blackface.) But now instead of triumph (the film has to run at least ninety minutes) there is an unfortunate pause for melodrama. The wedding (Connie and George). The baby on the way. The other woman. The baby is born and dies, while George is (unfairly) suspected of amorous dalliance. Go and never darken my door again. War. Victory. And Eddie meets George at a French hospital while singing:

> I don't want to get well,
> I don't want to get well,
> I'm in love with a beautiful nurse.

Would you believe that the rendezvous chosen for George's reconciliation with Connie is a club where the Other Woman is singing? Didn't they read the bills outside?

There is no reconciliation. Connie takes up half-heartedly with her agent

SHOW BUSINESS. Eddie Cantor is reprising his most famous song: 'Whoopee'.

(the ever decent Don Douglas) and George succumbs to the Demon Rum. A montage shows his descent, always with one day's growth of stubble, and Connie's rise to the point of having permanent backing by six gents in grey toppers. They both seem to sing nothing but 'It Had to be You'. Finally Eddie tracks down George in a low bar in San Francisco; George's voice is now husky and low, but it's nothing that a reel change can't cure. Eddie is full of tricks. He pretends to George that he, Eddie, is the drunk, so that George finds a mission in life, the reformation of both of them. Then Eddie tells Connie that George is despicable and irredeemable, so that she will rush to his defence, and before you can say Florenz Ziegfeld, Joan and the men are signed up to appear on Broadway in *Whoopee*, though all we see of it is Eddie singing the famous title song:

> Another June,
> Another bride,
> Another victim is by her side;
> Another season,
> Another reason
> For making whoopee.

She calls him toodles
And blinks her eyes;
She bakes him strudels and apple pies.
What is it all for?
It's so he'll fall for
Making whoopee.

Connie is in the audience, of course, with her faithful agent, and after the tumultuous applause dies down, Eddie has a little speech to make: 'This is request night for George Doan, and I made a little request.' It is of course 'It Had to be You', and Connie of course responds from the stalls, with tears in her eyes. As for the faithful agent, boy, does he know when to make a tactful exit. Sure, *Show Business* is a hastily-wrapped package of every showbiz cliché you ever heard, but that's precisely what it was meant to be. And seeing it again forty years later, without an audience to help, all the gags came up just as fresh as they have always done when heard from Benny Hill or Morecambe and Wise.

Show Business. US 1944; black and white; 92 minutes. Produced by Eddie Cantor for RKO. Written by Joseph Quillan and Dorothy Bennett. Directed by Edwin L. Marin. Photographed by Robert de Grasse and Vernon L. Walker. Music by George Duning. With Eddie Cantor as Eddie; Joan Davis as Joan; George Murphy as George Doan; Constance Moore as Connie; Nancy Kelly as Nancy.

Ready when you are, Mr de Mille
THE SIGN OF THE CROSS
A Roman officer is converted to Christianity by the love of a girl.

This, quite unsuitably, was one of the very first films I saw. I remember sitting in the mid stalls of the Queen's Cinema, Bolton, and asking my mother why, if in ancient Rome it was so dangerous to be a Christian, the Christians went round making crosses in the dust to attract each other's attention, and then forgetting to rub them out? I think she was at a loss for an answer; in fact the only one she could have given was that without this careless action on the part of the persecuted the film would have no plot, for it is from that one single mistake that the entire story, including betrayals and conversions and passionate love and jealousy, is unfolded within a twenty-four-hour span, thus fully satisfying the three unities of ancient drama but stretching the long arm of coincidence a bit.

242

THE SIGN OF THE CROSS. An unusually stylish composition for a de Mille picture, Irving Pichel lies dead, and Elissa Landi senses that the trouble's just beginning.

Coming back to the film fifty years later, it seems almost too painful for such flip comments. Despite the Victorian school of acting which prevails amid its Alma-Tadema-like production values – both quite appropriate since Wilson Barrett's stage work was first performed in the nineteenth century and was still drawing packed houses as late as 1947 in Edinburgh, where I caught up with it at a matinée when half the scenery fell down – it has an awesome effect upon the diligent viewer. This may be because its painfully unhappy ending is somehow unexpected in a 1932 epic, and the lovers' conviction that they will meet again on the other side of death seems quite unjustified in view of the fact that the villains have all the best lines. True, we are spared the details of Christians actually being eaten by lions, but the inevitability of it is enough; and the parade of perverse pleasures in the last half-hour has quite a nasty cumulative effect, what with gladiators, elephants, bears, tigers and entirely dispensable dwarfs, all killing or being killed in the arena, while Nero watches with a sickly grin, and trolley-loads of dead bodies are frequently drawn away. We have in fact been warned at the beginning of the sequence by a poster which announces that 100 Christians will be executed and adds

243

casually: 'The awning will be used and perfume will be sprinkled.' In such an atmosphere there are only wan smiles to be had from the half-heard domestic bickering as the Roman proletariat takes its seats:

> We won't see anything this high.
> – I couldn't get anything better. The gallery was good
> enough before we were married.

It is impossible now to evaluate this film in its original form, for in 1943, eleven years after it was made, Paramount devised a unique way of making it palatable to a modern audience in wartime. The original negative was edited to include a ten-minute prologue, credited in the new titles to Dudley Nichols, who should have been ashamed of himself, not least for allowing the music track to segue into 'The Wild Blue Yonder'. We are somewhere in Europe with the US Air Force. 'Gentlemen,' says the commander, 'today you bomb Rome.' He hastens to add that the bombs will contain nothing more explosive than pamphlets, and that two padres – one Catholic and one Protestant, of course – have asked to go along. These clerical gentlemen take it in turn to feed us scraps of history: 'Danger is no stranger to Rome, and nor are the Germans. Over those worn stones they brought the apostle Paul back for trial before Nero.' There follows some mention of Hannibal and his elephants ('tanks with tails'), and an awed comment when the forum comes into view: 'She's glorious, even in chains.' The crew consists of course of the usual mixture of Elmendorff, Horowitz, Morino and McGregor, and the best they can manage to chip in is on the level of 'I was born in Rome, Rome Ohio' and 'There are fourteen Romes in the United States.' At last we draw near to the nitty-gritty:

> The colosseum . . . where they killed so many Christians. Those martyrs gave their lives just as so many of you boys are doing today, because they refused to believe that might makes right. There's only one step in a man's mind from being a dictator to being a God. Nero thought he was a god.

And so we are back – you can tell by the increased photographic contrast – in the original film, with Rome in flames and Nero agreeing to a minion's subtle suggestion that the Christians might well be blamed for it. It is a surprise to find as the film progresses that Charles Laughton has only three short scenes and a few long-shots, but he certainly makes the most of them as a thumb-sucking homosexual, not at all worried by the loss of life but very concerned at his broken lyre. 'Look at this: I was in excellent voice, too.'

We move to the city streets, where a Christian girl is saved by the prefect of Rome, Marcus Superbus, for whom it is love at first sight. Not many heroes can recover from a first entrance lashing the Roman populace with a whip, and Fredric March just fails in the attempt, but then his role is pure dramatic manipulation, for once he is converted by love his real interest is at an end. Elissa Landi, however, as a Christian girl whose parents were coated with pitch and burned as torches to illuminate one of Nero's late-night orgies, creates something close to a genuine tragic figure, and one wonders why her career deteriorated so suddenly and irrevocably. We cut shortly for light relief to the Empress Poppea, Nero's presumably occasional mistress, in her famous bath of asses' milk; rumour and Claudette Colbert have told us that it curdled and stank on the set before all the necessary shots could be obtained. The scene is nicely handled, with cats lapping at the edge of the bath, and milk lapping against Miss Colbert's elegant breasts without ever displaying a nipple. 'May Morpheus give you deep slumber,' cries a guard as she passes. 'Thank you,' she murmurs sardonically, 'I'd rather have exciting dreams'.

It is Marcus Superbus' misfortune, on his way to rescue his captured Christian girlfriend, to run his chariot into Poppea's smart carriage and dash it to pieces. 'Excuse me,' he mutters in confusion, 'I'm in great haste tonight on the Emperor's most urgent business.' 'Come here,' she drawls in her best Mae West tones, '*I'm* the Emperor's most urgent business.' Marcus handles matters clumsily from then on, arriving too late to save most of the Christians but spiriting the girl away to his own quarters, where he proceeds to ignore her for most of the day, preferring, presumably in regret at his own sudden conversion, to attend an official orgy. We are spared the worst – or best – of this, since just as Antarea the lesbian is about to dance 'The Naked Moon' she is interrupted by Christians, singing on their way to the dungeons and thus setting the plot back on its inevitable course. The girl is arrested and sent off with them, so Marcus' only recourse is a personal appeal to Nero, who is still recovering from last night's exertions ('Delicious debauchery!'). He is inclined to shrug the matter off: 'If one Christian life will make our Marcus happy . . .' But the spurned Poppea – and here Miss Colbert gives a splendid tiger cat performance, even allowing us to see the wrong side of her face, which was taboo to cameramen for the next forty years – persuades him that Marcus is just a mad impulsive boy who needs saving from himself. Nero's attitude hardens, 'No, Marcus. We do not want barbarians laughing at Roman justice. The girl must publicly renounce her faith, otherwise . . . And now, have a little consideration. Would you have me late for the games?'

And so to the dungeon and the arena, and the remarkably disturbing scenes of self-sacrifice. But the film fades out discreetly as the lovers climb into the sunlit arena, and we mix to a final shot of those damned World War II bombers flying off into the sunset. In the circumstances it is remarkable that this film retains the power it does; perhaps it comes up all the fresher because of the subsequent years during which Christian faith has been dismissed as outmoded. Technically one might almost regard it as de Mille's best work, far more flexible in its grouping and camera movement than the much later *Samson and Delilah* or *The Ten Commandments*. Perhaps he simply responded well to Adolph Zukor's challenge when he returned to Paramount after three flops at MGM. The challenge was a very limited budget: no more than 650,000 dollars. The parsimony does not show: because of the dextrous storytelling we are more convinced that we have been in ancient Rome than we ever were in *Quo Vadis* or *The Fall of the Roman Empire*. True, the colosseum crowds seem to be faked, but the streets and marketplaces in which most of the story unfolds are as convincing as any sets could be in depicting the way things might have happened nearly 2000 years ago.

The Sign of the Cross. US 1932; black and white; 123 minutes. Produced by Cecil B. de Mille for Paramount. Written by Waldemar Young and Sidney Buchman from the play by Wilson Barrett. Directed by Cecil B. de Mille. Photographed by Karl Struss. Music by Rudolf Kopp. With Fredric March as Marcus Superbus; Elissa Landi as Mercia; Claudette Colbert as Poppea; Charles Laughton as Nero; Ian Keith as Tigellinus; Nat Pendleton as Strabo.

Love Lies Bleeding
SPELLBOUND
The new head of a mental home proves to be an imposter and an amnesiac.

Queues ringed the cinemas in 1945 for Gregory Peck and Ingrid Bergman in love; but as a thriller this was never one of Hitchcock's best works, and contrary to tradition commentators have actually thought less of it as the years lengthened. Its psychiatric preoccupations now seem elementary, its plot elongated to snapping point, and its substance no more than a number of vague followings and phony frights, topped off by a dream sequence which certainly isn't worth what it allegedly cost. But in 1945 *Spellbound* was hailed because it never mentioned the war, and was Hitch's first real glossy since *Rebecca*. Besides, at the Tottenham Court Road Dominion it was supported by Laurel and Hardy in *The Chimp*, which got neon billing on the marquee. The combination was sufficiently irresistible to warrant the expenditure of one shilling and sixpence.

It is a film full of foolish premises, though one can see that Ben Hecht might be pleased with his scenario (which follows the book scarcely at all) for smoothly combining a number of diverse elements as well as the then new-fangled psychiatry. These days everybody in America has an analyst and attitudes to a crooked mind have become much more sophisticated: we ask not so much what has he done as, will he get away with it? In this case we know Gregory Peck will, because he's the romantic hero, more sinned against than sinning; so it's a waste of his time having all those nervous hysterics because he thinks he might have murdered somebody. As for making fork marks in the tablecloth, then dashing away with excuses about his nerves having been bad lately, well, we really can't take that either. It's rather like the solemn hero of *Mourning Becomes Electra* saying he must just go off to clean his pistol; all too pat as a signpost to what might happen next. One thing is quite clear: this Dr Edwardes can't be the man who wrote that 'excellent work' *The Labyrinth of the Guilt Complex*.

246

SPELLBOUND. Fugitive Gregory Peck has trouble at the railway station, and that cop looks mighty suspicious despite Ingrid Bergman's explanations.

It takes us two hours to find out who Mr Peck really is, and apart from the mystery of his real identity, what we get once the love affair is established is a rehash of Hitch's favourite *The Thirty-nine Steps* routine. Peck must evade the police for long enough to establish (a) his real identity, (b) why he hates stripes, and (c) the name of the murderer of the real Dr Edwardes. Those who anticipate a twist on *The Cabinet of Dr Caligari* will be disappointed: there is a logical explanation for everything, even though it is arrived at by means of a dream sequence which doesn't hold water. This is Gregory Peck's narration for it:

> I seemed to be in a gambling house, but there weren't any walls, just a lot of curtains with eyes painted on them. A man was walking round with a large pair of scissors cutting all the drapes in half. Then a girl came in with hardly anything on and started walking round the gambling room kissing everybody. I was sitting there playing cards with a man who had a beard. He said: 'That makes twenty-one, I win.' But when he turned up his cards they were blank. Just then the proprietor came in and accused him of cheating. The proprietor yelled: 'This is my place and if I catch you cheating again I'll kill you. Then I saw the man with the beard. He was leaning over the sloping roof of a high building. I yelled at him to

watch out. Then he went over – slowly – with his feet in the air. And then I saw the proprietor again. He was hiding behind a tall chimney and he had a small wheel in his hand. I saw him drop the wheel on the roof. Then I was running and heard something beating over my head. It was a great pair of wings. They were chasing me and almost caught up with me when I came to the bottom of the hill. That's all I remember. Then I woke up.

Not all of these images are explained, but those with short memories may like to be reminded that wheel equals gun, eyes equal guards, gambling room equals asylum. And that'll be fifty dollars.

Luckily for our mystified hero, Ingrid Bergman is cast as a lady psychiatrist who has only to take off her glasses to look beautiful. She makes this gesture quite soon after meeting Mr Peck. Presumably his chief appeal to her is as material for a thesis, for he has said nothing to indicate an intellect to match her own, and she is no sexual pushover. She has earlier had a romantic brush with the staff Lothario, who tells her afterwards that it was like embracing a textbook. 'Your attitudes are very interesting,' she replies imperturbably. Kissing Mr Peck on the other hand is promptly described as 'like lightning striking', and provides Mr Hitchcock with another of his naughty visual metaphors: as the lips meet, we see in double exposure a door opening, and through that another . . . and another . . . It may be reminiscent of his better-known train-into-tunnel gag in *North by Northwest*, but *Spellbound* could certainly do with a few more like it.

You can tell when watching *Spellbound* that despite its heavy tone nobody took it seriously enough to make the plot either logical or plausible. Selznick himself appeared to regard it as a purely commercial enterprise, and was concerned mainly that it should outgross his previous production, the disappointing *Since You Went Away*. Every element was cynically manipulated to bring the public in: he even tried to get a Spellbound Concerto out of Miklos Rozsa's rather derivative score. Despite all these demerits, the picture is always watchable and sometimes very entertaining, in the lightest professional way. A lot of time and money were spent on getting the right photographic sheen. (Hitchcock, curiously, thought the dream should be in sharper focus than the rest of the picture.) The shots are carefully angled, and the actors positioned with skill into the dramatic and photogenic attitudes which will most effectively emphasize their physical attractiveness and cloak the bathos of their dialogue. All the ruses worked: Selznick came up with a 3 million dollar profit, but never again mentioned the film with affection.

Critics tolerate it today as a textbook of Hitchcockian style and Hitchcockian cheek. The paying customers forty years ago had a different reason for their enthusiasm: the flat lines were spoken by one of two superstars while looking into the other's eyes. When they are otherwise occupied, the film becomes a matter of routine suspense. Will they get out of the hotel before the fugitive is recognized? What is the amnesiac hero going to do with that razor? Who are the sinister men in the doctor's waiting room? What is the significance of the snow? The rest of the cast is decidedly subordinate. Michael Chekhov's mittel-European tutor is brought on as a turn to explain the plot. Rhonda Fleming is a decorative inmate. Leo G. Carroll, numerically Hitch's favourite actor, does at least get the climax to himself, having been identified by Miss Bergman as the murderer. Through his eyes we watch as he levels a gun on her. As though daring him to use it, she calmly walks to the door and leaves the room. He thereupon turns the weapon on himself, i.e. into the camera, and as he pulls the trigger there is a red flash – one frame of film – in this otherwise black-and-white movie. As usual, the trick is harmed because the plaster hand holding the gun as it rotates is very obvious; besides, wouldn't it be almost impossible to shoot oneself in this particular way without changing the position of one's fingers? Hitchcock always thought he'd failed if anyone asked that kind of question. Perhaps this time he did.

Spellbound. US 1945; black and white; 111 minutes. Produced by David O. Selznick. Written by Ben Hecht from the novel *The House of Dr Edwardes* by Francis Beeding. Directed by Alfred Hitchcock. Photographed by George Barnes. Music by Miklos Rozsa. Dream sequence by Salvador Dali. With Ingrid Bergman as Dr Constance Peterson; Gregory Peck as J.B.; Leo G. Carroll as Dr Murchison; Michael Chekhov as Dr Alex Brulov; Wallace Ford as Hotel Stranger; Norman Lloyd as Garmes; Rhonda Fleming as Miss Carmichael; Steven Geray as Dr Graff; John Emery as Dr Fleurot.

Thunderstorm Mystery
THE SPIRAL STAIRCASE

A New England town is terrorized by a killer of handicapped women.

When they remade *The Spiral Staircase* in 1975 I walked out of it after thirty-five minutes. Not that I have anything against remakes provided that the original remains in circulation; but by setting the action in a modern mansion the revampers not only sacrificed all the juicy atmosphere of a thunderstorm mystery but made it necessary to concentrate on nasty shocks rather than lingering menace. The glare of electric light also revealed the storyline as pretty rocky and the motivation extremely dubious. And so when Channel Four revived the original in 1984 I dutifully took a stayawake pill, only to be disappointed. The original is not nearly so good a film as I remembered, especially when broken up by commercials. But it has memorable moments among the *longueurs*, and can certainly go down in the history books as a superior gothic spine-chiller, if not, as Channel Four announced it, as 'one of the most terrifying films of all time'.

The spiral staircase has almost nothing to do with the action except as the setting of the final confrontation and shoot-out. It's an unlikely affair of iron,

THE SPIRAL STAIRCASE. Dorothy McGuire doesn't realize the danger she's in. Ethel Barrymore does, but she can't get out of bed. Stay tuned.

looking much too modern to be the cellar steps of the great Victorian mansion in which most of the action takes place. Boston, we're told, is the nearest big town, but we get no closer to it than the small local community, where on this wuthering winter afternoon in the 1890s ladies and gentlemen have congregated in the Village Hotel to watch motion pictures ('the wonder of the age'). Among them, thrilled by an item called *The Kiss*, is our heroine, the dumb servant girl Helen, who has lost her voice through shock at seeing her parents perish in a fire, and now works at the big house two miles up the road. As she absorbs the primitive emotion from the screen, the camera pans up, through the ceiling, in a well-remembered trick shot, to a bedroom in which a crippled girl is putting on her clothes. As she extracts a dress from the wardrobe we see what she fails to notice, that behind the line of hanging clothes an eye is watching her: the camera takes us right into a close-up of the mesmerizing pupil. And as the dress goes over the girl's head, to the sound of thunder outside, we close in on a second famous shot: her hands are twisting and crossing in pain, as the unknown assailant strangles her. By the time the sound of crashing furniture brings up the audience from downstairs, he has done a neat disappearing trick (through an upper storey window in broad daylight); and we learn from the sheriff that there have been other murders of women

250

with defects, a mental defective and a girl with a scar. He casts a critical look at Helen: 'You live up at the Warren house, don't you? Better hurry if you want to get home before dark.' As she hurries off, the hotel manager asks whether the sheriff has any line on the murderer. He shakes his head. 'Somebody we all know. Might be me. Might be you.'

The scene is set for Helen's fraught journey home under threatening skies. Although the idealistic young doctor (could he be the murderer?) gives her a lift for part of the way, she has to do the last stretch alone through the woods, past a rather extraordinarily phallic tree which makes one remember that her modest responses to the doctor's solicitude seemed to carry just a hint of suppressed sensuality. To cheer herself up against the impending cloudburst she rattles a stick against the cast iron railings, and fails to notice that watching her progress from under a tree is a sinister figure in a broadbrimmed hat and dark waterproof. Naturally we are not allowed to see his face; and of course it is just conceivable that he is not a man at all.

Inside, we are overwhelmed by carved oak, horsehair furniture, and potted aspidistras. We get the impression too that the basement boiler has been working overtime, heating every cubic inch of air in the wide corridors which allow such interesting vistas through doors which never seem to be closed, even when the occupants are having fierce arguments. The odd job man staggers in from the driving storm, and *he* wears a broad hat and a waterproof, but that connection has to be too easy. The cook is looking for means and encouragement to get drunk; when she trips over the bulldog, we wonder for a moment whether *he* can be the killer in disguise. We do know that the evil eye is in the house, because when Helen stops to look at herself in the landing mirror the eye is watching her too, except that it sees her with no mouth. (With his kink, the murderer would, of course.) Upstairs the nurse (too dumpy to be the murderer) has been made to sit on the landing by her tetchy patient, the aged mistress of the house (too infirm). Played in the grand manner by Ethel Barrymore, this ancient relic seems to be dying very slowly of an unspecified disease, and has to be constantly revived with ether; but she maintains enough strength to open an occasional eye, Ancient Mariner fashion, and warn Helen to 'leave this house tonight if you know what's good for you'. She seems also to be psychic, since she knows there has been another murder before anybody tells her. As the nurse comments with a shiver: 'Even with her eyes shut she seems to be watching you like an evil spirit.'

The family is complete when we are introduced to the old lady's son Stephen (Gordon Oliver) and her older stepson Professor Warren, who seems to have no first name and is played somewhat somnambulistically by George Brent. He appears to be a research botanist, overly conscious of having failed his dead father by not being the sort of man who can take life by the tail and swing it round. Both sons pay duty calls on mother, who only rolls her eyes and says: 'Why did you come back, Stephen? There's always trouble when you come back.' (A false lead if ever we heard one.) The likeliest trouble would centre on Professor Warren's glamorous secretary Blanche, with whom both men appear to have had romantic encounters. Into this uneasy menage, where

251

everyone seems constantly to be giving equivocal looks to everyone else, intrudes the sheriff with the information that 'we've traced the murderer to this vicinity'. He doesn't say how, and perhaps it doesn't matter, since the news conveniently restricts the range of the audience's suspicions.

The plot thickens. Old Mrs Warren's ether disappears, and the odd job man has to be sent miles through the storm to get more. The upstanding young medico turns up unexpectedly and wants to escort Helen to safety, but is called away to a baby case. The pneumatic Blanche is strangled in the cellar, her clutching hands strikingly visible at either side of a pool of darkness in which she and the killer are conveniently standing. (What *can* her defect be?) The cook meanwhile is sozzled in the kitchen; the nurse has given notice and is Off; Helen, suddenly and unreasonably suspicious of Stephen, has locked him in the cellar. Ain't nobody left to protect her except the old lady and the professor; and her faith in *him* is shattered when halfway up the stairs he tells her frankly that *he* is the murderer, with a mission to make his dead father proud by exterminating imperfection from the world and thus emphasizing his own strength. Regular filmgoers in 1945 cannot have been at all surprised by this development, since Mr Brent was too dull and too old to get the girl in the end, and unless he were the murderer, with a good hysterical speech at the climax, there would be no justification for having his name above the title. (There isn't much anyway, since Mr Brent in the role gives the worst performance of his career, hovering about like a man in search of the bathroom.) Anyway, the script manoeuvres both murderer and potential victim on to the aforesaid spiral staircase so that the professor can be shot several times from above by his stepmother, who has crawled out of bed for the specific purpose of crying 'Murderer!' at him and letting him have both barrels. She then expires on the spot, and poor dumb Helen, left with three corpses on her hands, is finally stung to action and speech. She runs to the telephone and utters the famous line: '189 . . . Dr Parry . . . come . . . it's I . . . Helen . . .' Upon which satisfying note the camera draws away, the scene fades out, and we can all stroll thoughtfully home to our Gothic mansions, carefully avoiding any shadowed areas on the way.

The Spiral Staircase. US 1945; black and white; 83 minutes. Produced by Dore Schary for RKO. Written by Mel Dinelli from the novel *Some Must Watch* by Ethel Lina White. Directed by Robert Siodmak. Photographed by Nicholas Musuraca. Music by Roy Webb. With Dorothy McGuire as Helen; George Brent as Professor Warren; Ethel Barrymore as Mrs Warren; Kent Smith as Dr Parry; Elsa Lanchester as Mrs Oates; Sara Allgood as the nurse; Rhys Williams as Mr Oates; Rhonda Fleming as Blanche; Gordon Oliver as Stephen.

That Old Black Magic
STORMY WEATHER

A black veteran of World War I becomes a dancing star.

When *Stormy Weather* was first released, publicity centred on the delectable young Lena Horne. 'Lovely Lena has a point of view,' ran a banner headline in *Picturegoer*, and the burden of the piece was her intelligence, her superior education and her determination to be taken as an equal, with no condescension because of her colour. It seemed a little odd to me that with these advantages and convictions she should consent to appear in an all-black musical which depicted most of its characters in Hollywood's old shuffle-footed way, as dim-witted folk with at best an instinctive knowledge of right and wrong. Sometimes they might know better than the white folk, but usually they played Dr Watson to somebody else's Sherlock Holmes. In most movies their existence, however, depended entirely on the whites, to whom they normally acted as servants or entertainers. I found it difficult therefore to understand how this movie could, as billed, contain no white characters at all; but it doesn't, not even among the applauding audiences, who are always shot from behind in an effort, one presumes, to preserve some sort of dramatic unity. It began to dawn on me that in Hollywood whites were not allowed to appear as supporting characters in a story in which blacks had all the star roles. Brought up in darkest Lancashire, I don't think I had ever met a black person, though I was anxious and curious to do so. Nor was I able to understand why Twentieth Century-Fox, so soon after Pearl Harbor, should want to make an all-black musical, when it was surely more urgent to show all ethnic groups marching side by side to war; but the penny dropped with the first scenes of the film, which show the blacks as loyal ex-soldiers in that earlier war, coming contentedly home in 1918 to their old subordinate positions lightened only by a limited eminence in the field of popular music.

The show is certainly intended as a tribute, opening on a magazine cover announcing a special issue spotlighting 'the magnificent contribution of the coloured race to the entertainment of the world over the last twenty-five years'. Flashbacks constitute the whole film. Bill Robinson, looking the same age throughout apart from a few grey hairs, is seen as 'Bill Williamson', chatting on the porch of his California home to a group of neighbourly kids about his dancing career. We are taken back to 1918 and the ticker-tape parade which greeted the return from the front of Bill and his friends, who after that, of course, were left to fend for themselves. He has a fast-talking buddy (Dooley Wilson) who is always getting into scrapes by pretending to be a big showbiz impresario; and the buddy has a sister (Lena Horne) with whom Bill promptly falls in love but who has her eyes fixed on stardom and does not consent to be his until a dozen or more show-stopping numbers have passed by. That's about all there is by way of plot, both principals ascending the ladder of fame with scarcely a foot misplaced on any rung. Not even Jolson in his own biopic had it so easy; and there are no pauses for sentiment at all. When in doubt, director Andrew Stone simply slides in another number. In other words, what we have is basically a revue, bringing together the very best black talent of its time, in both swing and jazz traditions, with a touch of bebop at the end and a smattering of comedy cross-talk along the way.

Dance directors with the imagination of Busby Berkeley were too expensive for Twentieth Century-Fox, so there are no kaleidoscopic numbers here, and with the exception of the 'Stormy Weather' finale (for which we have been prepared by electric thunder flashes during the main credits) everything is shot from the front stalls. But Fox knew how to stage a number that way, with perfect lighting, positioning and editing, and *Stormy Weather* is just as precise in these matters as, say, *Hello Frisco Hello* or *Nob Hill*. It may be simple, but it's professional all the way, and ingratiating from the word go. Even more important, all the songs are standards. In the early nightclub setting Lena sings 'There's No Two Ways about Love', and Bill joins her for a cakewalk. There follows a low point during which he has to work as a waiter in Memphis ('I ain't never been ambitious except to get three meals a day regular'), but on the way he is lured into a soft shoe shuffle on the riverboat and before long he is listening wistfully as Fats Waller sings 'That Ain't Right' and 'Ain't Misbehavin''. Given a chorus spot through Lena's pleadings, he is part of 'Dig a Dig a Doo, Dig a Doo Doo', and proves his star quality by upstaging the braggart leading man in a tom-tom number. Back on Broadway (or maybe it's Harlem) he is rescued from financial disaster by his buddy Gabe's impersonation of a big-time gent, and from the smash hit show which follows we are allowed to enjoy 'Salt Lake City Blues' and 'I'm Nobody's Sweetheart Now'. A pause for comedy is provided by two old-time performers (they put on blackface make-up) who go through the cherished routine in which they interrupt each other's drawling sentences. This is followed by 'I Can't Give you Anything but Love, Baby'. Cab Calloway, he of the fixed grin, the white suit and the loping gait, now appears to take over the last quarter of the picture, and offers his rendition of 'Geechy Joe' and 'I Lost My Sugar in Kansas City'. We are now ready for the spectacle of 'Stormy Weather', with liberal assistance from rain and wind machines as well as Katherine Dunham's ballet (seen perhaps at less than its best). 'There's No Two Ways about Love' is reprised; 'My My Ain't that Somethin'' is interrupted by the Nicholas Brothers in one of their most dazzling leaping dances; and we are all sent home happy to the strains of the 'Jumping Jive'. How do they cram all that into seventy-seven minutes? By not pausing for breath, that's how.

Stormy Weather remains an absolute knock-out, as deft and gleamingly monochromatic a show as when it was first allowed to slip out on release and appeared on a double bill at the Lido, Bolton, with a brilliant Frank Capra war documentary called *Divide and Conquer*, about the rise of the Nazis. An embryo critic even then, I wrote in my Film Notebook: 'Thoroughly entertaining: you will like Lena Horne.' Forty years later I paid my first visit to Harlem. The breadth of 125th Street was a litter-strewn disaster area, with

peeling placards on half-derelict buildings, and the Cotton Club, sitting in the middle of it at the western end, looked like a public lavatory. It seemed dangerous to stop outside the Apollo, for a number of layabouts were taking the wrong kind of interest in us, but we paused long enough to see that the foyer had not for some time been cleared of its garbage, and that although a show of some kind seemed to be current, the neon sign was broken and the words on the marquee misspelled. I don't know whether black New York ever was quite as clean and shining as it was depicted in *Stormy Weather*, but I'd certainly like to think so.

Stormy Weather. US 1943; black and white; 77 minutes. Produced by Irving Mills for Twentieth Century-Fox. Written by Frederick Jackson and Ted Koehler. Directed by Andrew Stone. Photographed by Leon Shamroy and Fred Sersen. Music direction by Benny Carter. Choreography by Clarence Robinson. With Bill Robinson, Lena Horne, Fats Waller, Cab Calloway, Eddie Anderson, Dooley Wilson, Katherine Dunham and her troupe, the Nicholas Brothers, Ada Brown.

SUMMERTIME (SUMMER MADNESS)

An American spinster becomes romantically involved on a holiday in Venice.

There would be no point in denying that in most of the preferred cinematic virtues this film is utterly defective. It has no plot to speak of, and muffs even the wisps of story which it places before us. We are told next to nothing about its heroine's character or background, and the thought processes through which she first gives in to her Italian Lothario and then rejects him are dimly perceived at best. The supporting characters to whom in the first reel we are rather amusingly introduced do not develop at all and become silent background figures. Even the editing is strange at times, as in the scene where Miss Hepburn sits on a flight of canal steps gazing at a pair of stone lions, upon which the camera fades out without ever making clear why she is so fascinated by them. And some of the dialogue is risible, which is an adjective we would never expect to apply to work by H. E. Bates and David Lean. 'All my life I've stayed at parties too long because I didn't know when to leave'. That sounds less like a real line than like a parody of Katharine Hepburn; to be followed by, 'The calla lilies are in bloom again.'

No, what we have here is a magnificently photographed travelogue of a sunlit city, with a star in the foreground. Mr Lean's camera explores every nook and cranny, both of Venice and of Miss Hepburn's incessantly mobile but essentially androgynous features. It could perhaps have been any romantic city, Rome or Rio or Toledo; but only Miss Hepburn of all our actresses could have taken the brunt of a hundred minutes of relentless probing, especially when as in this case there is no subtle characterization to bring out, only a thousand superb camera studies to treasure.

The clearest aspect of Jane Hudson as portrayed by Miss Hepburn is that she is a cine-camera fiend from Akron, Ohio (which in *Lost Horizon*, I remembered irrelevantly, is the source of Shangri-La's green porcelain bathtubs). In the train as Venice approaches she even photographs a travel brochure so that she can pan from it to the distant city. The Englishman opposite is amused:

> You like it?
> Oh, I've got to. I've come such a long way.

She has certainly brought a great deal of luggage, and in my experience of Italy she is lucky to keep all of it on her bewildering journey from the station to the Pensione Fiorini by canal bus, on which she meets another pair of American tourists of the comic postcard type. (They are called McIlhenny, another name remembered from a piece of writing, this time the delectable *Harvey* by Mary Chase; but *Summertime* has none of the fantasy which the association might suggest.)

256

The Pensione Fiorini is a modest miracle of elegance, as is its proprietress of whom we see too little. Like Miss Hepburn we are already drunk with apparently three-dimensional views of the Grand Canal, from whose actual squalor we are protected save for a shot of some rather clean garbage being thrown into it from an upper window. Venice is handed out as a great sensual experience to which we gladly succumb, since it has to be an experience of greater stature than the muddled sexual development which was the theme of Mr Laurents's original play, as evinced in its title *The Time of the Cuckoo*. (Venice could hardly have been got on to the stage.) We are left in little doubt that the central character is a middle-aged virgin, long on the shelf; she implies as much to the proprietress, who tries to comfort her:

SIGNORA FIORINI: In Italy, age is a virtue.
JANE: If it is, I'm loaded.

She is even made nervous when a street boy accosts her in his foreign tongue. As soon as she understands the situation she is glad to give him a coin in exchange for a postcard; but of course it turns out to be a dirty picture.

After forty minutes, what we have seen has been most enjoyable, but it has led in no particular direction. Fear not, for the plot is about to creep in, though it is so perfunctory that we might have enjoyed ourselves better in the end if Mr Lean had limited himself to dazzling our eyes. However. Our heroine is sipping a lonely coffee in the piazza when she notices that a man at the next table seems to be staring at her. When she goes into an antique shop to buy a glass goblet, he turns out to be the proprietor, Renato. Next day she passes the shop again and calls out of politeness. He is not in, but when he gets the message he turns into a randy Italian, assumes the call to be a gesture of availability, and is round at her pensione before you can say Wile E. Coyote. The approach he chooses for her is the most subtle he can think of, but she is still confused:

JANE: I don't know what your experience has been with American tourists . . .
RENATO: My experience has been that the tourists are more experienced than I.
JANE: I don't understand . . .
RENATO: Why do you want to understand? The most beautiful things in life are things we don't understand.

The film fails to make it clear why our heroine should capitulate at this point. Perhaps her famous comedy back-fall into a canal has something to do with it. But capitulate she does, even forgiving her Lothario in quick order for over-pricing the goblet and for already having a wife. All he has to do is make a few more magic passes in the moonlight ('Take a deep breath. Relax, and the world is beautiful . . .') and they are having an idyll on the isle of Murano, with fireworks in the night sky and she wearing an expression like the cat that swallowed the cream. And then, next morning, quite suddenly and with no apparent motivation, she is wiping back the tears and turning away as she tells him that her bags are packed and she is leaving in two hours. Naturally he takes this badly; his manhood has never been so insulted. But as the train pulls

SUMMERTIME. Katharine Hepburn in Venice hasn't a care in the world, but in just a moment Rossano Brazzi is going to look over the top of that newspaper . . .

out, there he is running up the platform with a gift and a gardenia, neither of which, symbolically, she can quite manage to grab. But the thought was there.

Summertime is a maddeningly inconsequential film, but few people can help liking it. Some people even mark it up among their top favourites; others use it as a means of recapturing the times when they also spent holidays drinking countless expensive cups of espresso in the piazza. I like it too, but for the rich background of Venice rather than for the thin drama which goes on in front of it. It's the only time Katharine Hepburn was ever upstaged by a city.

Summertime (GB title: *Summer Madness*). US 1955; Eastmancolor; 99 minutes. Produced by Ilya Lopert. Written by David Lean and H. E. Bates from the play *The Time of the Cuckoo* by Arthur Laurents. Directed by David Lean. Photographed by Jack Hildyard. Music by Sandro Cicogini. With Katharine Hepburn as Jane Hudson; Rossano Brazzi as Renato; Isa Miranda as Signora Fiorini; Darren McGavin as Eddie Yaeger; Mari Aldon as Phyl Yaeger; André Morell as man on train; Macdonald Parke as Mr McIlhenny; Jane Rose as Mrs McIlhenny; Jeremy Spenser as Vito.

Creatures of a Damaged Brain
THUNDER ROCK

A disenchanted political journalist takes a job as a lighthouse keeper and creates his own world.

I was no more than fourteen when I first saw *Thunder Rock*, but it was the first film to make me feel adult . . . and it boasted nothing more restrictive than an 'A' certificate. When it came out in 1943 the critics as one man feared that it would be far too intellectual for popular success, and there was much applause for the unflinchingly commercial ABC circuit which 'dared' to book it. I suspect that the bookers were influenced in this case not by the quality of the film itself but by the bullying tactics of MGM, which had somehow got this difficult film on its distribution lists and probably told the circuit that unless it played *Thunder Rock* it could whistle for the next Judy Garland musical. Whatever the truth, I was determined to lend my own support to so worthy an enterprise, and was able to catch up with *Thunder Rock* at ABC's Blackpool flagship the Princess, in whose dark vastnesses on a stormy Tuesday night a small band of enthusiasts applauded meaningfully when the entertainment ended. One of them walked back with me by the windswept lapping waves, all the way to South Shore, and said he felt 'enriched' by the experience. (I think he meant the film.) As for me, I perceived that I had been in the presence of one of those rare films with Something to Say, something about shouldering responsibility instead of opting out; and I resolved there and then that, although I had been too young to fight the war, I would certainly do my best to help win the peace.

Looking in 1983 at the battered, pock-marked print which seems to be the only remaining facility on *Thunder Rock*, I could swear that on that long-ago evening I never saw the initial sequence, a protracted and irrelevant joke set in the offices of the Great Lakes Navigation Company. Various petty officials are taking credit for having tracked down a loophole in the company accounts, the reason being that a lighthouse keeper on a rock in Lake Michigan has never cashed his pay cheques. The film proper then begins as the play does, with the monthly visit to the remote light of a quartermaster type whose second-in-command just happens to be an old buddy of Charleston, the moody lighthouse keeper. There is an attempt to render apocalyptic the approach through clouds to the silent rock, and in the original prints it may well have been so, but alas the lighthouse itself is an anti-climax, a cardboard creation with no sense of the sea around it. Best, then, to concentrate on the dialogue and the acting. Luckily the latter is first class and the former a distinct improvement on the play's sometimes pretentiously expressed sentiments, though Ardrey's very effectively-timed curtains have been abandoned in favour of a more rambling structure allowing for several flashbacks to give the momentary impression of something cinematic. It is an impression only; audiences unprepared to listen should not have bothered to come.

Charleston is not an especially rewarding part to play. The man has to be, from start to finish, angry, confused and brusque to the point of rudeness. He is Rodin's thinker, but more so: a symbol of isolationism, sitting on a rock. Once, however, he had been an ardent preacher, so Michael Redgrave must at the same time suggest that that part of him is not dead but only dormant. As Flanning says, he is getting out of touch. And as Charleston replies, if I wanted to keep in touch, what the hell would I be doing here? His buddy Streeter, still ardent for lost causes despite having failed in the Spanish Civil War, is on his way to fight with the Chinese:

CHARLESTON: Why China?

STREETER: Why a God-forsaken rock in the middle of Lake Michigan? All it's good for is a toilet for gulls. What do you do with yourself? Pick your nose, examine your navel?

That last sentence, by the way, is the censor's substitute for the play's 'You haven't even got a woman'. In fact Charleston doesn't *seem* to have anything; but he has, as we see for ourselves when the others have gone. Over the inner doorway of the lighthouse is a memorial tablet to the lost crew and passengers of a packet boat called *Land o'Lakes*, which perished on Thunder Rock in an 1849 storm, bringing to an abrupt halt the plans for a new life of several European immigrants. Charleston has found the salvaged log book, and in his loneliness and despair has recreated for his own comfort, in his mind's eye, the captain and five passengers, recreated them so vividly that they can hold conversations with him, even disagreeing, if they want to, with his own views. As he half explains to Streeter: 'It's good to live among hopeful people again. I've escaped from a world I can't help. I'm building up one that I can . . . in my own head.'

The dour Captain Joshua is closest to Charleston, helping him conjure up the others, who because of Charleston's own misanthropy are seen snapping and snarling at each other to such an extent that the Captain banishes them as mere caricatures and urges Charleston to think again: 'If you are so satisfied, why do I think as I do?' Charleston traces the causes of his own bitterness back through the thirties, and we see him as a travelling journalist all of whose warnings about Hitler and Franco and Mussolini went unheeded. His editor wouldn't print what he wrote, and the public wouldn't buy his books or turn up at his lectures. Having now a more complete understanding of himself, thanks to Captain Joshua, he is better able to put himself into a position to understand the others, though it has to be said that each successive flashback with its wealth of period detail weakens our sense of the inner strength by which Charleston creates these puppets, and makes us regard them as ghosts rather than mental projections. The recreated characters are alas rather predictable despite Charleston's best efforts: factory worker dying of TB, disillusioned suffragette, doctor hounded out of Vienna for using chloroform. But they speak fluently. Just as Charleston in Europe was told 'the fascist

260

THUNDER ROCK. Frederick Valk and Lilli Palmer have yet to learn that they're only figments of Michael Redgrave's imagination.

nations are like young puppies, they bark a lot but don't bite', so Dr Kurtz has a familiar kind of blind fatalism: 'If God had intended us to escape, he would have provided the means.' Their experiences all point to the same moral: if they had stuck it out just a few years longer in the face of opposition, they would all have had their way. 'Stick to your guns,' cries Charleston, 'men live among you who will be the leaders you despair of finding.'

Luckily for the film's dramatic structure, Charleston's puppets don't believe him at all; he is forced to prove his point by telling them that they have all been dead for ninety years, and that what they all hoped for but failed to get has already come to pass. The shock to all of them is imaginable; but having recovered their composure, they point out that by hiding on his rock he is committing the very crime of which he accuses them, i.e. not sticking to his guns. 'We no longer have the power to act in our lives,' they cry, 'and so we act in yours.' Not wanting to listen, he tries to banish them from his mind; but they refuse to go until he has promised to return and fight for what he believes in. Then they walk out into the sunlight and disappear, while he

261

settles down to await the next boat. 'You could stand by and watch for ever; there comes a time when you have to *do* something.'

Thunder Rock is perhaps the most elementary of fantasies, but it does seem to have a message for all times. That message was never more important than at the low point of the war, when we needed massive injections of propaganda to persuade us to the final effort. At least the film doesn't make its preaching too obvious: no Union Jack waves at the end, and the nearest it comes to direct political comment is in suggesting that throughout the thirties Churchill was right and everyone else was wrong. Its debaters from the *id* may now seem a faded device, but in world wars with their high death toll a suggestion of the supernatural seldom comes amiss, and at least the concept is distinctively theatrical: Ardrey's play could well stand revival on the South Bank, along with other fanciful dramas such as *Outward Bound* and *They Came to a City*. Meanwhile it served for one filmgoer as a stimulating entertainment which sent him out with a new sense of purpose to brave the sandy winds of Blackpool promenade.

Thunder Rock. GB 1942; black and white; 112 minutes. Produced by the Boulting brothers for Charter Films. Written by Jeffrey Dell and Bernard Miles from the play by Robert Ardrey. Directed by Roy Boulting. Photographed by Mutz Greenbaum. Music by Hans May. With Michael Redgrave as Charleston; Finlay Currie as Captain Joshua; Lilli Palmer as Melanie; Frederick Valk as Dr Kurtz; Sybilla Binder as Mrs Kurtz; Frederick Cooper as Briggs; Barbara Mullen as Ellen Kirby; James Mason as Streeter; A. E. Matthews as Mr Kirby.

Any Similarity to the Book is Purely Coincidental
TO HAVE AND HAVE NOT
An American charterboat owner in Martinique takes a stand against Nazis.

No matter how many times you see it, you can never quite remember the details afterwards. You just know that you had a pretty good time. The same of course is true of *Casablanca*, after whose success *To Have and Have Not* was deliberately fashioned. The same actor playing the same kind of unwilling hero; a similar pair of Allied fugitives in trouble with a Vichy government official (but all three lower down the cast list and somewhat ineptly played); an equally noisy if less salubrious café background, with another pianist thoughtfully watching the main action from the sidelines; the same sudden upholding of decent values at the end. The new elements are only two: a confused alcoholic who has no place in the plot (unless he stands for the nations reluctantly under arms who don't know what the war is all about); and, crucially, a cynical girl singer who gives the hero as good as she gets and finally wanders off with him into an extremely vague future. (Could she have been devised as a female version of the lamentably missing Captain Renault, with whom Rick Blaine started to have a beautiful friendship?)

So a shadow of *Casablanca* is what emerged. History is vague about any serious intent of filming the Hemingway book; the picture we have doesn't even bother to explain the title. Legend has it that Howard Hawks, who liked to make movies about heroes of the Hemingway type in the company of equally dauntless women, once wagered the author as follows: 'I can make a picture out of your worst story.' When Hemingway, bemused, inquired what story that might be, he was told *To Have and Have Not*, and it seems that from that point there was no turning back. If this version is true, then Hemingway might have saved his money by claiming that Hawks never did film *To Have and Have Not*, except by throwing away all its salient details and keeping the title. The book was set in 1933 Cuba, when army and police were fighting terrorist students, and Hemingway himself was filled with revolutionary sentiments. He actually wrote his somewhat picaresque story in 1936, soon after the outbreak of the Spanish Civil War, and took as hero a poor fisherman who smuggles rather than starve. He is finally depicted as one weak man who cannot succeed against large hostile political forces. The film even reverses this basic theme, for Humphrey Bogart is just as successful as his public would expect him to be. He is upgraded to a charterboat owner, and apart from the now irrelevant character of Eddy the alcoholic, and unless one counts Lauren Bacall as an amalgam of the three women in the novel, all that remains from the printed page is the early hiring of the boat by a crooked American tourist; and even the outcome of this situation is changed.

Whether Hemingway played any part in the wholesale changes – which might well have amused him – is not known. But Faulkner certainly deserves a major share of the credit or blame, though a good deal of work was also done by the reliable Jules Furthman, another writer who liked cynical action heroes (*Shanghai Express*, *China Seas*, *Only Angels Have Wings*). Between them these stalwarts produced myriad new characters and incidents which during 1943 and 1944 were reduced, expanded and intermixed under the eagle eye of Jack L. Warner, who was doubtless demanding another *Casablanca*-type hit.

Hawks himself must have added quite a number of touches, and by the time he started shooting he had handed himself the extra handicap of a new and untried female lead, only eighteen, whom he had seen on the cover of *Harper's Bazaar*. Bacall proved very nervous, forever trying to hide both her youth and her Jewishness (then unfashionable), and to make matters more complicated she soon found herself falling in love with her leading man, who was more than twenty years older. In these somewhat strained circumstances work proceeded as casually and jokily as Hawks could manage: he cast only the actors he liked, but having done so he liked to upset them as much as he could, especially by putting in new bits of business with inadequate rehearsal. There was a lot of drinking and horse racing, and Bacall eventually became one of the

TO HAVE AND HAVE NOT. Marcel Dalio has no doubt at all of the chemistry that's just exploded between Lauren Bacall and Humphrey Bogart.

boys. In the process the secondary female role, that of the fugitive Helene, was drastically reduced. Bogart slopped around playing his favourite image of himself, and when the film was released he was quite happy to let the publicity honours go to his new young girlfriend. ('Slinky, sultry, sensational!')

What the audience was left with may have been a somewhat rackety star vehicle, but it is seen now as an archetypal Hawks film, with men and women setting themselves against overwhelming odds and coming through rather spectacularly. It may not have the suspense of *Scarface*, the vivid action of *The Dawn Patrol*, the cynicism of *The Big Sleep*, the farce of *Bringing up Baby* or the frenetic black comedy of *His Girl Friday*; but within its own easy-going limits it is content to entertain, while giving the distinct impression that those who made it enjoyed themselves. On the debit side, it never reaches much of a climax; the memorable bits are just that; but value for money and customer satisfaction it certainly provides. A tragic ending might have been more in the spirit of the Hemingway original, but it would have ruined this particular film, which ends with the Nazi sympathizers vanquished and Bogart eloping with his Betty. 'Are you still happy?' asked Hoagy Carmichael from his piano stool. 'What do you think?' she answers blithely. By the time the movie came out, filmgoers knew that her happiness was real.

264

The humour may have been thought rather idiosyncratic at the time. Much of it consists of the rummy (Walter Brennan at his most toothless) asking strangers 'Was you ever bit by a dead bee?' (The point is left obscure.) The best of it is contained in the initial sparring between heroine and hero:

MARIE: You're not very hard to figure, Steve. Most of the time I know exactly what you're going to do. The other times, you're just a stinker.

MORGAN: What's all this for?

MARIE: Somebody has to make the first move. (*She kisses him.*)

MORGAN: Why did you do that?

MARIE: I've been wondering whether I'd like it.

The approach gets her nowhere, and she leaves his room moodily. Morgan grins:

MORGAN: You're sore, aren't you?

MARIE: I've been sore ever since I met you. One look and you had me placed. You didn't see me take Johnson's wallet, but you knew I had it. I brought that bottle up here to make you feel cheap. But I haven't made a dent in you. I'm the one who feels cheap. I never felt so cheap in my life.

MORGAN: What did I do?

MARIE: Nothing. That's the whole trouble. What's more, you don't have to do anything. Not a thing. Oh, maybe just whistle. You know how to whistle, don't you, Steve? You just put your lips together and blow.

With that one line the film's success was assured. Critics and public alike accepted it warmly, and I don't remember any of the usual outcry about a film being nothing like the novel on which it was based. Over the next twenty years two attempts were made, in *The Breaking Point* and *The Gun Runners*, to treat the Hemingway material more seriously. They were promptly forgotten, whereas Hawks's extremely cavalier treatment goes marching on, despite the occasional efforts of critics to make it more meaningful. *Vide* Robin Wood of the *Sight and Sound* school: 'It is one of the most basic anti-fascist statements the cinema has given us.' Well, OK, but there must be two films called *To Have and Have Not*, and he was watching the other one. Mine was just for fun.

To Have and Have Not. US 1945; black and white, 100 minutes. Produced by Howard Hawks for Warners. Written by William Faulkner and Jules Furthman from the novel by Ernest Hemingway. Directed by Howard Hawks. Photographed by Sid Hickox. Music by Franz Waxman. With Humphrey Bogart as Harry Morgan; Lauren Bacall as Marie; Hoagy Carmichael as Cricket; Walter Brennan as Eddy; Dolores Moran as Helene de Bursac; Sheldon Leonard as Lieutenant Coyo; Dan Seymour as Captain Renard; Marcel Dalio as Gerard.

UNFAITHFULLY YOURS

An orchestral conductor during a concert ponders three different ways of dealing with his supposedly unfaithful wife.

Aberrations in the career of a great man are acknowledged to be fully as interesting as the peaks of his achievement. In the case of Preston Sturges, the great films are crowded together between 1940 and 1944; after that, a combination of temperament and bad luck reduced his output to a series of greater or lesser shambles. A fight with Buddy de Sylva, head of Paramount, drove him to a partnership with Howard Hughes which was predictably troubled. He retreated in 1947 to the welcoming arms of Darryl Zanuck at Fox, who gave him a princely contract; but the one half-satisfactory film he made for that studio was a disastrous commercial flop and demonstrated that Sturges's giant talent was beginning to disintegrate. His freewheeling comic style had become a juggernaut on its way to a smash-up of cataclysmic proportions.

Unfaithfully Yours does at least have the big studio's professional gloss, on which Sturges had always relied, and it is full of his old manic energy; but it is energy without a centre. The basic idea had been whirling round in his brain since 1932 without finding development, and the truth is that it is incapable of development, for it is an idea for a revue sketch rather than a motion picture. Certainly it is not enough to fill 125 minutes, which was the length of *Unfaithfully Yours* at its first preview. You could come in half an hour late and pick up the storyline with no trouble at all; and although what we now have is painless to watch, the padding does show, the pacing is clumsy, and even the lines seem to be imitations of the Sturges manner rather than the distillation of pure Sturges. His enviable facility with words was coming to seem a liability. 'I spritz dialogue like seltzer water,' he had assured Zanuck, who was worried about a long shooting schedule. 'My trouble has never been in inventing it, but rather in throwing three-quarters of it away.' This time, not only did he throw too little away, but he based his comedy too closely on real people. Rex Harrison throughout, with his wisecracks and his rages, is a stand-in for Sturges himself, and his jealousy mirrors the insecurity of Sturges in his private relationship with a woman twenty-five years younger than himself. (He wrote the part of the unjustly suspected wife for her, and only a back injury kept her from playing it: it was a joke that would have appealed to both of them.)

Nor could Sturges any longer, it seemed, rely on his famous company of comedy characters. Though only six years had passed since the Ale and Quail Club assembled so riotously in *The Palm Beach Story*, such of its members as survive in *Unfaithfully Yours* look ill at ease, and some of them ill full stop. A breathless and wasting Robert Greig does indeed play the butler, but why is he

UNFAITHFULLY YOURS. Rex Harrison is thinking of murdering Linda Darnell. But it's only his fantasy.

called Jules when he speaks with a post-synched cockney accent? Al Bridge grabs a scene as the hotel detective, but he too seems at the end of his tether. Torben Meyer has an irrelevant moment with cymbals; Julius Tannen flits past as a tailor mistaken by our hero for a detective. ('About a blue serge suit my opinion is worth something. But from ethics . . .') Lionel Stander with a fake Russian accent is a noisy addition of no value, no substitute for William Demarest with whom Sturges had had a quite unnecessary row. The old face with the best chance is not a Sturges regular, but clearly should have been. He is Edgar Kennedy, who when the film was made was dying of cancer, and looks it; yet the scene in which he slurps into dithyrambs of enthusiasm about classical music ('For me, Sir Alfred, there's nobody handles Handel like you handle Handel') is not only in Sturges's best manner, it is the best chance Kennedy had had for years, and his playing suggests that he appreciated this last opportunity.

Rex Harrison, who subsequently helped to jinx the film's chances by his notoriety in connection with the suicide of Carole Landis, was clearly asked by Sturges for a repeat of his *Blithe Spirit* performance, i.e. a great deal of sarcastic talk with as few as possible pauses for breath. He plays a British orchestral conductor, scion of a family which has made millions from marketing a popular laxative. 'I am embarrassed,' his stuffy brother-in-law tells him, 'at the product your family makes its money with.' 'That product,' comes the reply, 'has kept England on time since Waterloo.' This rather heavy joke at the expense of Sir Thomas Beecham seems to have delighted Sturges rather more than it should, and one doubts whether many Americans understood it, even though the equivalent American laxative would be Carter's Little Liver Pills, and Harrison's character name is Sir Alfred de Carter. When first encountered, Sir Alfred is arriving by a much delayed plane, and the airport scene merely establishes the less important persons of the mini-drama: his young wife (Linda Darnell); his sister (Barbara Lawrence, apparently using up some wisecracks left over from Diana Lynn's role in *The Miracle of Morgan's Creek*); and her husband (Rudy Vallee, repeating his stingy millionaire role from *The Palm Beach Story*; his wallet has five zippers). Vallee is given to making pointless remarks such as: 'There is one very reassuring thing about aeroplanes. They always come down.' When Sir Alfred finally arrives, and embraces his wife, the millionaire and his wife have an enjoyable little matrimonial spat:

AUGUST: I don't think they ought to do that in public.
BARBARA: Better do it in public than never do it at all. Some men make you think of brut champagne, and others of prune juice.
AUGUST: Give me the simple viewpoint.
BARBARA: You got it, boy, you don't need to yearn for it.

Sir Alfred has no time for his brother-in-law, considering him a bore. His manager shrugs: 'He's worth a hundred million dollars. Don't be expecting also Mickey Mouse.' But brother-in-law it is who spins the plot finally into action. Having misinterpreted Sir Alfred's casual farewell remark, 'Keep an eye on my wife', and having other matters to attend to, he has set a private detective on the lady, and ventures now to offer his report. Sir Alfred is incensed: 'You dare to inform me that you have had vulgar footpads in snap brim fedoras sluicing after my beautiful wife?' Into the corridor go millionaire and report; and when the hotel detective later brings back the latter, Sir Alfred sets fire to it in a wastepaper basket, which brings on the fire brigade for a brief recreation of a Sturges free-for-all. But then, uncharacteristically, he starts to believe that his wife is really unfaithful, and while conducting the orchestra that evening he contemplates various forms of possible action. Rossini suggests a complex murder plot involving recording apparatus; Wagner is for forgiveness; while Tchaikovsky inspires a game of Russian roulette with the supposed other man. (On a technical note, the camera shot which swoops in on Sir Alfred at the beginning of each piece, heading unwaveringly for the black of his eyeball, is an achievement far outstripping Hitchcock's more famous track shot in *Young and Innocent*.)

After the concert Sir Alfred puts all three ideas, which have worked perfectly well in his mind, into abortive action. The murder plot becomes a prolonged farce, with none of the equipment being where it's supposed to be, or working properly when found. Sir Alfred rather tediously falls through the seat of several chairs, and it would take a very full house to keep the laughter alive until his abandonment of the whole idea. The other two methods are written off almost before they start, by the wife's satisfactory explanation of what the detective thought he saw. During the final embrace the rest of the cast edges into shot rather tentatively, just to remind us that they're still around, though they don't have anything to say, just as they haven't for the last forty minutes. It's as though Sturges started shooting before he had finished writing, and grew suddenly tired of his expensive joke. The laughter throughout has been hollow, and dependent more on the actors than on any wit in the script. That's an uneasy result, for the man is at his best as a preacher; an inverted one, perhaps, but a film-maker with something to say. *Unfaithfully Yours* is a very long after-dinner joke, a polished pleasantry which is still acceptable television fare provided there aren't too many commercial breaks. But it doesn't really remind you of the man who made *Sullivan's Travels*.

Of course, it will survive much longer than the 1983 'improvement' starring Dudley Moore. But then, what wouldn't be an improvement on Dudley Moore?

Unfaithfully Yours. US 1948; black and white; 105 minutes. Produced by Preston Sturges for Twentieth Century-Fox. Written and directed by Preston Sturges. Photographed by Victor Milner. Music by Alfred Newman. With Rex Harrison as Sir Alfred de Carter; Linda Darnell as Daphne de Carter; Rudy Vallee as August; Barbara Lawrence as Barbara; Kurt Kreuger as Anthony; Edgar Kennedy as Sweeney; Lionel Stander as Hugo; Al Bridge as House Detective; Julius Tannen as Tailor; Torben Meyer as Dr Schultz; Robert Greig as Jules.

Scent of Mimosa
THE UNINVITED

The new owners of a Cornish house find that it has ghostly inhabitants.

Not many serious ghost stories have found their way to the screen. This is the one that made the most vivid impression on me, probably because I was fifteen when it came out. Besides, the high death rate of World War II had brought about a new awareness of supernatural possibilities and an eagerness to wallow in them, so that a theme which five years earlier might have been regarded by most audiences as merely silly, came to attract large numbers of people wishing to be assured that death is not the end. Sensing from the write-ups that *The Uninvited* was something rather special, I travelled eleven miles to see it at the Manchester Odeon, where it was playing in a double bill with *Around the World*, featuring Kay Kyser and his band. With my usual flair for bad timing I went in at the climax, just as the haunted heroine narrowly escapes falling off the cliff; so that when I sat the film through I was acquainted with the surprise ending all the time. That seemed not to matter; indeed, it enabled me to give closer scrutiny to the steps by which the plot advanced, and I found them sturdy enough to satisfy my adolescent need for logic if not for probability. The story has elements of detection and deduction, and its mildly witty script is interrupted by genuine frissons. Looked at forty years later it remains enjoyable on all these counts, and it was pleasing to find that on television after a long absence it drew one of the largest audiences of Channel Four's first year.

Though the titles are very dull in their lettering style, they are agreeably accompanied by Victor Young's concerto-like music, much in the manner of the period melodramas then being popularized by Gainsborough. The establishing images still surprise one. It must have been no easy feat for Hollywood technicians, in the middle of a war, to build up so convincing an image of Britain's peaceful south west. In fact the shots of pounding sea, and of rocks which look like Bedruthan Steps (and which are endlessly repeated throughout the film, as though visible from wherever the characters happen to be) are probably Big Sur standing in for the old country. Over them a disembodied voice (someone had seen *Rebecca*) diligently sets the supernatural mood: 'They call these the haunted shores, the southern shores of Devonshire and Cornwall and Ireland . . . There's life and death in the endless sound of the waves . . . And eternity.'

An amiable brother and sister, the Fitzgeralds, are on holiday. By courtesy of a glass shot, they get a distant view of an old house on a cliff, and are entranced by it. Only spoilsports like me will complain mildly that when they get to the set of the house itself it's a different shape from the glass shot house; but at least we don't see the latter again. We remain in fact within Paramount's standard upper-class interior of the forties, with its elegant curving staircase which will be seen again in a dozen pictures from *The Strange Love of Martha Ivers* to *The Bride Wore Boots*. One more quibble, and I've done. Attention is particularly drawn to the reflection of the sea on the ceiling of an upstairs room; yet when we go into the next room, with a virtually identical view, there is no such reflection.

Local inquiry takes the romantic Fitzgeralds to the home of retired sea-dog Commander Bench (Donald Crisp at his doughtiest in what would now be a John Houseman part). He willingly sells them Windward House, as viewed, for £1,200. (This is a pre-war story.) When they take possession and open the one room which was locked, a rooftop studio, they are surprised to find it very cold, but fail to notice that their flowers wilt in it. The dog clearly senses something, for he shortly absents himself into the care of the local doctor, who brings into the story a character useful for background information and for marrying the unattached sister at the end. (Nobody in the picture, by the way, seems much interested in sex. The hero plays at being a music critic but is quite happy living with his sister until he finally pairs off with a wide-eyed girl whose previous idea of fun has been reading Dickens with grandfather. His sister marries a staid country GP more than old enough to be her father. Even the dog is more interested in hard-boiled eggs than in chasing squirrels, and everybody goes to church on Sunday after conversation about how much sherry to put into a tipsy pudding.)

The hauntings don't really start until about forty minutes in, when some moaning in the night drives the housekeeper straight off to the Jessups' farm up the road. The effects are helped along by the fact that the house doesn't have electricity: candelabras are so much more picturesque, and cast better shadows. The commander is disinclined to throw light on the matter beyond suggesting that the sounds may be 'an echo from a subterranean cave'. 'In any case,' he sternly points out to the bewildered buyers, 'your purchase of the property does not establish a social bond between us.' Obviously he has something to hide, for he forbids his pretty granddaughter to visit the house, which only means that she promptly does, feeling a natural empathy for the place where her mother died mysteriously. The story then put together from gossip is that the dead Mary Meredith had married an artist who misused her, and had an affair with his Spanish model. The latter was so jealous of Mary's baby that she tried to kill it, and in saving the baby (now Stella, the Dickens reader) Mary went over the cliff herself, by the dead tree. (Where else?) The evil Carmel then died of pneumonia and the artist went mad in an unspecified European country.

The Fitzgeralds gallantly try to sort things out by means of a seance, which first seems to put Stella in touch with her dead Mum but then starts her speaking Spanish and making a dash for the cliff. Meanwhile a crawling mist has been encountered on the staircase, but it backs away from the scent of mimosa. Fitzgerald deduces that there are two ghosts, one good and one evil, battling it out in the hereafter for the soul of the innocent girl. Angrily Commander Bench dismisses the stalwart doctor who has taken part in these shenanigans, and sends Stella into the distant care of a strange lady called Miss Holloway. She was once the baby's nurse (then why doesn't Stella like her?) and now runs the Mary Meredith Retreat on Bodmin Moor. In this funereal establishment distraught females are offered 'beautiful things to look at, music to hear, and a little sympathy'. Miss Holloway (a rare screen appearance by Cornelia Otis Skinner) is obviously a close relative of the sinister Mrs Danvers in *Rebecca*, for she spends much of her time gazing at a full-length portrait of her beloved Mary, and is easily prompted to describe the enthusiasm with which she and Mary once set out to conquer life. If the film is ever remade, the lesbian suggestions will, of course, be more explicit.

Meanwhile the mention of 'Holy Holloway, of Health Through Harmony' has set the doctor rummaging among his predecessor's files. Here he discovers in Carmen's case notes a suggestion of pneumonia accelerated by possible ill-treatment, i.e. the window having been left open to let the snow in. (Just what happened to poor dear Phyllis Calvert in *The Man in Grey*.) We begin to sense the truth. Stella is really the daughter of Carmel, the gentle ghost who haunts with mimosa. The malignant ghost is the jealous Mary, who, having herself 'feared and refused motherhood', tried to kill Carmel's child and went over the cliff in the process. There is a frantic dash to Bodmin Moor to rescue

THE UNINVITED. Crisis on what passes for a Cornish clifftop. Donald Crisp, Ray Milland, Alan Napier, Gail Russell, Ruth Hussey.

Stella, but the mad Miss Holloway has already sent the child alone to Windward House, where Mary's ghost can drive her to suicide. (We are back to *Rebecca* again, the mystery having been explained by a doctor, and a midnight drive being necessary to save the situation.) Luckily the repentant commander has gone to the house to confront the ghost of his own daughter, but dies of fright in the attempt. The Fitzgeralds and the doctor arrive just in time to intercept a second dash to the cliff edge by the distraught young girl, whose mind is cleared only when the puzzle of her parentage is explained. In a finale which is only slightly risible, our hero confronts Mary's still hovering spectre and hurls a candlestick at it, after which the way is clear for the first flush of dawn and a double wedding.

On second thoughts, no remake, please. The heavy hand of Hollywood today would do this fragile tale more harm than good: one can imagine the screams and the blood and the recollected sex and childbirth scenes. As it is, the curiously well-patterned plot lingers delicately in the mind, and although Lewis Allen's direction sometimes verges on the stolid, Charles Lang's limpid photography provides exactly the mood required.

There are two oddities connected with this film. First, in a unique piece of triple casting, the voice of Mary Meredith is played by Betty Farrington, the ghost of Mary Meredith by Linda Grey, and the portrait of Mary Meredith by Elizabeth Russell. One would like to know the thinking behind *that*. Second, when the movie first came out it was applauded by the British critics for its subtlety in not actually showing the ghosts but leaving them to the audience's imagination. In 1944 I went along with this, but felt slightly cheated. When I next saw the film twenty years later, the print was American, and the ghost of Mary Meredith was there all right, for three very startling appearances, as a misty head and a trailing scarf: not at all the sort of thing one wants to meet advancing from a dark stairwell. Research produced the explanation. The British censor had insisted that if the ghosts stayed in, the film would be labelled 'H' for horror rather than 'A' for adult. Paramount, fearing a drop in takings, agreed to a few cuts, and so unwittingly brought about the critical approval. Some are born great, some achieve greatness, and some have greatness thrust upon them.

The Uninvited. US 1944; black and white; 98 minutes. Produced by Charles Brackett for Paramount. Written by Dodie Smith from the novel by Dorothy Macardle. Directed by Lewis Allen. Photographed by Charles Lang. Music by Victor Young. With Ray Milland as Roderick Fitzgerald; Ruth Hussey as Pamela Fitzgerald; Donald Crisp as Commander Bench; Gail Russell as Stella Meredith; Cornelia Otis Skinner as Miss Holloway; Alan Napier as Dr Scott; Dorothy Stickney as Miss Hird.

It Might Have Happened Here
WENT THE DAY WELL?

English villagers repel Nazi paratroopers.

If you drive west from Marlow along the enchanting north bank of the Thames; and if near Medmenham, where dissolute eighteenth-century aristocrats formed the notorious Hellfire Club, you turn right and by-pass the dreamy village of Hambleden, a few uphill miles will bring you, just before Fingest with its twin-towered Norman church, to a signpost which points left along a narrow road to the hamlet of Turville. Here you are surrounded by the richest, most paintable country scenery in the whole of Britain, in a realm which seems to have changed very little since medieval days.

   In 1942 a film unit travelled along that narrow road, as many have travelled since. What it saw at Turville, and what is still there to be seen with barely a change even of the smallest detail, is behind the credit titles of *Went the Day Well?* Turville is a tiny community, so unspoilt that visitors have been known to weep at the sight of it. There is a church, a pub, a shop, two minuscule side streets and a row of half-timbered cottages, while high on the hill to the north a windmill proudly stands. The grouping is so perfect that one is not surprised that it has been taken so often to represent the best of England, and during the war it had an added poignancy as a symbol of what we were fighting for and what might so easily be taken away from us. The sheer unthinkability of its being harmed or even changed lent a note of horror to this steely fantasy about what might have happened if the Nazis had chosen it as a centre for invasion.

Bramley End, it's called in the film, and the opening music by William Walton serenely offers patriotic emotion with no suggestion of the terrors to come. There is however a rather disquieting superimposed quotation:

> Went the day well?
> We died and never knew.
> But, well or ill,
> Freedom, we died for you.

And there is Mervyn Johns welcoming us into the churchyard at a date which we quickly gather (or did then) is in the future, well after the war. He's the verger: 'Good day to you. Come to have a look at Bramley End, have you? Pretty little place.' People usually come, he says, for a look at the strange memorial to which he now directs our attention. 'Look funny, don't they, those German names in an English churchyard? They wanted England, those Jerries did – and this is the only bit they got.' We are led back in time to the Whitsun weekend of 1942, which is roughly when the film was shot; though since by the time of its completion the invasion threat had gone away, its release was held up for over a year, no doubt due to Whitehall ditherings about how audiences would receive so stark a warning.

For a few minutes we are lulled into a sense of false security, not only by the idyllic sunlit setting but by the presence of so many faces which we instinctively associate with honour, the establishment and happy endings. Frank Lawton and Elizabeth Allan, who had carried the flag to Hollywood. Leslie Banks, who could never quite shake his *Sanders of the River* image. Marie Lohr, the indomitable Lady Brit of *Major Barbara* (qv). C. V. France, the benign old vicar. Basil Sydney, the leader of the army platoon which arrives unheralded on manoeuvres, was last seen sharing a bridge with Banks in *Ships with Wings*. But we soon guess, or are allowed to know, that all is not well in Bramley End, that the soldiers are German paratroopers preparing the ground for Hitler's onslaught, and Banks is a traitor who will help them even if it means watching his own village folk die. (The actor's war-damaged face, which had so often lent him added suavity, is in this case useful in suggesting the character's duplicity.)

It takes quite a few lapses on the part of the Nazis for the villagers to cotton on. A soldier 'behaves like a Hun' when a small boy is too curious about his equipment. Another, supposed to come from Manchester, doesn't seem to know that there's a Piccadilly there as well as in London. A third, when playing cards, keeps score with elongated fives and crossed sevens. And

WENT THE DAY WELL? Everything in the English garden is not quite lovely. Valerie Taylor, Basil Sydney, Marie Lohr, C. V. France.

Sydney himself, tut tut, leaves in his kitbag a bar of chocolate embossed 'Chockolade – Wien'. Cornered and accused, he herds all the villagers into the churchyard and threatens them with summary execution: 'Yes, we are Germans, my men and I.' The white-haired old priest tries to ring the church bell and is callously shot down, as are the Home Guardsmen on their way home from an exercise. Leslie Banks, not yet revealed in his true colours, gets busy with his radio transmitter while outwardly maintaining his self-styled 'portrait of an English gentleman submitting reluctantly to superior forces'; this gives him charge of all messages out, which he then prevents from reaching their destination.

The situation eventually erupts into a climax of the most hair-raising violence, which must have shocked a good many people at the time. Banks is shot down in slow motion by the vicar's daughter (a performance of delicate English reticence by Valerie Taylor). Cuddly Muriel George, giving a splendid performance as the postmistress, throws pepper into her captor's face and brains him with an axe. Marie Lohr is exploded by a hand-grenade. And the churchyard is the setting for deadly sniping and bayoneting. By the time the credits roll up, fewer than half the characters are left alive.

275

The war ended less than two years after the release of *Went the Day Well?*
The invasion never happened, so its strong warning was unnecessary, and like
most outdated propaganda it was quickly forgotten. Its quiet ruthlessness had
made people uneasy, and many years passed before anyone was prepared to
remember the war in such terms. Looked at from the standpoint of the
eighties, however, it can be seen as an undoubted masterpiece of an entirely
unexpected kind. Its practised direction and its sharp editing have survived as
effectively as its cold and crisp photography, and for older viewers it recalls
with hair-raising vividness the days when they all thought they might have to
swing into unwelcome action of the same kind, and some of them of course
had to. Some war films have dated badly, and heroics of the Errol Flynn kind
are greeted with a pinch of salt and a hearty laugh; but *Went the Day Well?*
seems more like a chilling documentary than like fiction, and is guaranteed to
stop every cynic in his tracks.

Almost exactly the same spirit can be detected in a brilliantly mounted
six-minute propaganda piece put out by the Ministry of Information in 1941.
The rustic setting is equally idyllic and the plot is almost like a sketch for *Went
the Day Well?* It concerns two single ladies who are able to detect a German
paratrooper in disguise because he asks for directions to Yarvis Cross when he
means Jarvis Cross. Not only is this cinematic miniature highly entertaining, it
contrives to pack into its brief running time additional messages about saving
sugar, immobilizing vehicles, locking away maps, listening to radio instructions, keeping your nerve and being cheerful about rationing. The title is *Miss
Grant Goes to the Door*, and I can't recommend it too highly.

Went the Day Well? (US title: *Forty-eight Hours*). GB 1942; black and white; 92 minutes.
Produced by S. C. Balcon for Ealing. Written by John Dighton, Diana Morgan and Angus
MacPhail from a story by Graham Greene. Directed by Alberto Cavalcanti. Photographed
by Wilkie Cooper. Music by William Walton. With Leslie Banks as Oliver Wilsford; Valerie
Taylor as Nora; Basil Sydney as Major Ortler; Marie Lohr as Mrs Frazer; C. V. France as
Vicar; Frank Lawton as Tom Sturry; Elizabeth Allan as Peggy; Thora Hird as the Land Girl;
Mervyn Johns as Sims; Muriel George as Mrs Collins; Edward Rigby as the poacher; and
David Farrar, John Slater, Patricia Hayes, Harry Fowler, Norman Pierce, Grace Arnold.

Top of the World, Ma!

WHITE HEAT

A mother-fixated gangster gets his comeuppance.

Even as the credit titles fade into place, a steam train is rushing at us with a
roar, and the suitably thrusting background music seldom lets up for the next

108 minutes. Part of its burden is an ominous minatory note which tells us at once that all is not well and healthy; and as the plot progresses we come to associate this note with the off-key whine of the hero-villain as he lurches into one of his bouts of homicidal madness. *White Heat* is one of the two dozen negatives which the various owners of the Warner library have kept in pristine condition, so that on television today, allowing for commercials, it grasps you as fiercely and mercilessly as it did in the cinema nearly forty years ago. Even now you have to allow yourself a second viewing in order to appreciate the forward-careering direction of Raoul Walsh or the sharp new angles of the script by Ivan Goff and Ben Roberts. But the quivering central performance of James Cagney takes your breath away first time, on cue, exactly as was intended. He doesn't exactly dance through his villainy, but he's on tiptoe all the time.

Cody Jarrett's men are aboard the train with orders to stop it just as it emerges from a long tunnel. The rest of the gang waits in the sunshine, guns at the ready. Jarrett himself can't resist a dramatic but quite unnecessary leap from the top of the arch into the train's tender. He disarms the drivers with little more than a look. 'What's this,' they cry, 'a hold-up?' 'Naw,' he tells them sneeringly, 'you're seven minutes late, so we're just changing engineers.' Then to his men: 'You know what to do, just do it and stop the gabbing.'

The loot is secured, but not everything goes according to plan. A nervous minion gives away Cody's name to the footplate men, which means that they have to be shot dead. 'Why didn't you give my address too?' snarls Cody as he pulls the trigger. But even the master-criminal can't cover everything: one of the bodies falls on a steam escape switch which scalds the face of another gang member.

A shocking start, but the gang has got away to its mountain retreat where the restless Big Ed rumbles on (when Cody is out of earshot) about the leader's incipient madness and the possibility that he may take over himself. 'Where do you want the body sent?' someone asks disparagingly. The men seem further humbled by the presence of two women: Cody's glamorous, frustrated wife Verna and his hawk-like Ma. The older lady clearly taught Cody all he knows about the criminal way to the top; she is a cross between the real-life Ma Barker, who led her famous Boys against the FBI, and the fictional Ma Grissom from *No Orchids for Miss Blandish*. At the moment she only stirs the stew and glowers; but the time approaches for one of Cody's frightening, violent headaches, which now seem to haunt him as a punishment for having faked them as a boy. He falls to the floor in a heap, his revolver firing in sudden helpless incontinence; and only Ma's soothing massage can help him regain his equanimity and his confidence. 'Top of the world, son,' she coos admiringly at him as the forty-year-old sits on her knee. And a minute later, back to form, he is socking one of the gang. 'I told you to keep away from that radio. If that battery's dead, it'll have company.'

Eventually it seems safe to split, though once outside the house Cody has an afterthought and sends back his rawest recruit to kill the scalded man, who is too ill to move. It's a mistake, for the pair of them fake the shooting, and later

WHITE HEAT. James Cagney and Margaret Wycherly agree that it's not quite safe to leave a wounded man in the hideout: he might talk . . .

a bandaged body found in the hills provides a few clues for the US Treasury Department. The hunt is on, and the gang hides out in a motel. This time it's Ma's turn to make an error of judgement: she goes out to buy Cody a pound of his favourite strawberries. By ingenious police surveillance she is trailed back to the motel, and after another shoot-out Cody evolves a desperate plan: he will high-tail it to a neighbouring state and there give himself up for a minor crime, which will clear him of the train robbery since it will be tied to the same night. 'And what do I do for the next two years?' complains Verna. 'Same as ya did before ya married him,' mutters Ma with heavy innuendo. 'You'd better not,' threatens Cody, 'I'll be back.'

Enter Edmond O'Brien as the Treasury's undercover man, Fallon. Sent on a framed-up charge into the Illinois prison to mingle with '27,000 of the roughest and toughest', he has a hard time gaining the confidence of the suspicious Cody, whose view of him is: 'I don't know you, and what I don't know I don't trust.' But Fallon has running through his brain his superiors' warning of urgency: 'Any moment he's likely to crack open at the seams, so you'll be working against time.' Soon Fallon has a couple of breaks. During one of his psychotic headaches Cody discovers that Fallon can massage the pain away 'just like Ma'. And Fallon instinctively saves Cody's life when a rival inmate tries to crush him under a ton of steel bits. Now the psychopath begins to treat Fallon like a kid brother, and there is a lovely shot of them relaxing, Cody with thumb in mouth, which dissolves into a picture of Ma, back at the ranch, watching a torrid romance develop between Verna and Big Ed. Eventually she visits Cody in jail to tell him that the guilty pair have run out, and that she intends to extract revenge on his behalf. Impotently he pleads with her to do no such thing . . . but the next thing he hears, during a prison meal, is a message passed along by a new inmate to the effect that Ma is dead, shot in the back. (You can see Cody's neighbour wince as he has to tell him.) Cagney's sustained eruption at this moment is justly celebrated in the annals of film. Hundreds of convicts gaze aghast as he climbs mewling and screaming on to the long table and crawls along it, scattering plates. He punches five warders to the ground before he is finally overpowered and taken away, leaving behind him a huge room full of stunned and silent men.

That night, by rather contrived means, Cody effects an escape, at the same time killing his deadliest enemy. The latter is hiding in the boot of the getaway car, and finds it stuffy. 'Want some air?' asks Cody. 'I'll give you some.' And he empties his revolver into the soft metal, as an aperitif before proceeding to polish off Big Ed. Then grudgingly he takes the terrified Verna back, without ever discovering that it was really she who shot his beloved Ma.

It may be wondered by now what there is to deserve repeated viewing in this torrid and apparently unhealthy *mélange* of violence and implied sexual frustration. Certainly the present writer would not care to watch the modern variations on similar themes: *The Grissom Gang* and the remake of *Scarface* were sickening in their emphasis on the gory details. But *White Heat* contrives to remain exhilarating throughout its running time because there is no attempt to create sympathy for the criminal and because the story is superbly told as a piece of filmic narrative. While it is unreeling, the viewer is simply not given time to think, and revels in the entertainment; afterwards, perhaps, he reflects on the moral issues involved. Mind you, some pretty odd things do happen. In the lull before the violent climax there is a beautifully-lit night scene in the garden of the hideout when Fallon, caught trying to sneak out and warn the cops, implies that all he was after was a couple of hours in which to make love to his wife. There can be no doubting the homosexual nature of Cody's disappointment; but he is not ready to believe his new friend capable of betrayal.

CODY: Ok, kid, you're just lonesome, like me.
FALLON: But what about Verna?
CODY (*shaking his head*): Ain't never been nobody but Ma.

Yet as though on the rebound he snaps out of his mood, pays amorous attention to Verna, and carries her off to bed piggyback; and next morning she is moist-lipped and affectionate as never before. She even spits out her chewing-gum before kissing him. But Cody is off on what proves to be his final raid, a violent assault on the Long Beach gasworks. Every film buff knows the outcome: after ten minutes of shoot-outs amid the tear-gas clouds, Cody atop a gasometer is the only criminal left alive, and he fires his gun into the cylinder as it explodes and he is engulfed in flame. His last words are: 'Made it, Ma! Top of the world!'

White Heat. US 1949; black and white; 108 minutes. Produced by Louis F. Edelman for Warners. Written by Ivan Goff and Ben Roberts from a story by Virginia Kellogg. Directed by Raoul Walsh. Photographed by Sid Hickox. Music by Max Steiner. With James Cagney as Cody Jarrett; Edmond O'Brien as Hank Fallon; Virginia Mayo as Verna; Steve Cochran as Big Ed Somers; Margaret Wycherly as Ma Jarrett; Fred Clark as the trader; Paul Guilfoyle as Roy Parker.

Let Right be Done
THE WINSLOW BOY

A father defends his young son who has been expelled from naval college for supposedly stealing a postal order.

I saw it first on a wet Tuesday afternoon in Torquay. It seems only yesterday, yet almost all those concerned in its making are now long dead. I was mouldering myself, in the army, and had gone to the seaside to be cheered up, but it rained, and so a cinema was the only recourse. *The Winslow Boy* was the kind of prestige stuff I liked, and I'd enjoyed the play at the Manchester Opera House ('direct from its outstanding London run'), yet on the ABC screen it seemed less enlivening than I'd hoped. For one thing it was so long that it precluded a second feature, and the supporting programme consisted solely of one of those intolerable British four-reel documentaries which were thrown together at the time with a guarantee of circuit release because if they ran 33 minutes they filled the second feature quota requirement: something about the king's guards, I think it was, and very dreary indeed.

The Winslow Boy, despite its impeccable credentials and its basis in the real-life Archer-Shee case, was not one of those copper-bottomed cinematic treats which, like *Citizen Kane*, grab your attention with the opening shots and hold it firmly for two hours. Its titles were unimaginatively presented against that over-familiar background of crumpled satin, which meant only that the art director could think of nothing livelier. A good chance was thereby lost of drawing us instantly into the drama; as it is, the first thirty minutes of the film consist of scene-setting, and the professed star, the only performer to get a screen to himself in the credits, doesn't appear for fifty. (Come to think of it,

THE WINSLOW BOY. Robert Donat has a lonely time in the House of Commons.

he is seen remarkably little even after that.) The music, which might also have been helpful, dithers around irritatingly, with the volume turned up at the slightest dramatic excuse, such as an opening door or a kiss. And Freddie Young's photography, despite his eminence in the field, is undeniably flat and grey.

Nearly forty years later, while these remarks still apply, the criticisms seem hardly to matter. *The Winslow Boy* now presents itself as an entirely cherishable item, its cast list representing the cream of British theatre in the mid-forties; and nobility does not run fast. The identical production team was not in a race when two years earlier it made the wistful wartime masterpiece *The Way to the Stars*, and it is not in a race now. Its aim is gently, almost by implication, to recreate the not-too-distant past, and within that framework to allow its actors, by courtesy of Terence Rattigan's always supple and elegant dialogue, to move at their ease. It is an aim which should have been respected. When *The Winslow Boy* was reissued in the fifties it was cut by nearly thirty minutes, an obvious temptation. At the original length only one rather damaged print seems to remain; but when Channel Four revived it in the eighties it was revealed as a perfect thing in its own terms, a classic audience-pleaser. Slow-moving in film terms as they may be, the passages of character-building dialogue are marvellous stuff to listen to, and also to watch

281

because (as usual) Anthony Asquith catches his actors with precisely the right expressions to convey the thoughts *behind* what they actually say. Three of those actors, incidentally, were confirming their British heritage after earlier Hollywood success: Donat as the Count of Monte Cristo, Lawton as David Copperfield, and Hardwicke as innumerable colonels, politicians and saturnine villains, none of them with a tenth of the value of his Arthur Winslow.

We soon know our way around the rather dull Edwardian house in Wimbledon where the Winslows live, with its uncomfortable furniture, its dark wallpaper, and its stained glass conservatory leading to a walled garden. In the play it was all we had to look at, but the film does some rather curious opening–out, taking us twice to the theatre (to hear Cyril Ritchard and Stanley Holloway in full song), once into the House of Commons for a debate, and of course finally into the courtroom for the case which Mr Winslow, having obtained a Petition of Right, has brought against the King; though after (one presumes) a great deal of thought it was decided that as in the play we should be deprived of the sudden courtroom climax, so that Kathleen Harrison as the loyal family maid might keep her excited entry (much applauded even in cinemas) with the news of Mr Winslow's unexpected triumph over his majesty's government.

We have meanwhile been kept well in touch through dialogue with contemporary history; with Mr Balfour's 'Wait and see', with the German threat across the Channel, and with the activities of the Suffragettes, of which Kate Winslow, Arthur's eldest, is a keen member. However, she tells her rather prissy boy-next-door that she is not the militant type: 'I promise not to chain myself to your railings.' Rattigan refrains from the usual joke about income tax going up to sixpence in the pound, but Mr Winslow, finding his elder son dancing to the gramophone, does contrive within the same sentence to get laughs out of both modern music and the change in monetary values:

MR WINSLOW: I do not spend £200 a year to keep you at Oxford to do the Bunny Trot.

DICKIE: Bunny Hug, father.

MR WINSLOW: The exact description of the contortion is immaterial.

Mr Winslow, a bank manager prematurely retired through arthritis, has much the same character as Mr Bennet in *Pride and Prejudice*, valuing above all the peace and quiet of his study, but proud of his family and ready with a turn of wit when required. Though stern, he can be kindly. Having discovered his young son, a naval cadet, skulking in the garden because he has been expelled from Osborne for stealing, he displays none of the anticipated wrath, and finishes his interrogation with: 'In future I trust that any son of mine will have enough sense to come in out of the rain.'

That remark draws a line under the film's preliminaries: from now on the direction is forward, as Mr Winslow, determined that right shall prevail, is lucky enough to get on his side a haughty and nationally famous barrister-politician, Sir Robert Morton, who after first calling on the Winslows with an air of great disdain, and reducing young Ronnie to tears by his ruthless examination, casually announces as he departs that the boy is plainly innocent and he will take the case. This is one of the great scenes of modern theatre, and, by its canny direction and editing, of cinema too. When Sir Robert ringingly demands of the boy whether he can honestly deny that he is a liar, a forger and a thief, the camera on the last word makes a small forward movement which is a stroke of genius.

Even Sir Robert has trouble at first in furthering the case, but he meets all hostile comment with a quiet 'Do you really think so?' Fortunately encountering the First Sea Lord on the golf course, he finds geniality mixed with stone-wall tactics: the Admiralty transcripts of the inquiry must remain secret.

SEA LORD: I assure you however that the evidence is irrefutable.
SIR ROBERT: Nevertheless I intend to refute it.

Is Donat's famous asthma the reason why, during this outdoor scene, he is discovered seated, and remains so? He certainly looks twice his age at this point, and throughout the film his illness almost helps, by the downward turn of his mouth, to give a self-mocking quality to his performance and a wistfulness to the idealism which surfaces in his oft-repeated phrase 'Let right be done.' (I remember incidentally an episode of the then-current radio comedy series 'Take it from Here' in which a similar tale involves a hero called Wright, who finally turned out to be guilty. And the judge's verdict? Of course: 'Let Wright be done!')

Donat certainly makes the most of his Disraeli-like performance in the House of Commons, which as Sir Robert he describes as 'a trying place: too little ventilation and too much hot air'. Despite the semi-triumph which follows – the case can now come to court – Mr Winslow is beginning to feel he must give in. We have watched approvingly when, after being warned by a friendly banker to think very hard before spending another penny, he drops coins into the hat of the first beggar he sees; but he has finally run out not only of money but of further economies to make. Morton, who has the bit between his teeth by now, senses that it is not the father's pride but the daughter's idealism on which he must henceforth play. 'What are my instructions, Miss Winslow?' he asks. Because of her own views she can only say proceed, despite the fact that her fiancé is threatening to end their engagement because of the notoriety of the persistent Winslows. When he does, the middle-aged solicitor who is a long-standing family friend offers himself as a replacement, and she tells her father she will think it over. As usual Mr Winslow has a wry answer: 'Think it over by all means, and decide against it.'

Somewhat uncharacteristically, Sir Robert makes a second visit to the Winslow home with confirmation of the final triumph, just as reporters are beating on the door. 'What shall I say?' asks Mr Winslow helplessly. 'I hardly think it matters, sir,' responds Sir Robert, 'whatever you say will have very little bearing on what they write.'

And so the now-available Kate is left alone with the hitherto unapproachable Sir Robert, and the audience is quite suddenly tantalized by the possibility that a romantic spark may have been lit between them:

KATE: I have a confession and an apology to make to you.

SIR ROBERT: My dear lady, I am sure the one is rash and the other superfluous. I should make neither . . . (*They go on to speak of her feminism.*) It's a lost cause, you know.

KATE: How little you know women. (*He shrugs and prepares to take his leave, fixing her meanwhile with a thoughtful eye.*) I doubt if we shall meet again.

SIR ROBERT: Oh – do you really think so? How little you know men, Miss Winslow.

Above all its other virtues, *The Winslow Boy* has pages of dialogue which any scribbler would give his eye teeth to have written.

The Winslow Boy. GB 1948; black and white; 117 minutes. Produced by Anatole de Grunwald for London Films. Written by Terence Rattigan and Anatole de Grunwald from Rattigan's play. Directed by Anthony Asquith. Photographed by Frederick Young. Music by William Alwyn. With Robert Donat as Sir Robert Morton; Cedric Hardwicke as Mr Winslow; Marie Lohr as Mrs Winslow; Margaret Leighton as Katherine Winslow; Jack Watling as Dickie Winslow; Frank Lawton as John Watherstone; Basil Radford as Esmond Curry; Kathleen Harrison as Violet; Francis L. Sullivan as Prosecuting Counsel; Neil North as Ronnie Winslow; Wilfrid Hyde White as Watkinson; Ernest Thesiger as Ridgeley-Pearce.

The Case of the Triumphant Comeback
WITNESS FOR THE PROSECUTION
A convalescent QC takes on a murder defence.

For a film with several senses of strain about it, it always comes up as an immensely enjoyable entertainment. The original story, even when it was expanded into a successful stage play, was a bland affair operating on a single gimmick which prevented characterization of any interest. The story never made headlines, but the play ran and ran, partly because people like courtroom scenes and partly because of some effectively timed curtain revelations including a typical Christie twist in the tail which may not have been very plausible but sent audiences home happily working out its compatibility with the odd things which had happened previously.

Who knows why the waspish and mercurial Billy Wilder decided to film this theatrical warhorse, so very different from anything else in his canon? Necessary box office insurance, perhaps. Having made the decision, for whatever reason, he must have foreseen that quite a percentage of his potential audience might stay away because they already knew the ending. They had to be given another reason for going, and the reason Wilder decided on was to have a good laugh, not *at* the material but *with* it. To this end he encouraged writer Harry Kurnitz, no doubt with help from the actor, to flesh out the rather stodgy defence counsel into a full-length Charles Laughton caricature, complete with a dicky heart, a tendency to invective, and a nanny-like nurse, in which latter role Elsa Lanchester, Laughton's own wife, was cast for ready audience identification. The first fifteen minutes of Wilder's entertainment, before the plot is wheeled on, devotes itself to badinage between these two in the manner of *The Man Who Came to Dinner*. 'If I'd known how much you *talked*,' he tells her for a start, 'I'd never have come out of my coma.' Nor can he stand the tactful weeping of his own staff as he returns for the first time in months: 'Any more sentimentality around here and I shall go straight back to the hospital.' He scowls at the chair lift which has been installed, though his eye shows a small boy's gleam of pleasure at the new toy. 'We'd better go upstairs now and get undressed and lie down,' announces the nurse. 'We?' he snarls. 'What a nauseating thought.'

One reads all too often of Laughton's agonies in getting into the right mood for his roles – he walked off *David Copperfield*, leaving Micawber to W. C. Fields, and after weeks of tiresome delay on *Jamaica Inn* he announced gleefully to Hitchcock that he had decided to play a key scene in the mood of a small boy who had just wet his pants – but by 1958 he was clearly an old party who had reason to be grateful for any plum parts which came his way. If he modelled Sir Wilfrid Robarts on anybody it was probably himself. He plays with lines like a cat, stretching some and compressing others, usually giving the reading you least expect but always getting the laugh intended. It is the performance of a man who, although billed third, knows that the entire show is his to do as he likes with and that the audience will be with him all the way.

So Laughton is fine; but the Laughton role is basically an excrescence, a piece of comic relief. Mrs Christie must be served, and Mrs Christie is very English, so the first strain comes when the movie is made in California by a cynical Austrian whose motive is very possibly to get himself a quick and easy box office hit after a succession of expensive flops. There is almost nothing of Wilder in *Witness for the Prosecution* save the basic skills of a master of his craft. He puts in a few sly jokes, such as the Tyrone Power character going to the movies to see Jesse James (in which Power himself once starred) or Marlene Dietrich showing her famous legs in a Hamburg *boite* which is surely intended to remind viewers of *The Blue Angel*. This is in a totally dispensable flashback which holds up the plot still further; rumour has it that the sequence was included at the insistence of Miss Dietrich, to beef up her part and give her a song, but she sings very badly and in a blonde wig looks not so much like her old self as like Stanley Baxter in drag.

There is further unnecessary strain in the harsh photographic style, which is boring to look at and does not even obliterate the lines on Miss Dietrich's face. Nor can she adequately manage the climactic impersonation on which the plot turns: though make-up can alter her appearance, her Cockney has a distinct Germanic ring, and to be truthful her only real asset is her facial immobility, which gives nothing away in the courtroom scenes. Her casting made it

WITNESS FOR THE PROSECUTION. Ian Wolfe knows his place, which is to shut up while Charles Laughton talks to Elsa Lanchester.

necessary to add a few years to her husband, who in the play was described as an eager and likeable young ex-serviceman. Even so, the casting of Tyrone Power was an unhappy choice, for at forty-five he had lost his physical attraction, and may well have been ill, for he died in the following year.

Nothing but quibbles so far. But the piece as redesigned is an infallible crowd-puller, providing only that Laughton plays Sir Wilfrid. The twists still take an average audience's breath away, and though depleted of lines the supporting solicitor types (John Williams, Torin Thatcher, Henry Daniell) can usually raise a smile by raising an eyebrow. And just at the point when interest might flag, Una O'Connor bobs out of retirement and into the witness box to give us an aged version of her chirpy, lip-pursing housekeeper; while Norma Varden, whose career goes right back to the Aldwych farces, has her moment too as the murdered dowager.

As for suspense, the outcome of the mystery becomes less important to the audience than two questions: a) whether Sir Wilfrid will take the case and b) whether he will live through it on his diet of pills and his vacuum flask of cocoa which is really brandy. We disbelieve his apparent disinterest right from his first interview with the solicitor, whom he tells: 'I have done a very unethical thing. I have taken your cigar and I am not taking your case.' As for his health, he is really obliged to give us a happy ending in order to balance the fact that his co-stars, by reason of the plot, are prevented from doing so. One wonders indeed why they took on such equivocal and almost unactable parts. Dietrich is limited to three sharp-suited and very restrained appearances, one outburst (discreetly filmed in long shot), and the aforesaid disguise. Power in the solicitor's office has nothing to do but look innocent; in court he is limited to brief answers and tirades from the dock, including that hoary old standby 'You've got to believe me.' In the very last minutes both are allowed to relax their masks, and the notorious line 'Want to kiss me, ducky?' still provokes a sharp intake of breath. But the essence of the entertainment remains in such irrelevant moments as Lanchester chasing the departing Laughton with the quadruple cry: 'Your bath, your tablets, your massage, your injection!' Whereupon he stops in his tracks, thanks her, takes the hypodermic syringe and pierces his cigar with it.

Witness for the Prosecution. US 1958; black and white; 116 minutes. Produced by Arthur Hornblow Jnr for United Artists/Edward Small. Written by Billy Wilder, Larry Marcus and Harry Kurnitz from the play by Agatha Christie. Directed by Billy Wilder. Photographed by Russell Harlan. Music by Ernest Gold. With Charles Laughton as Sir Wilfrid Robarts; Marlene Dietrich as Christine Vole; Tyrone Power as Leonard Vole; Elsa Lanchester as Miss Plimsoll; John Williams as Brogan-Moore; Henry Daniell as Mayhew; Ian Wolfe as Carter; Una O'Connor as Janet.

Femme Fatale
THE WOMAN IN THE WINDOW

A professor befriends a girl who innocently gets him involved in murder.

Though it encountered considerable criticism on its first release, for an untenable reason which I'll come to later, and although it moves at a jog-trot rather than a canter, this is a movie for which I suspect a goodly number of middle-aged-to-elderly film buffs harbour considerable affection. You could call it a cleaned-up version of a smoking room story; at any rate it's a very clubbable picture, a cautionary tale for susceptible men. Appropriately it begins, or very nearly begins, in a New York gentlemen's club. Two rather clumsy prefaces have established our mature hero as an assistant professor at Gotham College, lecturing on 'some psychological aspects of homicide'. 'The man who kills in self-defence,' he states firmly, 'must not be judged by the same standards as the man who kills in anger.' The lecture fades abruptly to show him bidding farewell at the railroad depot to his thoroughly boring family, who are off on a summer trip. So he is free to walk along 42nd Street – then a respectable promenade – in the dying heat of the day, not exactly looking for excitement but able to bask peacefully in his temporary freedom. Bang on cue, his two friends at the club, a doctor and an assistant district attorney, start up a morose conversation about middle age as 'the end of the brightness of life, the end of spirit and adventure'. They speak of a picture in the window of the art gallery next door. They have all noticed it, and metaphorically licked their lips, for it is an oil painting of a glamorous modern woman, aloof and dangerous but very desirable. They wonder what they would do if they met the original. The professor chuckles ruefully: 'If I met her, I'd probably mumble something idiotic and run like the devil.' But it does seem a little revealing that, left to himself, the book he selects in the club library, before sinking into his accustomed armchair, is that respectable piece of erotica the Song of Songs.

Aroused at ten-thirty by the steward, he emerges blinking into the warm night and takes one last look at the portrait . . . only to find the exotic subject of it doing the same. She likes to watch men's reactions, she says: they vary between a solemn stare and a long low whistle. As for the professor, she thinks if he hadn't been interrupted he might have given a long low *solemn* whistle. Embarrassed by this analysis, he makes the mistake of admiring the artist's technique, whereupon the lady invites him up to her place to see, not etchings, but other sketches by the same man. She is persuasive: 'I'm not married, I have no designs on you, and one drink is all I care for.' Smiling but shaking his head ('I was warned against the siren call of adventure') he follows, and by courtesy of a cinematic dissolve or two he is shortly to be found opening a *second* bottle of champagne: 'I should say no, but I have no intention of saying it.'

The plot now takes a sudden turn with the violent entry of an unattractive jealous lover, clearly the provider of the luxury amid which the lady lives. Without pausing to hear an explanation he tries to strangle the professor, who on the point of gasping his last contrives to stab the intruder to death with a pair of scissors kindly handed to him by the lady. After a decent pause for the enormity of the situation to sink in, the survivors decide that for everybody's sake (i.e. their own) they must dispose of the body; and here begins the most enjoyably Hitchcockian section of this three-section film. With the body in the back of his car (and a couple of eerie shots of it are among the film's best effects), the fugitive professor is forced to converse with a tollkeeper and a cop at a stop light, running the risk of being remembered by both. As a criminal he is either clumsy or very unfortunate; while dumping the body in a wood he manages to leave both tyre tracks and footprints, to tear both his jacket and his hand on barbed wire, and to plunge his other hand into poison ivy. All these regrettable oversights very nearly come home to roost a couple of days later, when his clubbable friend from the DA's office genially invites him, as a theoretical expert on such matters, to study the scene of the crime. Looks of dawning suspicion are turned on him when he almost blunders into self-

THE WOMAN IN THE WINDOW. The smoking room story that got a professor into trouble. Raymond Massey, Edward G. Robinson, Edmund Breon.

incrimination. But the moments pass with no unfortunate sequel, and the scene is set for the final stage of the melodrama.

This is an attempt at blackmail by the dead man's crooked bodyguard, who has deduced exactly what happened. He wants 5000 dollars as a starter, and humorously shrugs off the lady's attempt to poison him with the professor's sleeping powders. Hearing by phone of her failure, the professor takes an overdose himself, and is too far gone to be roused by her further call, which is to say that the blackmailer, carrying incriminating evidence, has been ambushed and shot dead by the police on leaving her apartment, and that the case has therefore been closed without their being involved.

A nice ironic end, you might think; and so it is. But what so unnecessarily annoyed the critics (who can't have been following the plot very closely) is that the apparently fatally drugged professor is now awakened, at ten thirty, by the club steward, and goes home, recognizing on his way out the familiar cloakroom attendant and the doorman as the villains of what has plainly been a dream. This was taken as a scriptwriter's easy way out of an impossible situation, and the critical abuse has continued to attach itself to the film down the years; yet it is a false accusation, for as we have seen, the dream is only a flip twist to a tale which had already ended very satisfactorily, if unhappily. As in J. B. Priestley's *Dangerous Corner*, we have watched a story of what might have been, but Mr Priestley added to his telling a touch of the surreal, in the form of a time spiral, and so won the applause of the highbrows. True, there were too many dream movies towards the end of the war, for they offered easy comfort in a time of trial: George Sanders, for instance, found in the film version of *Uncle Harry* that the murders he had committed were not real. (In Thomas Job's original play, they were.) But nobody ever complained about the dream endings of *Roman Scandals* or *The Blue Bird* or *The Wizard of Oz* or *Fiddlers Three*.

I find *The Woman in the Window* an almost entirely commendable entertainment, well worthy of the normal high standards of its author-producer Nunnally Johnson. I am less enthusiastic about the direction of that increasingly moody and inflexible German Fritz Lang, which too often seems stolid when it should be imaginative, distant when it should be detailed. A remake by, say, Sidney Lumet might be interesting. Yet Lang must have been pleased with his work, for three years later he got together with the same trio of leading actors for a serious redraft of the same situation, from Jean Renoir's *La Chienne*. It was called *Scarlet Street*, and this time the unwise middle-aged hero murders with an ice-pick the trollop who has lured him, allowing the pimp-blackmailer to be executed for his crime. The movie caused controversy in America as the first in which a guilty man is allowed to go free; showing him twenty years later as a conscience-ridden derelict was apparently not enough for the puritans.

A sartorial note. Why do so many of the males in this picture wear straw boaters? Assistant DA, victim, blackmailer, assorted extras all follow the fashion, which must have lasted through very few New York summers. Another oddity which fans of long standing may sense is the feeling of *déjà vu* likely to creep over them in the professor's scenes with the top cop, played by Thomas E. Jackson, not an especially familiar actor but the same Jackson who in *Little Caesar* routed and killed the same Edward G. Robinson, who was playing the title role. Did Robinson suggest the casting? And is it an in-joke that the character is called Inspector Jackson? A further curiosity is the case of the vanishing antimacassar; in one shot it is behind Mr Robinson's armchaired head, but not in the next. Finally, there is the matter of the deduction about the footprints being deeper when the murderer was carrying his burden and lighter when he returns. It is adapted from something said in a Sherlock Holmes story, but when I watched *The Woman in the Window* on television early in 1983, it had been used earlier on the same evening in a recent television movie called *The Return of Frank Cannon*. Which shows at least that Hollywood is still imitating the best masters.

The Woman in the Window. US 1944; black and white; 99 minutes. Produced by Nunnally Johnson for International/United Artists. Written by Nunnally Johnson from the novel *Once Off Guard* by J. H. Wallis. Directed by Fritz Lang. Photographed by Milton Krasner. Music by Arthur Lang. With Edward G. Robinson as Richard Wanley; Joan Bennett as Alice Reed; Raymond Massey as Frank Lalor; Edmund Breon as Dr Barkstone; Dan Duryea as Heidt; Thomas E. Jackson as Inspector Jackson; Arthur Loft as Claude Mazard; Dorothy Peterson as Mrs Wanley.

Remember Him to Nelson Square

YANKEE DOODLE DANDY

The life of playwright and vaudevillian George M. Cohan.

I shall always associate it with Hawaii, for the unlikely reason that I last saw it there in 1982 when on my way home from Australia. The local television station was making it the main attraction on Sunday 4 July, and even went to the trouble of publicizing the forty-year-old film in the streets by dint of a procession of drum majorettes bearing banners. It all seemed irresistibly inappropriate, for most of them had Polynesian eyes and skin colour; but on Honolulu Beach, I was told, anything goes these days. Being reminded by the noisy crowds of Blackpool at its worst, I had soon had enough, and retreated to the Kahala Hilton for a quiet afternoon. Here Hawaiians in white marry ceremoniously as dolphins play in ornamental pools; but for me, in view of the humid weather, the warm Pacific waters were a greater attraction. I was pleasantly submerged in the shade of a handy palm tree when it came to my attention that every bather around me – and they numbered about three score – was leaving the water rather hurriedly. 'Sharks!' I muttered to myself, leaping for the shore; but the urgency seemed to be of a lesser kind, and in puzzlement I followed the crowds into a large deck chair storehouse. Here I found them avidly grouped round a television set to watch, not the solemn presidential announcement which I momentarily feared, but professional tennis live from Wimbledon . . .

That evening at eight I settled in my palatial room to watch *Yankee Doodle Dandy*. As it came on I was toying with a local pork dish called *pau pau*, followed by a whole fresh pineapple whose innards had been cleverly chunked without their being disturbed. It seemed rather difficult at first to regain the mood in which I had first approached this same film, forty years earlier at a shabby Lancashire cinema called the Regal, where it caused a mild sensation by being booked for a whole week instead of three days. (I had missed the first local run by going on holiday to the Isle of Man.) My time key was turned only by a small mistake which seemed as irritating in 1982 as I remembered it in 1942. When George M. Cohan goes to London, the script puts him in a hotel which has a view of Nelson's Column and is called the Nelson Square Hotel. That, for me, pleasantly fixed the entertainment back in the days when

291

not everybody knew everything, and even Hollywood scriptwriters had not necessarily been to London. Somehow it also reminded me that the real reason for a biopic of George M. Cohan in 1942 was the large number of patriotic songs which could be worked into the production, for in and around the real London, not the fake Hollywood one, a real war was then raging, and once again America was volunteering its help. Given the need, what theme could be more stirring than the one which Cohan wrote in 1917?

> Over there, over there!
> Send the word, send the word, over there!
> For the yanks are coming, the yanks are coming,
> The drums rum-tumming everywhere . . .

Cohan himself, Cohan the Broadway song-and-dance man, playwright, actor and producer, was dying of cancer as the film was made; but he lived long enough to see and enjoy its success. During production his contract gave him the right to check and approve every detail, and he even wrote a full script, though very little of it was used. Perhaps the movie could not escape infection by the wartime urge to exaggerate, for even though Cohan's notorious ego was toned down in the finished production, his daughter said of it: 'That's the kind of life Daddy would *like* to have lived.'

For most of its considerable length *Yankee Doodle Dandy* remains a great show, not perhaps among the slickest of Hollywood musicals, but a thoroughly likeable entertainment shot through with the electricity of one great performer being played by another. James Cagney had been a top star for twelve years, but most typically as a cocky young hoodlum; never before had he fully unleashed his stunning ability as a tap dancer. His dance numbers in this film went straight into the Hollywood Hall of Fame, and of their kind they have still not been excelled. Apart from them, and for understandable reasons, the picture provides a fairly smooth and straightforward account of a pretty nice guy; if it omits a few black spots and a bad marriage, that was the way Cohan and the public both wanted it. The disappointment is that despite the presence of Michael Curtiz behind the megaphone, it contains no masterstrokes of direction, only a moderately professional job of sewing the elements together. The cleverly constructed ambience of *Casablanca*, made within the same year, is never in evidence.

It begins with the flashback without which few films of the forties would have felt complete. Cohan, triumphant in a Broadway spoof of Roosevelt called *I'd Rather Be Right*, is summoned to a late evening appointment at the White House (presumably on a Sunday when the show isn't on). Cohan did meet the president several times, but always during the day; presumably the late hour was invented to make it more reasonable that he should settle down and tell Roosevelt his whole life story, which occupies the rest of the film. Cohan did claim to have written the two lines which cement the relationship, and they certainly seem to be in his style:

COHAN: Where else in the world could a plain guy like me sit down and talk things over with the head man?

YANKEE DOODLE DANDY. James Cagney is about to take wing.

ROOSEVELT: Well now, you know, Mr Cohan, that's as good a description of America as I've ever heard.

After the session the old performer is given a warm handshake by the president (played by Captain Jack Young but seen only in shadow) and dances downstairs to find soldiers marching past and singing 'Over There' on their way to the war:

SOLDIER: What's the matter, old timer? Don't you remember this song?
COHAN: Seems to me I do.
SOLDIER: Well, I don't hear anything.

Cohan naturally finds his voice and marches off with the troops into the night mist. Fade the picture, increase the sound track, bring up the house lights: not a dry eye anywhere.

The vaudeville scenes of Cohan's infancy and youth are edited with predictable verve and tension, snatches of a dozen acts merging into an agreeable kaleidoscope as the Three Cohans become the Four Cohans. The problem of the star's real age (forty-two) when he makes his first appearance at the supposed age of seventeen is cunningly got over by having him first seen as a bearded old fogey in a play. In this guise he plays a whole scene to a critical young fan who becomes his future wife, and when he removes the whiskers we accept him as a much younger man than he is, while the film, by one of Hollywood's marvellous compressions, has contrived to advance the plot at the same time. Problems or not, the ebullient Cagney won his first Oscar for this performance, and marked the occasion, after Greer Garson had rambled on for an hour, with a four-sentence acceptance speech: 'I've always maintained that in this business you're only as good as the other fellow thinks you are. It's nice to know that you people think I did a good job. And don't forget it was a good part too. Thank you very much.'

Cohan was an Irish-American phenomenon. Author of forty plays, composer of 500 songs, star or producer of more than a hundred Broadway shows, he was the firework that illuminated American light theatre during the first third of the century. He was shrewd enough to know that his script for the film lacked perspective. 'Frankly,' he said, 'it turned a blind eye to all my faults.' The film which emerged didn't have much depth either, and it has survived as a classic largely because of its star and its handful of great songs. It is an attractive watercolour of a subject which deserves one day to be painted in rich oils.

Yankee Doodle Dandy. US 1942; black and white; 129 minutes. Produced by William Cagney for Warners. Written by Robert Buckner, Edmund Joseph and Julius and Philip Epstein. Directed by Michael Curtiz. Photographed by James Wong Howe. Songs by George M. Cohan. With James Cagney as George M. Cohan; Walter Huston as Jerry Cohan; Rosemary de Camp as Nellie Cohan; Joan Leslie as Mary; Richard Whorf as Sam Harris; George Tobias as Dietz; Irene Manning as Fay Templeton; S. Z. Sakall as Schwab; Jeanne Cagney as Josie Cohan; Eddie Foy Jnr as Eddie Foy.

The Penguin, the Pup and the Flying Wombat
THE YOUNG IN HEART
A family of charming confidence tricksters moves in on a rich old lady.

When sometime in 1939 I saw the trailer for it at the Bolton Odeon, I half-expected an all-star musical spectacular. There were so many of my favourite people in it, all of them smiling happily, plus a cute puppy, plus a penguin, plus a futuristic car called a Flying Wombat, plus a rather modest train crash; and all these elements were heralded in the promotional reel by the word SEE followed by three exclamation marks. On reflection I decided that music was the one element lacking, but in any case I had no doubt that I would go, for it was clearly a very pleasant film in which there would be plenty of laughs and no murders, the sort of thing I could take my Auntie Flo to in the confident expectation that she would revise her low opinion of The Pictures. ('They put years on me,' she used to say. 'Sitting in the dark, and no talking!')

The Young in Heart proved to be a very pleasant film indeed, unlike anything else my mother and I had seen, and we both looked forward to encountering again its mixture of sentiment and self-mockery. (We noted that like the already much promoted *Gone with the Wind* it was a Selznick production, which seemed to be some kind of hallmark of quality, though we were not quite sure what a Selznick might be.) But it never seemed to turn up at our suburban locals. This was just about the time of the outbreak of war, and light comedies such as *The Young in Heart* must for a few months have seemed quite irrelevant, especially when they were peopled by upper-crust confidence tricksters used to wintering on the Riviera: that life had no place in the new world of stirrup pumps and Anderson shelters. Besides, the movie was a full stop of another kind: Janet Gaynor had announced that with it she would terminate a career which had lasted since before I was born, and that seemed a very long time indeed, apart from making mother feel sad. Neither of us ever got the movie out of our mind, and throughout the war I scanned the columns of the *Manchester Evening News*, which encompassed upwards of a hundred cinemas, for news of its turning up in Middleton or Radcliffe or Walkden, all within a ten-mile radius in the doomladen landscape of South Lancashire. But I never heard of it again until the summer of 1948, when I was an army education sergeant in Portsmouth and set off one rainy Thursday evening to do my duty by John Ford and sit through his critically acclaimed but clearly depressing Mexican enterprise *The Fugitive*, adapted from Graham Greene's *The Power and the Glory*. It was playing at an obscure cinema in Fratton called the Troxy; but when I reached this haven, it seemed that a virtual nil attendance on Monday had persuaded the management to take it off in a hurry. The substitute programme now on offer consisted (joy of joys!) of a Laurel and Hardy two-reeler called *County Hospital*, and as feature attraction *The Young in Heart*, the latest acquisition of a reissue distributor called New Realm. Sudden demobilization could scarcely have pleased me more, especially when this ghost from my past (all of nine years old) came up fresh as paint and sent me whistling all the way back to the barracks.

It was in 1948, with the commercial failure of *Portrait of Jennie*, that David Selznick began to lose interest in film-making. Soon after, all his films were withdrawn from the market, and it was only ten years later, about the time I began my long career as a television buyer, that they were bought up by the American ABC network and began to creep back into circulation. Sadly, *The Young in Heart* was not among them, some complication having developed over the international copyright. Local collectors did get their hands on 16mm prints, and in the mid-seventies I saw one and enjoyed the experience despite inadequate projection; but it was not until the early eighties that an enterprising television distributor in New York cleared the world rights. Most of his clients, I gathered, were acutely disappointed to find that what they had bought was *not* the Frank Sinatra/Doris Day starrer of the fifties, *Young at Heart*; I was probably the only prospect in the world to be absolutely delighted

THE YOUNG IN HEART. The charming Carletons have spotted a rich prey. Roland Young, Janet Gaynor, Billie Burke, Douglas Fairbanks Jnr.

at this chance of sharing my treasure with a wide audience. My joy increased when tests revealed that we had received a 35mm print in perfect condition apart from a few neg scratches which only a hypercritic would notice. I scheduled it on a Sunday evening in the autumn of 1984. At the appointed time I took the phone off the hook, set a decanter of brandy at my side, turned the lights down low . . . and was saddened by what I saw.

Four commercial breaks may have had something to do with ruining the pace; perhaps I had a cold coming on; or it may simply have been too late in the evening. Whatever the reason, for all the quality ingredients on which Selznick the perfectionist had insisted, the mixture obstinately refused to rise. I began to notice thinly written lines and overwritten scenes; fades to black which should have been replaced by dissolves; a lack of real thrust in the plot. The car and the puppy and the penguin were still pleasant distractions, but I found myself waiting for them because the plot didn't hold me. And it seemed to go on for hours, with the romantic leads looking embarrassed by their long repetitive speeches. Yet at the end, the off-screen announcer said 'What a nice film,' and said it with every indication of genuine enthusiasm; while over the next few days a dozen or more people told me how much they had enjoyed it and what a find it was. After that I very willingly set myself down as a hardened old cynic, and awaited my opportunity to take another look at *The Young in Heart* when I was in a better mood. My verdict after the second viewing is a softer one. *The Young in Heart* is indeed full of fine things, even though they don't include the over-emphatic, almost frantic score by the usually reliable Franz Waxman, who really does underline every joke to death, and often seems at odds with the flow of the dialogue.

The rather crass roller caption which begins the proceedings is not encouraging:

THE RIVIERA!
Coney Island with a Monocle, where the Beach twinkles like a gold piece and the Moon comes rolling out of a slot machine. Here Millionaire Mama seeks a glamorous son-in-law, while Tired Papa looks for new ways to get trimmed; and here come the Carletons, a merry little family exuding charm and a touch of Larceny with every fortune-hunting Smile . . .

That must have been written by the studio janitor, but it matches nothing else in the movie. We are instantly shown a clipping announcing the betrothal of the son of Sahib Anthony Carleton to the daughter of Senator Albert J. Jennings the Georgia millionaire, and from this we fade to the Sahib himself, Roland Young at his most dreamily laconic, accepting the senator's cheque for 34,000 dollars:

SAHIB: Many a hot Indian night my dear old Lancers and I have whiled away the hours with poker. Bit out of touch with the game lately. Which may account for the cards tonight seeming somewhat obstinate.
JENNINGS: Obstinate? I thought they did everything but push the money towards you.
SAHIB: Well, keeping it in the family, you know, my dear Jennings. A domestic jackpot. Of course, once the dear children are married, everything I have is yours. And everything you have . . . is mine.
JENNINGS: You mustn't let your generosity sweep away your reason, sir.

The men are overlooked by their women, and Sahib's slightly batty wife Marmy exclaims to her in-law-to-be: 'I think it's wonderful the way the Sahib has taken Mr Jennings – to his heart, I mean.'

Mrs Jennings inquires what exactly the Sahib does for a living, and Marmy babbles on vaguely: 'Part of the Brain Trust, you know . . . labour conditions, wages, unemployment. The Sahib thinks the only way to do away with unemployment is to do away with *employment*. If nobody works, there can't be any unemployment – and so the Sahib hasn't done a stroke of work for years.' But retribution is on its way to the Carletons: the police have discovered an old Toronto theatrical poster, in which one Thomas Higgins, who looks very like the Sahib, once played Col. Anthony Carleton in *Sweethearts of the Bengal Lancers*. In fact the Sahib has never been to India at all, and is a known cardsharp . . . of the most elegant kind, naturally. He is forced to return the senator's cheque in return for four second-class tickets to London. His son Richard is not displeased to cease his amorous attentions to the fat Georgia heiress with the squeaky voice, while his daughter George-Ann is happy to run away from a serious young Scot in case she makes the mistake of falling for him: 'How can I be in love with him? He hasn't any money! Young Duncan, however, is sufficiently serious to follow her on to the train: 'Your father's a worthless fortune hunter but I forgive you because you're only daft and I can cure you.'

But the Carletons already have their eye on another sucker: a lonely, wealthy old lady who has a big house in London and, entranced by their gentility, wants them to share it. She is not even put off by Marmy's rather vague notions of India: 'The children were born there, you know . . . somewhere in the Himalayas. A dreadful place, what with the ayahs and the whatnots.' And so the penniless Carletons arrive in London with great expectations, defying the suspicious eye cast upon them by Miss Fortune's lawyer. Time passes pleasantly enough, but the Sahib eventually becomes impatient at the lack of any sign of a new will: 'If the old girl doesn't cough up something soon after all we've done for her I shall lose my faith in human nature.' As Marmy adds, they *have* eaten all their meals with her, though needless to say Miss Fortune has paid for them. Something must certainly be done, before the lawyer starts making inquiries. Sahib puts it bluntly: 'For the sake of all of you I am prepared to make the surpreme sacrifice.' He means he will take a job, instead of spending his days watching other men work at a construction site. And Junior must do the same. And how the penguin, the pup and the Flying Wombat come into all this, the reader must find out for himself. I only wish that I could experience again the joy with which this modest comedy filled me when I first encountered it forty-five years ago.

The Young in Heart. US 1938; black and white; 90 minutes. Produced by David O. Selznick. Written by Paul Osborn and Charles Bennett from the book by I. A. R. Wylie. Directed by Richard Wallace. Photographed by Leon Shamroy. Music by Franz Waxman. With Janet Gaynor as George-Ann Carleton; Douglas Fairbanks Jnr as Richard Carleton; Roland Young as Sahib Carleton; Billie Burke as Marmy Carleton; Minnie Dupree as Miss Fortune; Henry Stephenson as Anstruther; Richard Carlson as Duncan McCrea; Paulette Goddard as Leslie; Eily Malyon as Sarah.

BEST OF THE BAD ONES

The first film I ever saw was pretty bad by any standard: *Madame Butterfly*, with Sylvia Sidney committing hara kiri, Cary Grant in a snow white uniform, and no Puccini except as background music. Seen again fifty years later, it did not so much creak as groan. These days, most of the new films seem pretty bad, by normal decent entertainment standards as well as by professional and technical ones, to the extent that it doesn't interest me to see them even for the sake of throwing critical brickbats. But like everyone else I have favourite bad films, and the term needs qualifying. Anything can be lousy, that's not difficult. In the old days of double features and quota quickies, appalling British rubbish was churned out by the mile in the knowledge that it would pay its way providing it filled the space between ice-cream intervals. Most of the titles are best forgotten, and no wise man would even try to bring them to mind. Just a handful, by their sheer awfulness, won't go away. Would you believe that New Realm once put out a thirty-three-minute filler (thirty-three minutes made it a feature for quota purposes, and that was important) under the title *Who's Baby?* All that money pouring in for next to no work, and they couldn't even get the spelling right. What was it about? It was a tour of baby animals in the London Zoo, and it wasn't even the worst British film I ever saw. I was wont for years to put on that particular pedestal something called *I Was a Dancer*, a wholly amateurish backstage melodrama with Diana Napier. Then I caught up with *He Found a Star*, a late-thirties comedy-musical starring Vic Oliver and that silvery hotel-bedroom gleam which British studios in those days persistently mistook for a sophisticated lighting effect. (Top feature titles like *They Met in the Dark*, *The Squeaker*, *The Lion Has Wings*, *Goodnight Vienna*, *In a Monastery Garden* and *Hatter's Castle* all suffered from it, though in the case of the last-named it did help to tone down the grinding overacting of Robert Newton.) The fifties made things worse for British second features, and I haven't even mentioned the name Danziger. I shudder to remember *Fire Maidens from Outer Space*, an abject piece of *papier mâché* science fiction for which some masochist called Cy Roth took full responsibility, with a flowing signature on the main title. *The Man Without a Body*, in which Robert Hutton tried to revive the head of Nostradamus on a kitchen table, and *Womaneater*, in which George Coulouris (Walter Parks Thatcher of *Citizen Kane*, no less) grew in his cellar an indoor plant which hungrily shook its fronds whenever a nubile beauty approached, were two apparently enticing horror attractions which proved to have nothing behind their titles but six reels each of total boredom. Between 1938 and 1948 I saw two different but equally overlong versions of the old music-hall sketch *A Sister to Assist'er*, and ran screaming in revulsion from the second (not that the first had not tried my patience sorely). A Tommy Trinder army comedy called *You Lucky People* was advertised as being in Camerascope, but the anamorphic lens which Mr Arthur Dent of Adelphi Films had bought for the purpose (presumably on Berwick Market) had a dark blemish right in the middle, and it kept getting in the way of the actors' faces. Over *The Devil's Hand*, and *Death in the Hand*, and *The Hand* itself it is merciful to draw a veil – merciful to my peace of mind as well as to the perpetrators.

Some American supports did of course find a permanent place in my little sink of iniquity, but at least most of them were quite sharply edited, and ended in half a reel of violent action which could be guaranteed to bring one out of one's torpor. Exceptions were the Joe Palooka series – a shameful waste of Leon Errol – and almost anything made by PRC, which my school friends and I once agreed must stand for a Pretty Ribby Concoction. The Medveds have made Edward D. Wood Jnr famous as the worst film-maker of all time, but I was unable to add him to my collection while at an impressionable age, since his efforts were at so low a level as to be rejected even by the British circuits, and none of them ever came my way until they were exhumed by Channel Four in the eighties.

All these films were guaranteed to contain no redeeming qualities. One suffered through them. For a film to be enjoyably bad, however, for it to qualify as a Best Bad Film, it must attain a certain production stature and contain within it talents which one would normally enjoy even though in this case they were sadly misapplied. *The Story of Mankind*, for instance, was so replete with personages usually welcome that it would have been impossible in 1957 for me to stay away from the Hammersmith Commodore, whatever the critical reports. Ronald Colman had emerged from a seven-year retirement to play the Spirit of Man, and very attractive he still looked in his trench coat, wandering through an eternity of dry ice, for all the world as though he had just stepped over the hill from Shangri-La. It was only when one listened to what he was saying that one began to wince, especially since Vincent Price, as his leader of the opposition in a tour through history, was overacting as usual. Soon it became boringly clear that the movie was going to come down from its astral plane only when the editor could cut in a few clips from older and better films, or new sequences capable of being acted out against the simplest of backdrops. Mr Hendrik Van Loon, who wrote the original 'work', must have been spinning in his grave to see it whittled into fragments and illustrated by distressed old actors. He might possibly have been pleased to see the Marx Brothers billed. But not seen together: oh no, Mr Irwin Allen was more subtle a producer than that. The Marxes found themselves separated not merely by scenes but by centuries. Harpo was Sir Isaac Newton, with apples positively raining on his head. Chico was a half-visible monk at the court of Columbus. Groucho at least had a scene or two to himself on a set representing Manhattan Island, which (as Peter Minuit) he proceeded to buy from the Indians for twenty-four dollars. Other names to conjure with found themselves in tricks which misfired equally. Peter Lorre through the smoke of Rome muttered a couple of lines as Nero. More smoke billowed around Hedy Lamarr as a Joan of Arc who had plainly come straight to the stake from the beauty parlour. Edward Everett Horton was listed, intriguingly, as Sir Walter Raleigh, but one barely had time to recognize the doublet-and-hosed figure who entered, smoking a pipe, before a courtier hilariously threw water over him on the assumption that he was on fire. End of scene, end of performance. The most enjoyment to be obtained from this witless and desiccated film occurred in the dialogue between Reginald Gardiner as Shakespeare and Agnes Moorehead as his Queen. The only possible explanation of their absurd performances is that they knew themselves to be sunk by the script and decided that they might as well have a bit of fun. The resultant exchange of gesture, grimace and exclamation is, I believe, without peer since the days of Sarah Bernhardt and Edmund Kean.

Even the greatest directors have things to be ashamed of. Often, sadly, they come right at the end of a career, when the big studio has younger fish to fry or the inventive mind is at the end of its tether. How else is one to explain William Dieterle's *Quick, Let's Get Married*? Or Carol Reed's *Flap*? or Josef von Sternberg's *Jet Pilot* and *Anatahan*? Or Michael Curtiz's *A Breath of Scandal*? Or George Cukor's *Rich and Famous*? or Frank Borzage's *The Big Fisherman*? Or Mervyn Le Roy's *Moment to Moment*? Or Leo McCarey's *Satan Never Sleeps*? Or Vincente Minnelli's *A Matter of Time*? Or Mitchell Leisen's *Bedevilled*? Or Ernst Lubitsch's *That Lady in Ermine*? Or John Ford's *Donovan's Reef*? Or Edmund Goulding's *Mardi Gras*? Or Raoul Walsh's *Marines Let's Go*? Or William Wyler's *The Liberation of L.B. Jones*? Or Frank Capra's *A Pocketful of Miracles*? Or Billy Wilder's *Buddy Buddy*? In the case of Otto Preminger the brick-thrower can take his choice of any item from *Hurry Sundown* in 1967 to *The Human Factor* in 1979, though he may have no real doubt that the nadir was reached with *Skidoo*. Detractors of Chaplin often aver that the rot set in as early as *The Great Dictator* in 1940, and that the débâcle of *A King in New York* and *A Countess from Hong Kong* was easily predictable. There is, of course, a faction averring that Hitchcock's *Family Plot* is a work of senility. As for George Stevens's *The Greatest Story Ever Told*, which he shot in Utah because he saw nothing in Israel that looked like Israel, the director confidently predicted that it would be an 'instant classic', showing until the end of the century and after. I think it must have been accidentally cut up and resold as Christmas card designs, for I haven't seen it around lately.

One does not always have to wait until the end of a great director's career for the sound of the hiccup. Hitchcock fans have quite a number of 'interesting failures' to explain away, including *Rich and Strange, Rope, The Paradine Case, Under Capricorn* and *The Wrong Man*. John Ford made the dreary *Three Godfathers* at the height of his powers, in 1948, the year of Billy Wilder's equally lamentable, nay inexplicable, *The Emperor Waltz*. Fritz Lang's best-forgotten *You and Me* came after he had been three years in Hollywood. Lubitsch's *Angel* was the flattest of his frou-frous to emerge in the mid-thirties, between *Trouble in Paradise* and *Ninotchka*. Leo McCarey's *Once Upon a Honeymoon*, made eighteen months before *Going My Way*, was a compendium of stiff writing and muddled thinking. Who is to be blamed for *Honky Tonk Freeway* but John Schlesinger? He took the money. Ditto Joseph L. Mankiewicz for the awful 1962 *Cleopatra*, re which catastrophe the only witty comment was made by macabre cartoonist Charles Addams at the premiere: 'I only came to see the asp.' Lindsay Anderson even believed that he had a winner in *Britannia Hospital*, but he found few to agree with him. Perhaps John Frankenheimer also believed in *The Extraordinary Seaman*, and William Wellman in *Track of the Cat*, and Fred Zinnemann in *Behold a Pale Horse* (the first American film to show a toilet flushing), and Karel Reisz in *The Gambler*, and Robert Rossen in *Mambo* and *Lilith*. I'm quite certain that the old MGM intellectual Albert Lewin had faith in *Pandora and the Flying Dutchman*, even though his alma mater wouldn't finance it; the arty fantasy, which wore Omar Khayyam's moving finger to the bone, backed their judgement. But nobody could have believed in *The Cool Mikado*, not even Michael Winner.

John Huston throughout his career virtually alternated one goodish film with one pretty bad (remember *The Barbarian and the Geisha* and *A Walk with Love and Death?*), though he seldom matched the disastrous *Annie* which he made at the age of seventy-six, or *Under the Volcano* which came two years later. Jean Renoir made so many masterpieces that stinkers like *The Woman on the Beach, The Golden Coach* and *Paris Does Strange Things* tend to be overlooked. David Lean, Rouben Mamoulian and Joseph L. Mankiewicz, on the other hand, made so few that each as it came along was treated by critics as a cause for celebration, and only many years later did it become clear how seldom they measured up to the expected standard. Foreign-speaking directors, however internationally acclaimed while they stay home, are usually at risk when their fame takes them to the big British or American studios. Remember François Truffaut's *Fahrenheit 451*? Remember Serge Bourguignon's *The Reward*? (Remember Serge Bourguignon?) Remember Marc Allégret's *Blanche Fury*? Remember Jan Troell's *Hurricane*? Remember Michael Cacoyannis's *The Day the Fish Came Out*? (Don't, it's too painful.) Michelangelo Antonioni was allowed to do as he liked with *Zabriskie Point* because of the surprisingly good receipts from *Blow-up*; but after its appalled reception he was never allowed to darken Hollywood's doorstep again, and even *Blow-up* is now seen only as a freakish fragment of swinging London. Richard Lester, a prophet without honour in his native America, came to London and had a fashionable success with *A Hard Day's Night*. The fashion soon waned when he served up such unpalatable and impenetrable items as *How I Won the War* and *The Bed-sitting Room*, and in order to survive he had to go back to making movies which somebody might possibly pay to see. (After what he'd done to the industry, he was lucky to find the work.)

Many disasters are caused by letting talent have too much of its own way. Peter Ustinov, dear fellow at home I'm sure, is to my knowledge an actor and raconteur of precision and wit, but results showed long ago that he should never be allowed behind a camera, especially not to direct his own scripts. *School for Secrets, Vice Versa, Private Angelo, Romanoff and Juliet, Billy Budd* and *Lady L* were surely sufficiently awful warnings; *Memed My Hawk* has to be the clincher. Sean Connery gets parts because of his dominating personality, yet he has never been box office except as James Bond: *Marnie, A Fine Madness, Shalako, The Molly Maguires, The Red Tent, The Offence, Zardoz, Ransom, The Wind and the Lion, Robin and Marian, The Next Man, Cuba* and *Wrong is Right* are surely proof enough of that. Elizabeth Taylor and Richard Burton between them were allowed essential creative control over far too many films, and since in the case of *Hammersmith is Out* Mr Ustinov was also involved, the dire result should have been no surprise to anybody. Merle Oberon sank her own finances into her last films, *Of Love and Desire* and *Interval*, and the results sagged even lower than her cosmetic surgery. Burt Reynolds may be a bankable star with the best toupé in the business, but his control of his own career has not been encouraging, with a list of clinkers far outnumbering his hits: *Skullduggery*, *Fuzz*, *Shamus*, *White Lightning*, *The Man Who Loved Cat Dancing*, *W W and the Dixie Dancekings*, *At Long Last Love*, *Hustle*, *Lucky Lady*, *Gator*, *Nickelodeon*, *The End*, *Rough Cut*, *Paternity*, *Stroker Ace* and *The Man Who Loved Women*. As for Clint Eastwood, it must be a bad thing for the industry, though a good one for his bank balance, that his movies continue to make millions when they are as irredeemable, as charmless, witless and uncontrolled, as *Hang 'em High*, *The Beguiled*, *Play Misty for Me*, *Joe Kidd*, *Magnum Force*, *The Eiger Sanction*, *The Enforcer*, *Every Which Way But Loose*, *Any Which Way You Can*, *Honkytonk Man*, *Firefox* and *Tightrope*. The man with the most mysterious influence over financiers is Stanley Kubrick, who has made a publicity campaign out of his own megalomania, and managed to write his own ticket for such absurdities as *2001: A Space Odyssey*, *A Clockwork Orange*, *Barry Lyndon* and *The Shining*. His contracts even give him ultimate control of where, when and whether his films shall be shown; thank goodness he has decided against releasing most of them to television. The man who has *lost* most influence is undoubtedly Ken Russell, who totally threw away a brilliant talent when he became obsessive about what someone called digging up dead composers and throwing rocks at them. The physical repulsion of *The Devils* was certainly no more objectionable than the crass taste of *The Music Lovers*, *Mahler*, *Valentino* and *Lizstomania*. In the last of these Lizst was given a line, 'Piss off, Brahms', which seems, together with a scene in which the composer is threatened by a giant phallus, to have finally frozen the loans from Russell's misguided benefactors.

The unreliability of Orson Welles is of course a story in itself. He barely seems to have finished a film since 1960. One has visions of odd reels lodged in vaults all over Europe and America, and even when he gets something finally in the can, more or less, it proves, like *Confidential Report*, *Othello* and *Chimes at Midnight*, to be riddled with technical imperfections of a kind which would never have been tolerated by the Hollywood moguls who gave him a free hand to make *Citizen Kane*. As early as 1948 he produced at Republic a crazy version of *Macbeth* in accents nobody could understand, within a castle set constantly dripping with damp. Duncan would have perished of pneumonia long before Macbeth made up his mind to stab him. Meanwhile Mr Welles continues on his steady progress as an actor, from fairly good to atrocious.

Among actors, it is not only Merle Oberon who should have given in gracefully to the ageing process. Even if the scripts had been better, Mae West should never have attempted *Sextette*, nor Laurel and Hardy *Robinson Crusoeland*, in the sad condition in which they found themselves, and Katharine Hepburn's involuntary headshake has all but ruined her performances since the early seventies. All credibility was lost when Leslie Howard and Norma Shearer were cast as teenagers in MGM's *Romeo and Juliet*; while in *Lilacs in the Spring* and *King's Rhapsody* Errol Flynn sometimes seemed to find difficulty in merely standing upright. But other factors besides age and infirmity render players unsuitable for certain roles. When Irwin Allen (that man again) decided to do a disservice to Conan Doyle's *The Lost World*, surely Claude Rains, about five feet high and dapper, can't have been even *his* first choice for the gorilla-like, crockery-smashing, body-threatening Professor Challenger, formerly played by Wallace Beery? Who at Paramount cast Paulette Goddard as a lady welder in *I Love a Soldier*? Even though the role won him an Oscar (for past services, presumably) did Ronald Colman, he of the measured gentlemanly tones, really think himself suitable for the role in *A Double Life* of a Shakespearean actor driven homicidal and sexually obsessive by months of playing Othello? Who cast Davie Niven as American spy Aaron Burr in *Magnificent Doll*? Come to that, who cast Ginger Rogers as Dolly Madison? Was it wise for Ingrid Bergman to play the saintly *Joan of Arc* at a time when her affair with Rossellini was the talk of the world? Did Marlon Brando think he made a good job of Napoleon in *Desiree*? (He called her Daisy Ray.) Was he pleased with his British accent as Fletcher Christian in *Mutiny on the Bounty*? (The British weren't). Whose idea was it to cast Marlene Dietrich in *Golden Earrings* as a gypsy with a carefully dirtied face, chasing Ray Milland half across war-torn Europe? (A poster showed him prone and her crawling over his back, saying 'Now you know how a gypsy loves.' Very interesting.) At the time of *The Stranger* Orson Welles, then twenty-eight, was not nearly old enough to play an escaped Nazi war criminal hiding out as a professor in a small American college town. (At the climax he was impaled very unconvincingly on a sword brandished by one of those slow-moving heraldic figures which Hollywood used to find below the faces of town hall clocks.) They say the avenger's role was originally conceived for Agnes Moorehead; I suppose Edward G. Robinson was the closest resemblance they could manage. And what of *Deception*? A menopausal Bette Davis is uncharacteristically anxious lest her former lover should find out about her present one. Her gloomy paramour (who else but Paul Henreid?) has with the help of Erich Wolfgang Korngold composed a cello concerto, to preserve the purity of which she shoots her ex, thereby robbing the movie of its only entertainment value, since the deceased gentleman was played by Claude Rains and supplied with lines by John Collier. While Mr Rains is in it, this is a movie of almost ecstatic badness: the scene in which he unnerves the guilty pair by taking them to a swank restaurant and ordering all the most recherché dishes on the menu has to be experienced to be disbelieved.

All big stars have lapses to be ashamed of; though come to think of it, Cary Grant may have been rather proud of going serious in *None but the Lonely Heart*. He played a downtrodden cockney called Ernie Mott, with a mother dying of cancer; the public stayed away in droves. Gary Cooper should never have seen himself as an architect with ideals in *The Fountainhead*. Steve McQueen hid himself behind a bushy beard in *An Enemy of the People*, as though afraid that he might be recognized: he needn't have bothered, people didn't go. Spencer Tracy was a crashing bore as the lonely fisherman in *The Old Man and the Sea*. Fredric March, well liked as a modern man, was all at sea as *Christopher Columbus*. Anna Neagle alienated her loyal public by playing an apparent Nazi spy in *Yellow Canary*, and it didn't do any good to make her sympathetic at the end, for the damage had been done. The Marx Brothers split their resources in *Love Happy* and gave the lion's share of the action to a new sentimental Harpo: that wasn't what the public wanted either. It seemed like sacrilege when Garbo paraded in a swim suit in *Two Faced Woman*. Burt Lancaster played a vitriolic columnist in *Sweet Smell of Success*: the critics applauded, the public rebelled. Dignified Greer Garson sought a change of pace by throwing up her skirts in *Julia Misbehaves*: it was the beginning of the end for her. Lana Turner had very little talent apart from a talent for looking pretty: when she lost that, her film titles read like a roll call of the dead. Peter Sellers did well to find in the awful Clouseau a character at whom the public could laugh, for since his elevation to stardom he had appeared in a series of perfect dogs: *The World of Henry Orient*, *After the Fox*, *The Bobo*, *I Love you Alice B. Toklas*, *The Magic Christian*, *Hoffman*, *Where Does it Hurt?*, *The Optimists of Nine Elms*, *Soft Beds and Hard Battles*, *The Ghost in the Noonday Sun*, *The Blockhouse*, *The Great McGonagall*, *The Prisoner of Zenda*, *The Fiendish Plot of Fu Manchu*. Fred Astaire can't have pleasant memories of himself as a wartime layabout in *The Sky's the Limit*. Rock Hudson was hardly ideal casting as a missionary in *The Spiral Road*. Marlon Brando did not suggest a career diplomat in *The Ugly American*. Peter O'Toole could have done without the incest in *Brotherly Love*.

Sometimes a single name rings bells, or should do so. It's a fair bet that no film directed by the self-styled visionary John Boorman will contain much to commend itself to straight-thinking folk, who may have sat and suffered through such *jeux d'esprit* as *Leo the Last*, *Zardoz*, *Exorcist II: The Heretic* and *Excalibur*. Similarly, neither subtlety nor competence should be expected of any item written or directed by Harry Alan Towers (or his alter ego Peter Welbeck). Critics and public have given up by now on the messily shot-scattering Blake Edwards, and on the uncontrollably fundamental Mel Brooks and the inscrutably verbose Robert Altman and the crudely violent Robert Aldrich and the interminably long-winded John Cassavetes. Likewise, so-called comedies starring Jerry Lewis and Frank Randle and Norman Wisdom and Wheeler and Woolsey are to be avoided except by dedicated cultists. (A cult movie is one which is admired not even despite its imperfections, but because of them.) One cohesive group of disasters was financed (but not necessarily released) in the sixties by Universal, whose British arm under Jay Kanter was clearly possessed of more money than sense. Listen to this string of commercial dogs: *Privilege*, *A Countess from Hong Kong*, *Fahrenheit 451*, *Charlie Bubbles*, *Work is a Four Letter Word*, *Boom!*, *Secret Ceremony*, *Three into Two Won't Go*, *Isadora*, *The Bofors Gun*, *The Night of the Following Day*, *The Adding Machine*, and *Can Heironymus Merkin Ever Forget Mercy Humppe and Find True Happiness?* The last-named, an ego trip for Anthony Newley, is a clear nominee for the title of worst film ever made, but of Mr Kanter's entire output only moments of *Charlie Bubbles* can now be looked at without embarrassment.

Sometimes a piece of racial miscasting will entirely ruin a film's chances, as did the placing of Alec Guinness as a Japanese businessman in *A Majority of One*: even the thought was too funny for words, like Stan Laurel playing Hamlet, and to make matters worse he had beside him Rosalind Russell as a Jewish momma. John Wayne was Genghis Khan in *The Conqueror*, playing the whole thing as a western and uttering the famous line: 'This Tartar woman is for me, and my blood says, take her!' The mind boggles. Slant eyebrows could not turn Nils Asther into a Chinaman for *The Bitter Tea of General Yen*. Cary Grant could not possibly be French for *I was a Male War Bride*. Alec Guinness again was not conceivable as a German in *Situation Hopeless but not Serious*, and certainly not as Adolf in *Hitler: The Last Ten Days*. (We accepted the stereotype of high-ranking Nazis played by British actors during World War II, but that pretence stopped on VJ Day. Even before that, when Fox were shooting *The Purple Heart*, the conception that the Japanese judges should be played by C. Aubrey Smith and Cedric Hardwicke caused so much hilarity on set that production ceased for re-casting.) In the thirties sheer novelty made us accept Paul Muni and Luise Rainer as Chinese in *The Good Earth*, but Katharine Hepburn could not repeat the trick in *Dragon Seed*. (Incidentally, Muni's much-applauded *Juarez* now seems only a matter of dark greasepaint and facial immobility.) More recently, Peter Ustinov was all make-up and hair dye in the leading role of *Charlie Chan and the Curse of the Dragon Queen*, and incidentally there's another film to join *Heironymus Merkin* in competition for *that* award: to sit through it is an endurance test, and the joke at the end, when the cars drive away reading JUST MARRIED and JUST ARRESTED respectively, leaves one speechless.

Horror films are almost too easy a target: some would say that all of them are worthless, and they do proliferate like weeds on Poverty Row. It may be instructive, however, to enumerate a few of the unhorrific atrocities which have emerged from major studios whose standards were lowered for the occasion. The *Captive Wild Woman* series at Universal is not even good for a laugh. *The Mole People* must surely have been intended as a Saturday morning special. *She-wolf of London* wins the prize for the most inept British setting; *The Cat Creeps* and *House of Horrors* tie for the sleaziest production, and *Curse of the Undead* has the risible idea of taking a vampire out west. Over at RKO, some of the works of the much-vaunted Val Lewton aren't looking so good these days. Can *anyone* make sense of *The Seventh Victim*? And was *Curse of the Cat People* ever much more than a hollow joke? Certainly Paramount was never cut out for the horror trade, as *Island of Lost Souls* and *The Monster and the Girl* amply demonstrate. Twentieth Century-Fox generated the right physical atmosphere in *The Undying Monster*, but the feeble script could come up with nothing better in the way of a family curse than:

> Beware thy bane
> On the rocky lane

which wouldn't make even a toddler's hair stand on end. (Better the doggerel from *Son of Frankenstein*:

> If the house is filled with dread,
> Place the beds at head to head.)

Warners, having made a fine start in the early thirties with *Dr X* and *Mystery of the Wax Museum*, then made only second feature horrors until the fifties, when they came in on the monster animal cycle with the excellent *Them!* and the woeful *The Black Scorpion*, which took place mostly in the dark and contained the very worst work of trick technician Willis O'Brien. It did however provoke a publicity campaign which, including as it did the following strictures, should be prized:

WE URGE YOU NOT TO PANIC OR BOLT FROM YOUR SEATS!

SHOWN UNCUT! EVERY TERROR EXACTLY AS FILMED!

THE MANAGEMENT RESERVES THE RIGHT TO PUT UP THE LIGHTS
ANY TIME THE AUDIENCE BECOMES TOO EMOTIONALLY DISTURBED!

William Castle, né Schloss, was El Cheapo of the horror field, a should-have-been fairground showman whose every two-bit shocker was distinguished by a publicity gimmick to draw the suckers in. *The Tingler* had certain seats electrically wired to give a mild shock at the moment of climax. *Homicidal* had a 'fright break' for the audience to steady its nerves, or get its money back if it dared follow the yellow streak painted on the floor leading to the paybox. *House on Haunted Hill* brought with it something called Emergo, a plastic skeleton which at a crucial moment was trundled above the heads of the audience on a wire. (It usually stuck.) *Thirteen Ghosts* had Percepto: if you wanted to see the ghosts you looked at the screen through special glasses. And *Macabre* offered you a thousand dollars-worth of free insurance if you died of fright. Boredom would have been more likely.

From horror to exploitation, films made on a shoestring with an apparent social purpose. I remember the queues that ringed my local Odeon in 1939 for *The Birth of a Baby*. I wasn't allowed to go, but older companions who slipped in somehow, assured me that 'you didn't see nothing'. I did later get to see *Social Enemy Number One*, which was apparently about VD, but I can't say I understood it: there was a little dialogue suggesting that drinking was associated with the disease, to which a lady asserted: 'My girls don't drink,' and the doctor answered quietly: 'Not even water?' *There* was food for thought. I grew wary after that of these starless, studio-less mini-movies, and began to avoid such as *Damaged Goods* and *Damaged Lives*, and *The Shame of Patty Smith* and *Amok*, which was about abortion in the Far East. When later I came to run a cinema in Cambridge, I did play *Ecstasy*, but it proved to be short of the ecstatic bits, and *The Devil's Weed*, starring Robert Mitchum's jail partner Lila Leeds. We drew the line at *Chained for Life*, screened for us by some fly-by-night distributor: it was about genuine girl Siamese twins who were both in love with the same man. What happened when one married him? The Watch Committee didn't seem to mind, but I did.

Some stars from other fields get only one chance in Hollywood: if they don't bring in the shekels, then goodbye. That happened to Lunt and Fontanne in *The Guardsman* back in 1932; though their name is still honoured on Broadway, they never made another film. Liberace was too overwhelming even for the wide screen: *Sincerely Yours* is his only star part. Little Jimmy Savo bombed resoundingly in *Once in a Blue Moon*. Jackie Gleason still hangs around, as he did before *Gigot*, but *Gigot* was his big chance and he fumbled it. Bette Midler is unlikely to be asked back after *The Rose*: she is another artist who can't be contained on film. Gwen Verdon was thought to be 'unphotogenic' in *Damn Yankees*, but went on to dazzle them on Broadway for thirty years. Kim Stanley was not asked back to Hollywood after *The Goddess*, but then she wasn't ideal casting for Marilyn Monroe. Singers can be unlucky: we never saw Georges Guetary again after *An American in Paris*, or Oreste Kirkop after *The Vagabond King*, or John Raitt after *The Pajama Game*, and we suspect that Luciano Pavarotti may find films hard going after *Yes Giorgio*. Ethel Merman was unlucky in a different way: she was around Hollywood for thirty years, but always considered a second string, so that when her big Broadway hits *Annie Get Your Gun* and *Gypsy* came up, she was passed over for both films; and they were certainly the poorer without her.

In the case of religious films it is sometimes difficult to distinguish the naïvely sincere from the merely crass. But surely in the latter category belongs Frank Sinatra in *The Miracle of the Bells*, salvaging the blessed memory of a deceased film star; Humphrey Bogart having his character changed when he impersonates a priest in *The Left Hand of God*; Bing Crosby getting Father O'Malley mixed up with show business in *Say One for Me*; Richard Burton being tempted to renounce his vows in *The Sandpiper*; David Niven as an extremely innocent bishop in *The Bishop's Wife*; Rex Harrison as a very secular Pope in *The Agony and the Ecstasy*; Henry Fonda, whisky sodden in *The Fugitive*; and Clifton Webb as an anti-communist cleric in *Satan Never Sleeps*. Mysterious but saintly figures, especially if light in the shape of a cross breaks through trees behind them, can usually be safely identified as Christ come back to guide the living: thus Conrad Veidt in *The Passing of the Third Floor Back*, thus Ian Hunter in the mercifully unique *Strange Cargo*. God himself appeared on the radio (though not on the sound track) in Dore Schary's inane *The Next Voice you Hear*. Angels are of course a related species and have appeared frequently in the cause of cinematic whimsy. The least worst of them have been Henry Travers in *It's a Wonderful Life*, Cary Grant in *The Bishop's Wife* and (surprise, surprise) Jack Benny in *The Horn Blows at Midnight*. Definitely on the far side of paradise, however, were Clifton Webb in *For Heaven's Sake*, Jeanette MacDonald in *I Married an Angel*, Robert Cummings in *Heaven Only Knows*, James Mason in *Forever Darling*, and Harry Belafonte in *The Angel Levine*.

Since 1970 or so, when cinemas all over the world began to close at an alarming rate, the floodgates of the remainder opened to let in trash. The old studios found themselves helplessly in the hands of independent producers motivated only to make a buck. They spent less and less on films requiring little professional expertise: cheap horror, cheap sex, cheap rough-house. 'Two men looked through the prison bars, The one saw mud, the other stars,' wrote Oscar Wilde in *The Ballad of Reading Gaol*. The old moguls, concerned for their prestige, had looked heavenwards at least occasionally; the new moguls looked only downwards, for they thought that through the mud they could see gold, which relieved them of any need for inspiration.

A little exploitation might have been forgiven in the troubled times, but these cheap movies contained little else. *The Sentinel*, *The Evil Dead*, *The Texas Chainsaw Massacre*, *Friday the Thirteenth*, and their various derivatives, took horror to a level so degraded that it could not have been contemplated a decade previously. In the case of violence there was a deterioration from Sam Peckinpah's poetically gory *The Wild Bunch*, down through *Prime Cut*, *The Possession of Joel Delaney*, *Death Wish*, *Bring Me the Head of Alfredo Garcia*, *The Island*, *Sharkey's Machine*, and *48 Hours*. *Straw Dogs*, which some said had started the trend towards senseless brutality, was still banned by British television in 1984 (I had found it more risible than horrifying, especially for a pub song which I was at pains to note:

> Some men goes for women
> And some men goes for boys,
> But my love's warm and beautiful
> And makes a baaing noise.)

Along with the violence of action had come a violence of language, slightly shy at first, but then at full flood when it was taken up by distinguished stars: by Dustin Hoffman in *Lenny*, by Paul Newman in *Slap Shot*, by Robert de Niro in *Raging Bull*, by the entire cast of *The Boys in Company C*. Along with this tendency to let everything hang out came a sudden tolerance of overt sexual activity. That famous row of asterisks was banished for ever as established stars, having insisted for years that they would never do such a thing, were viewable one after the other in bed scenes, and table-end scenes, that sometimes seemed longer than the films. Even Lord Olivier was hard at it in *The Betsy*. By the early eighties sex had been brought down to the level of schoolboy smut: the nearest one could get to serious consideration of the subject was the adolescent *The Blue Lagoon* and the smouldering *Body Heat*. Otherwise it came at you with teenage pimples and giggles, in *Meatballs*, *Caddyshack*, *National Lampoon's Animal House*, *Risky Business* and *Porky's*. There was straight porno too, of course, lots of it, but that is outside the scope of this essay.

A few films seemed to strive for a smoky combination of sex, violence and language: *Cruising*, *The Sailor who Fell from Grace with the Sea*, *Dressed to Kill*. Others were content to compete for the bad taste award. In *Harold and Maude* an eccentric teenage boy had an affair with a seventy-five-year-old woman. *The Adventure of Sherlock Holmes' Younger Brother* began with Queen Victoria saying 'Shit!' *Monty Python's Life of Brian* had something to offend Christians and non-Christians alike. In *Demon Seed* Julie Christie was raped by a computer, and seemed to enjoy it. In *Where's Poppa?*, an alleged comedy, George Segal tries to murder his senile mother. In *In God We Trust*, God turns out to be Richard Pryor, and what could be in worse taste than that? In *Lipstick*, a top model gets her revenge on a rapist who has attacked her sister, by shooting him in the private parts. In *The Greek Tycoon*, the love affair of Kennedy's widow and Aristotle Onassis was portrayed as a sensational fiction. In *The Killing of Sister George*, an amusingly waspish play about lesbians was given a ploddingly literal treatment but failed to turn into tragedy, or anything but an unwholesome mess. (The director deliberately left the key seduction scene without music, so that local authorities could cut as much as they chose.) In *S.O.B.*, a title which we were told stood not for son of a bitch, but for standard operational bullshit, Miss Julie Andrews bared her breasts and a film director's body was stolen from a mortuary and given a Viking funeral off the coast of Santa Monica. *Eating Raoul* looked to cannibalism for fun. *Mother, Jugs and Speed* was about ambulance chasers, and Jugs was Raquel Welch. *The Best Little Whorehouse in Texas* turned to a new field for cheap laughs (but found none).

There was also a cycle of films depicting gritty urban realism in the form of roaming gangs of violent teenagers: *The Class of Miss McMichael*, *The Warriors*, *Class of 84*. Another genre seemed to advocate total escape from reality, whether by fantasy (*Xanadu*), nostalgia (*1941, Grease*), musical madness (*Sergeant Pepper's Lonely Hearts Club Band*), science fiction (*Brainstorm*) or sheer incomprehensibility (*Night Moves*). All were acts of desperation in a medium where none of the roads had useful signposts. Stars were no longer a guarantee of box office: think of Sylvester Stallone in *Escape to Victory*, of Henry Winkler in *The One and Only*, of John Travolta in *Moment by Moment*. Well-known book titles cut no ice, not for instance in the case of *The World According to Garp*; and the star of that, a popular television comedian, found the going even tougher as *Popeye*, a film which was a disappointment and an embarrassment to all concerned, especially to those who thought Robert Altman might be a good choice to direct a comic strip.

Naturally a few good films did get through, but not enough to guarantee one a week to the American television networks, which henceforth upped the production of their own stories, with their own fireside stars. Hollywood had even forgotten how to make adventure spectaculars, as instanced by *The Swarm, When Time Ran Out, Beyond the Poseidon Adventure* and *Meteor*. It fumbled its own nostalgia in the dire *Nickelodeon* and *The Day of the Locust*. In *At Long Last Love* it failed to copy Astaire and Rogers, in *Alien* it failed to copy *The Thing* (or at least did so very boringly), in Michael Winner's *The Big Sleep* it failed to copy Howard Hawks's *The Big Sleep*. Even the aura of *Lost Horizon*, that classic of cinema kitsch, eluded it now: Ross Hunter's 1973 version had a big enough budget and a halfway decent cast, but marooned them in dreary sets with an unspeakable script and unsingable songs. Horror had descended to the level of *It's Alive*, about a new born baby with claws and a lust to kill. Of course fashion and publicity created occasional big successes, but they look pretty silly ten years later. Despite its frank language *Love Story*, with its meaningless tag line 'love means never having to say you're sorry', has a smell of the thirties rather than the seventies, and *The Godfather* is a Mafia-whitewashing absurdity compromised by the leading performance of a Marlon Brando so facially wired that he can scarcely talk.

Even the most popular comedians have a stinker or two to their discredit. (With Wheeler and Woolsey the situation is reversed: it's the good ones that are hard to find. And if one regarded Cheech and Chong as funny in the first place, the same would apply to them in spades.) Harold Lloyd would not particularly have wished to be reminded of *Professor Beware* or *Mad Wednesday*, nor Danny Kaye of *A Song is Born*. Laurel and Hardy had nothing to be proud of in the nine films they made after 1940. Abbott and Costello never made a thoroughly good film, except perhaps when they met Frankenstein, but usually the routines saved them: that could not be said of *The Noose Hangs High* or *Africa Screams* or *Lost in Alaska*. Anybody who has seen Buster Keaton in *Boom in the Moon* will not believe that the same man appeared in *The General*. Jack Benny made jokes about *The Horn Blows at Midnight*, but *George Washington Slept Here* has less to laugh at. Red Skelton should have returned to television *before* making *Public Pigeon Number One*. Rowan and Martin couldn't get a release for *The Maltese Bippy*. The Ritz Brothers sadly allowed their career to peter out in Universal programme fillers, of which the worst may have been *Behind the Eight Ball*. (They certainly were.) Phyllis Diller should have given up after *Did You Hear the One About the Travelling Saleslady?* Eddie Cantor tried, and failed, to play straight in *Forty Little Mothers*. Olsen and Johnson were funny only once, in *Hellzapoppin*: their earlier and later efforts are hard to watch. The Hope-Crosby *Road* shows are far less amusing than they seemed at the time, and *Road to Hong Kong* is dire indeed. As for W. C. Fields's *You Can't Cheat an Honest Man*, the title is much funnier than the film.

The thought of doing a remake should deter far more producers than it does: there have been so many failures. *The Mad Room* was a vulgar travesty of *Ladies in Retirement*, as was William Castle's *The Old Dark House* of its namesake. *Barricade* was, hilariously, *The Sea Wolf* on dry land, with a stagecoach standing in for the San Francisco ferry. *The Fiend Who Walked the West* performed a similar disservice for *Kiss of Death*. *High Society* put the chill on the delectable wit and subtlety of *The Philadelphia Story*. Martin and Lewis appeared *chiefly* in remakes, always to their disadvantage. *Living it up* was a disguised *Nothing Sacred* (Lewis as Carole Lombard); *You're Never Too Young* was *The Major and the Minor* (Lewis as Ginger Rogers); *Scared Stiff* was *The Ghost Breakers* (Lewis as Willie Best); *Pardners* was *Rhythm on the Range* (Lewis as Bob Burns?). One of the most awful warnings of recent years was the Russian-American *The Blue Bird*, with Elizabeth Taylor in several parts too many; but consider also the horrors of Peter O'Toole in *Goodbye Mr Chips*, with that soporific Leslie

Bricusse score; of Mai Britt in *The Blue Angel*; of Peter Sellers in *The Prisoner of Zenda*; of Edward Fox in *The Cat and the Canary* (playing a sadistic doctor who wasn't even in the original); of *The Spiral Staircase*, so crudely overlit that nothing spooky could possibly happen; of Disney's *Babes in Toyland*, with its Laurel and Hardy impersonators; of Rod Taylor in *Trader Horn*. Paul Henreid in the 1947 *Of Human Bondage* was bad enough in all conscience, but in 1964 we had to tolerate Laurence Harvey, with Kim Novak as Mildred. The third version of *And Then There Were None* was set in an isolated desert hotel in Iran; having found the location, the director did nothing whatsoever to make it interesting. As for *Stagecoach* – you remember there *was* a remake of *Stagecoach*? – the writer-producer Martin Rackin came to London and held a press conference to say that his new film would have an all-star cast led by Alex Cord (Alex Cord?), far more impressive than the collection of deadbeats who cobbled together that old black-and-white version some of us older ones might remember. Everyone present wished devoutly for Mr Rackin's version to be a stinker . . . and it was.

   No category of film is a safe bet for a producer. Certainly not musicals: think of the long stretches of dead celluloid involved in *Les Girls*, *Yolanda and the Thief*, *I Married an Angel*, *The Barkleys of Broadway*, *Down to Earth*, *The French Line*, *Gentlemen Marry Brunettes*, *Something in the Wind*, *The Pirate*, *The Belle of New York*, *Second Chorus*, *London Town*, *West Point Story*, *The Kissing Bandit*, *Xanadu*, and *Can't Stop the Music*. Nor are biographical pictures, biopics as the trade calls them. Think of Gable as *Parnell*, of Harris as *Cromwell*, of Huston as *Abraham Lincoln*, of Knox as *Wilson*, of Jackson as *The Incredible Sarah*, of Jagger as *Brigham Young*, of Ameche as *Alexander Graham Bell*. Music seems to make bad films of this genre especially risible: thus *A Song to Remember* (Chopin), *Song Without End* (Lizst), *Song of Love* (Brahms); thus certainly poor Grieg in *Song of Norway* and Strauss in the 1972 version of *The Great Waltz*. Animals are not always surefire box office, not at least *Jonathan Livingston Seagull* or *An Alligator Named Daisy* or the feathered denizens of *Bill and Coo*, an item which James Agee described as 'by conservative estimate, the God-damnedest thing ever seen'.

   So much pondering on bad films sends new titles spinning through the brain, many of them unique in their foolishness. How are we to categorize Billy Wilder's bewildering *Kiss Me Stupid* except as a desperately unfunny smoking room story, with Dean Martin as a hero who gets a headache if he doesn't have sex every day, but gets too much of it from all angles when he drives 'along Paradise Valley, past Warm Springs, to Climax'? To be categorized and swiftly put aside are Hollywood's anti-communist films of the McCarthy era: *My Son John*, *The Red Danube*, *The Woman on Pier 13*, *I Was a Communist for the FBI*. They are even worse than the pro-Russian films of six or seven years earlier: *North Star*, *Mission to Moscow*, *Song of Russia*. *Red Planet Mars*, another product of the cold war, had to be seen to be believed, setting forth the premise that spiritual messages from Mars inspire the Russian peasantry to revolt against their tyrannical rulers; it is further suggested that 'the man from Nazareth and the man from Mars are the same'. Robert Newton as a murderous cockney, chasing Burt Lancaster through Hollywood's idea of London's dockland in *Kiss the Blood off my Hands* was merely risible. Katharine Hepburn and a whole battalion of top stars so overloaded the flimsy whimsy of *The Madwoman of Chaillot* that under Bryan Forbes's listless direction it sank without trace in a sea of ennui. John Barrymore spoofing himself in *The Great Profile* should have been a hoot, but the man had already destroyed himself and the real tragedy showed through. *Deadline at Dawn*, the only film directed by Group Theatre genius Harold Clurman, turned a New-York-by-night low-life mystery into something as doom-laden as Aeschylus: he should have learned something from Santell's version of *Winterset* ten years earlier. And whereas screenwriter Ben Hecht had been enjoyably over the top about newspapers in *Nothing Sacred*, the same Hecht over the top about ballet in *The Spectre of the Rose* produced an unintentional absurdity, with lines like: 'I am but a faded carnation in the buttonhole of Broadway.' (Hecht was two men, a skilled commercial hack and a pretentious jerk.) Dudley Nichols must have wanted to film *Mourning Becomes Electra* very badly; he filmed it very badly indeed, with obviously suicidal Michael Redgrave dashing to the door and announcing: 'I must go and clean my pistol.' 'Gable's back and Garson's got him,' ran the tag-line for *Adventure*: but whoever thought they had chemistry? James Mason was overkeen to display himself as a cortisone addict in *Bigger Than Life*; the movie was much smaller. Bob Hope produced himself in *Boy Did I Get a Wrong Number* and a succession of burlesque-oriented comedies: each was worse than the last. *Helter Skelter* is an inane British answer to *Hellzapoppin*, filled at random with BBC in-jokes, a girl with hiccups and ten minutes of an old silent comedy with Walter Forde. *The Chase* (1947 version, not that the later one was much better) is a murky melodrama taking place mainly in the dark and involving Michèle Morgan and Peter Lorre in double crosses so complex that not even the writers can have known what was going on. *Whirlpool* was based on the absurd supposition that Jose Ferrer could hypnotize himself into rising from his bed and committing murder a few hours after he had undergone the major surgery which provided his alibi. *Reflections in a Golden Eye* teamed Elizabeth Taylor as a nympho, Marlon Brando as a homosexual, Robert Forster in the altogether, and Julie Harris as a character who cut off her nipples with garden shears. *The Man Who Understood Women* was a mysterious Thespian aberration by writer-producer-director Nunnally Johnson, who usually kept his feet on the ground. As for *Matilda*, that so-called comedy about a boxing kangaroo, surely Messrs Gould and Mitchum should have opted out when they found that no kangaroo was trainable and they would be acting with a man in a skin? *A Canterbury Tale*, from the normally reliable team of Powell and Pressburger, concerned a justice of the peace who in the wartime blackout goes around pouring glue on girls' hair as a warning that they shouldn't consort with GIs. *Three Wise Fools* had little Margaret O'Brien adopted by crusty old Lionel Barrymore, sentimental old Lewis Stone and bluff old Edward Arnold; Thomas Mitchell was also around to dispense Irish whimsy, and everyone kept saying: 'God be on your pillow.' *Green Mansions* unwisely starred that fashionable vision from the Rue de la Paix, Audrey Hepburn, as a magic nymph in a steamy South American jungle. *The Long Goodbye* foisted upon an audience which deserved better Elliott Gould as a Philip Marlowe who was in every respect the antithesis of Raymond Chandler's character – so why film the book? *The White Cliffs of Dover* was a clumsily weepy three-decker attempt to show, after the world-wide success of *Mrs Miniver*, that America too had played a part in a couple of world wars. *Till the End of Time* had the delicate Dorothy McGuire as a war widow guiltily giving herself to service veterans, to a theme tune borrowed from a Chopin Polonaise. *Won Ton Ton* began life as an amiable spoof of Hollywood in the twenties, with a cast of sixty fading stars making cameo appearances; but the assignment was handed to the hard-boiled Michael Winner, who viewed the old timers as old bores and cut down their screen time to so few frames each that if you blinked, you missed them. *Ragtime*, the novel, is a multi-storied kaleidoscope of America in the century's first decade; in filming it, Czech Milos Forman virtually discarded all the stories except one, blew that up into a statement about freedom, and to an already overlong movie added a twenty-minute comeback appearance by octogenarian James Cagney as a character not in the novel and irrelevant to it.

And now, two favourite bad films, both from Warners during World War II. It must have been difficult for the brothers to explain away Paul Henreid's Viennese accent. Once he was given a Viennese mother, and on another occasion a Viennese schooling. I forget which it was when he played the Revd Nicholls in *Devotion*, the story of the Brontës, but it added a measure of humour to a film already rich in the unintentional kind. If Mr Henreid seemed a little lost in the Yorkshire surroundings – Richard Winnington in the *News Chronicle* once said he looked as though his idea of fun would be to find a nice cold damp grave and sit in it – he was no more so than Olivia de Havilland and Ida Lupino as Charlotte and Emily, who were depicted as living in something closer to a country manor than the drab, bare parsonage of reality. *Devotion* included the famous literary exchange in a London street between Sydney Greenstreet and a bearded extra: 'Morning, Dickens.' 'Morning, Thackeray.' Who was devoted to what, or why, I have no idea, but the script invented a dream of death for Emily, in the shape of a night rider on a black horse; when she did die, he swooped down and carried her off. At the time of release it appeared that various departments at Warners were not talking to each other, for production kept making costume movies and promotion kept pretending they hadn't. Thus the poster campaign for *Devotion* tried to turn it into a modern melodrama about incestuous lesbians ('It tells ALL about those Brontë sisters!') with Greenstreet (playing Thackeray, remember) even more sinister as 'the *Friend*, the furious fat man'. If you don't believe me, check the file.

Even more ridiculous, but thoroughly enjoyable, is *Desperate Journey* in which, during a chase through Europe, Flynn and Reagan as downed Allied flyers outwit the Nazis personified by Raymond Massey, whose dialogue is very nearly limited to the utterance:

'*Schweinhund!*' Mr Flynn's last observation, as he soared above his pursuers in a stolen plane, was: 'Now for Australia and a crack at those Japs!' In comparison, *Objective Burma* was a model of reticence and plausibility.

Cinema is a mere child among the arts, so one should not be too surprised when it behaves childishly. What is surprising is that financiers in the eighties still make readily available such vast amounts of money for other people to waste: nearly 50 million dollars in the case of the space-fiction epic *Dune*, which as released was so dark as to be almost invisible and so cut down as to be quite incomprehensible. Being also fairly inaudible, it was certainly the bore of 1984. Paul McCartney at least spent his own money on the witless *Give My Regards to Broad Street*, a lesson in the folly of believing that one can do no wrong. The most celebrated flop of the eighties was the highbrow western *Heaven's Gate*, which illustrates the sad fact that simply because a director enjoys a freak success such as *The Deer Hunter* he does not necessarily have the wisdom necessary to spend 40 million dollars on an untested script.

And so at last to the top of the bill, which has to be *Myra Breckinridge*. The novel was probably unfilmable, but Twentieth Century-Fox gave Mike Sarne money to film it anyway. The result was a pseudo-satire so vulgar when it wasn't obscene, and so boring when it wasn't inexplicable, that one actually welcomed the appearances of an incredibly aged Mae West as an oversexed agent who told her platoon of virile bodyguards: 'I'm feeling a little tired today. One of you fellows'll have to go home.' (She also expressed a distinct interest in policemen's balls.) After *Myra Breckinridge* the record must end: it is so bad a film that nobody has yet aspired to making a worse. Remember as you wend your disgusted way home from an uncomfortable cinema that only one film in ten these days makes money; and fewer than one film in twenty is any good at all. It's the hunt for the exceptions that's exciting.

Halliwell's Hall of Humility

Twenty films with plenty to be humble about

Myra Breckinridge (Sarne)
A Clockwork Orange (Kubrick)
Straw Dogs (Peckinpah)
Lisztomania (Russell)
Zabriskie Point (Antonioni)
Casino Royale (various)
How I Won the War (Lester)
The Madwoman of Chaillot (Forbes)
Mame (Saks)
Hammersmith is Out (Ustinov)
At Long Last Love (Bodganovich)

Kiss Me Stupid (Wilder)
Reflections in a Golden Eye (Huston)
1941 (Spielberg)
Zardoz (Boorman)
The Story of Mankind (Allen)
Dune (Lynch)
Looking For Mr Goodbar (Brooks)
Boom! (Losey)
Can Heironymus Merkin Ever Forget
  Mercy Humppe and Find True
  Happiness? (Newley)

Books of the Film

A MOVIE LIBRARY

From the beginning until the 1980s, a period of nearly a century, the magic of the movies was hard to recapture once one had left the cinema: one waited anxiously for a reissue, or cultivated a 16mm home movie enthusiast, or joined the National Film Theatre. Now most films can be savoured time and again, either through buying or renting a video, or by a theoretically illicit taping of a television transmission. It has been quite the reverse with books about the movies. At one time there were very few, but all the free libraries carried them. Now the copies of those old classics have fallen apart or become unpleasant to touch, and most libraries were unable or unwilling to cope with the flood of film books, many of them redundant or poorly researched, which deluged us in the seventies when the nostalgia craze was at its height. These notes are an attempt to satisfy young correspondents who ask which books about film they should read above all others. Making such a list presents no great difficulty; getting the books may be something else again. I can do no more than give the dates and publishers: enthusiasts who are really dedicated in their pursuit will doubtless discover that their patience, with the help of one of the specialized second-hand film book distributors, will eventually be rewarded.

Histories to begin with. There are far too many, and many are too partial. Start, perhaps, with a good pictorial handbook: Ernest Lindgren's *A Picture History of the Cinema* (London, Vista Books, 1960) rather than Paul Rotha's better-known *Movie Parade* (London, Studio Press, 1936, revised 1950), which has fine stills but insufficient information. The next step could be Lindgren's *The Art of the Film* (London, Allen and Unwin, 1948, revised 1963), an excellent introduction to film appreciation; then back to history proper with David Shipman's two-volume set *The Story of Cinema* (London, Hodder and Stoughton, 1982 and 1984). In recommending the Shipman version I would not wish to minimize the achievement of Rotha in his *The Film Till Now* (London, Vision, 1930, revised by Richard Griffith 1967), but it does concentrate on the silent period and is intended for serious students of film aesthetic. While mentioning silents, the most sympathetic accounts of that period and its performers have been provided by Kevin Brownlow in his magnificent *The Parade's Gone By* (New York, Knopf, 1968) and *Hollywood: The Pioneers* (London, Collins, 1979), a version of his fine thirteen-hour television series. In similar vein, but stretching into the sound period, is Bernard Rosenberg and Harry Silverstein's *The Real Tinsel* (New York, Macmillan, 1970). Richard Schickel's *Movies: The History of an Art and an Institution* (New York, Basic Books, 1964) and Arthur Knight's *The Liveliest Art* (London, Macmillan, 1957, frequently reprinted) are brief, well-written surveys, ideal for a journey. Serious readers may wish to tackle Lewis Jacobs's *The Rise of the American Film* (revised version New York, Teachers' College Press, 1968; originally published 1939) or even Rachael Low's multi-volumed but still incomplete *History of the British Film* (London, Allen and Unwin, from 1948). By now you may need more detailed information about particular actors, in which case there is another brightly-written two-volume set by Shipman, *The Great Movie Stars* (London, Hamlyn, 1970 and Angus and Robertson, 1972). Finally in this group, do acquire another picture book with elongated captions, *The Movie* (New York, Bonanza, 1957, frequently reprinted and updated): this lively piece of writing by Richard Griffith and

Arthur Mayer underlines better than any book I know the trends in film fashion and the way movies are publicized.

I suppose most people equate the film business with Hollywood, which as we have all been told is a state of mind rather than a geographical location. True, true, but it's a state of mind chiefly located to the north and west of Los Angeles. The trouble is that the visiting outsider will find nothing to reward his inquiring gaze. I therefore recommend first of all one of the 'inside' books written by intelligent reporters using the fly-on-the-wall technique. Surprising how frequently highly-placed executives fall for the flattery implied in this method, and then wish they hadn't when they find their juicy offhand remarks splattered all over a bestseller. The sharpest of these I know, though written in 1951, is still Lillian Ross's *Picture* (London, Gollancz, reprinted in Penguin), which told more than anyone at MGM wanted to read about the making, revising and virtual abandoning of *The Red Badge of Courage*, and also about the sentimental bullying technique adopted by Louis B. Mayer as head of the studio. In 1969 John Gregory Dunne in *The Studio* (New York, Farrar-Straus-Giroux) performed a similar hatchet job on Twentieth Century-Fox at the time of the atrocious but expensive *Doctor Dolittle*. I particularly liked, and believed, the story of has-been director Henry Koster proposing to Richard Zanuck a sentimental patriotic musical which would clearly have starred, had they been available, Deanna Durbin, Grace Moore, Yehudi Menuhin, Leonard Bernstein, Bobby Breen and George M. Cohan.

Once-eminent producer Walter Wanger, who seems in his last years to have been a bit loony on Elizabeth Taylor, turned the axe unwittingly on himself in *My Life with Cleopatra* (New York, Bantam Books, 1963), undoubtedly the funniest and most revealing account of what went on in Rome in 1961 during the making of *that* film. (Spyros Skouras had thought that only a few revisions would be needed to the old Theda Bara script of 1917: his mistake cost him his job as company president.) Revelations, in a more professionally gossipy style, are the main matter of Garson Kanin's *Hollywood* (New York, Viking, 1974); the best parts are the early chapters about his life as a gopher for Samuel Goldwyn. Two Hollywood hotels, where lovers were changed more often than the bedsheets, also provide good gossip: try for bedtime reading Sheilah Graham's *The Garden of Allah* (New York, W. H. Allen, 1970) and Sandra Lee Stuart's *The Pink Palace* (New York, Lyle Stuart, 1978), the latter being the story of the Beverly Hills Hotel.

Any filmgoer naïve enough to think that the Hollywood myths were created by Americans should next read Philip French's *The Movie Moguls* (London, Weidenfeld and Nicolson, 1969) and John Baxter's *The Hollywood Exiles* (London, MacDonald, 1976), about the stream of executive and creative talent from Europe. In the latter I especially like the sad sagas of Emil Jannings and Edgar Wallace, both so typical of Hollywood, and the chapter intriguingly called Take Your Balls in your Hand and Chuckle. The English colony is separately treated in Sheridan Morley's *Tales from the Hollywood Raj* (London, Weidenfeld and Nicolson, 1983). Aspects of the film city at specific times are headed by Alexander Walker's *The Shattered Silents* (London, Elm Tree, 1978), which covers the traumatic takeover by sound films, and Colin Shindler's *Hollywood Goes to War* (London, Routledge and Kegan Paul, 1979), a witty treatise which exceeds its brief and explains how the war themes were carried through into the austerity years. A glance at R. J. Minney's *Hollywood by Starlight* (London, Chapman and Hall, 1935) will assure the reader that little essential to the film city has changed over the years. One thing that has gone however is the influence of the gossip queens who kept stars in abject terror for forty years, but you can read about them in George Eels's *Hedda and Louella* (New York, Putnam, 1972), including the incident when Louella Parsons was booted up the backside by Joseph Cotten.

The Movie Moguls may have whetted appetites for more information about each cigar-chomping studio head. Jack L. Warner was fondly assumed by most people to be only semi-literate, and when accused of not having read a book all the way through he probably did reply: 'I read *part* of it all the way through.' But in *My First Hundred Years in Hollywood* (New York, Random House, 1965) he gives a racy and entertaining account of his own career without making himself out to be either an intellectual or a saint. On a similar lowish level of book-learning was Harry Cohn, who once asked his writers to produce no more period scripts 'about people who go out of the room backwards'. This arch-tyrant of Columbia distrusted words of more than four letters, and claimed to know if a film was no good because it made his fanny itch. In *King Cohn* (New York, Putnam, 1967) Bob Thomas lists some of the funeral comments made in lieu of eulogy by people with whom he had crossed swords during his long career:

> He was a great showman, and he was a son of a bitch (George Jessel). He never learned how to live (Samuel Goldwyn). He liked to be the biggest bug in the manure pile (Elia Kazan). He was a song plugger and a louse (Lou Holtz). He wanted to pull everyone down to his level (Edward Dmytryk). He was the wandering Jew: he had no soul (Sam Bischoff). He was the last of the pirates (Everett Riskin). He was a sadistic son of a bitch (Hedda Hopper). He was the meanest man I ever knew – an unreconstructed dinosaur (Budd Schulberg). He was absolutely ice-cold in his self-interest (Norman Krasna). He was not all good and not all bad; he had star quality (Lewis Milestone). He was a son of a bitch (John Wayne).

At least he was interesting. Mr Thomas performed a similar if less sensational service for *Thalberg* (New York, Doubleday, 1969) and *Selznick* (New York, Doubleday, 1970), though Selznick, the memo-writer of all time, is rather more interestingly handled in three books which are all worth reading because they demonstrate different aspects of the man who was perhaps the worthiest of the moguls: intellectual, commercially quick-thinking, chance-taking, totally involved and unstoppable (until overtaken by financial failure in 1948). *David O. Selznick's Hollywood* (New York, Knopf, 1980) is an immense, and immensely expensive, coffee-table book by Ronald Mayer which takes the reader right into the script conferences and weekend parties which spawned all the great Selznick movies of the thirties and forties; it also reproduces superb colour stills and publicity material which are available nowhere else. *Memo from David O. Selznick* (New York, Viking, 1972) is a fat and juicy compilation by Rudy Behlmer of the great man's memos to his underlings; his disagreements with Hitchcock over *Rebecca* are particularly instructive. (Hitch said in a 1966 speech: 'David Selznick sent me a memo in 1940. I've just finished reading it.') Finally the mogul's ex-wife, Irene Mayer Selznick, produced in *A Private View* (London, Weidenfeld and Nicolson, 1983) a portrait with few holds barred of the husband who was so tired that he constantly fell asleep at dinner and almost missed his own honeymoon, and of the father, Louis B. Mayer, who took his family to Rome when locations for the silent *Ben Hur* were being scouted, but was primarily concerned to find a kosher butcher who would supply better food than the five-star hotel could offer. Mayer crops up again as the subject of Bosley Crowther's *Hollywood Rajah* (New York, Holt-Rinehart-Winston, 1960), which presents a rich picture of life at MGM during his reign. None of the biographies of Samuel Goldwyn is really satisfactory – one feels he was a remote man whose life is best expressed in his work and his alleged malapropisms – but Darryl F. Zanuck was well treated by Mel Gussow in *Don't Say Yes Until I Finish Talking* (New York, Doubleday, 1971) which presents Zanuck as writer, gambler and ladies' man as well as studio head and bon viveur.

Studies of individual studio output have been lavishly provided in recent years by Crown in New York and Octopus in London, who intend to keep all the volumes in print. So far published are *The MGM Story* by Douglas Eames, *The Warner Bros. Story* by Clive Hirschhorn, *The Universal Story* by Clive Hirschhorn and *The RKO Story* by Richard B. Jewell and Vernon Harbin. The last-named is particularly fascinating because Mr Harbin is a long-time studio accountant who is able to say which films made money and which didn't. In the works are Fox and Paramount, both of which have been treated before with partial success in *Mountain of Dreams* (London, Granada, 1977) by the present author, and *The Films of Twentieth Century-Fox* (New York, Citadel, 1979) by Tony Thomas and Aubrey Solomon. Also a partial success is *Universal Pictures* (New York, Arlington House, 1977) by Michael G. Fitzgerald. In Britain, *Movies from the Mansion* (London, Elm Tree, 1976) is a look at the Rank-Pinewood output by George Perry; and Elstree Studios were rather dimly celebrated in Patricia Warren's *Elstree: The British Hollywood* (Elm Tree, 1983). *Ealing Studios* by Charles Barr (London, Cameron and Tayleur, 1977), is far more analytical and satisfying.

Now for a few fairly recent overviews of the Hollywood scene, dating from the declining years of the studios. Beth Day's *This Was Hollywood* (New York, Doubleday, 1959) is seen mainly from the viewpoint of an MGM publicist, Frank Whitbeck, and all the better for it. Ezra Goodman's *The Fifty Year Decline and Fall of Hollywood* (New York, Simon and Schuster, 1961) has all the sharpness you would expect from a *Time* journalist, and begins with a befuddled and girl-chasing D. W. Griffith holed-up at the Knickerbocker Hotel; not at all Miss Gish's image. Paul Mayersberg's *Hollywood the Haunted House* (New York, Stein and Day, 1968) gives an admirable picture of life in Tinseltown at a time when even the ghosts seemed to be leaving, and a slightly later stage in the period of transition is tackled by Charles Higham in *Hollywood at Sunset* (New York, Saturday Review Press, 1972). If you want the seamy side of stardom, try Kenneth Anger's two volumes of *Hollywood Babylon* (New York, Bell, 1975 and 1984), but don't necessarily believe everything you read. A really joyous book is Arthur Mayer's *Merely Colossal* (New York, Simon and Schuster, 1953) which gives a wry account of the movies from an exhibitor's point of view.

Accounts of the British industry are less lively, though full of solid information. Charles Oakley's *Where We Came In* (London, Allen and Unwin, 1964) and George Perry's *The Great British Picture Show* (London, Granada, 1974) are the best of them; but the story of British films is often best told in the stories of individuals, notably Karol Kulik's *Alexander Korda* (London, W. H. Allen, 1975); Alan Wood's *Mr Rank* (London, Hodder and Stoughton, 1952); Geoff Brown's *Launder and Gilliat* (London, British Film Institute, 1977); Ian Christie's *Powell and Pressburger* (London, British Film Institute, 1979); and Michael Korda's tale of his father and two uncles, *Charmed Lives* (New York, Random House, 1979). On the exhibition side I can only humbly mention my own memoir *Seats in all Parts* (London, Granada, 1985). I don't know a first-rate comprehensive history of the French cinema, but for Germany between the wars the one to go for is Siegfried Kracauer's *From Caligari to Hitler* (London, Dobson, 1947).

Life stories of actors, directors and even writers are seldom worth reading for more than the basic facts. The 'Films of' series in their various forms can be disappointing too: look out for the ones that give background stories and critical comments, not just a plain synopsis. Usually good value are James Robert Parish's books of short linked biographies which he has issued with various collaborators under such titles as *The Paramount Pretties*, *The Fox Girls*, *The Glamour Girls*, *The Swashbucklers*, *Hollywood's Great Love Teams*, *The Debonairs* and so on. Scarcely a film creator has failed to be analysed at some length, but the least likely are sometimes the most rewarding: I like particularly Charles Higham's *Hollywood Cameramen* (London, Thames and Hudson, 1970) and Richard Corliss's *The Hollywood Screenwriters* (New York, Avon, 1970), both full of informed comment.

Full-scale biographies and autobiographies are legion, but here are a few with that something extra. Mae West's *Goodness Had Nothing to do with It* (New York, Prentice Hall, 1959). Charlton Heston's *The Actor's Life* (New York, Dutton, 1978). (How rare, an actor who keeps a printable diary!) A comedian's letters (even rarer): they are of course *The Groucho Letters* (London, Michael Joseph, 1967), and very funny too. Funnier still, if somewhat reprehensible, *The Marx Brothers Scrapbook* (New York, Darien House, 1973), which consists mainly of off-colour interviews recorded by Richard Anobile with a Groucho in his dotage. Then there is Mary Astor's briskly abrasive *A Life on Film* (New York, Delacorte Press, 1967). Ray Seaton and Roy Martin's *Good Morning Boys* (London, Barrie and Jenkins, 1978) is a detailed and sympathetic study of Will Hay. One of the first film biographies, and still among the sweetest, is John McCabe's *Mr Laurel and Mr Hardy* (revised edition New York, Grosset and Dunlap, 1966); a brilliant analysis of the work of these fine comedians is Charles Barr's *Laurel and Hardy* (London, Cinema One, 1968), and a multitude of stills from their films is collected in McCabe's and Al Kilgore's *Laurel and Hardy* (New York, Dutton, 1975). R. C. Sherriff's autobiography *No Leading Lady* (London, Gollancz, 1968) includes a hilarious episode about his being hired by James Whale to move to Hollywood and write *The Invisible Man*. Frank Westmore's *The Westmores of Hollywood* (London, W. H. Allen, 1976) is an amusing and affectionate account of a family devoted to making up the stars. *Hollywood Director* (New York, Curtis, 1973) by David Chierichetti is a full study, with Mitchell Leisen's cooperation, of a stylish but unsung director who made his mark upon the Paramount look. Raymond Chandler wrote vividly about Hollywood in his novels, but tended to see the film city through an alcoholic haze. Sample *Raymond Chandler Speaking* (London, Hamish Hamilton, 1962), a collection of letters edited by Dorothy Gardner and Kathrine Walker; it's full of sharp insights. Another alcoholic was W. C. Fields: he amused us because of his misanthropy. The standard biography is Robert Lewis Taylor's *W. C. Fields: His Follies and Fortunes* (New York, Doubleday, 1949), but more recently available are two fascinating books by the star's grandson Ronald J. Fields: *W. C. Fields by Himself, His Intended Autobiography* (New York, Prentice Hall, 1973) and *W. C. Fields: A Life on Film* (New York, St Martin's Press, 1984). Mel Torme's *The Other Side of the Rainbow: Judy Garland on the Dawn Patrol* (New York, Morrow, 1970) is an objective first-hand account of the last triumphs of a great star whose world was simultaneously going to pieces. Charles Higham's *Charles Laughton* (London, W. H. Allen, 1976), written in cooperation with the widow Elsa Lanchester, unsparingly tells of the star's homosexual torments. Francois Truffaut's *Hitchcock* (New York, Simon and Schuster, 1967) takes the form of a long interview in which, one feels, both participants were acting although they threw up some fascinating detail; John Russell Taylor's *Hitch* (London, Faber and Faber, 1978) is duller but more informative. Charles Chaplin's *My Autobiography* (London, Bodley Head, 1964) was long awaited, but revealed a bitter egoist striving in the wrong way to overcome a deprived childhood. John Kobler's *Damned in Paradise* (New York, Athaneum, 1977) gave a much more believable impression of the drunken downfall of John Barrymore than Gene Fowler's more sympathetic *Good Night, Sweet Prince* (New York, Viking Press, 1944). Robert Parrish's *Growing up in Hollywood* (London, Bodley Head, 1976) and Bessie Love's *From Hollywood with Love* (London, Elm Tree, 1977) are charming memoirs of life in the studios when the film city and the writers were all young. Whitney Stine's *Mother Goddam* (New York, W. H. Allen, 1974) has the benefit of acerbic footnotes by the subject herself, Bette Davis. I suppose David Niven's *The Moon's a Balloon* and *Bring on the Empty Horses* (London, Hamish Hamilton, 1971 and 1975) deserve a place for their popularity, though despite vivid portraits of Errol Flynn and others, both books are filled with misremembrances and fabrications. And there was value of a sort in Richard Lamparski's many-volumed *Whatever Happened to* series, with their affecting pictures of aged folk who seem to bear little resemblance to the glamour portraits on the left-hand page.

The social history of film largely remains to be written, though Margaret Farrand Thorp made a good start in *America at the Movies* (New Haven, Yale University Press, 1939). She showed how the movies of that period were sold to the public; Leo Rosten in his *Hollywood, The Movie Colony and the Movie Makers* (New York, Harcourt-Brace, 1941) produced a work of social science in which the studio personnel were analysed by questionnaire. Hortense Powdermaker's *Hollywood the Dream Factory* (Boston, Little-Brown, 1950) was an anthropological report, much duller than anyone expected, though its title was widely quoted. Roger Manvell's famous paperback *Film* (London, Penguin, 1945, much reprinted and revised) partly estimates the influence of film on society, though chiefly aiming at a film aesthetic which the man in the street can understand. And I like a recent picture book called *Flesh and Fantasy* (New York, St Martin's Press, 1978) in which Penny Stallings shows how we are all taken in by fake glamour and publicity.

Not enough films have been captured on the printed page as screenplays, and few indeed lend themselves to this treatment, but the serious scholar should find and study as many as he can; the British Film Institute's library in Charing Cross Road will provide a list of all that have been published. One of the best known, with two versions given, was turned by Pauline Kael into *The Citizen Kane Book* (Boston, Little-Brown, 1971), but her long introduction made authorial confusion worse confounded. Introductions are also appended to the scripts in the Wisconsin University series; all these come from Warners, and I found the background information on *Mystery of the Wax Museum* (no *The*) most intriguing. MGM issued six titles but found no demand: Meredith Corporation made a fascinating boo boo in issuing what it claimed to be the shooting script of *The Big Sleep* but was in fact a totally unknown version with many unshot scenes, variations of dialogue and a different solution.

A satisfactory facility for those aiming to recapture the fun and thrills they once had at the cinema was provided by Richard Anobile's Film Classics Library series, published around 1975 by Darien House, New York. In each case a full script was distributed as captions to about 1400 frames from the film itself, making a perusal of the book the next best thing to seeing the movie, even better in the sense that one could go backwards and forwards over especially enjoyable sections. Alas, there were too few buyers. The series collapsed almost at once, the only titles available being *Psycho*, *Frankenstein* (which has a curiously unsympathetic introduction), *Stagecoach*, *The General*, *The Maltese Falcon*, *Casablanca*, and the Mamoulian *Dr Jekyll and Mr Hyde*. Almost as satisfactory are the myriad informational books about the making of particular movies: Aljean Harmetz's *The Making of the Wizard of*

315

Oz (New York, Knopf, 1977) is a dandy, and not far behind are Orville Goldner and George E. Turner's *The Making of King Kong* (New York, Barnes, 1975), Donald Knox's *The Magic Factory* (about the making of *An American in Paris*) (New York, Praeger, 1973) and Hugh Fordin's *The World of Entertainment* (about the making of Arthur Freed's MGM musicals) (New York, Doubleday, 1975).

A few books now about particular types of film. Denis Gifford's *A Pictorial History of Horror Movies* (London, Hamlyn, 1973) has always seemed to me quite admirable: lively and amusing, yet as scholarly as his out of print *British Film Catalogue* (Newton Abbot, David and Charles, 1973). Carlos Clarens's *Horror Movies* (London, Secker and Warburg, 1968) is also scholarly but has insufficient detail. William K. Everson wrote a jolly book on *The Bad Guys* (New York, Bonanza, 1964) and another on *The Detective in Film* (New York, Citadel, 1972). Don Miller's *B Movies* (New York, Curtis, 1973) is a marvellous read even though one might never wish to see a single film he mentions. Of many books about musicals I recommend John Springer's *All Talking! All Singing! All Dancing!* (New York, Citadel, 1966) and Clive Hirschhorn's massive *The Hollywood Musical* (London, Octopus, 1981); of even more about westerns the choice is George Fenin and William K. Everson's *The Western From Silents to Cinerama* (New York, Orion, 1962). Those old enough to remember Leon Errol and Edgar Kennedy will relish Leonard Maltin's *The Great Movie Shorts* (New York, Crown, 1972), not to mention the same author's *Movie Comedy Teams* (New York, New American Library, 1970). Of several who have written about old-time series characters like the Saint and the Falcon, I choose James Robert Parish's *The Great Movie Series* (New York, Barnes, 1971). If what the censor saw, and you didn't, interests you, then seek out Murray Schumach's *The Face on the Cutting Room Floor* (New York, Morrow, 1964).

Positively finally, a little fiction. Raymond Chandler's *The Little Sister*, Scott Fitzgerald's *The Last Tycoon*, Nathanael West's *The Day of the Locust* and Richard Brooks's *The Producer* are all fairly widely available and go without saying; you may need to look a little harder for Gavin Lambert's short stories *The Slide Area* (London, Hamish Hamilton, 1959) which give a predictably jaundiced view of Hollywood. The funniest Hollywood spoof I know is called *A Biographical Epic at Imperial Pix; Subject, Bindle Biog* and was written in 1947 by F. Hugh Herbert for an issue of *Screenwriter*; alas, it seems not to have been published elsewhere except in anthologies. Jeffrey Dell's *Nobody Ordered Wolves* did a pretty thorough hatchet-job on the British industry in the mid-thirties, when it was overfilled with Hungarians. Perhaps the funniest film book of all, for those able to cast themselves back into the late silent era, is Elmer Rice's half-forgotten *A Voyage to Purilia* (London, Gollancz, 1930), which, in the form of a parody on *Gulliver's Travels*, visits the over-the-rainbow land of Hollywood cliché. Unquotable in a small space, it is a fine piece of writing from which not a cliché emerges unscathed. I have often had to lay it aside in public places for fear of being led away in a straitjacket.

Curiosities of Film Titles

WHAT'S IN A NAME?

The romance has gone from the title business. From actors' names too, of course: once upon a time Ira Grossel would change himself to Jeff Chandler, Issur Demsky to Kirk Douglas, and Tula Finklea to Cyd Charisse, but nowadays performers hang on doggedly to uncharismatic labels like Carrie Snodgress and Sissy Spacek and Duncan Regehr and Hanna Schygulla and Simon MacCorkindale: the less euphonious, it seems, the better they like it, and if we can't spell it or pronounce it then that's our fault and not theirs. Similar thinking clearly applies to titles, whose creators defy us to find them unattractive, as though to do so would be an admission of failure on our part. There can be no other explanation, surely, for films called CADDYSHACK and MEATBALLS and JINXED and BUSTED. At best they show a lack of inventiveness, almost as pronounced as that of producers who laconically label their packages PORKY'S 2 and JAWS 3 and ROCKY 3 and so on. These are not so much films in their own right as repeat orders for addicts.

Some have gone to an opposite extreme, dragging down their product with such cumbersome come-ons as: WHO IS HARRY KELLERMAN AND WHY IS HE SAYING THESE TERRIBLE THINGS ABOUT ME? or CAN HEIRONYMUS MERKIN EVER FORGET MERCY HUMPPE AND FIND TRUE HAPPINESS? or COME BACK TO THE FIVE AND DIME, JIMMY DEAN, JIMMY DEAN or OH DAD, POOR DAD, MAMA'S HUNG YOU IN THE CLOSET AND I'M FEELING SO SAD. Surely the owners of these properties can never have expected to do business with them? Did the titles, in fact, indicate some sort of death wish?

Here are some more fairly recent one-word titles:

EMBRYO	HAIR	CRAZE	TAPS
DOGS	STREAMERS	REDS	AXE
FAME	RUNNERS	SCRUBBERS	THIEF
CLASS	STRIPES	EXPOSED	ENIGMA

Fancy calling your own film an enigma! What do you suppose the audience is going to make of it? And why should they bother? In comparison with such laid-back labels, something like SO FINE seems embarrassingly over-descriptive, and BACK ROADS a positive cornucopia of encouraging information. Which is more than I can say for the current rash of titles affected by the present participle syndrome. You know them: RUNNING, CRUISING, LOVING, LIVING, MISSING, BREAKIN', and so on. When they are extended the effect becomes positively hypnotic, and I for one cannot guarantee to tell the difference between any of the following:

MAKING LOVE	BREAKING UP	STAYING ALIVE
BUSTIN' LOOSE	BREAKING AWAY	LOSING IT
LIVING IT UP	STARTING OVER	TAKING OFF
MAKING IT	RUNNING BRAVE	REACHING OUT
GETTING IT ON	FALLING IN LOVE	GOING BERSERK

I suppose EDUCATING RITA, EATING RAOUL, BREAKING GLASS and MAKING THE GRADE are horses of a somewhat different colour; while WALKING TALL, RIDING HIGH and SITTING PRETTY are old friends.

Nor can I understand why any producer, who would presumably like a profit, should want to afflict his work with a title which must deter potential customers from crossing the road towards it. It is not so very long since LOVE AND PAIN AND THE WHOLE DAMN THING and that saddest of admissions DON'T WORRY WE'LL THINK OF A TITLE. Then there was THE END, a comedy about dying. And HIGH ANXIETY, a reflection of Mel Brooks's own neuroses (and who would want to share those?). And OH GOD, YOU DEVIL, of which the best that could be said was that it was less offensive than OH GOD 3. And PATERNITY, which must have struck fear into the hearts of a sizeable fraction of the population. And S.O.B., the meaning of which, when you summoned the temerity to ask, turned out to be 'standard operational bullshit'.

It should surely be an axiom that the public will be unlikely to patronize a title which it can't remember because it is too complicated. Several cases have already been listed, and the admonition must apply equally to such composites as THE CONCORDE – AIRPORT 79. This does not flow trippingly from the tongue and can have arisen only from the desire to add something fresh to a fading series without entirely discarding the original. Similarly, lawyers sometimes let themselves in for a condition that the author's name must be part of the title, which is why we can seldom find in the index a film called ONCE IS NOT ENOUGH, because its official title is JACQUELINE SUSANN'S ONCE IS NOT ENOUGH. This leads to such absurdities as SIDNEY SHELDON'S BLOODLINE and RUSS MEYER'S UP!; and it is said that in the early sixties an eminent director had to be forcibly restrained from labelling his current work JOSHUA LOGAN'S FANNY. Does any of this help the movie's chances? Certainly not: the ticket buyers don't know who half these people are.

Producers once tried to make their titles amusing, intriguing or vaguely inspirational. This trend seemed to run out in the seventies, round about the time when the maker of A CLOCKWORK ORANGE used the allusive title of the book on which it was based but quite forgot (or disdained) to explain it. Sam Peckinpah went even further by adapting the novel *The Siege at Trencher's Farm* into STRAW DOGS, which title he took from a Chinese proverb not mentioned in the film. I for one used to enjoy working out the titles which derived from idioms or proverbs; that is to say, phrases popular in everyday speech which make a general meaning vivid by emphasizing some particular example. None of the following titles refers literally to the objects named:

A FLEA IN HIS EAR. The hero is discomfited, not plagued by insects.
THE IRON PETTICOAT. About a cold-hearted Russian lady, not chain-mail underwear.
TWO-FACED WOMAN. No female freak, but a lady who presents different identities.
CHIP OFF THE OLD BLOCK. Not a woodcutting saga, but a musical about a father-son partnership.
DUCK SOUP. Whether or not ducks make good soup, this American slang phrase came to mean anyone who is a cinch or a pushover. But perhaps the Marx Brothers simply chose it to continue their series of animal titles including ANIMAL CRACKERS, MONKEY BUSINESS and HORSE FEATHERS, none of which had any plot relevance whatever.

Here are some other idiomatic titles. The actual meaning of most of them is clear enough, but the reason for the meaning is often harder to find:

BOTH ENDS OF THE CANDLE	POT LUCK
LES QUATRE CENTS COUPS	SECOND FIDDLE
BREAK THE ICE	A CUCKOO IN THE NEST
ON THE CARPET	RAISING THE WIND
FEATHER YOUR NEST	SALT OF THE EARTH
HOUSE OF CARDS	THE HORSE'S MOUTH
THE BLACK SHEEP OF WHITEHALL	THE GIFT HORSE
CASTLE IN THE AIR	IN THE SOUP
FACE THE MUSIC	FRENCH LEAVE
THE DEVIL AND THE DEEP	CRY WOLF
ENOUGH ROPE	TORN CURTAIN
ONE WILD OAT	TROUBLE IN PARADISE

LES JEUX SONT FAITS	BY HOOK OR BY CROOK
FAST AND LOOSE	THE SEVENTH VEIL
WHILE THE SUN SHINES	THE FALLEN SPARROW
MAN ON FIRE	THE GRASS IS GREENER
SHAKEDOWN	THE MOON AND SIXPENCE

Several of the titles above contain animal references, because a comparison of familiar human and animal attributes, appearance and behaviour often results in an image or metaphor which everyone can understand. Here are some more titles in which the animals mentioned appear only in the form of human characteristics:

THE LEOPARD	DADDY LONGLEGS
THE SPIDER AND THE FLY	ROMMEL DESERT FOX
CAT ON A HOT TIN ROOF	THE EAGLE HAS LANDED
THE LITTLE FOXES	THREE BLIND MICE
POOR COW	THE FIREFLY
BROTHER RAT	THE FROG
OF MICE AND MEN	MADAME BUTTERFLY
THE CAT AND THE CANARY	THE EAGLE AND THE HAWK
COBRA WOMAN	BLUEBOTTLES
THE SEA HAWK	THE SEA WOLF
THE SANDPIPER	DRAGON SEED
WOLF'S CLOTHING	THE TIGER MAKES OUT
HE WHO RIDES A TIGER	MOTHER CAREY'S CHICKENS
THE BLACK SWAN	SPARROWS CAN'T SING
SWEET BIRD OF YOUTH	WHAT'S NEW PUSSYCAT?
THE FOX	AFTER THE FOX
THE BIRDS AND THE BEES	DRAGONFLY SQUADRON
FLYING TIGERS	A GATHERING OF EAGLES
THE IRON HORSE	THE BAT
BATMAN	THE GREEN HORNET
THE TORTOISE AND THE HARE	THE SLEEPING TIGER
THE SWAN	LOAN SHARK
DEAR OCTOPUS	A LION IS IN THE STREETS
THE FLIGHT OF THE PHOENIX	THE RABBIT TRAP
THE SNAKE PIT	DOG DAY AFTERNOON
THE VOICE OF THE TURTLE	WORM'S EYE VIEW

If canines seem notable by their near absence, perhaps we have to thank that title-creator who assured us that IT SHOULDN'T HAPPEN TO A DOG.

A title which baffled many was THE RAZOR'S EDGE, the film of Somerset Maugham's novel about a man seeking a purpose in life. The film itself did not help at all, but the title page of the original novel gives the answer in the shape of an oriental proverb: 'The sharp edge of a razor is difficult to pass over; thus the wise say the path to salvation is hard.' The publicity for the film ignored this and substituted: 'Between love and hatred there is a line as sharp as a razor's edge'!

Hundreds of film titles have taken the form of quotations from literary originals, and all too often the allusion is left unexplained. A little detective work may solve a number of nagging puzzles.

The Bible is a favourite source. No fewer than eight titles, and possibly more, come from the Song of Solomon alone:

The SONG OF SONGS, which is Solomon's. . .

. . . the time of the singing of birds is come, and THE VOICE OF THE TURTLE is heard in our land. . .

ARISE, MY LOVE, my fair one, and come away. . .

Take us the foxes, THE LITTLE FOXES, that spoil the vines . . . for OUR VINES HAVE TENDER GRAPES. . .

MANY WATERS cannot quench love, nor can the floods drown it. . .

For unto us A CHILD IS BORN, unto us a son is given. . .

And here are some other Biblical examples.

Genesis 3: And they heard the voice of the Lord God walking in the garden IN THE COOL OF THE DAY. . .

Genesis 4: Am I MY BROTHER'S KEEPER?

Exodus 21: Eye for eye (AN EYE FOR AN EYE), tooth for tooth, hand for hand, foot for foot. . .

2 Samuel 1: Saul and Jonathan were lovely and pleasant in their lives, and in their death THEY WERE NOT DIVIDED. . . I am distressed for thee, MY BROTHER JONATHAN. . .

2 Samuel 18: Would God I had died for thee, O Absalom, MY SON, MY SON. . .

1 Kings 19: And after the earthquake a fire, but the Lord was not in the fire; and after the fire a still small voice (THE SMALL VOICE)

Proverbs 13: He that SPARETH THE ROD hateth his son. . .

Hosea 8: They have sown the wind, and shall reap the whirlwind (REAP THE WILD WIND)

Joel 2: Multitudes in THE VALLEY OF DECISION. . .

Matthew 5: ye are the SALT OF THE EARTH. . .

Matthew 6: Consider the LILIES OF THE FIELD, how they grow . . . they toil not, neither do they spin. . .

Matthew 26: THE SPIRIT indeed IS WILLING, but THE FLESH IS WEAK. . .

Luke 1: Because there was NO ROOM for them AT THE INN. . .

John 18: NOW BARABBAS was a robber. . .

John 16: QUO VADIS? Whither goest thou?

Romans 12: VENGEANCE IS MINE; I will repay, saith the Lord. . .

1 Epistle Paul 3: The love of money is THE ROOT OF ALL EVIL. . .

Revelation 6: And I looked, and BEHOLD A PALE HORSE: and the name of him that sat on him was Death. . . And I saw in the right hand of him that sat on the throne a book . . . sealed with seven seals (THE SEVENTH SEAL). . . For the great DAY OF his WRATH is come. . .

Revelation 8: And when he had opened THE SEVENTH SEAL, there was silence in heaven about the space of half an hour. . . And the seven angels which had the seven trumpets prepared themselves to sound. . . (THE ANGEL WITH THE TRUMPET) And when he had cried, SEVEN THUNDERS uttered their voices. . .

Revelation 17: For he is lord of lords, and KING OF KINGS. . .

Nor can we forget THE TEN COMMANDMENTS, THE DEVIL AND TEN COMMANDMENTS, FORGOTTEN COMMANDMENTS, THE SEVEN DEADLY SINS.

After the Bible, the Book of Common Prayer has been most frequently plundered. The Lord's Prayer itself gives us five film titles: GIVE US THIS DAY, OUR DAILY BREAD, FORGIVE US OUR TRESPASSES, THE POWER AND THE GLORY, and WORLD WITHOUT END. The marriage service yields FORSAKING ALL OTHERS, TO HAVE AND TO HOLD, FROM THIS DAY FORWARD and FOR BETTER, FOR WORSE. And here are more titles of which the Book of Common Prayer is the sometimes surprising source:

The Litany: . . . deceits of THE WORLD, THE FLESH AND THE DEVIL. . .

2nd Commandment: I the Lord thy God am a jealous God, and visit the SINS OF THE FATHERS upon the children. . .

6th Commandment: THOU SHALT DO NO MURDER

Psalm 23: He shall feed me in a GREEN PASTURE[S]. . .

Psalm 30: Heaviness may endure for a night, but JOY cometh IN THE MORNING. . .

Psalm 91: Thou shalt not be afraid for any TERROR BY NIGHT. . .

Psalm 107: They that go DOWN TO THE SEA IN SHIPS. . .

Psalm 121: So that the sun shall not burn thee by day, neither [NOR] THE MOON BY NIGHT. . .

Psalm 128: Thy wife shall be as THE FRUITFUL VINE upon the walls of thine house. . .

Psalm 139: If I take the WINGS OF THE MORNING and remain in the uttermost part of the sea, Even there also shall thy hand lead me. . .

The third most popular title source is probably Shakespeare. He has been pillaged by novelists, though film-makers have sometimes regarded him as a jinx and fought more shy:

Hamlet
Whiles, like a puff'd and reckless libertine,
Himself THE PRIMROSE PATH of dalliance treads. . .

THIS ABOVE ALL: to thine own self be true. . .

MURDER MOST FOUL, as in the best it is. . .

TO BE OR NOT TO BE, that is the question. . .

    LEAVE HER TO HEAVEN,
And to those thorns that in her bosom lodge,
To prick and sting her. . .

I am but mad NORTH [BY] NORTHWEST; when the
wind is southerly, I know a hawk from a handsaw. . .

A Midsummer Night's Dream
ILL MET BY MOONLIGHT, proud Titania. . .

Henry V
But when the blast of war blows in our ears,
Then imitate the ACTION OF THE TIGER. . .

King John
BELL, BOOK AND CANDLE shall not drive me back
When gold and silver becks me to come on. . .

THIS ENGLAND never did, nor never shall
Lie at the proud foot of a conqueror. . .

Julius Caesar
CRY HAVOC, and let slip the dogs of war. . .

Macbeth
THE [THREE] WEIRD SISTERS. . .

Life's but a walking shadow. . .
    . . . it is a tale
Told by an idiot, full of sound and fury,
Signifying nothing. [THE SOUND AND THE FURY]

The Merchant of Venice
How sweet the moonlight sleeps upon this bank!
Here will we sit, and let THE SOUND(s) OF MUSIC
Creep in our ears. . .

Richard II
This royal throne of kings, this scepter'd isle. . .
This other Eden, DEMI-PARADISE. . .
THIS HAPPY BREED of men. . .

The Tempest
Misery acquaints a man with STRANGE BEDFELLOWS. . .

Sonnet 116
Love alters not with his [Time's] brief hours and weeks
But bears it out even to the EDGE OF DOOM. . .

His Will
Item, I give unto my wife my SECOND BEST BED, with the furniture.

Nursery rhymes have been astonishingly popular, presumably because of their instant familiarity to all comers. But they have been applied to a very wide assortment of films:

HI DIDDLE DIDDLE

THE CAT AND THE FIDDLE

LADYBIRD, LADYBIRD (fly away home; Your house is on fire and your children all gone)
COME BLOW YOUR HORN
SING FOR YOUR SUPPER
(London Bridge is broken down,)
MY FAIR LADY
THURSDAY'S CHILD (has far to go)
FIDDLERS THREE
HERE WE GO ROUND THE MULBERRY BUSH
RINGS ON HER FINGERS and BELL(E)S ON HER TOES,
SHE SHALL HAVE MUSIC / WHEREVER SHE GOES
THERE WAS A CROOKED MAN
THREE BLIND MICE, / SEE HOW THEY RUN!
WHO KILLED DOC ROBBIN?
SO LONG AT THE FAIR
ALL THE KING'S MEN
ROCK-A-BYE-BABY
ALL THE WAY HOME
MARY, MARY, (quite contrary)
UPSTAIRS AND DOWNSTAIRS (and in my lady's chamber)
WHEN THE BOUGH BREAKS (the baby will fall)
TEN LITTLE NIGGERS
MARY HAD A LITTLE

Well-known songs have much the same effect as nursery rhymes. Can you supply all these titles of non-musical films with their hummable tunes?

ALL THROUGH THE NIGHT
ALWAYS LEAVE THEM LAUGHING
BEYOND THE BLUE HORIZON
COMING THROUGH THE RYE
DOWN WENT MCGINTY
FINEGAN BEGIN AGAIN
FIRE DOWN BELOW
IF YOU KNEW SUSIE
ISN'T IT ROMANTIC?
IT HAD TO BE YOU
I KNOW WHERE I'M GOING
I'LL BE SEEING YOU
THE LAST TIME I SAW PARIS
LOVE IN BLOOM
MY DARLING CLEMENTINE
MY HEART BELONGS TO DADDY
MURDER HE SAYS
OH SUSANNAH
ONE HOUR WITH YOU
ONCE A JOLLY SWAGMAN
PRETTY BABY
SHE WORE A YELLOW RIBBON
SIDEWALKS OF NEW YORK
SOMEWHERE I'LL FIND YOU
THE STRAWBERRY BLONDE
THE SUN SHINES BRIGHT
THE STREETS OF LAREDO
THOSE ENDEARING YOUNG CHARMS
THE TRAIL OF THE LONESOME PINE
UNDER MY SKIN
UNDER THE YUM YUM TREE
THE YELLOW ROSE OF TEXAS

Another type of film purports to tell the life story of a particular composer, and uses as a title the name of one of his 'smash hits':

THE BEST THINGS IN LIFE ARE FREE: Brown, Henderson and de Sylva
DEEP IN MY HEART: Sigmund Romberg
I'LL SEE YOU IN MY DREAMS: Gus Kahn
IRISH EYES ARE SMILING: Ernest R. Ball
MY WILD IRISH ROSE: Chauncey Olcott
NIGHT AND DAY: Cole Porter
MY GAL SAL: Paul Dresser
OH YOU BEAUTIFUL DOLL: Fred Fisher
RHAPSODY IN BLUE: George Gershwin
ST LOUIS BLUES: W. C. Handy
SWANEE RIVER: Stephen Foster
THREE LITTLE WORDS: Kalmar and Ruby
TILL THE CLOUDS ROLL BY: Jerome Kern
YANKEE DOODLE DANDY: George M. Cohan
YOUR CHEATING HEART: Hank Williams
YOU WILL REMEMBER: Leslie Stuart

Sometimes, too, song titles are used for biopics of performers with whom they are especially identified:

AFTER THE BALL: Vesta Tilley
CHAMPAGNE CHARLIE: George Leybourne
LOOK FOR THE SILVER LINING: Marilyn Miller
LOVE ME OR LEAVE ME: Ruth Etting
ROSE OF WASHINGTON SQUARE: Fanny Brice
SHINE ON HARVEST MOON: Nora Bayes
WITH A SONG IN MY HEART: Jane Froman

Returning to the literary field, it is surprising how many well-known title-making phrases come from the works of little-known people. TIGHT LITTLE ISLAND, for instance, which America used for WHISKY GALORE, comes from a poem called 'The Snug Little Island' written about 1800 by one Thomas John Dibdin:

Oh what a snug little island!
A right little, tight little island!

Enough of that. THE MAN ON THE FLYING TRAPEZE, used by W. C. Fields as a film title and by William Saroyan for an autobiographical book, was written by George Leybourne (Champagne Charlie) around 1860:

Oh he flies through the air with the greatest of ease,
This daring young man on the flying trapeze.

Edna St Vincent Millay contributed BOTH ENDS OF THE CANDLE in the following form:

My candle burns at both ends;
It will not last the night;
But oh, my foes, and oh, my friends –
It gives a lovely light.

Ernie Pyle, the American war correspondent, appears to have given to the language the phrase WORM'S EYE VIEW, and THE WAY OF ALL FLESH was contributed by a seventeenth-century writer named Thomas Shadwell. It was the American Daniel Webster (personified by Edward Arnold in a famous film) who, when advised against entering the overcrowded legal profession, remarked: 'There is always ROOM AT THE TOP.'

Many famous phrases have come from American sources which may seem remote to Britishers. Perhaps Judge William Marcy, who died in 1857, was an important historical figure, but we shall remember him as the man who said: 'TO THE VICTOR belong the spoils of the enemy.' It was Julia Ward Howe who wrote the BATTLE HYMN of the American Republic, with its famous couplet which rather obscurely gave Steinbeck a title for a novel and Ford a title for a film:

323

Mine eyes have seen the glory of the coming of the Lord:
He is trampling out the vintage where THE GRAPES OF WRATH are stored.

And it was Francis Scott Key who gave us

'Tis the star-spangled banner; O long may it wave
O'er the land of the free, and the HOME OF THE BRAVE!

Still in the early nineteenth century, Samuel Francis Smith wrote his poem 'America', which is sung to the tune of the British national anthem, and concludes:

From every mountain-side
LET FREEDOM RING.

In the same strain, the hymn of the US Marines begins

From the HALLS OF MONTEZUMA
TO THE SHORES OF TRIPOLI

which explains why in those two films we never got as far as the places mentioned; and a few lines later comes the boast FIRST TO FIGHT, recently used as a film title. Concluding our selection from American patriotic songs is SO PROUDLY WE HAIL.

After Shakespeare, Rudyard Kipling seems to have contributed more film titles than any other British writer, of which the last one listed below may be the most surprising:

'Mandalay'
Ship me somewheres EAST OF SUEZ. . .
. . . on the ROAD TO MANDALAY. . .

'The Children's Song'
Teach us delight in simple things,
And mirth that has no BITTER SPRINGS. . .

'The Female of the Species'
For the female of the species is more deadly
[DEADLIER] THAN THE MALE. . .

'A Smugglers' Song'
BRANDY FOR THE PARSON, baccy for the clerk. . .

'The Vampire'
A FOOL THERE WAS and he made his prayer. . .
To a rag and a bone and a hank of hair. . .

'Gentleman Rankers'
To the LEGION OF THE LOST ones, to the cohort of the damned. . .
Gentlemen-rankers out on the spree,
Damned FROM HERE TO ETERNITY.

The most surprising lack is of any title from the works of Lewis Carroll, one of the most quoted writers in the English language. Otherwise, British writers seem to contribute one or two titles each, of which I give below a selection of the most interesting and least known.

Rupert Brooke: 'The Soldier'
. . . there's some corner of a foreign field
That is FOREVER ENGLAND.

Robert Browning: 'Life In a Love'
ESCAPE ME?
NEVER – beloved!

Robert Burns: 'Auld Lang Syne'
Should OLD ACQUAINTANCE *be forgot. . .*
. . . We'll take a A CUP OF KINDNESS *yet*

– 'To a Mouse'
The best laid schemes OF MICE AND MEN
Gang oft a-gley. . .

324

Winston Churchill
Never in the field of human conflict was so much owed by so many to so few (NEVER SO FEW)

This was their finest hour (THE FINEST HOURS)

This is not the end. It is not even THE BEGINNING OF THE END. But it is perhaps the end of the beginning. . .

An IRON CURTAIN is drawn down upon their front. . .

William Congreve: The Double Dealer
See how love and MURDER WILL OUT. . .
– *The Old Bachelor*
Thus grief still treads upon the heels of pleasure;
Married in haste, we may REPENT AT LEISURE.

John Donne: Devotions
But I do nothing upon myself, and yet am MINE OWN EXECUTIONER. . .

NO MAN IS AN ISLAND, entire of it self.
Any man's death diminishes me, because I am involved in mankind; And therefore never send to know FOR WHOM THE BELL TOLLS; It tolls for thee.

Thomas Gray: 'Elegy Written in a Country Churchyard'
The boast of heraldry, the pomp of pow'r,
And all that beauty, all that wealth e'er gave,
Awaits alike th' inevitable hour;
The PATHS OF GLORY lead but to the grave.

Can storied urn or animated bust
Back to its mansion call the fleeting breath?
Can honour's voice provoke the SILENT DUST,
Or flatt'ry soothe the dull cold ear of death?

FAR FROM THE MADDING CROWD's ignoble strife
Their sober wishes never learned to stray. . .

– 'Ode on a Distant Prospect of Eton College'
. . . Where ignorance is bliss
'Tis FOLLY TO BE WISE. . .

John Lyly: Maides Metamorphose
[THE] NIGHT HAS A THOUSAND EYES. . .

Christopher Marlowe: Dr Faustus
Was this THE FACE THAT LAUNCHED A THOUSAND SHIPS?

– 'The Passionate Shepherd'
COME LIVE WITH ME and be my love. . .

John Milton: Comus
Come, knit hands, and beat the ground
In a light fantastic round (THE LIGHT FANTASTIC)

SABRINA FAIR. . .

– *Lycidas*
FAME IS THE SPUR that the clear spirit doth raise. . .
To scorn delights, and live laborious days. . .

– *Samson Agonistes*
O dark, dark, dark, amid the BLAZE OF NOON. . .

Christina Rosetti: 'Song'
When I am dead, my dearest,
Sing NO SAD SONGS FOR ME. . .

Percy Shelley: 'To a Skylark'
Hail to thee, BLITHE SPIRIT!
Bird thou never wert. . .

— *Ode to the West Wind*
IF WINTER COMES, can spring be far behind?

— *Sonnet*
Lift not THE PAINTED VEIL which those who live
Call Life. . .

Robert Louis Stevenson: 'Requiem'
'Here he lies where he longed to be;
Home is the sailor, home from the sea,
And the hunter HOME FROM THE HILL.'

Alfred Tennyson: 'Lady Clara Vere de Vere'
Kind hearts are more than coronets
And simple faith than Norman blood (KIND HEARTS AND CORONETS)

– 'Locksley Hall'
In the spring a YOUNG MAN'S FANCY
Lightly turns to thoughts of love. . .

The list could be extended almost indefinitely with phrases which have passed into common usage before being picked up by writers to express a particular attitude, probably not the one intended by the original creator, but one which suits a purpose and has the kind of ring that a good title needs. Would it be fair to credit Disraeli with coining the phrase THE DARK HORSE? Or Matthew Arnold with BETWEEN TWO WORLDS? The seventeenth-century Matthew Henry certainly coined the phrase ALL THIS AND HEAVEN TOO, but Rachel Field put quite a different emphasis on it when she wrote a novel of that title 300 years later. Similarly, when around 1800 Valentine Blacker instructed his soldiers to 'Put your faith in God, my boys, and KEEP YOUR POWDER DRY' he had no way of knowing that during World War II the title could be used for a romantic film in which the powder referred to would be applied to Lana Turner's face.

One might have expected that Dickens and Wilde would provide a title or two, with their flair for picturesque speech, but I cannot find one. And Edward Fitzgerald's translation of Omar Khayyam, which seems to be built of thinly-mortared quotations, yields only two:

COME FILL THE CUP, and in the Fire of Spring
The Winter Garment of Repentance fling. . .

I sometimes think that never blows SO RED
THE ROSE as where some buried Caesar bled. . .

Politicians in general seem to speak only for their own day, though one might instance the following as well as Churchill:

Thomas Jefferson
THE TREE OF LIBERTY must be refreshed from time to time with the blood of patriots
    and tyrants. It is its natural manure.

Abraham Lincoln
The ballot is stronger than the bullet (BULLETS OR BALLOTS)

Franklin Roosevelt
I see ONE THIRD OF A NATION ill-housed, ill-clad, ill-nourished. . .

Christopher North (1829)
His Majesty's Dominions, on which THE SUN NEVER SETS. . .

Of all the films I have seen and discussed, the title to which I have most frequently been asked to provide a key is NOW VOYAGER which Bette Davis made in 1942. Perhaps because the original novel by Olive Higgins Prouty was only briefly published in England, perhaps because the key phrase is muttered aloud by Miss Davis during the film, it has whetted a great deal of curiosity, and a recent TV screening provoked much fan mail on the subject. The quotation comes from Walt Whitman, and could hardly be simpler, being used as an encouragement to the leading character to lead a more adventurous life: 'Now, Voyager, sail thou forth, to seek and find.'

Having dealt rather superficially with titles borrowed from literature and popular speech which therefore bring with them an established and familiar quality, let us return to some simpler types of title in which film producers persistently place faith . . . and let us wonder why.

The lure of the female sex is obvious to half the population, but surely it is strange how many different *genres* of film have been sold on the basis of a single female first name (i.e. discounting such compounds as MIN AND BILL, VICTORIA THE GREAT and even THE STORY OF RUTH). There have been *murder melodramas*:

LAURA	BEDELIA	IVY	SAPPHIRE
STELLA (US)	ANGELA	ELLEN	GILDA
JULIE	JENNIFER	MARNIE	REBECCA
MADELEINE	VICKI	SERENA	

There have been *sophisticated comedies*:

NINOTCHKA	SABRINA	ROSIE	KIKI
SUZY	JESSICA	FEDORA	PETULIA

And *family comedies*:

BLONDIE	LOUISA	EMMA	KATHY'O
KATHLEEN	JANIE	PEGGY	TAMMY
JACQUELINE	MOLLY	GERALDINE	BERNADINE
GLORY	MARY LOU		

And *assorted comedies* such as MAISIE, JEANNIE, ANGELINA, ROSITA and MIRANDA, which bring in heroines as diverse as a gold-digger, a Scottish spinster, an Italian MP and a mermaid. There was even a man in a kangaroo suit called MATILDA.

Next we come to the *musicals*:

ROSE MARIE	ROBERTA	ATHENA	KATINA
SALLY	SUNNY	LILI	GIGI
IRENE	MARGIE	ROSALIE	ANNIE

If we include the field of opera, CARMEN turns up most often.

Then, the *costume dramas*:

JASSY	SALOME	JEZEBEL	NANA
DIANE	KITTY	FABIOLA	ZAZA
ANGELIQUE			

And assorted *sex melodramas*:

DEDEE	TONI	OPHELIA	OLIVIA
MADDALENA	CABIRIA	LU	LOLITA
LULU BELLE	STELLA (Greek)	EVA	MURIEL
ELECTRA	PHEDRA		

And a few *horrors*:

CARRIE	CHRISTINE	RUBY	DOMINIQUE
VAMPIRA			

And even some reasonably straightforward *romances* of the old school:

CARRIE (1952)	GABY	LOLA	FRIEDA
CLAUDIA	FANNY	ANNA	JOANNA
CYNTHIA	TERESA	LYDIA	MELODY
ADA	JESSICA	ISABEL	

One can scarcely include in any of these categories such oddballs as Dreyer's GERTRUD, the spy story LISA, the gangster story GLORIA, the ghetto-set JUDITH, the memoir JULIA, the factory floor drama NORMA RAE, or the filmstar biopic FRANCES. Other small groups include films for children (HEIDI, POLLYANNA) and about problem children (MANDY, PAULA); there is the biopic of a national heroine (ODETTE) and one of an eccentric dancer (ISADORA). There is even a western called FRENCHY; and something called BRIGHTY in which the heroine turns out to be a donkey.

Wouldn't you think that producers would take more trouble to indicate what kind of film is on offer? Of course, the title alone doesn't sell tickets, but it's a great help; and cinemas showing these first-name movies must have been packed through the years with patrons vaguely expecting something different.

Boys' names are clearly felt to be a less effective magnet. The only ones which come to mind – a mixed bag – are JUBAL, HUD, KIM, MARTY, PEPE, MARIUS, CESAR, MICKEY, MARCELINO, ORPHEUS, HANNIBAL, HONDO, DINO, PYGMALION, OLIVER, SIMON, ARTHUR, CAL – and HARVEY, if you count white rabbits six feet tall. Men's surnames on the other hand have frequently connoted strength, sometimes of the superhuman variety, and the visual publicists have conceived some of these as etched out of towering rock:

HARPER	CAHILL	PATTON	MADIGAN
BLOOMFIELD	MCLINTOCK	BULLITT	BRANNIGAN
HOOPER	MCQ	DESTRY	KLUTE
LASSITER	BRUBAKER	MARLOWE	SHANE

There is also an honourable historical section, hoping to suggest that there's a man inside the fancy costume:

PARNELL	DISRAELI	DANTON	VOLTAIRE
NIJINSKY	JUAREZ	CROMWELL	

NAPOLEON had a similar effect, but Napoleon was in fact a first name; BONAPARTE would not have had quite the same ring.

Television has adapted these conventions to its own purposes. The list of comedies about cute, conniving, domineering or cuddlesome ladies seems almost endless, and most are attached to a simple first name:

HAZEL	MAUDE	JULIA	RHODA
NANCY	PHYLLIS	ALICE	DIANA
FAY	TAMMY	GRINDL	DINAH

Even a tough police psychiatrist, adept at kneeing suspects where it hurts, is known as JESSIE, and whoever referred to the Lucille Ball show as anything but LUCY, whatever the current season may have been called?

Male television heroes, on the other hand, tend to be known by surnames only, even if the surname is a jawbreaker:

DELVECCHIO	EISCHIED	PETROCELLI	BARETTA
HUNTER	KOJAK	QUINCY	SERPICO
MANNIX	LONGSTREET	LANCER	HENNESSY
SHANNON	RAFFERTY	MAGNUM	BRONK
STONE	BANYON	HAWK	STACCATO
NEWHART	CANNON	IRONSIDE	SHANE
NICHOLS	MAVERICK	BOONE	MACGYVER

A curious title development of the fifties was the attempt to elevate routine movies by saddling them with an antithesis of alliterative intangibles, as in THE PRIDE AND THE PASSION, a pretentious adventure movie which, since the title had no discernible relation to the movie's plot, would have done better to keep C. S. Forester's original THE GUN. I suppose one can trace this device back to Jane Austen's PRIDE AND PREJUDICE and SENSE AND SENSIBILITY, but at least her attributes were precisely fitted to the leading characters and indeed formed the pivot of the story. In the thirties and forties there were occasional nods towards this form, as in YOUNG AND INNOCENT, YOUNG AND WILLING, FLESH AND

FANTASY; but the use of the definite article made the fifties deluge pompous and self-defeating:

THE HIGH AND THE MIGHTY
THE PROUD AND PROFANE
THE FLAME AND THE FLESH
THE BRAVE AND THE BEAUTIFUL
THE YOUNG AND THE GUILTY
THE NAKED AND THE DEAD
THE BAD AND THE BEAUTIFUL
THE BOLD AND THE BRAVE
THE YOUNG AND THE DAMNED
THE WILD AND THE WILLING

Actor John Hurt said of the last named (it was his first film) that he never did find out who was which. The vogue petered out rapidly though not before time, and the attempt in 1963 to give it a fresh lift with OF LOVE AND DESIRE fell very flat indeed.

Another irritating style in double-decker titles was launched with the attempt in 1943 to perpetuate two fading series by combining their leading characters in one film: FRANKENSTEIN MEETS THE WOLF MAN. Subsequent examples include:

THE BOWERY BOYS MEET THE MONSTERS
MOTHER RILEY MEETS THE VAMPIRE
BELA LUGOSI MEETS A BROOKLYN GORILLA
ABBOTT AND COSTELLO MEET FRANKENSTEIN
  (and THE KILLER, and THE MUMMY, and
  THE INVISIBLE MAN, and THE KEYSTONE KOPS,
  and DR JEKYLL AND MR HYDE)
BILLY THE KID MEETS DRACULA
JESSE JAMES MEETS FRANKENSTEIN'S DAUGHTER
DRACULA VERSUS FRANKENSTEIN

Other films have simply listed their ingredients:

MONEY, WOMEN AND GUNS
GUNS, GIRLS AND GANGSTERS
LOVE, HONOUR AND OH BABY
WIFE, DOCTOR AND NURSE
WIFE, HUSBAND AND FRIEND
LOVE, SOLDIERS AND WOMEN
SHAKE, RATTLE AND ROCK
THE WORLD, THE FLESH AND THE DEVIL
PAPA, MAMA, THE MAID AND I
MUMSY, NANNY, SONNY AND GIRLY
BREAD, LOVE AND JEALOUSY (etc)
TEXAS, BROOKLYN AND HEAVEN
YESTERDAY, TODAY AND TOMORROW

If M and Z are the shortest ever film titles, odds are still being taken on the longest. There were occasional biggies in the thirties and forties: THE MAN WHO BROKE THE BANK AT MONTE CARLO beat NEVER GIVE A SUCKER AN EVEN BREAK by six letters and two spaces. But it was not until the advent in 1953 of the super-wide CinemaScope screen that producers felt constrained as a matter of policy to think of extra-wide titles to fit it. BEYOND THE TWELVE-MILE REEF, HOW TO MARRY A MILLIONAIRE and THERE'S NO BUSINESS LIKE SHOW BUSINESS were only the beginning: in recent years double-barrelled and deliberately clumsy titles have become fashionable:

DR STRANGELOVE, OR HOW I LEARNED TO STOP
  WORRYING AND LOVE THE BOMB
THOSE MAGNIFICENT MEN IN THEIR FLYING
  MACHINES, OR HOW I FLEW FROM LONDON
  TO PARIS IN 25 HOURS AND 11 MINUTES
THE FEARLESS VAMPIRE KILLERS, OR PARDON ME BUT
  YOUR TEETH ARE IN MY NECK
DARLING LILI, OR WHERE WERE YOU THE NIGHT
  YOU SAID YOU SHOT DOWN BARON VON RICHTHOFEN?

The trophy in this department was recently won by Peter Weiss with the film of his play THE PERSECUTION AND ASSASSINATION OF MARAT AS PERFORMED BY THE INMATES OF THE ASYLUM AT CHARENTON UNDER THE DIRECTION OF THE MARQUIS DE SADE. If his subsequent play is ever filmed, he will have beaten his own record, its title being: DISCOURSE OVER THE PREVIOUS HISTORY AND THE LONG CONTINUING FREEDOM FIGHT IN VIETNAM AS AN EXAMPLE OF THE UNNECESSARY WEAPONED BATTLE FOR THE UNDERDOGS AGAINST THOSE PRESSING THEM UNDER AS WELL AS OF THE ATTEMPT OF THE UNITED STATES OF AMERICA TO DESTROY THE CAUSES OF THE REVOLUTION

A type of title I find especially annoying is that which sounds enjoyably mysterious but turns out to be merely the name of the house, hotel, or nightclub where the action takes place:

    THE BLUE ANGEL
    THE BLUE GARDENIA
    THE BLUE DAHLIA
    THE GREEN COCKATOO
    THE HALFWAY HOUSE
    THE GREEN MAN
    THE BLACK RAVEN
    DIAMOND HORSESHOE
    SEVEN SINNERS
    THARK
    JALNA
    THE FURIES
    DRAGONWYCK
    THE QUIET WOMAN
    WUTHERING HEIGHTS
    THE FRANCHISE AFFAIR

The same annoyance is felt when an intriguing title turns out to be only the name of a fictitious town (WARLOCK, FIRECREEK), a book written by the hero (FOOTSTEPS IN THE DARK) or a play (THE HIGH TERRACE, FORTY NAUGHTY GIRLS).

And somehow it still doesn't seem right for a title to ask a question, though this has always been a popular gimmick if discreetly used. It would be a diligent filmgoer indeed who could provide the correct answer in each of the following cases:

WHO DONE IT?
WHO KILLED AUNT MAGGIE?
WHO KILLED DOC ROBBIN?
WHATEVER HAPPENED TO BABY JANE?
WENT THE DAY WELL?
DID YOU HEAR THE ONE ABOUT THE TRAVELLING SALESLADY?
WHO GOES THERE?
WHERE DO WE GO FROM HERE?
WHO'S MINDING THE STORE?
WHERE'S CHARLEY?
WHO IS HOPE SCHUYLER?
WHO'S BEEN SLEEPING IN MY BED?
WHAT'S THE MATTER WITH HELEN?
WHAT'S NEW, PUSSYCAT?
WHAT NEXT, CORPORAL HARGROVE?
WHAT DID YOU DO IN THE WAR, DADDY?
WHEN YOU COMING BACK, RED RYDER?
WHAT PRICE HOLLYWOOD?
WHAT'S SO BAD ABOUT FEELING GOOD?
WHERE WERE YOU WHEN THE LIGHTS WENT OUT?
ISN'T LIFE WONDERFUL?
WHERE'S POPPA?

WHERE'S THAT FIRE?
WHO KILLED MARY WHATSHERNAME?
WHAT'S BUZZIN', COUSIN?
WHO IS KILLING THE GREAT CHEFS OF EUROPE?
WHO IS HARRY KELLERMAN AND WHY IS HE SAYING THESE TERRIBLE THINGS ABOUT ME?
WHO'S AFRAID OF VIRGINIA WOOLF?
IS EVERYBODY HAPPY?
ARE HUSBANDS NECESSARY?
WHO?
DARLING, HOW COULD YOU?
WHO'S GOT THE ACTION?
HAS ANYBODY SEEN MY GAL?
WHO'S MINDING THE MINT?
WILL ANY GENTLEMAN?
ARE THESE OUR PARENTS?
SHALL WE DANCE?
WHAT BECAME OF JACK AND JILL?
WHAT'S UP TIGER LILY?
ARE YOU WITH IT?
ISN'T IT ROMANTIC?
WHAT PRICE GLORY?

WHATEVER HAPPENED TO AUNT ALICE?   WHO'LL STOP THE RAIN?
WHAT'S UP, DOC?   WHY WORRY?
WHERE'S JACK?   IS PARIS BURNING?
WHAT WAS THAT LADY?   ARE YOU BEING SERVED?
WHO SLEW AUNTIE ROO?   QUO VADIS?

One at a time, please.

Another form of punctuation used to give a film pretensions above its natural station is the exclamation point or screamer, which has been arbitrarily attached in official publicity to such diverse films as:

HELP!	HATARI!	RHINO!	STAR!
ANNIE!	OLIVER!	OKLAHOMA!	GERONIMO!
POINT BLANK!	RETREAT, HELL!	GUNG HO!	OH SUSANNA!
OH MEN, OH WOMEN!		OH BOY, OH GIRL!	

Punctuation by full stops is fairly unusual. S.O.S. SUBMARINE and THE BRIDE CAME C.O.D. and THE V.I.P.S are clear enough, but other abbreviated titles have required parenthetical explanation:

F.P. 1	(floating platform)
O.S.S.	(on secret service)
THE D.I.	(drill instructor)
D.O.A.	(dead on arrival)
P.T. 109	(patrol torpedo boat)
T.P.A.	(the president's analyst)

P.J. seems to have no more significance than a man's initials, and the same applies to B.F.'S DAUGHTER, though in Britain a B.F. was something else again, so that title was changed to POLLY FULTON. S.W.A.L.K. was known by some people to mean 'sealed with a loving kiss' but the title was changed for safety to MELODY. S.N.A.F.U. was an old army term, untranslatable in either country unless bowdlerized as 'situation normal, all fowled up'; in Britain it was changed to WELCOME HOME. As for the opus played in Britain as DEADLINE MIDNIGHT but in America under its original title

–30–

– well, we'll leave the producer to explain that. We have explained S.O.B., and everyone knows that E.T. means extra-terrestrial; so we come to two cases in which asterisks were used instead of dots, for no reason except to add a little flavour. M★A★S★H means 'mobile army surgical hospital', but S★P★Y★S means only that M★A★S★H is being aped. For sheer impossibility of promotion Richard Brooks's comedy

$

took some beating. How was the girl on the phone to tell a patron what was playing? In the end the title had to be changed, in America to DOLLARS and in Britain to THE HEIST. Business could have been better even then.

An easy way out for a producer with no imagination is to call his film THE BIG this or that. Here are some of the words which have been so adorned in movie titles:

LIFT	BANKROLL	BEAT	BLUFF
BONANZA	PAY-OFF	BOODLE	CAPER
COMBO	CARNIVAL	CAT	CHASE
SLEEP	SOMBRERO	TREES	CIRCUS
CITY	CLOCK	COUNTRY	CUBE
FISHERMAN	FIX	FRAME	GUSHER
HANGOVER	HEAT	TIP-OFF	WHEEL
STEAL	KNIFE	LAND	LEAGUER
NIGHT	NOISE	OPERATOR	PUNCH
SHOW	SHOW-OFF	SKY	HOUSE
MOUTH	STORY		

THE GREAT also has its adherents, but is often followed by two words rather than one:

331

From the quality of the films listed it is clear that both BIG and GREAT should be retired from title service.

Psychological thrillers have long been popular, but it was PSYCHO which led the fashion for labelling them as such. Hollywood quickly followed with PYRO and HOMICIDAL; then Hammer Studios got into the act with PARANOIAC, MANIAC, FANATIC and HYSTERIA. SCHIZO was an independent also-ran. Whether more than one fan in a dozen knows what these words mean is open to doubt; but then we have cheerfully accepted for forty years and more titles consisting entirely of foreign words, which may or may not be explained in the script but whose meaning is generally forgotten by the time the end title comes up:

BONJOUR TRISTESSE	KISMET	SAADIA	JIVARO
ZANZABUKU	BANDIDO	TIARA TAHITI	MARA MARU
SAYONARA	HATARI	SABAKA	JACARE
SIMBA	RIFIFI	MAMBO	TEMBO
AVANTI	LA LUNA	MANDINGO	PAPILLON
TELEFON	QUEIMADA!	THE YAKUZA	EUREKA
WOLFEN	TORA! TORA! TORA!	LA CAGE AUX FOLLES	

There has lately been a rash of titles which are utterly meaningless in relation to the content of the film to which they are attached. There is no sense in arguing about the choices of Michelangelo Antonioni, who claims to choose 'by intuition', but I would like to challenge the perpetrators of the following to relate them to the films concerned:

BEDAZZLED
DEAD HEAT ON A MERRY GO ROUND
I'LL NEVER FORGET WHATSHISNAME
THE DEADLY AFFAIR
THE GLASS BOTTOM BOAT (yes, we did see such a thing, but
  it wasn't part of the plot)
QUATERMASS AND THE PIT (there was no pit in the film version)
MURDERERS' ROW
THE AMBUSHERS
THE QUILLER MEMORANDUM (*what* memorandum?)
LORD LOVE A DUCK

These examples seem more the result of laziness than of any attempt to deceive. There have been titles in the past which made me wonder if the producer was having a quiet laugh at the audience's expense. Were we expected to know that TWENTIETH CENTURY and BROADWAY LIMITED were trains? That SARATOGA TRUNK was a railroad line, like the DENVER AND RIO GRANDE? That the baby in BRINGING UP BABY was a leopard? That A SONG TO REMEMBER and SONG WITHOUT END were about classical composers who wrote no vocal music at all? That THE MAGNIFICENT REBEL would turn out to be Beethoven? That the NORTHWEST PASSAGE, in the film from the book of that name, was never sought and only vaguely referred to (because only part one of the book was used)?

More complaints. HELL TO ETERNITY is a phrase that makes no grammatical sense and has no contextual meaning. SANTA FE TRAIL was not the western it sounds, but an account of the rounding up of racial fanatic John Brown. MILLION DOLLAR LEGS was a title conceived by Joe Mankiewicz for a totally different film from the one to which Paramount casually attached it. Who or what was enchanted in ENCHANTMENT was never clear. STAND UP AND CHEER was apparently an injunction to the audience, and a pretty impertinent one at that.

SHE DONE HIM WRONG is not only ungrammatical but an incorrect description of its own plot, in which if anything he done her wrong. ANOTHER PART OF THE FOREST must be utterly bewildering except to smart-alecs who know that it deals with the same characters as THE LITTLE FOXES at a different time of their lives. PHFFFT was thought to be a clever title for a divorce comedy because it represented 'the sound of an expiring match'.

Horror films have fared especially badly from the title creators, who are inevitably anxious to promise more than they can possibly fulfil. The vampire count has frequently had his name taken in vain: it isn't his son in SON OF DRACULA, or his house in HOUSE OF DRACULA, or his brides in BRIDES OF DRACULA. Poor old Baron Frankenstein suffered in much the same way, being frequently confused with his own monster, as in FRANKENSTEIN MEETS THE WOLF MAN and ABBOTT AND COSTELLO MEET FRANKENSTEIN; while FRANKEN-STEIN CREATED WOMAN is an utter misnomer, as he does no such thing. No feline has any connection with the plot of either the 1934 or the 1941 film called THE BLACK CAT, though in each film such an animal crosses the screen once or twice as the ultimate in red herrings. Nor, despite his screen credit, is either film based in any way upon the works of Edgar Allan Poe; the poor man has suffered particularly badly at the hands of Hollywood, for none of the various films called THE RAVEN is based on his poem. Finally, THE BEAST WITH A MILLION EYES proved to be a miscount by several hundred thousand.

Occasionally a film title refers not to the plot but to the stars. The hero and heroine of TOGETHER AGAIN met only during the course of the film and were never separated; the title plainly referred to the re-teaming of Charles Boyer and Irene Dunne. Similarly, filmgoers seeing WHERE THERE'S LIFE were clearly supposed to mutter 'there's Bob Hope'. NEVER GIVE A SUCKER AN EVEN BREAK is a title justified by nothing in the film, but it does express the philosophy of its star, W. C. Fields. DOUBLE DYNAMITE was generally supposed to refer to Jane Russell's superstructure, as it bore no other conceivable reference to the film. The ultimate in this kind of title was ABBOTT AND COSTELLO MEET THE KILLER, BORIS KARLOFF, an unhappy amalgam apparently caused by a contractual commitment to give Karloff's name equal prominence with those of the two comedians; the disastrous effect was accentuated by the fact that the character played by Karloff turned out not to be the killer after all.

FURY, FLESH, NAKED and HELL are great words for title-writers. Over-use has reduced their effectiveness to such an extent that they are almost interchangeable: who can tell the difference between FLESH AND FURY, NAKED FURY, DEVIL IN THE FLESH, THE FLAME AND THE FLESH and NAKED HELL? Or between any of the following:

THE NAKED DAWN	THE NAKED EDGE
NAKED ALIBI	THE NAKED HILLS
NAKED EARTH	THE NAKED SPUR
THE NAKED HEART	THE NAKED GUN
THE NAKED SEA	THE NAKED MAJA
NAKED PARADISE	THE NAKED STREET

Another much misused word is DEVIL, which has come to imply little more than evil, danger or daring, usually in routine action dramas:

THE DEVIL'S BRIGADE	THE DEVIL'S HAIRPIN
THE DEVIL'S MASK	DEVIL'S HARBOUR
THE DEVIL TO PAY	DEVIL'S CANYON
THE DEVIL'S PASSKEY	THE DEVIL AND THE DEEP
DEVIL SHIP	THE DEVIL AT FOUR O'CLOCK
DEVIL BAT	TALK OF THE DEVIL
DEVIL GODDESS	DEVIL ON WHEELS
THE DEVIL MAKES THREE	THE DEVIL THUMBS A RIDE
DEVIL SHIP PIRATES	THE DEVIL'S DISCIPLE
DEVIL'S CARGO	THE DEVIL'S GENERAL
DEVIL'S DOORWAY	THE DEVIL IS A WOMAN
THE DEVIL DOLL	THE DEVIL AND MISS JONES
THE DEVIL'S HENCHMAN	FLESH AND THE DEVIL
THE DEVIL IS A SISSY	THE DEVIL NEVER SLEEPS
THE DEVIL'S PLAYGROUND	THE WORLD, THE FLESH AND THE DEVIL

In none of these films did Satan himself appear, but he did take part, more or less, in EYE OF THE DEVIL, THE DEVIL IN LOVE, THE DEVIL AND DANIEL WEBSTER, DEVILS OF DARKNESS and THE DEVIL RIDES OUT.

Genuine wit is something one rarely encounters in the titling business, and few of the instances below, mostly using a play on words, have done big business:

ADVANCE TO THE REAR
A BIG HAND FOR THE LITTLE LADY (poker)
CINDERFELLA (with Jerry Lewis as Cinders)
ROBIN AND THE SEVEN HOODS
THE DESK SET (office workers)
FULL OF LIFE (account of a pregnancy)
A JOLLY BAD FELLOW (a villainous university don)
STATE OF THE UNION (marriage and politics)
MISS GRANT TAKES RICHMOND (General Grant did the same)
TALES OF MANHATTAN (about a tail coat)
TAKE A LETTER DARLING (wife becomes secretary)
SMASHING TIME (literally and metaphorically)
CALLAWAY WENT THATAWAY (western spoof)
HEAVEN ONLY KNOWS (the hero is an angel)
THE HEAVENLY BODY (Saturn or Hedy Lamarr?)
THE HIGH COST OF LOVING
A PAIR OF BRIEFS (set in a law court)
STAGE FRIGHT
TAKE HER SHE'S MINE
TOP SECRET AFFAIR (politics too!)

Suggestiveness is at least equally common. I refer not to the recent crop of club movies with such titles as HOT HOURS, INDECENT DESIRES and THE UNSATISFIED SEX, but to films from major renters who have had to approach their objectives through innuendo:

LET'S DO IT AGAIN
PLEASE TURN OVER
RAISING THE WIND
LADIES WHO DO
LOVE ON A PILLOW
NO SLEEP TILL DAWN
SOME LIKE IT HOT
THE PAJAMA GAME
ONLY TWO CAN PLAY
LET'S MAKE LOVE

As far back as the early thirties Lubitsch was doing pretty well at this game with titles like ONE HOUR WITH YOU and TROUBLE IN PARADISE; in the latter case he left no doubt of his intention by fading in a double bed behind the word 'Paradise' in the main title.

You could practically compose a world gazetteer from the films which have used place names in their titles. It is interesting to note the cities and countries which are thought to suggest by their very names so much mystery and romance that no further build-up is needed. Sometimes there are special reasons: World War I made VERDUN and YPRES and MONS world famous; World War II did the same for DUNKIRK and EL ALAMEIN, ANZIO, BENGAZI and TOBRUK. Otherwise the majority of these 'exotic' locations seem to be in the African continent:

MOZAMBIQUE	SUDAN
PORT SAID	CASABLANCA
ZANZIBAR	TIMBUKTU
TANGIER	KHARTOUM
MOROCCO	CAIRO
SAHARA	ALGIERS
TRIPOLI	TANGANYIKA

334

Almost as many hail from the mysterious east:

CALCUTTA	SINGAPORE
TEHERAN	MANILA
SUEZ	SAIGON
HONG KONG	BAGDAD
MACAO	ISTANBUL
BORNEO	CHINA
MALAYA	

Australasia accounts for none. Southern America provides

RIO	BRAZIL
SANTIAGO	TAMPICO
VERA CRUZ	

And Europe has a mere sprinkling of suitable places:

SOFIA	LISBON
MALAGA	BERLIN

It will be observed that Britain is well out of the running: no multitudes could be imagined flocking to see a film called WIGAN, or even TUNBRIDGE WELLS. But the United States are much better at trumpet-blowing: nearly a third of the states have passed the test as film titles.

CALIFORNIA	UTAH
NEVADA	MONTANA
NEW MEXICO	ARIZONA
TEXAS	OKLAHOMA
CAROLINA	DAKOTA
HAWAII	IDAHO
MISSISSIPPI	LOUISIANA

So have many of the old western towns where the lead flew most dangerously:

TOMBSTONE	DODGE CITY
CARSON CITY	WACO
DALLAS	ABILENE TOWN
TULSA	RENO
SAN ANTONIO	SANTA FE
CHEYENNE	TUCSON
EL PASO	VIRGINIA CITY
CIMARRON CITY	CRIPPLE CREEK
LARAMIE	WICHITA

When it comes to compound titles, of all the places in the world New York clearly has the most appeal: and the following list excludes many second features starring the Bowery Boys and the East Side Kids.

DOCKS OF NEW YORK	PORT OF NEW YORK
LITTLE OLD NEW YORK	NEW YORK NIGHTS
THE COLOSSUS OF NEW YORK	SUNDAY IN NEW YORK
SO THIS IS NEW YORK	THE KILLER THAT STALKED NEW YORK
SIDEWALKS OF NEW YORK	THE BELLE OF NEW YORK
NEW YORK TOWN	NEW YORK CONFIDENTIAL
BROADWAY	BROADWAY MELODY
LITTLE MISS BROADWAY	BROADWAY RHYTHM
ANGELS OVER BROADWAY	LULLABY OF BROADWAY
JUST OFF BROADWAY	GIVE MY REGARDS TO BROADWAY
THE ROYAL FAMILY OF BROADWAY	BROADWAY BILL
BOWERY TO BROADWAY	MEET ME ON BROADWAY
BROADWAY LIMITED	BLOODHOUNDS OF BROADWAY

DOCTOR BROADWAY
WALKING DOWN BROADWAY
ON THE BOWERY
TWO LATINS FROM MANHATTAN
TALES OF MANHATTAN
THE KID FROM BROOKLYN
NEATH BROOKLYN BRIDGE
GREENWICH VILLAGE
MIRACLE ON 34TH STREET
52ND STREET
THE PHANTOM OF 42ND STREET
IT HAPPENED ON FIFTH AVENUE
MADISON AVENUE
BREAKFAST AT TIFFANY'S
CONEY ISLAND
EAST SIDE, WEST SIDE

TWO TICKETS TO BROADWAY
THE BOWERY
MANHATTAN ANGEL
MANHATTAN MELODRAMA
A TREE GROWS IN BROOKLYN
WHISTLING IN BROOKLYN
PARK ROW
ROSE OF WASHINGTON SQUARE
42ND STREET
THE HOUSE ON 92ND STREET
FIFTH AVENUE GIRL
TENTH AVENUE ANGEL
UP IN CENTRAL PARK
GRAND CENTRAL MURDER
WEST SIDE STORY
MANHATTAN
ELLIS ISLAND (TV mini series)

London provides a comparatively meagre list:

LONDON TOWN
POOL OF LONDON
DARK EYES OF LONDON
LONDON BELONGS TO ME
WEREWOLF OF LONDON
TOWER OF LONDON
LONDON MELODY
HYDE PARK CORNER
BERKELEY SQUARE
THE LAVENDER HILL MOB
23 PACES TO BAKER STREET
A WINDOW IN LONDON

SOHO INCIDENT
EAST OF PICCADILLY
PICCADILLY INCIDENT
WATERLOO BRIDGE
PASSPORT TO PIMLICO
I LIVE IN GROSVENOR SQUARE
SPRING IN PARK LANE
MAYTIME IN MAYFAIR
PEG OF OLD DRURY
WATERLOO ROAD
THE GHOSTS OF BERKELEY SQUARE

Geography seemed to become unpopular in the seventies. The only recent additions to the American range have been DEATH VALLEY and ZABRISKIE POINT. (The latter, oddly enough, lies within Death Valley.) Abroad, there's CUBA and GALLIPOLI, and that's about it.

A child could learn to count from film titles, up to eighteen anyway:

IT HAPPENED ONE NIGHT
TWO TICKETS TO BROADWAY
THREE VIOLENT PEOPLE
FOUR FRIGHTENED PEOPLE
FIVE CAME BACK
THE SIX MEN
THE SEVENTH CROSS
EIGHT AND A HALF
NINE GIRLS
TEN DAYS IN PARIS
OCEAN'S ELEVEN
TWELVE ANGRY MEN
THIRTEEN GHOSTS
FOURTEEN HOURS
X-15
SIXTEEN FATHOMS DEEP
SEVENTEEN
EIGHTEEN AND ANXIOUS

After that there are gaps as you count your way past THE ATTACK OF THE FIFTY FOOT WOMAN, NINETEEN EIGHTY FOUR and CELL 2455 DEATH ROW.

336

Of the days of the week, Monday has been remarkably unpopular but the rest are adequately covered:

BLACK TUESDAY
ANY WEDNESDAY
IT HAPPENS EVERY THURSDAY
FRIDAY THE THIRTEENTH
SATURDAY NIGHT FEVER
NEVER ON SUNDAY

Of the months, February seems still to be at liberty:

THE NIGHT OF JANUARY 16TH
THE MARCH HARE
APRIL LOVE
MAYTIME
JUNE BRIDE
CHRISTMAS IN JULY
THE TEAHOUSE OF THE AUGUST MOON
SEPTEMBER AFFAIR
THE OCTOBER MAN
SWEET NOVEMBER
A WARM DECEMBER

Years in titles make the films very difficult to reissue. FASHIONS OF 1934, VOGUES OF 1938 and SENSATIONS OF 1945 returned in light disguise as FASHIONS, VOGUES and SENSATIONS; but the BIG BROADCAST, GOLD DIGGERS and BROADWAY MELODY series were never revived at all.

Some well-known and affectionately remembered films have titles which even the most enthusiastic filmgoer would find it difficult, in retrospect, to explain, usually because of some specific reference which may or may not have been explained in the film. THE CARPETBAGGERS, for instance, was not explained and the title must have been totally bewildering to all but American audiences, who knew from their civil war history that carpetbaggers were itinerant northerners who took advantage of unsettled conditions. The reference in the film was to unscrupulous characters who grabbed success at the expense of other people. THE THIRTY-NINE STEPS were vaguely explained in the film as a band of international spies; John Buchan's original explanation was rather different. ANGELS ONE FIVE is RAF slang for an altitude of 15,000 feet; ICE COLD IN ALEX referred to two glasses of lager to which the leading character was looking forward when he reached Alexandria. THE BLIND GODDESS and THE WALLS OF JERICHO are easy. THE SEVENTH VEIL was the last reserve discarded by a patient under hypnosis. THE MINISTRY OF FEAR was understood in World War II to mean the Gestapo; THE SHEEP HAS FIVE LEGS is a French proverb the significance of which I entirely forget. BLACK NARCISSUS, THE BROWNING VERSION and THE INN OF THE SIXTH HAPPINESS were all explained on screen, but ULYSSES (Milo O'Shea, not Kirk Douglas) was not, and I never knew anyone who could explain the significance of THE MOON AND SIXPENCE, a phrase which does not occur in Maugham's book, until I read the Maugham biography by Ted Morgan, who avers that the title was borrowed from a phrase in a *Times Literary Supplement* review of *Of Human Bondage*. The writer described Maugham's hero as being 'like many young men, so busy yearning for the moon that he never saw the sixpence at his feet'.

Titles are getting more interesting, and certainly more outlandish. This is partly due to television, which has proved that provided a title is intriguing it does not have to express solely the basic stimulants of sex and action. Mind you, television sometimes over-reaches itself: there was an episode of NAKED CITY called KING STANISLAUS AND THE KNIGHTS OF THE ROUND STABLE, which wouldn't have sold many tickets. Alas, some of the best film titles never reach the marquees, being changed at the last minute by chicken-hearted distributors. These gentlemen may at least be comforted to know that their problems are shared by theatrical managements. In 1967 a farce was opening in London's West End under the title STAND BY YOUR BEDOUIN, and a national newspaper listed all the alternative titles which had been seriously considered. They were:

A LOAD OF ISTANBUL
FLORENCE OF ARABIA
FEZ TO FEZ
GET WELL OILED
UP A SAND DUNE WITHOUT A CADDIE
I'VE GROWN ACCUSTOMED TO HER FEZ
THREE SHEIKS IN THE WIND
WHO FLUNG DUNN?
THE FOUR-MINUTE NILE
FOLLOW THAT CAMEL
BETWEEN THE SHEIKS
WHEN DID YOU LAST CHANGE YOUR SHEIKS?
CLEAN SHEIKS ON THE BEDOUIN
RED SHEIKS IN THE SUNSET
JUST DESERTS

How did they come to omit OIL BE SEEING YOU and UP THE PYRAMIDS?

INDEX

NB: Only principal references are noted, and the three essays, being entirely composed of minor ones, are not covered at all.